THE FACILITATIVE LEADER IN CITY HALL

Reexamining the Scope and Contributions

Advancing excellence in public service . . .

American Society for Public Administration
Book Series on Public Administration & Public Policy

Evan M. Berman, Ph.D.
Editor-in-Chief

The Facilitative Leader in City Hall:
Reexamining the Scope and Contributions
by James H. Svara

Mission: Throughout its history, ASPA has sought to be true to its founding principles of promoting scholarship and professionalism within the public service. The ASPA Book Series on Public Administration and Public Policy publishes books that increase national and international interest for public administration and which discuss practical or cutting edge topics in engaging ways of interest to practitioners, policy-makers, and those concerned with bringing scholarship to the practice of public administration.

CRC Press
Taylor & Francis Group

THE FACILITATIVE LEADER IN CITY HALL

Reexamining the Scope and Contributions

JAMES H. SVARA

ASPA
Advancing excellence in public service

American Society for Public Administration
Series in Public Administration and Public Policy

CRC Press
Taylor & Francis Group
Boca Raton London New York

CRC Press is an imprint of the
Taylor & Francis Group, an **informa** business

CRC Press
Taylor & Francis Group
6000 Broken Sound Parkway NW, Suite 300
Boca Raton, FL 33487-2742

© 2009 by Taylor & Francis Group, LLC
CRC Press is an imprint of Taylor & Francis Group, an Informa business

International Standard Book Number-13: 978-1-4200-6831-3 (Hardcover)

Library of Congress Cataloging-in-Publication Data

The facilitative leader in city hall : reexamining the scope and
      contributions / editor, James H. Svara.
          p. cm. -- (Public administration and public policy ; 151)
      Includes bibliographical references and index.
      ISBN 978-1-4200-6831-3
      1. Municipal government--United States. 2. Political leadership--United
States. 3. Mayors--United States. 4. City councils--United States. I. Svara, James
H. II. Title. III. Series.

JS331.F27 2009
352.23'6216--dc22   2008021911

Visit the Taylor & Francis Web site at
http://www.taylorandfrancis.com

and the CRC Press Web site at
http://www.crcpress.com

Dedication

To William N. Cassella, Jr., and Terrell Blodgett for their lifelong
contributions to advancing leadership in local government.

Contents

3   FACILITATION IN THE COUNCIL–MANAGER FORM
A.   CLASSIC SITUATIONS: WHEN LEADERSHIP LOOKS EASY (EVEN THOUGH IT'S NOT)

B.   COUNCIL–MANAGER COMMUNITIES WITH ADVERSITY AND CONFLICT

Preface

A perpetual challenge facing city governments is the quality of political leadership. Effective mayors provide a sense of direction and help ensure that all parts of city government are working in a coordinated and purposeful way with community support for the city's goals. Ineffective mayors leave their cities to drift, allow city departments and staff to work ineffectively, and fail to make a connection with citizens. With increasingly complex problems to address, the need for leadership is even greater.

Although there is general agreement about the "ends" of mayoral leadership, there is disagreement about the "means." One purpose of this book is to examine the nature of leadership and how mayors can be effective using an approach to leadership that empowers other officials rather than seeking power over them. The book explores how mayors can make a difference and get better results in city government by providing vision, strengthening the governance role of the council, harnessing the professional leadership of the city manager or city administrator and staff, building partnerships in and beyond the community, and developing strong linkages with citizens. This approach reflects a *facilitative* style of leadership that is generally recognized as preferable to an *authoritarian* or *power-based* style in the general leadership literature (but not in the bulk of the mayoral leadership literature).

The book is also a critical examination of governmental structure and political process in cities. By examining mayors, it illuminates the nature of city government and clarifies the similarities and differences in cities that use the two major forms of government as their constitutional basis. Discussions of the topic of mayoral leadership in the United States usually start with the premise that "strong" mayors in mayor–council cities are real leaders, and council–manager mayors with no separate powers are figureheads and ribbon cutters. The potential and actuality of leadership in council–manager governments is still poorly understood.

Mayors in council–manager cities operate in conditions that are more favorable to developing a constructive leadership style—one that stresses working with rather than trying to control others, and they are more likely to get support from the city manager and administrative staff, rather than feeling the need to establish control over administrative staff. Mayors in council–manager cities who attempt to "take charge" in their cities are not only acting in ways that contradict the logic of the form of government, they are also attempting to use a style that is less effective even if it could be achieved. It may be more productive for mayors in mayor–council cities to pattern themselves after their council–manager counterparts by incorporating facilitative methods in their leadership behavior.

These choices are not academic questions. Mayoral leadership has been the key issue in referenda to change the form of government in a number of large council–manager cities. By clarifying this core issue in designing effective city governments, the book contributes to understanding the dynamics of urban politics and city government.

This book updates and moves beyond the 1994 book *Facilitative Leadership in Local Government*. The format is the same, but the book provides more critical analysis of the mayor's office. In the introductory chapter, I examine the model of facilitative leadership and analyze the responses provided by city council members in a national survey conducted in 2001 about the nature of mayoral leadership and how it affects the performance of the city council. There are strong similarities in the characteristics of effective mayors in both council–manager and mayor–council cities. The book presents fourteen case studies of mayors from a variety of cities who have served in the past ten years. The studies examine the factors that contribute to effective leadership and the challenges that mayors face. The concluding chapter uses the findings in the case studies to analyze the nature of leadership in its formal and political setting.

This book provides a transforming view of the mayor's office and identifies leadership issues related to the form of government in American cities. The case studies and survey data suggest that mayors in council–manager cities are better positioned to develop positive and effective leadership than their so-called "strong" mayor peers in mayor–council cities. Furthermore, mayors in mayor–council cities can be more effective by incorporating facilitative methods in their leadership behavior as well.

Who is this book for?

This book is important for a wide range of readers. It is obviously relevant for persons who occupy the mayor's office or are considering whether to run for mayor. It blends idealism and reality by showing how to be a mayor who brings people together and moves a city forward, while being a practical guide to being effective. The book demonstrates that these two characteristics tend to go together. It is useful to city managers, chief administrative officers, and department heads who work with mayors. Administrators cannot determine the behavior of politicians, and subordinates cannot dictate the behavior of their superiors, but having a positive model of the behavior that is desired is an important part of "managing" your boss. The model that the subordinate encourages must also be consistent with the superior's interest, and the facilitative model can meet this criterion. When superiors are collaborative, they get greater buy-in and better results.

The book is also useful for administrators at lower levels in the organization and for young professionals to understand the context in which they work and the possibilities for positive political leadership. Persons close to the start of their careers are likely to have negative stereotypical views of top politicians. The common perception these days is that elected officials are so power oriented and intrusive that it is unwise to move into top administrative positions. Acquiring a more balanced and positive assessment of mayors could influence whether these next generation professionals remain in local government service and seek to become a city manager or city administrator. It is important for lower and midlevel administrators to understand what goes on at the top of the organization in the interactions between the top elected officials and the top administrators. Although they may feel far removed from the interactions that occur among upper level administrators and elected officials, the book illuminates and demystifies these dynamics. It demonstrates that partnerships are possible and that mayors often incorporate the recommendations of top administrators and by extension of staff throughout the organization. It also conveys the important message that politicians make important contributions to shaping the future of local government and improving the administrative process. Administrators who understand the role of elected officials have a deeper appreciation of the democratic process.

Acknowledgments

I would like to thank the contributing scholars who have shared this scholarly endeavor. They each explored their subject with perception and thoughtfulness. They have provided both vivid portraits and important insights that advance our understanding of mayoral leadership. I appreciate their support and responsiveness throughout the process of creating this book.

The publication of this book provides an appropriate opportunity to acknowledge my profound appreciation to William N. Cassella, Jr., former long-time executive director of the National Civic League, and Terrell Blodgett, the Mike Hogg Professor Emeritus in Urban Management at the LBJ School of Public Affairs at the University of Texas. Bill and Terrell have been friends and advisers for a long time. They have been at the forefront of efforts to recognize and advance the contribution of elected officials, and they helped with the development of *Facilitative Leadership in Local Government*. This book is dedicated to them.

I am grateful for the encouragement of my colleagues in the School of Public Affairs at Arizona State University. I am indebted to Allyson Ross for her assistance in organizing the workshop on Mayoral Leadership and the Future of Council–Manager Government held in April 2007, and to the League of Arizona Cities and Towns for their co-sponsorship of the workshop. It provided the occasion to present the model and get constructive feedback from the mayors and council members who are confronting the challenge of leadership on a daily basis.

My wife Claudia has been patient and helpful throughout this project. She provides the dual gift of being interested in my work and reminding me to pursue interests other than my work.

James H. Svara

Contributors

Robert Benedetti, PhD, is professor of political science and executive director of the Jacoby Center for Public Service and Civic Leadership at the University of the Pacific in Stockton, California. He was a member of the faculty and later provost at New College in Sarasota, Florida, where he taught and wrote about urban politics in Florida. He also served as dean of the college at the University of the Pacific. Currently, he is engaged in a comparative analysis of the office of the mayor in seventeen California cities. He received his doctorate from the University of Pennsylvania in 1975.

Rikke Berg, PhD, is an associate professor at the Department of Political Science, University of Southern Denmark. Her field of research is public administration and local government, particularly in the roles of local elected officials, political leadership, and local government forms. Research results of the latter are published in Rikke Berg and Nirmala Rao (eds.) (2005): *Transforming Political Leadership in Local Government,* Hampshire, U.K.: Palgrave Macmillan.

Raymond W. Cox III, PhD, is a professor in the Department of Public Administration and Urban Studies at the University of Akron. He received his PhD in public administration and policy from Virginia Tech. Dr. Cox is the author of more than fifty academic and professional publications—ten reports for government agencies as well as more than forty professional papers. He serves as the chair of the Local Government Management Education Committee of NASPAA (National Association of Schools of Public Affairs and Administration).

Janet Denhardt, PhD, is a professor in the School of Public Affairs at Arizona State University. Her teaching and research focus on democratic values, organizational behavior, and leadership. Her recent books include *The Dance of Leadership, The New Public Service, Managing Human Behavior in Public and Non-Profit Organizations,* and *Street-Level Leadership.* She earned her doctorate from the University of Southern California.

Roger J. Durham, PhD, is professor of political science at Aquinas College. His primary research agenda revolves around post Cold War crises and American foreign policy issues. He is chair of the department, as well as coordinator of the international studies degree, and has led Aquinas College students to Haiti, Honduras, and Ireland for intense study. He has been at Aquinas College for twelve years after receiving his PhD from the University of Oregon.

Gerald T. Gabris, PhD, is a distinguished teaching professor and the director of the Division of Public Administration at Northern Illinois University. His primary research interests involve public sector leadership, innovation management, organization development, and human resources administration primarily within a local government context. He is a former managing editor of *Public Administration Review*, and consults regularly with numerous local governments in the area of strategic planning and executive evaluation.

Wendy L. Hassett, PhD, has over twelve years of experience in local government management. Currently, she teaches as a clinical associate professor of public affairs in the School of Economic, Political, and Policy Sciences at The University of Texas at Dallas. Her scholarly work has appeared in *Public Administration Review, Public Performance & Management Review, Review of Public Personnel Administration, Journal of Public Budgeting, Accounting & Financial Management,* and other journals.

Ulrik Kjaer, PhD, is associate professor in the Department of Political Science, University of Southern Denmark, and has been visiting research scholar at Stanford University (1996) and the University of Colorado (2006/2007). Among his research interests are political leadership, political recruitment, and local elections. His most recent book is on local political leadership (written together with Rikke Berg and published in Danish).

Kenneth A. Klase, PhD, is an associate professor of political science at the University of North Carolina/Greensboro, where he is also the director of the Master of Public Affairs program. His teaching and research interests include public budgeting and finance and public financial management. His recent research has focused on budget execution, performance budgeting, and local government structure and management.

Shayne Lambuth graduated with a bachelor's degree in political science from the University of the Pacific in 2007. She is currently pursuing a California teaching credential. Lambuth is also the co-author with Robert Benedetti of an upcoming article exploring the changing relationships between mayors, councils, publics, and managers in major California cities.

John Nalbandian, PhD, is a faculty member and former chair in the Department of Public Administration at the University of Kansas. He is a member of the National Academy of Public Administration. From 1991 to 1999 he served on the Lawrence City Commission, including two one-year terms as the commission's mayor. Nalbandian consults with local governments nationally and has spoken to groups of local government officials internationally.

Sarah Negrón earned her bachelor of arts degree in political science from Wellesley College and her MPA from the University of Kansas. Her public sector work experience includes positions with the city of Merriam, Kansas; Johnson County, Kansas; the City of Pompano Beach, Florida; and Fairfax County, Virginia. Currently, Negrón is a doctoral student in the Department of Sociology at the University of Kansas. Her research interests include gender, feminist theory, and social inequality.

Bart Olson holds a bachelor of science degree in political science and a master of public administration degree, both from Northern Illinois University. He is the assistant city administrator for the United City of Yorkville, Illinois. In March of 2006, Olson was hired as the city's first assistant city administrator, and served a three-month term as the interim city administrator from June 2007 to September 2007.

Alicia C. Schortgen, PhD, is assistant professor of public affairs at the University of Texas at Dallas. Her multidisciplinary research interests focus primarily on leadership and nonprofit studies, and she has authored several manuscripts in these content areas. Prior to earning her PhD, Schortgen worked in various professional capacities in the voluntary sector.

John T. Spence, PhD, AICP, is a lecturer in political science at Thomas More College. He received his doctorate from the University of Cincinnati in 2003, simultaneous to serving two terms on the Covington, Kentucky, board of commissioners: one of five elected officials responsible for overseeing a city government of over three hundred employees and a $50 million budget. Dr. Spence's primary research focus is municipal government, electoral and voter behavior, and civic engagement.

James H. Svara, PhD, is professor in the School of Public Affairs and director of the Center for Urban Innovation at Arizona State University. He is a fellow of the National Academy of Public Administration, an honorary member of the International City/County Management Association, and former member of the National Council of the American Society for Public Administration and chair of its section on Intergovernmental Administration and Management (SIAM), as well as recipient of SIAM's Stone Award for outstanding research contributions.

Vaughn Mamlin Upshaw, EdD, DrPH, is a lecturer in government and public administration at the University of North Carolina at Chapel Hill School of Government. Upshaw provides local elected officials and senior managers training in public administration, governance, and leadership. Upshaw has more than twenty years experience working with and serving on public and nonprofit governing boards at the local, state, and national levels.

Martin Vanacour, PhD, served the cities of Phoenix and Glendale, Arizona, for thirty-five years and retired as city manager of Glendale. He is a professor of practice and associate director of the School of Public Affairs at Arizona State University. He is a nationally known speaker and facilitator specializing in council manager relations. Vanacour received a PhD from ASU.

Douglas J. Watson, PhD, is professor and director of the public affairs program at The University of Texas at Dallas. He is the author or editor of *Local Government Management: Current Issues and Best Practices* (2003), *Spending a Lifetime: The Careers of City Managers* (2006), and *Civic Battles: When Cities Change Their Form of Government* (2007), and four other books. His work has appeared in *Public Administration Review, Review of Public Personnel Administration*, and other journals.

Craig M. Wheeland, PhD, is professor of political science at Villanova University and serves as associate vice president for academic affairs. He received an MPA from the University of South Carolina and a PhD from The Pennsylvania State University. His research interests include leadership by elected officials and professional administrators in city and suburban governments; collaborative problem-solving approaches, such as community-wide strategic planning; and municipal government institutions.

Curtis Wood, PhD, is an assistant professor in the master of public administration program at Northern Illinois University, where he teaches courses and conducts research in public management, ethics, and regional governance. He is a co-author of *The Adapted City: Institutional Dynamics and Structural Change* with H. George Frederickson and Gary Alan Johnson. He has twenty years of municipal government experience, seventeen years as a finance director.

Kaifeng Yang, PhD, is an assistant professor at the Askew School of Public Administration and Policy, Florida State University. His research interests include public and performance management, citizen involvement, and institutions. His work has appeared in *Public Administration Review, Public Performance & Management Review*, and *Public Integrity*, among others.

Eric S. Zeemering, PhD, is assistant professor of public administration at San Francisco State University, where he teaches urban administration and intergovernmental relations. He completed his PhD at Indiana University in 2007. His dissertation examines the role of local elected officials in the development of interlocal collaboration in Michigan.

Yahong Zhang, PhD, is an assistant professor at the School of Public Affairs and Administration (SPAA), Rutgers University at Newark. Her research involves local government, public policy, institutions, and gender issues in the public sector. She teaches research methods and urban policies.

CONCEPTUALIZING THE FACILITATIVE MODEL

Chapter 1

Reexamining Models of Mayoral Leadership

James H. Svara

Contents

1.1 Introduction

The mayor's office in city government is an inherently challenging position. Mayors have constituents who are in close proximity and expect attention to matters that are extremely specific, localized, and sometimes only partially within the sphere of city government action, if at all. Mayors can never have enough knowledge, authority, or resources to deal with all the myriad problems brought to their attention, but they are still expected to be the "problem-solver–in-chief" in their community. At the same time, mayors are expected to provide a sense of direction and purpose for their cities even though cities are subject to many forces in the larger government system, in the society, and in the economy over which they have very little control. They even create a sense of civic identity for their jurisdictions. Thus, mayors are expected to make their cities work in small and large matters, and these expectations are probably quite similar across cities of different sizes and across countries.

Mayors differ considerably, however, in the formal setting and the cultural milieu in which they operate. Some have extensive direct administrative powers in their organizations and separate authority vis-à-vis the city council in establishing and carrying out policy. Others are part of the council with limited or no direct independent administrative authority. The responsibilities of the mayors to their communities may be very similar, but the capacity of the organization in which they work and the tools of leadership and the resources on which they can draw differ substantially. They also fill their positions in a national political culture that shapes norms about what leaders do and how they operate. Approaches that are consistent with norms seem natural and are considered to be appropriate, whereas approaches that counter norms may be criticized in the media or misunderstood. It is likely that formal structures and cultural norms generally reflect and reinforce each other, but this is not always the case and is not possible when differing structural approaches are used in the same country, as is the case in the United States (Mouritzen and Svara, 2002).

Persons selected to the top elected office in their cities bring a number of personal characteristics to the position that interact with the formal features of the office. Of particular concern are the factors that shape the mayor's key interactions and the mayor's impact on the direction of city government. These are the leadership style of the mayor and the mayor's sense of vision. Other personal factors are important as well, such as the mayor's ability to communicate in a variety of settings and the mayor's level of energy and commitment, but in this discussion we will assume that mayors who are effective in the other two areas—style and vision—are also capable of getting their message across and devote sufficient energy to the position. Style and vision interact in a number of important ways, but they will be considered separately. Style and vision differ in how they are impacted by structural features. Mayors can be highly visionary even if they have limited formal powers, just as formally strong mayors can lack vision.

Style of leadership as it pertains to how one interacts with others is more likely to be shaped by formal structure. For example, the classic types of leadership styles are autocratic or controlling, democratic or participative, and laissez-faire. Considering the first two styles, it is likely that a controlling style will be more common in cities where mayors have extensive formal powers to reward and punish others, whereas the sharing style will be more common where the mayor and the city council have similar formal powers. Still, leaders make choices about how they interact with others that can run counter to these expectations. Beyond form of government, cultural values may also reinforce one style or another.

The situation in the United States is unique because two forms of local government in American cities are widely used.* The two forms differ in formal structure. The mayor–council form is based on the constitutional principle of separation of powers between the mayor and the council, and the council–manager form is based on the unitary principle with all authority assigned to the city council that appoints a professional city manager (Newland 1985). The two forms tend to differ in their internal process with conflict common in the mayor–council form and cooperation common in the council–manager form (Svara 1990), and this difference persists even when controlling for a wide range of other characteristics of the city, such as size, growth, and socio-economic status, as well as city government features, such as council size and partisanship (Nollenberger 2008). There is recurring debate about the advantages and disadvantages and strengths and weaknesses of the two forms. The last fifteen years has been a time of relatively high intensity in the debate (Gurwitt 1997; Ehrenhalt 2004; O'Neill 2005).

The difference in the mayor's position is one of the most important sources of variation between the two forms of government. It has been common to use the same criteria to assess the mayor's potential for leadership regardless of form. When the preconditions of mayoral leadership are assumed to include formal authority over staff and financial resources, it is common to view the mayor in council–manager cities as an incomplete figurehead who fills only ceremonial functions (Pressman 1972; Bowers and Rich 2000). There is another well developed but still not widely recognized approach. Mayors in council–manager cities can provide leadership that is appropriate to the structural setting in which they function (Wikstrom 1979). These mayors can be effective and can make a difference in their cities using an approach to leadership that differs from that found in mayor–council cities. I have proposed a leadership model that identifies what is unique and potentially positive about the mayors in council–manager cities. These mayors can be facilitative leaders (Svara 1987) who guide their cities rather than drive them (Svara 1990). The characteristics of the office in the major forms of government are appropriate to different logics of leadership (Wheeland 2002).

Mayors who are effective at filling the facilitative model improve the performance of the city council and the city government overall as indicated by survey

---

* This was formerly the case in Germany and to a slight extent is now found in England, where eleven local authorities have opted to change to a form of government based on an elected executive mayor.

data and by case studies of successful mayors in city governments and chairpersons in county governments (Svara et al. 1994). There is limited evidence from case reports and a small sample study that mayors in mayor–council cities can be effective using the facilitative approach (Svara et al. 1994).

The Facilitative Leader in Local Government (Svara et al. 1994) presented the facilitative model of leadership illustrated by eight case studies of mayors in council–manager cities and one from a city that had recently changed from the commission to the mayor–council form of government. This book builds on that work conceptually and presents ten case studies from council–manager cities, three from mayor–council cities, and one from a city in Denmark that uses a quasi-parliamentary form that is similar to the council–manager form as a form of government with unified authority, but like a mayor–council form in the sense that the mayor has executive authority. This book will reexamine facilitative leadership in council–manager cities, and also consider to what extent mayors in mayor–council cities incorporate a facilitative approach in their leadership style and what effect it has. The Danish case study helps us to clarify the cultural values in which leadership is embedded by examining facilitation in the context of another country.

The topic needs to be reexamined for several reasons. Cities face new conditions including demographic change and increased fiscal pressures that make it more difficult to sustain facilitative leadership. In the past fifteen years, the importance of the mayor's office has come to be more widely recognized in council–manager cities. Some cities have made structural changes to "empower" the mayor and enhance the office as a focal point of political leadership in council–manager cities, and some have changed to an elected executive form of government (Frederickson, Johnson, and Wood 2003; Mullin, Peele, and Cain 2004), although both kinds of changes are uncommon and other cities have rejected change in structure. City councils have become more diverse and members are more actively committed to their own agendas for political action (Svara 2003). The case studies will examine how mayors deal with divergent views on their councils and foster a sense of shared commitment in the face of opposition and conflicting priorities in their cities. Many cities are confronting a critical question: Can mayors without separate formal powers be effective leaders? Other cities might examine the opposite question: Can mayors with formal powers provide more effective leadership by using facilitative approaches?

Assessment of mayoral leadership takes place in the context of the two major forms of government used in American cities. As background to the exploration of the mayor's office, it is important to review how use of forms of government is changing in the United States.

1.2 Distribution of Forms of Government

There are two trends with respect to the use of form of government in American cities since 1990. The proportion of cities that uses the council–manager form of government continues to increase. At the same time, changes within form or change of form are being made or considered in some large cities.

The use of the council–manager form in cities has steadily increased since its appearance in the first decades of the twentieth century, and the trend continues. Since 1990, the number of cities over 2,500 in population using the council–manager form has increased by over 1,000, and the number of mayor–council cities has decreased by over 500 during this time period. The overall percentages of cities using the major forms and other forms of government in 1990 and 2005 are presented in Table 1.1.

There is substantial change in form for cities under 10,000 in population. It is likely that the increased number of council–manager cities comes from newly incorporated cities that adopt the form, and from growing cities that change from the mayor–council to the council–manager form. In cities over 10,000 in population, there has been relative stability over the past fifteen years in the use of the mayor–council form and other forms of government, along with a dramatic increase in the number of council–manager cities. Because growing Sunbelt and suburban cities are more likely to use the council–manager form (Frederickson, Johnson, and Wood 2003), council–manager cities tend to move up the population scale. Still, the council–manager form is used more than the mayor–council form in central cities (Svara 2005), and council–manager governments represent a slightly larger share in all but one city-size category in 2005 compared to 1990.

In council–manager cities, there is increasing recognition of the importance of mayoral leadership (National Civic League 2003). In a number of large council–manager cities, the role of the mayor has expanded and, in some cities, the office has been formally "empowered," e.g., Cincinnati, Kansas City, Long Beach,

Table 1.1 Change in Use of Major Forms of Government: 1990 to 2005

All Cities over 2,500 in Population	1990 % (number)	2005 % (number)	Change	Change: Cities under 10K	Change: Cities over 10K
Mayor–council	54.5 (3645)	43.3 (3096)	−11.2 (−549)	−540	−9
Council–manager	36.2 (2420)	49.1 (3505)	12.8 (1085)	561	524
Other	9.2 (617)	7.6 (543)	−1.6 (−74)	−48	−26
Total	99.9 (6682)	100.0 (7144)	– (462)	1990 (3914) 2005 (3887) Diff = − 27	1990 (2768) 2005 (3257) Diff = 489

Source: Data from *The Municipal Year Book,* 1991 and 2006.

and San Jose. The mayor in the cities other than Long Beach has the authority to nominate the city manager, although the selection is still made by the entire city council. In Long Beach, the mayor can veto the council's selection or removal of the manager. The mayors in these cities also present their own budget recommendations to their councils in addition to city managers' recommended budgets that are also presented to the council. Since 1990, the council–manager form has been replaced with the mayor–council form in nine cities with population over 100,000: Fresno, California; Hartford, Connecticut; Miami, Florida; Oakland, California; Richmond, Virginia; St. Petersburg, Florida; San Diego, California; Spokane, Washington; and Toledo, Ohio. During this time period, the council–manager form replaced the mayor–council form in Topeka, Kansas, and El Paso, Texas. Abandonment of the council–manager form was rejected in Cincinnati, Ohio; Dallas, Texas; and Kansas City, Missouri. The debate over form of government and/or powers for the mayor in large council–manager cities will probably continue as more council–manager cities move into very large city status. The number of council–manager cities over 250,000 in population has increased from 23 to 27 between 1990 and 2005. The population of Phoenix, Arizona; San Antonio, Texas; and Dallas, Texas, exceeds one million, and San Jose, California, is approaching the million-person threshold.

The perceived need for stronger political leadership along with criticism of divided councils and, on occasion, incompetent city managers are offered as arguments for the shift to the mayor–council form (Hassett and Watson 2007). In contrast, the potential for stalemate, misuse of mayoral powers, and lower levels of professionalism are used by critics as arguments against the strong mayor form, and the council–manager form is promoted for its stronger council governance and professionalism in policy advice, administration, and management (Svara 2006).

Mayors tend to use different styles of leadership depending on form, but they share some characteristics. All mayors can be visionary and seek to identify new approaches and goals for their cities. In large cities, mayors generally are becoming more media-based in their campaigns rather than relying on parties, and promote change through appealing directly to voters over the heads of members of the city council (Flanagan 2004). Mayors, like other political leaders at all levels of government and worldwide, are asserting themselves more in their relationship with administrative staff. The greater control and expanded involvement in administrative matters evidenced by Margaret Thatcher and Tony Blair in the United Kingdom, and Ronald Reagan, Bill Clinton, and George W. Bush at the, U.S. national level has been illustrated in city politics by mayors such as Rudy Giuliani (New York City) and Stephen Goldsmith (Indianapolis) in mayor–council cities, as well as the expansion of formal powers or the visibility of the mayor in some council–manager cities (Svara 2007). This expanded involvement by the mayor could significantly alter the roles of the mayor and manager, impact mayor–council relationships, and affect administrative operations depending on how it is carried out.

The issue to be explored in this chapter and in the case studies is how mayors manifest their expanded involvement. Mayors do not necessarily seek to diminish the contributions of other officials or to impose their views on others while increasingly asserting themselves. Council–manager mayors typically are not able to use a power-oriented style to control city government, but they can be visionary and strive with others to shape the city's agenda. In mayor–council cities, although the structure may predispose mayors to use their power to overcome conflict with other officials, the mayor may adopt a cooperative mode of interacting with the city council. As we shall see in data presented in this chapter, it is a choice made fairly often even though it has been rarely recognized. Although form creates constraints and predispositions, it does not dictate style.

1.3 Dimensions of Mayoral Leadership

There are two dimensions that shape how leaders interact with followers: their relationship style and their approach to shaping purpose and direction. In this section, we will examine a style based on facilitation, and direction setting based on creating a vision of the future.

1.3.1 The Facilitative Model

It is possible to conceive of leadership in government as collaborative and focused on accomplishment of common goals.* The facilitative model presumes that relationships among officials are essentially cooperative, although it is not clear whether this is a prior condition of a facilitative approach or a result of using the facilitative approach.†

1.3.1.1 Facilitative Model in the Leadership Literature

This view of the mayor's office is consistent with a number of studies of leadership that emphasize facilitation rather than power or control as the basis for leadership. These include studies that focus on the private sector, such as Bennis (1985 and 1989), Gilmore (1988), and Kouzes and Posner (2002). The key leadership attributes identified in these studies are creating a vision and securing broad commitment and participation from organizational members. The two dimensions identified in the mayor's leadership—coordination and direction setting—parallel dimensions in

---

* For a review of previous research on alternate approaches to leadership in government and facilitative leadership in the private sector, see Svara et al. (1994, chap. 1.) This section summarizes the main arguments from that chapter.

† In the mayor–council form, separation of powers is supposed to lead to conflict as one official checks the power of another.

the "seven habits" identified by Covey (1989) in his assessment of the qualities that are associated with effectiveness. Effective leaders stress empathetic communication, think in "win/win" terms rather than seeing their interests in conflict with those of others, and use synergy to make the whole greater than the sum of the parts. Furthermore, effective leaders are proactive, have a clear sense of the ends they wish to achieve, and prioritize tasks to achieve long-term goals. Thus, effective leaders improve process and sharpen the sense of purpose.

These elements are also found in the leadership traits of facilitative team managers described by Rees (1991). Leaders improve the process of interaction by empowering participation and developing consensus and focus on the purpose toward which the group is working. To Cufaude (2004), facilitative leaders "make connections and help others make meaning" and "provide direction without totally taking the reins."

Two styles of leadership and two types of organizations are posited in these writings. One is an authoritarian style with one-way or top-down communication. The leader seeks to use powers of the office and manipulate people and resources to establish control. The counter style stresses the following skills: helping groups solve problems, listening, communicating, developing team capacity, coaching, motivating, inspiring (Rees 1991). The roles of the facilitative leader are to "listen, ask questions, direct group process, coach, teach, build consensus, share in goal setting, share in decision making, [and] empower others to get things done." When people are not in charge, Bellman (1992) points out that they are "primarily in the business of supporting other people in the accomplishment of their own goals." Consequently, to be effective you must "lead from the middle" (Bellman 1992). A strong advocate of viewing leadership in terms of service rather than power is Richard Greenleaf, whose concept of servant leadership is finding support in the business world (Kiechel, 1992). The servant-leader is one who "wants to serve, to serve *first*." In time, "conscious choice brings one to aspire to lead." This leader is "sharply different from one who is a *leader* first." (Greenleaf 1977).

The organization that matches the control or power-oriented style is hierarchical in nature. Increasingly, organizations are flatter and loosely knit. This counter view sees organizations as networks with fluid authority, ambiguous limits, and overlapping domains. Crosby and Bryson (2005) argue that the world is characterized by shared power. Leaders in this setting "inspire and motivate followers through persuasion, example, and empowerment, not through command and control. Such leaders foster dialogue with their followers and the situations in which they find themselves, and they encourage collective action to address real problems" (Crosby and Bryson 2005) They cannot rely on formal authority or position power to get things done.

Kouzes and Posner (2002), in their review of the practices and commitments of successful leaders, stress the importance of facilitation. They find that effective leaders enable others to act by fostering collaboration and strengthening others. They inspire a shared view of the future and enlist the support and involvement of others. Leadership comes through modeling rather than commanding, and effective leaders set an example. Finally, they elevate followers—"encouraging the heart"—by recognizing the contributions of others and celebrating accomplishments (as opposed to taking personal credit.) This kind of leadership presumes an inclusive approach and working with others rather than achieving power over them or manipulating resources to secure their support. As Covey (1989) puts it, leaders must inspire "creative cooperation." Taken together, these writers articulate a distinct paradigm of leadership. The paradigm appears to be a startling departure from what we expect to find in the corporate world associated with a "think big and kick ass" philosophy (Trump and Zanker 2007), but it is becoming the accepted leadership style (Gergen 2005). The facilitative model might seem completely alien to the political process, although, as noted, it is appropriate to a shared power world (Crosby and Bryson 2005) and an era of "new governance" with widespread partnerships and networking across sectors and jurisdictions (Kettl 2002).

The superiority of the facilitative approach in all sectors is supported by the *Good to Great* research of Jim Collins (2001; 2005.) Successful companies, nonprofits, and governments that sustain excellence for the long term have "type 5" leaders. They combine selflessness and a focus on making the right decisions that will advance central goals. They perform better over the long term than the highly visible and charismatic change agents who produce only short-term gains. The type 4 leader can also be effective and "catalyzes commitment to and vigorous pursuit of a clear and compelling vision, stimulating higher performance standards" (Collins 2005). This approach, however, is leader-centered rather than enlisting the support, ideas, and energy of a wide range of actors. The distinction is similar to the difference between the "transformational" leader who attempts to drive change (Couto 1995), and James Macgregor Burns' ideal: "transforming leadership." This occurs when "one or more persons *engage* with others in such a way that leaders and followers raise one another to higher levels of motivation and morality" (Burns 1978). In Burns' view, "the genius of leadership lies in the manner in which leaders see and act on their own and their followers' values and motivations" (1978).

The characteristics of the facilitative leader in top elected positions in local government can be divided into three categories: the attitude toward other officials, kinds of interactions fostered, and approach to goal setting. Table 1.2 presents the characteristics of the facilitative leader.

The leader who uses the facilitative approach is committed to helping other officials accomplish their goals. He or she promotes open communication among officials. The approach to managing conflict stresses collaboration in which the interests of the leader and others are mutually satisfied. The leader shares leadership and seeks to coordinate efforts among officials. Finally, the leader seeks to create a shared vision that incorporates his or her own goals *and* the goals of others, promotes commitment to that shared vision, and focuses efforts of all involved on accomplishing the vision. In view of the importance of broad participation in shaping vision, some might conclude that the leader has no significant role. Robert

Table 1.2   Characteristics of the Facilitative Leader in Local Government

Attitude Toward Other Officials:
■ The leader does not attempt to control or diminish the contributions of other officials.
■ The leader empowers others by drawing out their contributions and helping them accomplish their goals.
■ The leader values and maintains mutual respect and trust.
Kind of Interactions Fostered:
■ The leader promotes open and honest communication among officials.
■ The leader seeks to manage conflict and resolve differences in a way that advances the mutual interests of all officials.
■ The leader is willing to share leadership and form partnerships.
■ The leader fosters understanding of distinct roles and coordinated effort among officials.
Approach to Goal Setting:
■ The leader fosters the creation of a shared vision incorporating his or her goals and the goals of others.
■ The leader promotes commitment to the shared vision.
■ The leader focuses the attention and efforts of officials on accomplishing the shared vision.

Source: Svara et al. 1994. *Facilitative Leadership in Local Government: Lessons from Successful Mayors and Chairpersons in the Council–Manager Form*, San Francisco: Jossey-Bass. With permission.

and Janet Denhardt (2006) reject this conclusion and assert that the leader retains a central role in the visioning process.

> It's just a different role. Instead of coming up with the vision, the leader must "integrate and articulate the group's vision." In some ways, this is more difficult than the leader's deciding alone.

In the facilitative process, the leader ensures that there is a vision that is understood and widely accepted and that it is the focal point for action.

Facilitative leadership is the style that is natural (or at least has fewer impediments) in the council–manager form of the government. The mayor is the leader of a collective body with few if any separate powers. The mayor in mayor–council cities with separate powers can choose to use facilitation or rely on formal and informal resources to use an asserting and controlling style of leadership.

1.3.2 Visionary Leadership

It seems reasonable to assume that having a clear sense of purpose has always been an important factor in leadership, and it appears that having vision is becoming even more important. In contrast to the approach taken in *The Facilitative Leader* when the visionary quality was subsumed in the larger facilitative model, it is now singled out as a characteristic to be examined separately. New methods of communication and new media for reaching more people more quickly over greater distances make it easier to inform and align a wide array of actors and make it possible to engage and enlist more people in the cause the leader espouses. These potentialities presume, however, that the leader is conveying ideas that capture the imagination and secure support. A leader with a vision of the future can bring followers together. A leader who lacks vision—and fails to bring group members into a process to create a vision—leaves followers in a state of uncertainty and confusion. They may follow different leaders or pursue their own separate ends.

Kouzes and Posner (2002) identify a number of practices that pertain to visionary leadership. To them, "envisioning the future" is the practice that "most differentiates" leaders from other persons we respect. It is important for leaders to challenge the process by searching for opportunities, experimenting, and taking risks. By enlisting others, leaders seek to inspire a shared vision. It provides "a clear picture of what it would look and feel like if [the organization] were achieving its mission" (Crosby and Bryson 2005). Beyond the content, a shared vision creates an emotional connection between people and the leader (Denhardt and Denhardt 2006).

There are interconnections between a facilitative style and vision. To Kousez and Posner (2002), they are entirely intermixed because enlisting and sharing are linked to vision. Leaders who base their leadership on formal or informal powers may have some advantages in promoting their ideas and securing the support of some backers, but ultimately a leader is not viewed as a visionary by offering rewards or threatening sanctions. Mayors and other leaders cannot "impose a self-motivating vision on others" (Kouzes and Posner 2002). Denhardt and Denhardt (2006) argue that we increasingly recognize that "broad participation in setting the goals, directions, and vision of a group or organization is helpful in arriving at the most comprehensive and creative statement, as well as the one most likely to be implemented."

Still, facilitation is not enough by itself. The official who uses the facilitative style has difficulty reaching the highest level of leadership without being visionary. According to Kouzes and Posner (2002), "before you can inspire others, you have to be inspired yourself." Although the facilitator without vision can move the organization forward by helping to get the ideas expressed by others accepted as shared goals, it is also possible that others will not have the ideas that generate widespread support. The mayor must be able to step forward, articulate goals that others are willing to accept, and persuade others to support them. Many officials and citizens alike are conditioned to look to the mayor for leadership. Mayors have the opportunity to meet this expectation and may frustrate followers if they are not able to offer ideas about future projects and goals.

There is no reason why mayors should differ greatly in the level of visionary leadership based on form of government, although differences may be produced by resources, expectations, or the type of persons who seek the office and are then elected. In surveys of city administrators in 1997 and city elected officials in city government in 2001, respondents were asked the following question:

> Do you agree or disagree with the following statement? The mayor is a visionary person who constantly initiates new projects and policies for the city.

The council–manager mayor can act in this way by developing ideas for other council members to consider. Mayor–council mayors are expected to act in this way and have more latitude to operate independently. Indeed, the ideal leadership type in city government is the innovator or policy entrepreneur who would behave in ways consistent with this definition (Dahl 1961; Talbot 1967; Ferman 1985). Despite these considerations, we shall assume that visionary leadership can be found in any setting. Furthermore, we will *not* presume that a mayor will display both vision and facilitation, but rather look for the actual variation in the combinations in each major form of government.

1.4 Mayoral Leadership and Form of Government

A number of measures of leadership and governmental performance were included in a survey conducted for the National League of Cities in 2001 (Svara 2003). This survey was the first to allow the comparison of the level of facilitative and visionary leadership by mayors in both mayor–council and council–manager cities. The survey was conducted in cities over 25,000 in population, and the response rate was 33 percent. Table 1.3 reports the responses of council members (with the mayor excluded) on a number of indicators of the mayor and council's performance. It offers some general comparisons of cities with the two major forms of government. These indicators will be analyzed in greater depth later in this section.

The mayor in mayor–council cities is much more likely to be viewed as a visionary by council members, although the difference is not as great when only mayors in council–manager cities who are directly elected are considered.* On the

---

* For those directly elected, 45.6 percent were considered to be visionaries, compared to 34.5 percent of the mayors selected within the council.

Table 1.3 Council Member Ratings of City Government Features by Form of Government

	Mayor–Council (%)	Council–Manager (%)
Mayor is a visionary[1]	57	42
Mayor and council have a good working relationship[1]	64	80
Mayor accomplishes council goals[2]	43	n/a
Mayor helps council set goals[2]	n/a	46
Effectiveness of council at long-term goal setting[3]	46	69
Effectiveness of council at oversight of administration[3]	39	61
Number of respondents	227 (21 mayors excluded)	320 (67 mayors excluded)

[1] *% agree;*

[2] *% very good/good rating;*

[3] *% excellent/good rating.*

other hand, the council–manager mayor more commonly has a positive working relationship with council members. Ratings are similar on two measures dealing with the mayor's support for council goals setting or accomplishment of council goals. In both forms of government, just under half of the mayors work closely with the council in determining the direction of the city. The implications of not working together on goals are likely to be different. In the council–manager form, the absence of mayoral attention means that the council members must wrestle with setting goals on their own with the advice of the city manager. In the mayor–council form, the failure of mayors to incorporate the goals of council members probably means that mayors work on their own agenda and expect the council to fall in line.

When comparing how well key functions are performed by the council, the council–manager councils perform substantially better at setting long-term goals and at overseeing the performance of administrative staff. In the following sections, we will examine how the mayor's characteristics affect council performance and how the council assesses the mayor in council–manager and mayor–council cities.

1.4.1 Council–Manager Cities

In this section and the next, a number of measures of mayor a characteristics and council performance will be presented for cities with respondents divided by different forms of government. In all the data analysis, mayors have been excluded.

1.4.1.1 Facilitative Roles of the Mayor

The mayor in the council–manager form occupies a strategic location at the center of communication channels with the council, the city manager, and outside actors including citizens, community leaders, other governments, and the media (Svara 1990). Although occasionally dismissed as a ribbon cutter or ceremonial head of the government because of their lack of formal powers, close examination of these mayors indicates that they fill a wide range of roles, which fall into three broad categories (Svara 1994). The first set of roles are traditional or "automatic" in the sense that they are built into the office, and all mayors will fill them unless they are inept or make an effort to avoid them. Mayors perform *ceremonial* tasks and act as a *link to the public, presiding officer*, and *representative/promoter* for the city. A second set of roles involves active coordination and communication; active in the sense that the mayor must recognize and choose how to fill them. In these roles, the differences between more and less active mayors are likely to emerge. The mayor is an *articulator/mobilizer* of issues for the city, promotes *liaison and partnership with the manager*, and *strengthens teamwork*. In this role, the mayor works to coalesce the council into a cohesive team and establishes a positive "tone." Similarly, the mayor can *build networks* that connect individuals, groups, organizations, and other governments inside and beyond the community. Finally, the third category encompasses three additional roles that deal with policy leadership and guiding the work of the council. In the *goal setter* role, mayors engage in activities to create a sense of direction or a climate for change. As *delegator/organizer*, the mayor helps the council and manager understand and maintain their roles, including helping the council members understand their responsibilities. Finally, in the *policy initiator* role, the mayor develops programs and policies to address problems. If active in this role, the mayor is instrumental in shaping the city's or county's policy agenda and creating a shared vision.

These roles are mutually reinforcing and success in one enhances success in others. Further, they go on concurrently. Still, the performance of mayors will vary from city to city in two respects: how many roles are filled, and how well they are filled.

1.4.1.2 Indicators of Performance

The survey of council members in council–manager cities in 2001 contained four measures of the mayor's performance that relate to aspects of the facilitative model. These include:

1. Promoting communication within the council
2. Promoting a positive relationship between the council and the manager
3. Helping the council set goals and priorities
4. Articulating broad goals for the city

With cluster analysis, three types of mayors have been identified. The first tends to perform poorly in all four activities (35 percent of the mayors). The second is consistently between good and satisfactory in performance (33 percent). Finally, the third has ratings close to very good for all four areas (32 percent). Given the patterns of performance, the three types are labeled (1) caretaker, (2) coordinator, and (3) goal setter.

The three types of leader are associated with substantial differences in performance by the city council, and with different assessments of their own characteristics by council members. In Figure 1.1, a number of key governance functions handled by city councils are presented. When goal-setter mayors and, to a slightly

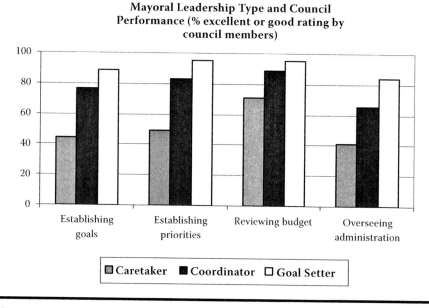

Figure 1.1 Mayoral leadership type and council performance (percent (%) excellent or good rating by council members).

lesser extent, the coordinator-type mayors are present, councils according to their own self-assessment perform much better in goal setting, establishing annual priorities and objectives, and overseeing administrative performance. In contrast, only two in five councils perform at an excellent or good level when mayoral leadership is limited. There is less variation in reviewing the budget.

Similar differences are found when council members assess their contribution and how they function as a governing body. Almost all members agree that the council provides sufficient direction and leadership when the mayor is a goal setter, whereas just over half agree when the mayor is classified as a caretaker. The differential is also found in the view that the council is not simply a reacting and vetoing body, that it avoids a short-term focus, that there is not sufficient time to consider policy issues, and that the council provides adequate appraisal of the city manager's performance. As was the case in performance in filling council functions, the coordinator-type mayor is associated with higher assessments that are close to those when the goal-setter type is found.

The type of leadership also makes a difference in handling problems or obstacles to performance. Council members were asked to identify whether certain conditions are a major problem that cause frustration to them as elected officials. Conflict among council members was identified as a source of frustration in almost three councils in five with caretaker-type mayors. In contrast, only one in five councils with a goal setter have this condition. In addition, lack of clear goals and unclear division of labor were less likely to be present when the mayor is a coordinator or goal setter.

Finally, in Figure 1.2, some indicators of the mayor's characteristics and performance are presented.

The goal setter and coordinator mayors almost always have a positive working relationship with the other members of the council and receive good ratings as a spokesperson for the council. The goal setter is also more likely than either of the other types to be seen as a visionary and to be effective at promoting the economic development of the city. Whereas the coordinator serves the council well and has a positive relationship with members, the goal setter is much more likely to provide an innovative quality. The caretaker often has a negative relationship with the council, not a positive one, and is seen to be an ineffective spokesperson or promoter of the city. Most strikingly, the caretaker is almost never considered to be a visionary.

1.4.1.3 Visionary Leadership

The connection between facilitative leadership and visionary leadership cannot be simply assumed. As indicated in Figure 1.2, most—over three quarters—of the goal setter-type mayors are also perceived to be visionaries, but almost a quarter are not. Does the presence or absence of the visionary quality make a difference when it is found alone or in combination with an indicator of facilitation? To make this determination, mayors are divided into four groups based on the ratings of council

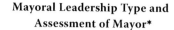

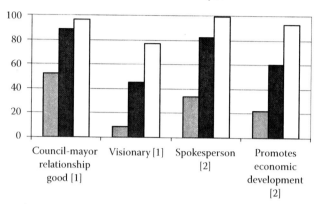

Figure 1.2   **Mayoral leadership type and assessment of mayor.**

members about whether the mayor is a visionary and how effective the mayor is at helping the council set goals. Most mayors either have both qualities or lack both. Almost a third of the mayors are visionaries and also are effective at helping the council set goals and objectives (32 percent), or they are not visionary and are ineffective at goal setting (44 percent). The breakdown is presented in Table 1.4. Only one-quarter have a mixed rating with a higher assessment in one dimension than the other.

In Figure 1.3, it is possible to see the impact of the combination of these characteristics on the council's performance in setting long-term goals. The figure presents the proportion of council members who rate their performance as excellent or good in setting goals. (Those who rate performance as satisfactory or poor are not included in the figure.)

When neither quality is present, less than half of the councils perform at an excellent or good level. The theoretically possible situation can occur when the mayor promotes his or her own ideas, but leaves the council out of the process of goal setting. The mayor, who is visionary but not effective at working with the council on goal setting, is associated with the second highest proportion of excellent ratings, but just seven in ten councils with this kind of mayor perform above the satisfactory level. Mayors who help the council, but offer few new ideas themselves, contribute to a generally good level of performance, but less often to very strong performance. These councils are able to draw on the recommendations of the city manager as well as their own ideas, but the absence of a visionary leader makes a difference in their level of accomplishment. The combination of vision and

Table 1.4   Council Member Assessment of Mayor's Visionary Leadership and Support for Council Goal Setting in Council–Manager Cities

	Effectiveness at Helping Council Set Goals	
Visionary	Very Good or Good	Fair or Poor
Yes	31.5	10.7
No	14.1	43.6

Note: All columns = 100%, number = 298.

facilitation achieves as much success over all, and almost half of the council members in these cities feel that they achieve excellent performance. These councils are apparently better able to focus not only on the process of goal setting, but the substance as well, in part because the mayor is contributing innovative ideas to advance the city. Figure 1.3 indicates that when mayors are *only* visionaries or only *help* the council, the city council is less likely to achieve the highest level of performance.

The relative importance of the mayor in enhancing the performance of the council does not imply that there is a competitive relationship with the city manager over the future direction of the city when the mayor is an effective and visionary goal setter. In fact, it appears that the mayor who assists with goal setting and is visionary has the highest level of complementarity with the city manager. Almost all council members agree that these mayors have a positive relationship with the city manager, and 71 percent agree completely when the mayor is both facilitative and visionary. With the other three combinations of qualities, most agree that the relationship is positive, but just over half agree completely when the mayor is either a visionary *or* a goal setting assister, and only one-third agree completely when the mayor is neither. When the mayor fails to bring one or both of these qualities—innovative ideas or attention to the goal setting process—to the governing process, there is a vacuum in leadership. The city manager helps fill the vacuum to some extent. Still, based on council members, assessment of their performance, the council does not perform as well when these leadership contributions from the mayor are missing, and city managers experience some weakening in the relationship with the mayor when the mayor's leadership is weaker.

In sum, facilitation is the model for leadership in council–manager cities. Mayors who combine this approach with their own sense of vision can greatly improve governmental outcomes and processes. The coordinator-type mayor also makes a contribution by improving internal communication, building cohesion within the council, and strengthening the interaction between the council and city manager. When the mayor is a caretaker, the council and manager work around the mayor rather than being guided by the mayor.

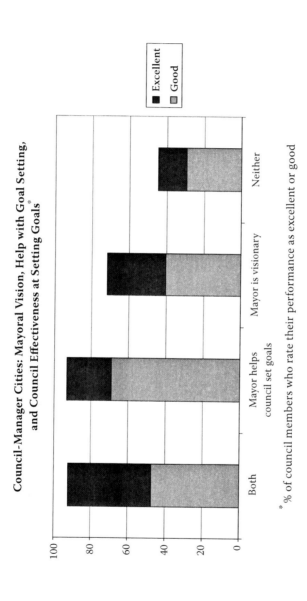

Figure 1.3 Council–manager cities: Mayoral vision, help with goal setting, and council effectiveness at setting goals.

1.4.2 Mayor–Council Cities

Most of the research on facilitative leadership by mayors has focused on council–manager cities. A major question that warrants further attention is whether this kind of leadership style is possible in mayor–council cities where the top elected official has a number of formal and informal powers on which to draw? The thrust of the literature of mayoral leadership in these cities in the United States has been to explore the mayor as the "driving force" in city government (Svara 1990). The ideal is an innovative or entrepreneurial leader who takes charge of the development of policy initiatives and makes sure that the implementation of policies is consistent with purpose. In both aspects of leadership, it is typically presumed that the effective mayor will generate a majority in favor of change from the disparate interests within the city and overcome resistance to change from other political and administrative actors (Yates 1977).

1.4.2.1 Facilitative Leadership

There are two contrasting perspectives on the question of whether these mayors can use the facilitative approach that presumes sharing of responsibility: working with other actors in a cooperative way, and focusing on accomplishing the policy goals of others as well as one's own goals. These behaviors may be ineffective when dealing with other actors who have incompatible goals, and may even leave the mayor subject to exploitation by others who could take advantage of the mayor's inclusive approach. The approach also seems to contradict the expectations of the media that the mayor *runs* the city. Significant sharing with others may create the impression that the mayor is weak. On the other hand, there is a long-standing recognition in research on presidential leadership that the greatest potential for leading others comes from the "power to persuade" (Neustadt 1980), a theme pursued by Wheeland in his case study of former mayor Ed Rendell of Philadelphia. This quality refers to the ability to bring others to understand and accept the leader's point of view by the quality of the ideas presented and by the leader's effectiveness at persuasion. This approach does not depend on rewards and threats to win supporters. Presumably, effectiveness at persuasion requires that the leader be open to the ideas of followers and peers and find ways to include their ideas in his or her own goals. This is an essential feature of facilitation. Another well-established principle in leadership research is that effective leaders vary their leadership style depending on circumstances, including the characteristics of the followers (Hersey and Blanchard 1993). Relying on a directive approach when interacting with others who share goals and values with the leader and who possess the capability to act on their own initiative fails to tap into the resources that followers can offer. Participative and team-oriented leadership broadens the capacity for change by aligning the talents and energies of the leader and followers. Having power over others does not mean that one uses it exclusively to fashion leadership or ignore other approaches to building support.

There is evidence of mayors using a facilitative approach in mayor–council cities (Gurwitt, 1993). A mayor from a strong mayor–council city concluded that mayors may be more effective if they stress cooperation with other participants in local government. Michael B. Keys (1990), mayor of Elyria, Ohio, who interviewed six other strong mayors, reported these findings:

■ Effective city government is characterized more by cooperation than by conflict.
■ The mayor should serve a team-building function, working to build consensus in the council.
■ The mayor should blend direction to the council in some areas with facilitation of the council's decision making in other areas.

Keys' conclusion was that the "executive mayor can, and has the desire to, serve a facilitative function with council on certain matters." To do so, elected chief executives need to understand this alternative approach to leadership and have training in the skills needed to operate successfully with a facilitative approach.

The survey of council members conducted in 2001 contains questions that permit an initial examination of the extent to which mayors in mayor–council cities use facilitative methods as part of their total leadership style. The responses will be examined to estimate how common it is to find facilitators in the mayor's office in mayor–council cities. Three case studies presented in Chapter 4, Chapter 14, and Chapter 15 will examine in depth how these mayors operate.

In the survey, respondents were asked to assess the quality of the performance of mayors in the following areas:

1. Providing the council with sufficient alternatives for making policy decisions
2. Providing the council with sufficient information and performance measures to assess the effectiveness of programs and services
3. Accomplishing the goals established by the council

The first examines whether mayors share information with council members and empower them to make policy choices drawing from a full array of policy options. Mayors that use the facilitative approach would inform the council about all appropriate options. Mayors that attempt to control the council emphasize their own preferred alternative and/or manipulate information in such a way as to restrict the council's capacity to make a free and informed decision. An example is dumping on the council large amounts of information supporting the mayor's preferred policy option with limited time to digest it or obtain information about alternatives. City councils usually have limited staff resources to undertake independent policy research.

The second indicator measures information sharing at the implementation and service delivery end of the governmental process. Providing adequate information about performance supports the council's oversight role. If there is tension in the relationship between executives and legislatures, oversight can be used as tool for the legislature to steer administrative action in directions preferred by the members and different from the priorities of the executive. Investigations by the council can be conducted in such as way as to be intrusive and damaging to the mayor. A former administrator observed that the mayor and his staff were suspicious of council investigations. "Investigation was war," he noted, and the way that council members come out as "stars" before the media was to make administrators "look bad" (Chase and Reveal 1983). From the council's perspective, an investigation may be the only way to secure information that the mayor is withholding from them. In circumstances like these, mayors may insert themselves between the council and administrative staff to limit the kind and amount of information that is provided to the council. Being forthcoming (providing information voluntarily), on the other hand, can promote cooperation and enhances the capacity of the council to monitor the administrative process.

The third measure is the clearest indicator of a facilitative approach. This set of survey questions was developed to evaluate the performance of the executive—either the city manager in the council–manager form or the mayor in the mayor–council form. Given our standard expectations of executive–legislative relations, it almost seems inappropriate to ask how well strong mayors work to accomplish the council's goals. It is easy to assume that in mayor–council cities, the usual question is how well the council accepts the mayor's goals. A common expectation is that if the council members don't get on board, a "strong" mayor will pressure or entice them to support his or her proposals. In actuality, as we saw in Table 1.2, over two-fifths of the council members in the survey indicated that the mayor does an excellent or good job of accomplishing his goals. This could indicate that the council's goals are the same as the mayor's goals and, therefore, the mayor is being self-centered in accomplishing what the council has decided. It appears, however, that there is a sharing of views that has led to mutuality of purposes. This is the same condition achieved by the goal setting facilitative mayor in council–manager cities.

Cluster analysis of the three ratings of the mayor by council members produces three types of mayors that differ with regard to their relationship to the council. The results are presented in Table 1.5.

The first type is largely separated from the council and has low ratings on providing policy options, providing information for oversight, and accomplishing the council's goals. The second type is fairly reserved in the relationship and receives intermediate or satisfactory ratings on the three measures. The third type is supportive of the council and receives excellent to good ratings. The three groups are close to equal in size with the supportive type having a slight plurality.

When mayors have a supportive relationship with the council, the performance of the city council is substantially stronger than in cities where the mayor is more distant. As indicated in Figure 1.4, the differential is similar to that found in council–manager cities with mayors of the goal-setter type.

Table 1.5 Types of Mayoral Relationships to City Council in Mayor–Council Cities

| Type of Relationship | Average Ratings by Council Members: How Well Does the Mayor ... | | | Proportion of Cities |
	Present Policy Options*	Provide Information for Oversight	Accomplish Council Goals	
Separate	3.9	3.9	3.6	32.4%
Reserved/ cool	3.0	2.7	2.9	31.1%
Supportive	1.7	1.8	1.6	36.5%

* Scale: 1 = excellent; 4 = poor. No. = 219.

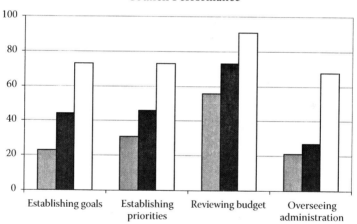

Mayor Relationship to Council and Council Performance*

*% Excellent or good rating by council members

▨ Separate   ■ Reserved   ☐ Supportive

Figure 1.4   Mayor relationship to council and council performance.

Most councils with supportive mayors perform at a high level. With the exception of budget review, most city councils with reserved mayors are poor or only satisfactory in performance; just over two in five of the council members give themselves an excellent or good rating at establishing goals and setting priorities, and only one in four provide a good rating for overseeing administration. Less than a

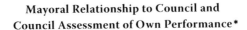

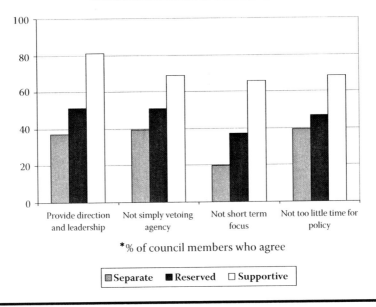

Figure 1.5 Mayoral relationship to council and council assessment of own performance.

quarter of the councils with separate type mayors perform at a good or better level in three areas.

The same differentials are present in indicators of council characteristics, as shown in Figure 1.5. With supportive mayors, four-fifths of the councils provide direction and leadership to their cities, and seven in ten are not simply reactive bodies that accept or reject recommendations of the mayor. These councils that work with supportive mayors are not likely to have a short-term focus or lack the time to address policy issues. When the mayor is separated from the council, only two in five council members agree that they provide direction, do not simply try to check the mayor, and have enough time for policy. Only one in five feels that the council does not focus on short-term matters.

The mayor's style in relating to the council has an impact on internal relations in the council, despite the fact that mayors do not typically chair the council. In over half of the councils in cities with a separate or reserved mayor, internal conflict within the council is a major source of frustration for council members. In contrast, this condition is found in only one-quarter of the cities with a supportive mayor. As would be expected, the relationship between the mayor and the council is positive in over 90 percent of the cities with supportive mayors. In comparison, 60 percent and 35 percent of the council members with reserved and separated mayors, respectively, consider the relationship with the mayor to be good.

In cities that have a chief administrator or chief administrative officer (CAO), it is always an important question whether the CAO is considered to be the agent of the mayor alone, or an official who serves both the mayor and council.* When the mayor has a supportive relationship with the council, the CAO is viewed by nearly three-quarters of the council members to be equally accountable to the mayor and the council. In cities with reserved mayors, approximately half the council members take this view. When mayors separate themselves from the council, only one in ten agree that the CAO is equally accountable. In these councils, the predominant view is that the CAO's accountability is tied to the mayor alone.

Thus, the interactions between the mayor and council in mayor–council cities are more varied than we have recognized in previous research. Mayors who seek to accomplish the goals of the council can be found in cities of all sizes.† When mayors (and council members) set aside separation of powers and work together, council performance is enhanced and working relationships are more positive. A reserved and cool relationship produces some, but fewer, benefits. When mayors separate themselves from the council, the council flounders and is ineffective, has extensive internal dissension, has a conflictual relationship with the mayor, and receives little information from the CAO.

1.4.2.2 Visionary Leadership

As noted in the discussion of council–manager mayors, it is possible that mayors will come up with their own new ideas, but not be very good at helping the council develop goals. The qualities of being visionary and helping others develop goals usually either go together or are both absent in council–manager cities. Only 10 percent were visionary but not effective at promoting council goal setting, and 15 percent were good at goal setting but not visionary (presented earlier). The survey used in mayor–council cities permits a similar assessment. In these cities, the comparison can be made between being visionary and being effective at accomplishing the goals of the council. As indicated below, there are two substantial groups of mayors who are either visionary and help accomplish the council's goals or not visionary and, therefore, ineffective. In addition, however, one in five is visionary, but not attentive to the goals of the council. These mayors might be labeled go-your-own-way innovators because they come up with new ideas, but do not incorporate the council's goals in a way that the council members consider to be effective. Only one in twenty mayor–council mayors are good at council goal accomplishment, but

---

* In mayor–council cities over 10,000 in population, approximately 45 percent have a city administrator. Among the respondents to this survey, 41 percent report having a city administrator.
† In mayor–council cities 25,000 to 50,000 in population, 45 percent of the mayors receive very good or good ratings at accomplishing the goals of the council. In the 50,000 to 99,999 population range, 37 percent received this rating. In cities of over 100,000, 41 percent received this rating.

Table 1.6   Council Member Assessment of Mayor's Visionary Leadership and Effectiveness at Accomplishing Council Goals in Mayor–Council Cities

	Accomplish Goals of Council	
Visionary	*Very Good or Good*	*Fair to Poor*
Yes	37.3	20.3
No	5.5	36.9

Note: All columns = 100%; number = 217

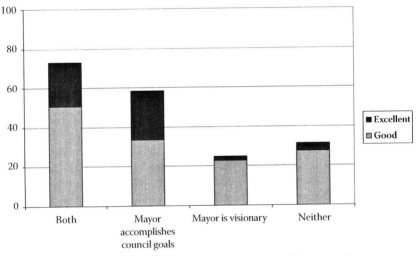

M-C Cities: Mayor as Visionary and Accomplisher of
Council Goals and Council Effectiveness at Setting Goals*

*% of council members who rate their performance as excellent or good

Figure 1.6   Mayor–council cities: Mayor as visionary and accomplisher of council goals and council effectiveness at setting goals.

are not visionaries themselves. The combinations are presented in Table 1.6. These combinations of mayoral leadership are related to the effectiveness of the council in setting long-term goals.

Figure 1.6 is similar to Figure 1.3 presented above regarding council–manager mayors. The mayors who are highly rated in both areas are associated with councils that are generally effective at setting long-term goals. Three of five councils with mayors who accomplish council goals, but are not visionary themselves, are excellent or good at goal setting, although there are few mayors in this category (only 5 percent of the total). The mayor's vision does little to help the council's performance when the mayor gives limited attention to the council's goals. Only one-quarter of these councils are effective, even less than the proportion that works with mayors who are neither visionary nor concerned with the council's goals. This result is quite different than the one found in council–manager cities. Whereas one-quarter of the councils that work with a council–manager mayor who is only visionary do not achieve a good or excellent level of performance, three-quarters of the councils in mayor–council cities with visionary-only mayors are not highly effective at setting long-term goals.

The lack of council effectiveness with visionary-only mayors does not necessarily mean that these mayors are not effective in areas over which they have substantial control. Two-thirds of this group are seen as excellent or good at improving efficiency, and three-quarters get this rating in promoting economic development, although in the assessment of efficiency, the good ratings outnumber the excellent ratings. Among mayors who are nonvisionary and do not help the council, only 26 and 36 percent are good or better at improving efficiency and promoting development, respectively, and few receive an excellent rating.

In contrast, among those who advance their own ideas and also help accomplish the council's goals, almost all get high marks from the council, and those with excellent ratings outnumber those with good ratings by a two-to-one margin. It is possible that mayors who work constructively with the council are able to come up with more innovative ideas and to be more effective because they are spending less time and energy in conflicts or boundary disputes with the council, and are getting support rather than resistance from the council. To expect the strong, yet solitary, mayor to be an effective innovator who keeps the council at a distance is not consistent with the assessment given by council members. A majority of these mayors make a mark and achieve effectiveness, but far fewer succeed and they achieve a lower level of effectiveness than the visionary mayors who adopt an inclusive approach to leadership and promote the council's goals as well as their own.

Considering the evidence, the facilitative approach manifested in sharing information with the council, empowering the council's policy-making and oversight functions, and incorporating the council's goals into the goals of the mayor, appears to achieve better results than a power-over approach vis-à-vis the council. Innovative mayors have sufficient power to have an impact on city government acting on their own, but they will have greater impact if they work with the council to expand the power to address the problems of the city. The emphasis in the general leadership literature on the importance of inclusion and collaboration appears to be appropriate for mayor–council cities as well. Facilitators and visionaries who seek to foster a shared vision achieve higher levels of effectiveness than those who seek to maintain control and accomplish their own goals alone.

1.5 Conclusion and Issues to Be Explored

Mayors may pursue different approaches to filling the responsibilities of their office depending on form of government, but there are shared aspects of leadership and flexibility as well. Mayors in council–manager cities can improve the performance of their governments by promoting better communication between the key actors inside and outside of government. Mayors that attend to the process of setting goals and also have a sense of vision, appear to have greater impact on achieving both clearer direction and greater cohesion within the city council. In these pursuits, they are assisted by a city manager who supports both the mayor and the council as a whole, and offers professional direction to the administrative organization under the continuous oversight of the council. The mayors in council–manager cities are not "burdened" with powers that can distract them from governance responsibilities and also tempt them to rely on formal resources to induce or compel support. Rather than relying on formal powers, they can build leadership through the skillful execution of automatic roles and the effective promotion of coordination and communication.

Mayors in council–manager cities make the greatest contribution when they monitor and adjust the governmental process, ensure that the council is setting goals, and contribute their own ideas about the future direction of the city. Some of the case studies to be presented here demonstrate how this process occurs in a seemingly effortless way with mayors that take advantage of the characteristics of the form of government to fill coordinative and directive roles in well-functioning cities. When positive conditions prevail and official actors work together smoothly, it is easy to overlook the important contribution that mayors make to fostering and maintaining these characteristics. In other case studies, that contribution will be explicit as mayors help to overcome problems and reestablish the constructive working relationships that have been lost. The mayor's contribution is also clear in cities where major new policy initiatives have successfully been launched. Still, substantial leadership has been provided in all three situations. They represent examples of leadership that maintains a positive process, restores a constructive working relationship, or initiates new policy approaches.

Mayors in mayor–council cities face different choices, but they may wind up in a place similar to their counterparts in council–manager cities. The separation of powers context in which they operate provides the opportunity to set an independent course and to use the power of the office to induce support from inside and outside the council. The problems with this approach are that power alone is typically not sufficient to achieve substantial policy change or improvement in government performance, and the exercise of power to help friends and punish enemies is likely to generate a reaction from critics of the mayor and can lead to stalemate or corruption. Mayors can choose instead to work with the council in their policy-making activity, or to allow their CAO to provide information and assistance to the city council rather than being exclusively the agent of the mayor. Mayors who are supportive of the city council can reduce the likelihood of conflict among officials in the separation of powers setting. By providing appropriate alternative policy options and sufficient information for oversight, and by supporting the accomplishment of council goals, mayors enhance the performance of the council, improve internal relationships, and reduce conflict. Mayors who are somewhat distant from the council members or clearly separated from them have councils that perform worse and give themselves lower ratings for their performance. The supportive mayors strengthen a shared power to solve problems, while other mayors stress their distance from or power over the council.*

There is a strong association between use of the facilitative approach and vision. On the positive end of the interaction, it seems reasonable to expect that innovative persons are open to new ideas and receptive to the contributions of others. When both qualities are present, there is a strong boost to council performance. In contrast, a strong negative effect is found when both are absent. When mayors are visionaries, but are not supportive of council goal setting or accomplishing council goals, the impact is substantially different depending on the form of government. Most councils still perform well in council–manager cities, while most display moderate to low levels of effectiveness when the mayor goes his or her own way in the mayor–council form. The negative impact of less effective mayoral leadership is not as strong in council–manager cities because councils have collective responsibility to set direction and oversee performance, and the city manager is responsible for assisting the entire council. The council is less able to govern on its own in the separation of powers setting. City administrators are not present in over half of the mayor–council cities, and when present they may be more closely aligned to the mayor than the council.

Both kinds of mayors can be visionaries, but many are not. It is inherently difficult to envision the future. It is easy to be trapped by the assumptions and constraints of the present. It is also difficult to achieve balance between one's own sense of what a preferred future world would be, on the one hand, and being open to the visions that others have or, on the other, that emerge from a collaborative visioning process. The visionary may get caught up in his or her own dreams and ambitions and never get around to facilitating. Consequently, the visionary-first mayor may never learn of the goals of others, never be able to create a *shared* vision, and never be able to enlist the support of others. A charismatic and creative leader will attract followers based on the quality of the ideas presented, but those who do not get on board may be viewed as opponents who need to be bought off or pressured into providing support. This mayor's vision could be enlarged as a result of compromises made to secure key supporters, but this quid pro quo approach is not the same as creating a shared vision with broad support.

---

* Stone (1989) makes the distinction between "power over" and "power to." The former term implies control, and the latter refers to the capacity to act.

This reexamination began with an emphasis on the distinctions between forms of government in American cities and leadership approaches appropriate to each. Analysis of survey responses from city council members indicates that there is a substantial possibility that mayors in both council–manager and mayor–council cities can use the facilitative approach with positive results, and both make a contribution when they bring their vision to the consideration of the city's future. Form continues to be important because it defines the context in which vision and facilitation are used. It does not dictate, however, the leadership style the mayor will choose.

These findings suggest some issues to explore in reading the case studies. When presented evidence that facilitative leadership by the mayor is associated with positive working relationships with the council and with the top administrators, it is appropriate to ask which comes first? Does cooperation make it possible to be a facilitative leader, or does such leadership contribute to positive relationships? How do mayors handle behavior that is counter to the normal expectations of the form? How do council–manager mayors deal with conflict? How do mayor–council mayors establish trust and broaden their support? Is there a dual mode of leadership that mayors in either form may pursue—one based on facilitation and another based on a more forceful interactional style? Do the similar results from both forms of government suggest that there is a convergence of major forms of government? Finally, what are the implications of this evidence for the debate about empowering the mayor and which form of government to choose, particularly in large cities?

The case studies that follow offer evidence to answer these questions. The information and insights from the studies of individual cities will be summarized in the concluding chapter. The facilitative approach fits the norms and distribution of resources in council–manager cities, and it is an option in mayor–council cities. The results of effective use of the facilitative approach and the presence of visionary leadership are the same in both types of cities: the city is better at setting direction and the performance of government is improved. There is great variation in the personalities and styles of the mayors profiled in the case studies, and differences in the ways that they fashion leadership. The mayors do not cover their leadership roles equally well, and they differ in their success. Still, the case studies present strong evidence that in the top elected office in local government, as well as in leadership positions in other kinds of organizations, an inclusive democratic style of leadership that empowers followers is more effective than approaches that stress power over other actors or simply focus on helping people get along with each other. Furthermore, a vision of the future provides purpose and direction that is missing when officials react to current problems. The ideal leader is the visionary facilitator. Here the statistical evidence has been offered that supports this view. In the chapters that follow, detailed portraits are offered of this kind of leader in action.

References

Bellman, G. M. 1992. *Getting Things Done When You Are Not in Charge*. San Francisco: Berrett-Koehler Publishers.

Bennis, Warren, 1985. *Leaders: Strategies of Taking Charge*. New York: Harper & Row.

Bennis, Warren, 1989. *Why Leaders Can't Lead*. Reading, MA: Addison-Wesley.

Bowers, James R., and Wilbur C. Rich, eds. 2000. *Governing Middle-Sized Cities: Studies in Mayoral Leadership*. Boulder, CO: Lynne Rienner Publishers.

Burns, James McGregor. 1978. *Leadership*. New York: Harper Torchbooks.

Chase, Gordon, and Elizabeth C. Reveal. 1983. *How to Manage in the Public Sector*. Reading, MA: Addison-Wesley.

Collins, Jim. 2001. *Good to Great*. New York: HarperCollins.

Collins, Jim. 2005. *Good to Great and the Social Sectors*. Boulder, CO: Jim Collins.

Covey, Steven R. 1989. *The Seven Habits of Effective People*. New York: Simon & Schuster.

Crosby, Barbara C., and John M. Bryson. 2005. *Leadership for the Common Good: Tackling Public Problems in a Shared-Power World*, 2nd ed. San Francisco: Jossey-Bass.

Cufaude, Jeffrey, 2004. The Art of Facilitative Leadership: Maximizing Others' Contributions, *The Systems Thinker® Newsletter V15N10, Pegasus Communications*, http://www.pegasuscom.com/levpoints/facilitativeleader.html (accessed November, 2007).

Cuoto, Richard A. 1995. The transformation of transforming leadership. In *The Leader's Companion*, ed. J. Thomas Wren, New York: Free Press, 102–107.

Dahl, Robert A. 1961. *Who Governs?* New Haven, CT: Yale University Press.

Denhardt, Robert B., and Janet Vinzant Denhardt. 2006. *The Dance of Leadership: The Art of Leading in Business, Government, and Society*. Armonk, NY: M.E. Sharpe.

Ehrenhalt, Allan. 2004. The mayor–manager conundrum, *Governing Magazine*, October.

Ferman, Barbara. 1985. *Governing the Ungovernable City*. Philadelphia: Temple University Press.

Flanagan, Richard M. 2004. *Mayors and the Challenge of Urban Leadership*. Lanham, MD: University Press of America.

Frederickson, H. George, Gary A. Johnson, and Curtis H. Wood. 2004. *The Adapted City: Institutional Dynamics and Structural Change*. Armonk,NY: M. E. Sharpe.

Gergen, David. 2005. Forward: Women leading in the twenty-first century. In *Enlightened Power*, eds. Linda Coughlin, Ellen Wingard, and Keith Hollihan, New York: Jossey-Bass, xv–xxix.

Gilmore, Thomas N. 1988. *Making a Leadership Change*. San Francisco: Jossey-Bass.

Greenleaf, Robert K. 1977. *Servant Leadership*. New York: Paulist Press.

Gurwitt, Rob. 1993. The Lure of the Strong Mayor. *Governing* 6 (10) (July): 36–41.

Gurwitt, Rob. 1997. Fragmented cities: Nobody in charge. *Governing Magazine,* September.

Hassett, Wendy L., and Douglas L. Watson. 2007. *Civic Battles: When Cities Change Their Form of Government*. Boca Raton, FL: PrAcademics Press.

Hersey, Paul, and Kenneth H. Blanchard. 1993. *Management of Organizational Behavior*. Englewood Cliffs, NJ: Prentice Hall.

Kettl, Donald F. 2002. *The Transformation of Governance: Public Administration for Twenty-First Century America*. Baltimore: Johns Hopkins Press.

Keys, Michael B. 1990. Facilitation: Next stop — city hall? Unpublished paper, Elyria, OH.

Kiechel, Walter, III. 1992. "The Servant as Leader." *Fortune*, (May 4), 121–122.

Kousez, James M., and Posner, Barry Z. 2002. *The Leadership Challenge*. 3rd Edition. San Francisco: Jossey-Bass.

Mouritzen, Poul Erik, and James H. Svara. 2002. *Leadership at the Apex: Politicians and Administrators in Western Local Governments.* Pittsburgh: University of Pittsburgh Press.

Mullin, Megan, Gillian Peele, and Bruce E. Cain. 2004. City caesars? Institutional structure and mayoral success in three California cities. *Urban Affairs Quarterly,* 40: 19–43.

National Civic League, 2003. *Model City Charter,* 8th ed. Denver: National Civic League.

Neustadt, Richard E. 1980. *Presidential Power: The Politics of Leadership from FDR to Carter.* New York: John Wiley & Sons.

Newland, Chester A. 1985. Council–manager governance: Positive alternative to separation of powers. *Public Management,* 67 (July): 7–9.

Nollenberger, Karl. 2008. Cooperation and conflict in governmental decision making in mid-sized U.S. cities, *The Municipal Yearbook 2008.* Washington, DC: International City/County Management Association.

O'Neill, Robert J., Jr. 2005. *The Mayor-Manager Conundrum That Wasn't.* Washington, DC: International City/County Management Association. http://www.icma.org/main/ns_search.asp?nsid=1543 (Accessed November, 2007.)

Pressman, Jeffrey L. 1972. Preconditions of mayoral leadership. *American Political Science Review.* 66: 511–524.

Rees, Fran, 1991. *How to Lead Work Teams: Facilitative Skills.* Amsterdam: Pfeiffer & Company.

Stone, Clarence, 1989. *Regime Politics: Governing Atlanta.* Lawrence: University of Kansas Press.

Svara, James H. 1987. Mayoral leadership in council–manager cities: Preconditions versus preconceptions. *Journal of Politics.* 49: 207–227.

Svara, James H. 1990. *Official Leadership in the City: Patterns of Conflict and Cooperation.* New York: Oxford University Press.

Svara, James H. 2003. *Two Decades of Continuity and Change in American City Councils.* Washington, DC: National League of Cities.

Svara, James H. 2005. Exploring structures and institutions in city government, *Public Administration Review,* 65: 500–506.

Svara, James H. 2006. Mayoral leadership in one universe of American urban politics: Are there lessons for (and from) the other? *Public Administration Review,* 66: 767–774.

Svara, James H. 2007. Leadership by top administrators in a changing world: New challenges in political-administrative relations. In *Transforming Public Leadership for the 21st Century,* eds. Ricardo S. Morse, Terry F. Buss, and G. Morgan Kinghorn, Armonk, NY: M.E. Sharpe, 69–102.

Svara, James H., et al. 1994. *Facilitative Leadership in Local Government: Lessons from Successful Mayors and Chairpersons in the Council–Manager Form.* San Francisco: Jossey-Bass.

Talbot, Allan. 1967. *The Mayor's Game.* New York: Harper & Row.

Trump, Donald J. and Bill Zanker. 2007. *Think Big and Kick Ass.* New York: HarperCollins.

Wheeland, Craig M. 2002. An Institutionalist Perspective on Mayoral Leadership: Linking Leadership Style to Formal Structure. *National Civic Review* 91, no. 1 (Spring): 25–39.

Wikstrom, Nelson. 1979. The mayor as a policy leader in the council–manager form of government: A view from the field. *Public Administration Review.* 39: 270–276.

Yates, Douglas. 1977. *The Ungovernable City.* Cambridge, MA: MIT Press.

EXPLORING CONCEPTUAL ISSUES

Chapter 2

Defining Facilitative Leadership: A View from Inside the Mayor's Office in Lawrence, Kansas

John Nalbandian and Sarah Negrón

Contents

"On occasion ... a city commissioner becomes mayor and actually functions as more than a ribbon cutter, presiding officer, and symbolic head. In recent years, this occurred only when John Nalbandian, a student of city management, twice served as mayor for a year. ... He had the gumption to run for office, and he took his election seriously. He listened—at least most of the time—to his constituents. Then (and here's the rub) he'd make up his mind and seek to move forward with what he thought was the best program ... that he thought he could get the commission to support."

Burdett Loomis
Political Scientist, University of Kansas (2001, 413)

2.1 Introduction

What follows is a difficult but welcomed assignment. A social scientist is expected to be objective and analytical, but that is difficult when you are the subject of your own investigation. I will attempt to meet social science standards with what I believe are objective observations and will alert the reader when my own feelings or interests assert themselves.* But, I will also add a perspective that is not normally possible when the investigator is separated from the subject. I will comment on how the definitions of mayoral leadership in the literature relate to my own mayoral experience. I will identify revisions or additions that I feel should be made to better explain what it means to be a mayor.

For me, the opening quote nicely sets the stage for this chapter on my work as a facilitative mayor. Two parts of the quote stand out. First, the facilitative mayor is not a political neutral who solely advances the work of others. The effective mayor has a mind of his/her own. But, secondly, he/she moves within the context of a governing body and this involves helping other elected officials understand and realize their collective will. One must be able to act in ways that help structure political issues, facilitate the governing body's work, and instill community confidence. In short, an effective, facilitative mayor must act in ways that others respect sufficiently enough to alter their own attitudes or behavior, including their votes. But, it also involves acknowledging and advancing council goals, especially if you do not object to them.

Council–manager government naturally encourages a facilitative mayoral role if only because the mayor's formal authority is so limited. While citizens, the city's professional staff, outside agencies and governmental units, and many members of the council itself expect the mayor to provide leadership, he or she is required to

---

* This chapter is written in first person because it is the account of my experience as mayor. My co-author Sarah Negrón participated fully in the preparation of this chapter.

do so as a member of a governing body and in partnership with the city's professional staff. For me, the word *engagement* succinctly captures the role of the effective facilitative mayor. The mayor engages issues, citizens and community groups, the professional staff, and, most importantly, the mayor's number one constituency—the other council members.

I begin this chapter with some background information about the city of Lawrence. I follow with a section on campaigning to feature the ad hoc nature of local politics and how important loyalty is in politics, along with a very brief section on what it is like to be a professor of government *and* an elected official. Then I introduce some general comments about politics in the local governments I have worked with over the years as a trainer and consultant, also drawing upon my academic career and real life experience as an elected official for perspective. Finally, I have some case examples to illustrate the way I acted as a facilitative mayor. Throughout the chapter, I include quotes from a journal that I kept during my eight years in office.

2.2 Context

Lawrence, Kansas, had a population of about 72,000 in 1991. It has since grown to some 90,000 and is home to two universities: the University of Kansas and Haskell Indian Nations University. While the city has a large student population, for the most part, the students are uninvolved in local politics. Despite a lack of student involvement, Lawrence citizens are highly educated with a significant number actively engaged in local politics. Thus, many well-articulated interests come to bear on the commission's policy decisions.

Lawrence is located about an hour from the Kansas City metropolitan area, an hour from the airport, and forty-five minutes from the state capital in Topeka. We are a full service city, which means that the city offers services like providing water, managing storm water, operating a sewage treatment plant, and operating and maintaining its own parks and recreation programs. Separate authorities in some metropolitan areas might provide these kinds of services and others. Even though we are close to a major metropolitan area, we still are a free-standing city, not a suburb. The megaissue in Lawrence for the past thirty years is how we can grow and yet retain our identity, which geographically is centered in an ideal college-town downtown.

Since the early 1950s, Lawrence has been a council–manager city. The form is very well accepted, and even though we elect our five commissioners at-large, we rarely fail to elect a politically representative commission—especially reflecting perspectives on growth. Even though we have a 12 percent minority population, we rarely if ever have had a minority member of the community on the ballot. Economically, we are in good shape; we spend money frugally. The city commission reluctantly approves property tax increases when unavoidable. We swing back and forth around growth issues and, over time, there is balance. In the past thirty years, we have had only three city managers, and the last two had previously been assistant city managers in Lawrence.

By tradition, mayors serve one-year terms. The mayor's role largely is ceremonial, but as in other council–manager cities, citizens look to the mayor for leadership, and the commission does not resent mayoral leadership as long as it is not high-handed. I cannot remember a time when a mayor was selected because of a specific agenda. Mayoral agendas tend to rise from the issues at hand, with the mayor attaching to a few that are consistent with campaign promises either explicit or implied.

Elections for the five-member commission are held in the spring every two years. If more than six candidates formally declare their intent to run, a primary election reduces the field to six. I cannot remember when we did not have a primary election. Of the six candidates running in the general election, the top three vote getters are elected to the commission. The top two serve a four-year term while the third-place candidate serves a two-year term. The council selects the mayor, and, by tradition, the two top vote getters each serve a one-year term as mayor. I was elected to the city commission in 1991 in second place and served as mayor from 1993 to 1994. I was reelected to the commission in 1995 as the top candidate, served as mayor from 1996 to 1997, and completed my second term as commissioner in 1999. I chose not to run again.

2.3 The Campaign and the Decision to Run

My family and I came to the University of Kansas in 1976. Soon after we arrived, I remember a knock on our door at home preceding a gubernatorial election. "Hello, I'm John Carlin. I am the Democratic candidate for governor, and I would like your vote." We had come from Los Angeles where I had completed my doctoral studies and where I had grown up, and that NEVER happened in L.A. I thought to myself, "John, you can become anything you want in this town!" It is not as if I planned from this time to run for office; in fact, it rarely entered my mind. But, I knew that if I wanted to run for office, I could—anyone could.

I think I have been the president of every club, organization, or group I have belonged to since I was a kid. I have been the faculty's choice to chair the public administration department at the University of Kansas on two different occasions for a total of twelve years. So, I am accustomed to being the center of attention, and I like it. I became department chair in the mid-1980s, and, combined with my faculty responsibilities, it was more than a full-time job. The University of Kansas is known for its local government emphasis in public administration, and even though I did not come to KU as an expert in local government, one is expected to learn. So, I learned. When I finished my five-year term as department chair, I wrote a book on professionalism in local government and, when that was completed, I thought, "I ought to run for city commission." It was not a plan. It was not urged upon me by others. I just thought it would be an interesting thing to do. I had always been politically aware, but never really politically involved in campaigns, and I knew very few people in Lawrence outside of the university. Normally, this would be a disadvantage. But, the university is a strong political base for one of its own, and in terms of credibility within the university, being a professor of government started me off on the right foot. As KU Political Science Professor Loomis noted, "The chamber of commerce recruits its candidates, and a loose coalition of neighborhoods recruits its own. With occasional exception (Nalbandian comes to mind), candidates win with most of their backing from one faction or another." (2001)

I met Dan W. (I have omitted all last names) playing weekend basketball with a group of adults. I think Dan had been politically involved forever. Another teammate and friend of Dan's was a state senator. When I was thinking about running, I talked with Dan who later became my chief campaign advisor. Dan told me two things. First, he said, "You have to smile more." Second, he advised me to start talking with people to learn about issues. He gave me names of people to talk with, and then one name led to another until I had talked with quite a few people. I began these conversations in the summer of 1990. If I was going to run, I was going to give it a legitimate try even if it meant spending over six months in preparation.

Journal Entry: January 19, 1991

Carol (my spouse) reminded me that a lot of my support has come from the guys I used to play basketball with on Sundays: Dan and Bob T., and to a lesser degree from Wint with his letter, Steve H. with his encouraging words and offer to help, Mike W., Bird, and Paul S. Dan is the key and I can't see why he would be helping me like he is if we hadn't gotten to know each other better through basketball. I think we really enjoyed playing on the same team. This is the "old boys" network in action. It is supplemented by the years I spent working academically with Nader S., who has always displayed more loyalty to me than vice versa. Also, it is cemented with my relationship with Wendy M., which began when she was working with IPPBR (a university research center).

The lesson I learned initially from my involvement in politics focused on the importance of loyalty. We all casually talk about loyalty, but to a politician, it is the glue that binds relationships. The most important lesson for administrative professionals to learn is that organizational structure is crucial to their competence. For the professional

- There is always someone in authority above you.
- There are position descriptions.
- There are performance evaluations.
- There are established ways of getting things done that either are set out in policy and rules, or are learned as practices over time.

Once you enter the local political arena, you confront the reality that, for the most part, politics is unstructured; it can be haphazard and even chaotic. You have to create structure and order for yourself and those around you who want to work for you and with you. While employees rely on organizational structure for predictability and reliability, in politics loyalty can substitute for the absence of formal structure and established relationships.

Campaigns are about two things. First, you need a good candidate. There is no substitute for a candidate who is electable—a person who people can attach to intellectually or emotionally, or in some combination. Second, you need organization, and you have to create it in nonpartisan contests because it does not exist in the way that a new employee walks into an organization with its structure, roles, and statuses. Every campaign has key individuals. Some campaigns are more organized than others. Some involve the candidate as a key organizer and others do not. I was fortunate in my first campaign to have a person, Dan W., who had been involved in politics all his life.

Journal Entry: November 12, 1990

Dan picked out of our conversation and focused on "Invest in the future with respect for the past" as a possible main campaign theme. As we talked, he jotted notes about complementary themes and issues that I would have to work (develop positions) on: tax abatements; team builder and catalyst; a person who can make things happen while sensitive to process; independent thinker, thoughtful, and capable; family diversity suggests comfort with community diversity; dichotomous issues fail to capture real sentiments of Lawrence citizens—no one wants no growth or unlimited growth.

He and I developed thirty- to sixty-second responses to all the questions we thought people would ask during campaign forums. I memorized them. Dan was very good. He made sure that everything he wrote was something I could own up to. He asked me time and again, "Are you sure you believe this?" It is so easy in a campaign to tell people what they want to hear. You are the focus—always—and the attention is beguiling. You do not want to discourage the attention; it energizes people working on your campaign, and it is one of the attractions of holding office, but you do not want to be hijacked by it.

My campaigns were pretty traditional for Lawrence at the time. We raised money with letters and phone calls. We bought newspaper advertisements, printed and then handed out brochures, made telephone calls, and participated in numerous candidate forums. We posted hundreds of yard signs. I did not know about any of this stuff when I first started in 1990. But I learned, and a few years after I left office I headed a friend's campaign—we lost.

What really surprised me about running for office was the number of people who wanted to work on the campaign. I remember Randi T. calling and saying that in every city commission election she chose one candidate she would work for, and she would like to work for me. She became the "sign lady" and she did a great job—during both of my campaigns. But as strange as this may seem, I rarely talked with her during my eight years in office. This is true of others as well. I had a team of people working for me, but, after the election, the team dissolves and most people go their separate ways.

Journal Entry: April 1, 1991

> I am particularly struck by the initiative others took on my behalf. "D" mailed some forty letters to people he knew. Lew T. mailed some one hundred invitations to a coffee and said he was going to make phone calls for me. Nancy C. mailed postcards and so did Larry M. Randi T. accepted all kinds of responsibility. Dulcy S. organized all the Quail Run brochures into routes. Paul D. (now a state representative) was indispensable with yard signs. Unbelievable!

Because, in Lawrence, we all run at-large, it does not make sense to run a negative campaign focusing on any specific individual in the election. This influenced how I prepared for the candidate forums and what kind of material we put in my brochures and other mailings. I was a university professor of government, and we were trying to project the image of a candidate who was knowledgeable and who could put that knowledge to work in a facilitative fashion. In order to do that, I needed not only to make sure I knew about issues, but I had to mount an issue-oriented campaign.

Campaigning is exhilarating and debilitating depending on which hour of the day it is. I remember a cold January in Lawrence when I was knocking on doors, and the reception was miserable. "You are running for what?" "What is your name?" "When is the election?" Then, we wised up and got the names and addresses of people who had voted in the last local election from the County Clerk's office. On a particular block I might visit only three or four homes, but the reception was amazing. "Yes, I know who you are." "I have a question for you." "What do you think about...?" Or, even better, "I'm planning to vote for you!"

The first time I received a campaign contribution in the mail from a person I did not know, I realized, "There is no backing out now." Up to this time, as a candidate, you are surrounded by people whom you know or have come to know. Then, you receive a check from someone you do NOT know—what did they see, hear, or think that led them to send the check? You never really know the answer, but you campaign confidently as if you do.

2.4 Roles, Responsibilities, and Relationships

No major issue that comes to a legislative body has a "right" answer. You can search as long as you like and you can request as much information as you like, but ultimately it is going to boil down to creating a solution or policy that engages conflicting values like representation, efficiency, equity, and individual rights. The goal is working to build, maintain, and preserve a sense of community that is forged over time from the way these values play themselves out.

With the tremendous challenges that governing bodies face in their goal of community building and working with conflicting values, individual commissioners confront working conditions that they are unlikely to have faced before. In all of your working life, how many jobs have you had where there wasn't a supervisor, boss, or someone in charge and responsible? On the commission, no one is *in charge*. No matter how much power the mayor may accrue, his/her authority is limited. When commissioners disagree, the mayor cannot say, "I have heard enough, this is what we are going to do."

When one couples the fundamental value conflicts in policy making with the lack of authority, one sees the importance of facilitative leadership—the theme of this book. But facilitative leadership is not formulaic, even though it provides a nice conceptual lens. Because of the ambiguity that the value conflicts and lack of authority pose, politics is *socially constructed*; in other words, it is framed by largely unwritten, but understood, sets of expectations and obligations among commissioners that are developed and reinforced over time. No one knows how a complex political issue is going to turn out. Political issues unfold like the skin of an onion where there is no middle. You just keep unfolding and unfolding as leadership works toward a solution that will join what is politically acceptable with what is administratively feasible, all the while aiming toward building and preserving community identity and vitality.

More conceptually, I think it is possible to chart what kinds of bridges the facilitative mayor works to build. I have written elsewhere about the conflicting forces of administrative modernization and citizen involvement (Nalbandian 2005). Each of these forces is powerfully affecting governance at the local level, and they create tension that can be viewed along five dimensions. While the concept of citizen engagement is commonly understood, administrative modernization may not be. It includes adoption of innovations relating to areas such as performance management, performance measurement and benchmarking, goal-based performance appraisal, quality assurance, and performance budgeting, as well as the application of technology to the routinization of administration processes including uses of the geographic information system/global positioning system (GIS/GPS).

I will not discuss these five dimensions in detail. It is enough to see how there are gaps that in my judgment are growing and can be charted along the five dimensions as seen in Table 2.1. It is critical to bridge the gaps because the space between the two trends represents the distance between what is *administratively feasible* (represented by the modernization column) and what is *politically acceptable* (represented by the citizen involvement column). Those individuals who can help bridge these gaps add value to their communities because they are connecting the spheres of politics and administration. In a nutshell, this is the most valuable connection

Table 2.1 Gaps between Modernizing and Civic Engagement Perspectives

Modernizing the Organization	Gaps	Civic Involvement
1. Professional staff		Elected officials
2. Departments		Chief administrative officer
3. Institutions		Community-based politics
4. Specialist		Citizen focus and community problems
5. Policy		Place

that the mayor can facilitate because effective action can only result when these spheres come together effectively.

In retrospect, my goal as a commissioner was to help make these connections, and as mayor, I could take more of the lead than I could as a commissioner. The social construction comes into the picture as the mayor, in concert with the governing body, learns how to do this—how one joins others, cajoles others, learns from others, and persuades others in developing common frames, and then works toward consensus solutions so that bridges are built and the onion unfolds with implicit purpose, even if unpredictably. In retrospect, the path taken to resolve an issue makes sense, but when one is in the middle of the debate, it can feel like wandering hopelessly in a meandering stream.

The mayor's role is a set of expectations derived from personal expectations and from the expectations of those in various policy arenas, including the city's staff. The sometimes complementary and sometimes conflicting expectations create the working definition of the role. In crafting and enacting the role of mayor, one's self cannot be denied. The self initiates structure and is expressed through the structure that is created. Political ambiguity has to be reduced in order for competent work to occur. As mayor, I could see myself describing issues and ways of approaching them that were natural to me as a person, which naturally empowered my role as mayor. When elected officials now seek my advice, I tell them, "You have to deploy your strengths in ways that facilitate the work of the commission, and in ways that others will value." Your strengths are key because they help reduce the ambiguity just as much as the expectations that others have of you in your role as mayor. But, you have to deploy your strengths in ways that others value. It does no good to make decisions that result in comfort for you if they make work difficult for others, including the city's professional staff.

My strengths are very clear to me. I can conceptualize, organize, and collaborate, and I am flexible. It is who I am and what I do. I did it in high school and in college, and I have gotten used to working this way. It is what works for me and, most importantly, as mayor, it is what others valued. I know this from the comments my fellow commissioners made about me in tribute at my last commission meeting. A mayor who can help define the big picture, and who can help the commission understand where it is on an issue, all the while attempting to move with purpose, holds a special place among commissioners.

To illustrate some of these ideas in practice, I am going to quote extensively from a journal entry I made on May 18, 1993. This would have been a little over a month into my first term as mayor. I had been on the commission a little over two years at this time.

Journal Entry: May 18, 1993

I have been mayor now for over a month, and I cannot believe how time consuming it is. The ceremonial duties alone take up a lot of time. Trying to take some policy responsibility adds considerably to the time required because the mayor simply cannot proclaim or dictate direction. First, it takes some ideas, then you have to talk with people, and that takes a lot of time.

I also realize that I have to set some priorities for myself. I can get involved in a lot of projects, and take initiative on a lot, but to see something through takes persistence and time, and that requires setting priorities. What is evolving for me is the importance of "how do we pay for our growth?" And we need to approach this issue from a joint city/county/school board perspective. I talk about this theme on many occasions, and it seems to be catching hold. The other day, Dan W., the chair elect of the chamber, and Gary T., executive director of the chamber initiated a meeting where they discussed with me the desirability of establishing a joint city/county/school board citizens committee to review capital needs and revenue sources.

This is a great idea, and I sent them our city/county/school board goals statement that is very consistent with their suggestion. Their point was that the citizens committee can gain greater attention than government representatives and as the committee learns, the community will learn as well.

This is the kind of suggestion that would never come from staff in Lawrence, and I wonder if it would come from staff in other jurisdictions as well. In any case, to carry through is going to require a lot of discussion. For example, I have to get (Commissioner) S. on board or else I think it will fail with the city governing body. We have to get W. (county administrator) on board with the county, and W. (chamber of commerce president) is going to talk with county commissioner B. I am apprehensive about the school board because they generally see things fairly narrowly.

Another mayoral responsibility is helping others get things they want to initiate and which I favor on the political agenda. Yesterday, I called Jo A., a new commissioner, and we talked about her interest in summer parks and recreation programs for youth. She wants some things done this summer, which will probably drive the staff crazy. I told her that her best bet would be to prepare a written proposal for the city commission's consideration that could be included in the 1994 budget that we are now discussing. Further, I told her that a written proposal could lead to a discussion of city/school boards cost sharing—something I favor.

To further this theme, Chris M. (member of the Bert Nash board) talked with me about the needs of the Bert Nash Mental Health Center, and their facilities and my interests in developing a broader multi-agency healthcare perspective that is not dominated by the hospital. He knew of my interest, and was playing to it. During our conversation, I suggested that he prepare a concept paper that would identify the mutual interests of the healthcare groups at 4th and Maine, including the hospital, and the city/county/school district interests as well. Ray D. (faculty colleague), who is also on the Bert Nash board, prepared that document in draft and it will facilitate movement of our study session away from the immediate issue of a parking lot, to the broader issue of a multiagency, multigovernment perspective on healthcare issues. Ray and Chris' issue is to get the hospital more sensitive to the needs of the other agencies. So, all of our interests overlap. Then, I sent a letter to the president of the hospital board, Bob J., Sr., inviting him and the incoming president to talk with me about where the hospital was heading. My goal here is to broaden the public's participation on the hospital board. I was going to do it with appointments, but that would be political dynamite and would detract attention from my agenda. So, I am going slower, learning first, then I might increase the number of appointments on the board so I can make two appointments during my term. Ray would be one.

As a final example, Marilyn B., new president of the United Way board, called to talk with me about the broader perspective on United Way that she gained by going to a national conference. She was telling me about projects where the city and schools had cooperated. This indicates that she knows of my interest in the broader perspective. So, I need to try to find a way to get her interests on the political agenda. I think what I am going to ask her to do is to make a presentation to the Parks and Recreation Board, and then to request a report from the board to the city commission on where we can take her ideas. I will also share that report with the school district and possibly our joint committee.

This is the kind of thing that I am good at—thinking broadly and inclusively and then working to strategize. It is hard to make an impact with these skills as one commissioner, but as mayor it's a lot easier because people listen to you; they think you have more power than you actually have. Whereas, Commissioner W. used to tell people as mayor that he had just one of five votes, I don't remind anyone of that fact. I just try to move things along, focusing especially on inclusive projects."

One noticeable lesson from these vignettes is that the facilitative mayor who knows his/her strengths puts him/herself in the position of permitting others to play off them. We can see how others knew not only my interests, but also they knew my style, and they took advantage of it to advance what they wanted. I think this is an under-appreciated value of the facilitative mayor. He/she encourages similar behavior in others because that is what he/she responds to, and getting an influential mayor on your side is important to an advocate or interest group no matter how virtuous their cause.

2.5 Professor as Mayor

In Lawrence, Nalbandian was perhaps the perfect mayor in that the community is truly dedicated to the city manager form of government. Nalbandian was an elected official with the intellect and soul of a manager. (Loomis 2001)

Loomis' quote is on the mark. Even though I do not have the skill or temperament to be a city or county manager, I did understand the work prior to my first election based on extensive academic exposure, my interest, and connections to city management professionals nationwide. In a council–manager government, there are three crucial sets of relationships: with citizens and community groups, with other governing body members, and with the city's professional staff. I think for some council members, the staff partnership is the most difficult to grasp, in large part because so many council members do not have executive work experience in large, complex organizations. They do not necessarily have the experience to help them understand administrative complexity. But they are told they are in charge; they are supposed to set direction, and they have oversight responsibility for operations they often know little about compared to the professional staff. They are confronted with agendas that are ninety percent staff-driven. Nearly all of the problems they deal with are brought to them by the staff they are supposed to oversee and direct.

Frankly, I had few of these challenges. I basically knew about the governing body and staff relationship when I was elected. I trusted the staff. I knew the city manager and assistant. They respected me and vice versa. There is a word of caution here. Forms of government are different, and form does matter. I am a professor of public administration in a department that specializes in council–manager govern-ment. If I were a political scientist who was expert in the federal government (which means a structure based on a separation of powers), I might have a difficult time understanding the roles and relationships that are set out in council–manager gov-ernment, and I think that is an issue of confusion for some new commissioners.

In sum, my knowledge helped me a great deal, and I enjoyed learning what I did not know: about utilities, planning, and storm water management. But, in the end, it is not only about knowledge, good governance is about judgment. I wrote for a city newsletter in 1999:

> People often ask me what it is like teaching government and being an elected official. My answer has been the same from the beginning, and it surprised me. "There is not a lot of difference." Every Tuesday night we face the single most important question any political theorist asks: What should be the role of government? (*City Newsletter*, 1999)

2.6 Cases

I am going to illustrate two points with two cases. The first case will show how the facilitative mayor uses his/her authority and power to convene important conver-sations around issues he/she and the community care about. The second case will show how politics unfold in uncertain ways, and how the facilitative mayor must be flexible.

2.6.1 The Sales Tax

Early in my first term, I wondered why we had put ourselves in a reactive mode when it came to recreation facilities and programs. I particularly recall the Youth Sports Incorporated (YSI) nonprofit soccer group coming in several times asking for various improvements to our soccer fields. At one point at a commission meet-ing I asked whether it would be desirable to have a plan—a parks and recreation master plan. I had not thought this out beforehand, it was purely contextual. The commission agreed, and the Parks and Recreation staff was overjoyed at the com-mission's direction.

We hired a consultant who held community meetings to supplement his exper-tise, and he produced a plan. The question then became, "How do we fund the plan?" At that time, I was mayor for the first time. I had in the back of my mind for some time that a dedicated sales tax might be a feasible revenue source. As events unfolded, however, there were complicating factors. The school district, which for a number of years had been trying unsuccessfully to convince the community that Lawrence should have a second high school, finally had made its case successfully, and they were ready to put a bond issue on the April ballot. The county was being lobbied heavily by the Public Health Department, Visiting Nurses Association, and the Bert Nash Mental Health Center for more room, as the hospital's expansion was reducing available space for these agencies whose services were growing. Also, the county jail was overcrowded, and we needed new facilities. This was the financial environment we confronted as we were discussing the parks and recreation master plan.

The key event occurred when I used my position as mayor to call a meeting with Gary T., the executive director of the chamber of commerce, and Dan W., the president of the chamber and my former campaign director. Gary was especially important because he was a long-range thinker—which connected the two of us—and no bond issue passes in Lawrence without the chamber's backing. It is a progressive chamber, so that is not a great stumbling block, and they can mobilize their members as voters.

At our lunch meeting, I asked them how we could sequence elections so that the city, county, and school district would not be proposing competing bond issues. We talked and we talked, and then a light bulb flashed for Gary. He said that we should not sequence the votes, we should combine them. We should propose a countywide sales tax that would fund the city's and county's projects, and we should use the sales tax to reduce the property tax the equivalent amount it would take in a school district property tax increase to pay for the second high school. In effect, we could get the parks and recreation master plan, the jail, the health facilities, *and* the high school for a one-cent sales tax and no increase in property tax. It was brilliant, and it worked.

It worked in part because I had lent my mayoral status to help those who were already supporting more city, county, and school district cooperation. I suggested some cooperation, but mostly, I was just the voice for sentiments that others desired. I think this is one role that the facilitative mayor plays: You lend your status to others for projects that they are pushing and with which you agree. This cooperative base provided a framework to test out Gary's idea, which, of course, became associated with me because I was the one who publicly pushed it. As I look back on my eight years, this sales tax vote and the creative way we combined projects was my greatest accomplishment.

2.6.2 Municipal Golf Course

> I'm not sure I'm supposed to be talking to you. Can you look yourself in the mirror with any integrity?
>
> **Stan H.**
> *Lawrence Municipal Golf Course Committee*

Construction of Lawrence's municipal golf course is an issue that preceded my election and spanned both of my terms as commissioner. When I ran for city commission in 1991, a local advocacy group— the Lawrence Municipal Golf Course Committee— pledged to support me in exchange for my written support of their desire for a municipal golf course. I play golf and indicated to them that I favored reviewing this proposal and bringing it to the commission for consideration. My name was in newspaper ads that they placed supporting the candidates who favored a municipal golf course.

During my tenure as a new commissioner, we did consider construction of a municipal golf course on land to be leased from the Army Corps of Engineers. The commission was in favor of the plan, but two more public golf course options became available: A private golf course offered to sell their existing course to the city; another privately owned golf complex (offering a driving range and mini golf) presented plans to build an 18-hole course. The commission chose to allow the second businessman to pursue construction of a new course instead of pursuing the new municipal course option because it would achieve the same end result—increased capacity and affordable golfing for the general public—without expenditure of public funds. I supported that option.

In a newspaper interview after we entertained other proposals, I said, "I think what we agreed to in the campaign was the concept of a municipal golf course. … I think that, in endorsing Mr. G's proposal, all the goals and objectives of a municipal course are met. I don't think we're backtracking at all. It's just that the conditions are different from what they were." (King 1991)

This is an example of where my flexibility and my desire to facilitate the work of others rather than taking a strong, consistent stand worked against me and the city. From the perspective of the Municipal Golf Course Committee, I had sold out. The quote opening this section was made to me in commission chambers after the meeting where we endorsed the private initiative. I learned something from this experience. To facilitate you have to be respected. With only six months in office, I had not earned the respect needed in order to change my mind and still be seen as a credible commissioner. Thus, even though I was trying to facilitate the building of a golf course (the ultimate goal), my facilitative methods failed because I did not have the needed resources. I had lost the respect and loyalty of the Golf Course Committee.

> "They've accused us of having no integrity. And I'm really angry about that," Nalbandian said. "They failed to acknowledge that anything is different now than during the spring. In the spring, we had one option, the municipal golf course. Now we have two options. Why wouldn't any reasonable person look at both options?" (Toplikar 1991)

To make a long story short, none of the private initiatives panned out, and the Golf Course Association proved correct. It was not until 1996 when, ironically, the golf course had been included in the new parks and recreation master plan (for which I received a lot of credit) that we finally began construction.

I was the mayor in 1996 and 1997, and because I played golf and had been an initiator of the master plan and the sales tax initiative, I became the governing body's representative on this project. I went out with the construction team and they took me on a tour of what they were doing. My picture was in the paper, and I became reincarnated as champion of the golf course. It is so strange now to have people refer to me as the "father of our golf course," in light of what Stan H. said to me in 1991.

Lawrence's Eagle Bend Golf Course opened to the public on July 18, 1998. While on the city commission at the time, I was not the mayor when it came time to cut the ribbon to celebrate the opening of the course. When the mayor is at a ribbon cutting in Lawrence, by tradition the mayor speaks on behalf of the city commission. But at the end of Mayor K.'s remarks, he invited me to come to the podium and say a few words. That kind of political generosity is not lost among commissioners. His wife gave me a handmade Christmas card with my picture as part of the first foursome to play Eagle Bend.

As a side note to this story, when people used to call me the "father of the golf course," I would object and say that others had a very large role to play and that I was only one of a majority vote. After a while, I learned that people do not want to hear that. They really want to believe that someONE made a difference. As an elected official, it is foolish time and again to try and deflect credit that people want to give you as long as you understand that "it is really not about you."

In the two cases presented above, you can see how the world of administration is represented by a parks and recreation master plan. Master plans are a fundamental tool of administrative work, representing the culmination of "data, subplans, and reports." They exemplify administrative work as they create legitimized documents upon which professional analysis and recommendations can be made. The world of politics is messier. From the cases, it is clear that the notion of starting with a goal, creating a desired path with alternatives, and then working toward the desired end is not the politics I experienced. That world consisted symbolically of "passion, dreams, and stories" and it proceeded in fits and starts. Further, the facilitative mayor does not always choose his/her partners. As mayor, I relied on my connections, the connections of others, and their passion and dreams for energy and support, in order to collectively construct messages that we believed the electorate would find compelling as they considered a public vote on the sales tax, for example.

2.7 Conclusions

One lesson stands out for me about being a mayor and city commissioner: Respect and loyalty leading to trust count above all other elements for a facilitative mayor. Because a facilitative mayor does not have the authority of a chief executive, he/she has to continually cultivate less formal sources of influence. This is where respect, loyalty, and trust come in. Respect is necessary so that people will listen to you, and I think each elected official earns respect in different ways. I was a logical, big picture thinker who took others into consideration, and my respect for others was reciprocated. The one phone call I remember in all my eight years on the commission came from a citizen a couple of nights after we had made a decision about downtown. The caller, who I was acquainted with, but whom I did not count as a supporter of mine, said he had read the paper and was surprised at my vote because he considered it antidowntown. He went on to say that he knew I was a reasonable person, and he was calling because he wanted to know why I voted the way I did. This one phone call reinforced for me the idea that if one is true to one's beliefs and one's way of treating others respectfully, that respect will be recognized and returned.

While citizen respect is important, as I stated earlier, the respect of the other members of the governing body is most valued. It has to be continually earned and nurtured because it is so valuable yet fragile. Our commission requires three votes to pass a motion, and a facilitative mayor always is thinking, "How do we get this done?" Other commissioners may be content to say what they think needs to be heard, but the facilitative mayor is action-oriented.

Loyalty based on position, threats, or incentives is fleeting; loyalty built on respect can last. And, as I have indicated earlier, loyalty is the glue. To have someone's respect, loyalty, and trust enables you to look down the dais and with a nod of the head understand that you have someone's vote or he or she has yours. It is connecting to Mayor K., who went out of his way at the golf course ribbon cutting to invite me to speak for a project that he knew would help define my terms in office.

There are all kinds of opportunities to break trust, lose respect, and trash loyalty. I remember a particularly difficult night when I became pretty visibly and vocally upset at another commissioner, and he at me. After the meeting, he came over to me, held out his hand, and said "No hard feelings?" What can you say to that? You shake his hand, and you remember his generous gift of civility—one commissioner to another—and you try to learn from it.

I want to end on a personal note. I was in my first term on the city commission and the mayor had finished her one-year term and was stepping down. It is customary for other commissioners to make remarks and for the outgoing mayor to say a few words before the new mayor is sworn in. The outgoing mayor said that being mayor was the highlight of her life. Arrogantly, I thought to myself, "She must have led a pretty diminished life if this was it!" Little did I know. Now as I look back at everything that I learned about city government, about all the people I met, about all the projects we worked on, there is nothing that lifts my spirits more today than the greeting, "Hi, Mayor."

References

King, Mason. 1991. Golf group says promises broken, *Lawrence Journal World*, Oct. 23. http://www2.ljworld.com/news/1991/oct/23/golf_group_says_promises/ (accessed August, 2008)/

Loomis, Burdett. 2001. "Lawrence politics: Three themes, four notions, and a handful of stories," in *Embattled Lawrence: Conflict and Community,* eds. Dennis Dommer and Barbara Watkins. Lawrence, KS: University of Kansas Division of Continuing Education.

Nalbandian, John. 2005. Professionals and the conflicting forces of administrative modernization and civic engagement." *American Review of Public Administration* 35(4): 311–326.

Toplikar, David. 1991. Commissioners call charges unfounded," *Lawrence Journal World*, Nov. 27. http://www2.ljworld.com/news/1991/nov/27/commissioners_call_charges_ unfounded/ (accessed August, 2008).

Chapter 3

Facilitation in Its 'Natural' Setting: Supportive Structure and Culture in Denmark

Rikke Berg and Ulrik Kjaer

Contents

"I try hard not to steamroller anyone. Not that I am flabby, but I listen and make adjustments … I think I distribute it [the political leadership], and I try to unite the council … I believe everyone gets their part and that we are all taking part in pulling Middelfart in the right direction"

Steen Dahlstrøm
*Mayor of Middelfart**

3.1 The Limited Impact of Formal Power Structures

The opening quotation by a Danish mayor clearly indicates a political leader trying to involve other actors and share political leadership. What may not be obvious is that his intent is to gain support and accumulate influence as well. If facilitative leadership is defined as the effort to "improve the process of interaction by empowering participation and by developing consensus and focus on the purpose toward which a group is working" (Svara 1994), this particular mayor may be characterized as a facilitative leader. And, he is not alone. On the contrary, very few Danish mayors use their personal and formal political power to force through their ideas, goals, and visions in the council, in the administration, and to the citizens (Berg and Kjaer 2007).

As in the United States, facilitative leadership in Denmark is often explained by the local government institutions, i.e., the structural conditions provided for leadership in the municipalities. In the United States, the particular form of political leadership oriented toward coordination, communication, and cooperation is associated with the council–manager form, in which the council possesses all governmental authority (Svara 1994). In Denmark, the connection between facilitative leadership and the formal framework for mayoral behavior is due to the fact that the decision-making authority is clearly vested in the city council as in the council–manager form. Thus, in principle, the power is in the hands of a collective body, according to the local government form in Denmark. However, the structure is more complex and, in practice, the organization of the political executive is much more ambiguous because it is shared among several political bodies and actors: the city council, the standing committee, the finance committee, and the mayor. The city council is elected for a period of four years and typically consists of eleven to seventeen members (Ejersbo, Hansen, and Mouritzen 1998).

True to parliamentary systems, the executive comes from the legislative body, and there is no formal separation of powers. The city council elects the mayor as well as the members of the standing committees among themselves, the latter typically consisting of five to seven members being responsible for the "immediate administration of affairs" of each department (Berg 2005). The mayor chairs one of these

---

* Quotations attributed to officials and leaders in the city of Middlefart are from interviews conducted by the authors.

committees (the finance committee), which supervises all financial and administrative matters and appoints all personnel, except the CEO and the department heads, who are appointed by the council. The mayor also heads up the municipal administration (Figure 3.1). Thus, the position of the Danish mayor is considered as a full-time job—typically the only full-time job among the elected officials. The mayor can in certain urgent cases decide on behalf of the council, but has no authority to interfere with or block decisions taken by the committees. Thus, when it comes to specific, day-to-day administrative matters, the standing committees are fully in charge (Le Maire and Preisler 2000). In terms of personal power, the Danish mayor, therefore, is almost as "weak" as the mayor in the American council–manager form, except for the extensive responsibilities exercised by the Finance Committee.

Some special features of the electoral system in Denmark further limit the similarities between the American and the Danish mayor. Firstly, compared to the United States, the party system in Denmark is very strong. Very few mayors are elected from nonpartisan lists. The mayor is also a party leader. Secondly, due to the seat allocation system* in the Danish councils, the formal power of the Danish mayors tends to vary somewhat more. If it is necessary to form a coalition of two or more parties to create a governing majority, the mayor is constrained (because he is the leader of only one of the parties) by the other coalition members. These mayors are likely to use facilitative methods because of the unified authority assigned to the council, and also because of the need to secure support from other parties in their coalition (or who might be coalition partners in the future).

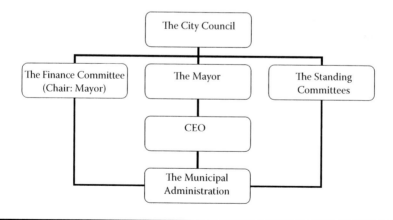

Figure 3.1   The political/administrative organization of a Danish municipality.

---

* The seat allocation system is a straightforward d'Hondt proportional representation system among competing lists, which represent either national political parties presenting local lists or local groups of concerned citizens (O'Leary, Grofman, and Elklit 2005).

From time to time, one of the parties in the council captures an absolute majority of the seats in the council, consequently assigning the mayor a large amount of formal power in terms of seats. This phenomenon is not typical for the Danish municipalities; however it is not unusual either. After the election in 2005, one out of four municipalities in Denmark was, in fact, led by a mayor from a majority party.

How does this affect the political leadership of Danish mayors? Will the facilitative approach be discarded when another option is available? From a structural perspective on political leadership, one may expect that a gain of an absolute majority in the council could mean the death of facilitative leadership. Since Weber first formulated the classical model of bureaucracy, basing political leadership on legal rational authority, there has been a general recognition that institutions have formative influence on political leaders (Peters 1999; Elcock 2001). Furthermore, the power structures in a specific setting will encourage or restrict different types of leadership behavior (Stone 1995). A more or less sudden replacement of one set of power structures with another, therefore, will be expected to lead to a transformation in the role of the mayor (Berg and Rao 2005). In the Danish case, the mayor's weak position in the executive system could be expected to be disregarded in favor of his strong position in the seat allocation system. Consequently, one would expect the mayor to replace the facilitative leadership model with a more classical power model, i.e., use his newly gained power to push his political visions and ideas through the council despite the opinion of the opposing parties. From this perspective, the mayor would also be expected to expand control over the bureaucracy.

According to a study of Danish mayors and the elected officials in the councils, this, however, seems not to be the case (Berg and Kjaer 2005). Independent of the relative strength of the mayor's party, indicators of facilitative leadership are still found in almost every municipality. As demonstrated in Table 3.1, a majority of mayors as well as councilors find the debate in the councils to be good and constructive, reflecting a positive atmosphere of communication, a low level of tensions, and few power struggles between the mayor and the council. Decisions do not take place in the "lobby" in a caucus of party members, but in regular meetings of the council and committees.

As illustrated in Table 3.2, both groups of actors also consider their mutual relations to be cooperative. In both tables, councilors who are outside the mayor's coalition have a less positive assessment, although even here a majority views relationships as cooperative. These findings support the conclusion that the facilitative leadership model is generally recognized by elected officials regardless of the strength of the mayor's electoral mandate in the council.

The same positive relationship is found between the mayor and top administrators irrespective of the strength of the mayor's party in the council (Berg and Kjaer 2005; Mouritzen and Svara 2002). Tensions and conflicts within the council

Table 3.1 Mayors' and Councillors' Assessment of the Work in the Council (percent)

		Councilors[a]		
	Mayors	Member of the Mayor's Party	Member of the Mayor's Coalition	Not Member of Either of These
Most Political Decisions Are Taken at the Council and Committee Meetings and Not in the Lobby				
Agree	54	62	50	42
Neutral	28	24	26	23
Disagree	18	14	24	35
Total	100	100	100	100
The Political Discussion at the Meetings Is Constructive				
Agree	81	85	68	61
Neutral	14	9	22	21
Disagree	5	6	10	18
Total	100	100	100	100
n =	213	287	190	286

[a] The councilors are split according to whether they are members of the mayor's party, the mayor's coalition, or neither of these.

Source: Berg, R., and U. Kjaer, *Den danske borgmester*, University Press of Southern Denmark, 2005. With permission.

often can rub off on the administration. The absence of variation related to differences in party representation adds to the view that the facilitative model is viable in a variety of settings. In defiance of the electoral system, which in one out of four municipalities enrich the mayor with a nontrivial power base, the facilitative leadership model seems to be the overall dominant style of local political leadership in Danish municipalities.

What accounts for this finding? If not the formal government institution and the power structures inherent in these, what else can explain this prevalent type of leadership among the Danish mayors? In order to pin down the answer, we will look into the Danish case from which the introductory quotation originates: The municipality of Middelfart led by Mayor Steen Dahlstrøm. As Dahlstrøm is one of the few Danish mayors who has experienced election terms both with and without

Table 3.2 Mayors' and Councilors' Assessment of the Level of Conflict (%)

		Councilors[a] with Mayor		
	Mayor with Councilors	*Member of the Mayor's Party*	*Member of the Mayor's Coalition*	*Not a Member of Either of These*
The Relationship Is				
Very conflict-ridden	0	1	5	5
Conflict-ridden	3	3	14	20
Neutral	16	10	11	28
Cooperative	62	32	51	38
Very cooperative	19	54	19	9
Total	100	100	100	100
n =	211	291	192	288

[a] The councilors are split according to whether they are members of the mayor's party, of the mayor's coalition, or neither of these.

Source: Berg, R., and U. Kjaer, *Den danske borgmester*, University Press of Southern Denmark, 2005. With permission.

an absolute majority in the council,* this case is particularly useful for the study of the issues outlined. While elaborating the case and illuminating the political leadership of Dahlström, we will pay special attention to the relations between the mayor and his potential political opponents. We examine these questions:

Why is the mayor trying so hard to establish alliances, cooperate, communicate and share his leadership, when he, in reality, has the power to make the council act according to his preferences?

Why is the cooperative style of leadership important to him? What kinds of alliances does he make?

How does he reach them?

Does his facilitative leadership in Middelfart prove to be successful?

---

* The case study was conducted in 2004 during the mayor's fifth election period, which is the only period in which his party, The Social Democratic Party, has held the absolute majority in the council. Due to this, the case data have been carefully considered in order to rule out that the role and behavior of the mayor is just a simple reflection of old habits from earlier periods when the mayor was not in possession of the power derived from the many mandates.

Before going into depth with these dimensions of the case, we shall, however, provide some contextual knowledge of the city and its mayor.*

3.2 The City and Its Mayor

Middelfart is a middle-sized Danish municipality with 20,186 inhabitants distributed among the city of Middelfart and the peninsula called Strib (the former accounting for the largest part of the population). The municipality is in the middle of the country, at the very western part of the island of Funen. Middelfart is situated by a beautiful coastline facing the sea and the western part of the country, Jutland. Though Funen and Jutland are joined by a bridge, starting (or ending, depending on the perspective) in Middelfart, the population of Middelfart has a long tradition of being affiliated with Funen. Just across the bridge, in Jutland, is found the so-called "Triangle area," which consists of three somewhat larger municipalities (Vejle, Kolding, and Fredericia) which form the apexes of a triangle, and four smaller surrounding municipalities (Lunderskov, Vamdrup, Vejen and Boerkop) (Figure 3.2). Together these municipalities account for the biggest economic growth within Denmark.† Despite the heavy competition from, especially, the three larger municipalities, Middelfart also has experienced substantial economic growth during the past fifteen years, and is now mainly dominated by whole-sale businesses, construction firms, and consulting firms. Traditionally, the population has mainly consisted of farmers and blue collar workers with low incomes, but now the population is slightly changing to white collar and self-employed workers. There is also a large increase in the value of the housing market in Middelfart. Compared to Danish municipalities in general, Middelfart has a tax rate below average and an average level of service. However, compared to all neighboring municipalities on the island of Funen, the citizens of Middelfart are better off in terms of low taxes and high services.

The municipality holds a long tradition of Social Democratic mayors, as it has been governed by Social Democrats for more than eighty-five years. Steen Dahlstrøm, who is only the fourth democratically elected mayor in Middelfart,‡ is no exception to this tradition. He was born in Middelfart fifty-five years ago and grew up in modest circumstances in the same city. As a child, he often listened to

---

* The analysis of the municipality of Middelfart and its mayor, Steen Dahlstrøm, is based on a study conducted from 2003 to 2004. Besides using documents from the municipalities and articles from the local newspapers, interviews have been conducted with the mayor, the chair of the Social Democratic group in the council, a backbench member of the Social Democratic group, the leader of the Liberal party, the chair of the local party branch of the Social Democratic Party, the CEO of the municipality, a journalist at the local paper, and the CEO of the local bank. Observations have also been made of a meeting in the council, a meeting in the economic committee, and a meeting at the local party branch of the Social Democratic Party. Furthermore, the mayor has been observed for an entire day, including meetings in and outside town hall. For a full description of the method used in the study, see Berg and Kjaer, 2007.
† Except for the capital Copenhagen.
‡ Until 1919, the Danish mayors were appointed by the king.

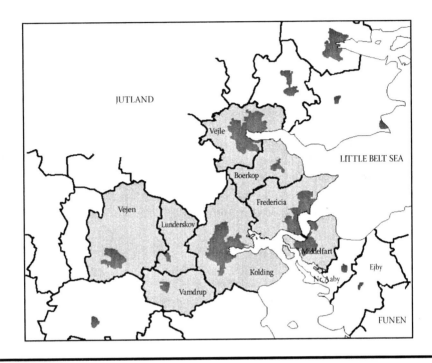

Figure 3.2   Map of Middelfart and the other seven municipalities in the Triangle area.

political discussions in the home of his grandmother, who was an avid supporter of the Social Democratic party. Around 1980, he graduated with a degree in education and, almost by coincidence, started his teaching career in one of Middelfart's public schools. In his teaching position, he got to know many of the inhabitants of the municipality, whether it was the young citizens (and future voters) of Middelfart or their parents. Even today he finds his personal knowledge of the citizens to be very important in his ability to make political decisions, whether it is about developing an industrial policy or supporting the administration in its decision making regarding individual citizens.

Steen Dahlstrøm was first elected to the council in 1981, when he was only 30 years old. After the election, he was appointed as the new chairman of the local party. His knowledge of the party organization from the inside and familiarity with all the local party members were the stepping-stones for his mayoral candidacy. At the election in 1985, the old mayor stepped down and Dahlstrøm was appointed by the council as the new mayor of Middelfart after serving just one term on the council (1982 to 1985). He has held the position since that time and now has more than twenty years of tenure.

At the beginning of his regime, Dahlstrøm found the position more troublesome than it is today. At the onset, he found it difficult to follow in the footsteps of the old, very experienced mayor, as he had to keep a balance between continuity and change, retaining old supporters while obtaining new ones. He also was more sensitive to criticism, and often lost his temper in either group meetings of the party or at council meetings, which clearly was to his disadvantage. Over the years, however, he has gained more confidence in the position, and, consequently, he is not affected to a great degree by the high expectations and criticism as he was in his earlier years as mayor. Dahlstrøm's ambitions have also been under development. In the beginning, his ambitions were more personal than political. He found it very important to be visible and to let the citizens and others know who he was. Later on, his political ideas and visions gained increasing importance and today his ultimate criterion for success is results rather than publicity:

> If you get to set your fingerprints on the development of the city, you are on the right track ... Some of the best moments are when you have had a good meeting with the council and you can see that there is a process on the go—that we take decisions, get things done, and that Middelfart develops.

Mayor Steen Dahlstrøm

In order to get and keep "the process" going, the mayor pays special attention to three major municipal arenas: (1) the political arena made up of the council and the Social Democratic group of party members within the council; (2) the external arena, in particular, the business community of Middelfart and the surrounding municipalities of the "Triangle area"; and (3) the administrative arena composed of the CEO and lower level managers of the municipal administration. In the following section, we will elaborate and analyze the mayor's leadership approach in each of these arenas.

3.2.1 'For Better or for Worse': Building Trust and Consensus within the Political Arena

During the past twenty years of governing, Dahlstrøm has been supported by various coalitions composed by multiple parties, ranging from conservatives to liberals. However, in the election in 2001, his own party, the Social Democratic party, won ten out of nineteen seats in the council, i.e., an absolute majority, which potentially enabled the mayor to form a minimum winning coalition. With the majority in hand, he did not have to depend on support from any other party than the Social Democrats, and all the important chairs of the committees could be distributed among his political friends within his party group. Yet he refrained from doing so. Instead, Dahlstrøm started to invite other members of the new council to join the coalition. Two parties agreed to this, the Social Liberals (a centrist party in Denmark) and the Conservative party. The latter, in return, received one of the committee chairs.

To pass up the formation of a minimum winning coalition may be unheard of in many western countries, including the United States, but is not, however, a unique finding for Denmark (Berg and Kjaer 2005; Serritzlew, Skjæveland, and

Blom-Hansen 2005). In many of the Danish municipalities, the mayors perceive forming a minimum winning coalition as both a risky and inappropriate affair; risky, because minimum winning coalitions tend to create more enemies than friends on the council. This would clearly be a disadvantage if the mayor's party should lose the majority again, as it would be much harder convincing the rest of the parties to appoint a former "enemy" for the position of mayor. Forming a broad coalition is thus perceived as insurance in the case of future election defeats, which would otherwise mean losing the mayoral position (Elklit and Pedersen 1995). Yet, minimum winning coalitions are also perceived as being inappropriate in the sense that they leave other parties out of the realm of influence, pulling the decisions in the direction of a single party's program and adding to the advantage of one particular group of voters, i.e., the ones voting for the majority party.

From Dahlstrøm's perspective, forming a minimum winning coalition, would be a violation of a very important norm in the Danish municipalities in general, and Middelfart in particular; that being the norm of consensus (Berg and Kjaer 2005).

> It's important that the mayor is the mayor of the whole city, not only the
> mayor of the Social Democrats ... It's important for people that we work
> together, that we cooperate ... The municipality must be run in a sensible
> manner, and by that I mean the whole municipality for all of its citizens.
>
> **Mayor Steen Dahlstrøm**

Dahlstrøm not only emphasizes the inclusion of other parties in terms of the distribution of seats, but also in terms of the day-to-day decisions in the council and in the finance committee. In general, he puts a lot of effort into communicating with the members of the council and committees. This is also why he has established a regular routine of "informal orientation" at every official meeting. This informal orientation is the first item on the meeting agenda and is deliberately used by the mayor to inform the councilors of matters that have not yet reached the formal agenda, but are nevertheless making their way through the administration and heading toward the official agenda. The informal orientation is then used by the mayor as a tool for inclusion, for developing a common understanding of the pending topics, building the council's confidence in him, and bringing about a sense of ownership for the issues at stake.

> I want them (the councilors) to be informed. I want them to be a part
> of the life in the municipality of Middelfart, and that they are a part of
> the basis for decision.
>
> **Mayor Steen Dahlstrøm**

The inclusion of other parties in the decision-making process from time to time impedes the clarity of who has really initiated the agenda. The mayor clearly believes he still is in charge of the decisions taken. According to former U.S. President Harry Truman, this is a true hallmark of political leadership. As Truman put it,

"A leader is a man who has the ability to get other people to do what they don't want to do and like it."* The mayor is, however, not the only one who seems to use a Trumanian strategy. The leader of the Liberal Party finds that his party indeed influences the political outcome, but that they do it by feeding the mayor with ideas and initiatives and accepting that he, in public as well as in his own mind, makes them his own. What seems to be going on in the consensual political setting of Middelfart, therefore, might be labeled a "double Truman."

Clearly the mayor feels that "the process" runs more smoothly with the support of the council. In fact, it is so important for him to reach broad decisions with all nineteen members of the council supporting them, that he would rather make compromises on his proposals than push party preferences through the council. An example of this is the budget for 2004. Here the council was divided on an issue concerning the financing of a local sports center. The Social Democratic party was clearly against the public financing of this center; however, two of the parties outside the coalition were in favor of letting the municipality be responsible for the construction. Steen Dahlstrøm convinced his party group that reaching an agreement on the entire budget was more important than getting all of their opinions through, and all nineteen members of the council ended up voting for the budget.

This case, as well as some other cases during this election period, has created some resistance for Dahlstrøm within his own party group. Some of the group members feel that the mayor tends to be more loyal to the council than to his own party group. Dahlstrøm is, however, very conscious that the atmosphere and the cohesiveness of the group are vital for his political leadership. In order to overcome the tensions in the group, he has decided to share his leadership roles with the chair of the Social Democratic group. Informally, the two of them have divided two important roles of the political leadership between them; the mayor primarily focusing on the coherence of the council, and the chair of the Social Democratic group primarily focusing on the coherence of the party group (for this distinction, see Leach and Wilson 2000). Within the council, the mayor is quite often perceived as the "good cop," i.e., the all-embracing political leader seeking broad support and consensus across the traditional political party lines; while the chair of the Social Democratic group is perceived as the "bad cop," i.e., the leader of the Social Democratic group promoting a thorough and confronting party line in the council (but pleasing the members of the Social Democratic group). The role sharing has two important consequences: (1) the members of the mayor's party are able to express their cultivated Social Democratic policy in the council, without running the risk of pushing the other parties away; and (2) the mayor is able to reach broad agreements, while not creating too many frustrations within the party group.

This strategy seems to pay off. Not only are most of the decisions in the council agreed upon by all nineteen members, but also none of the Social Democratic

---

* Truman quoted from Elcock (2001, 85).

members has been tempted to leave the group at the wrong moment during Steen Dahlstrøm's governing period. As we will demonstrate in the following section, the successful outcome of facilitative leadership in terms of coherence and cooperation in the political arena also seems to have a positive spillover to the external arena.

3.2.2 Entering 'Nonholy' Alliances in the External Arena

It is a well-known view in Denmark that mayors elected from the Social Democratic party have particularly close bonds to the trade unions, while mayors coming from the Conservative or Liberal parties have tight bonds to the business communities. Accordingly, cooperation between Social Democratic mayors and private sector firms has been perceived as mostly inappropriate and as a nonholy alliance. However, this common wisdom has been shown to be nothing but a myth. According to a survey among Danish mayors (Berg and Kjaer 2005), all mayors—irrespective of party affiliation—have extensive contact with the business community in their municipalities. In fact, the business community is one of the mayors' most frequent contacts in the external arena, only exceeded by the contacts to citizens and the media (Berg and Kjaer 2005). Steen Dahlstrøm is no exception to this pattern. He pays a great deal of attention to the external arena, including the private sector firms, the media, and nongovernmental organizations (NGOs). However, the focus here will be on his relations with the business community of Middelfart, and partly on his relations with the neighboring municipalities in the "Triangle area," which have been of vital importance to the economic and cultural development of the municipality in the later years of his mayoralty. By cooperating with both the private sector firms and the other public authorities in the area, Dahlstrøm has been able to take advantage of the growth in the "Triangle area," consequently attracting new firms and creating jobs in the municipality. He has also succeeded in developing Middelfart from a traditional provincial town into a modern city with cultural facilities, supporting the positive trend with new firms and new employees coming to the municipality.

One of the mayor's most important external alliances is with other local governments in the region: the seven municipalities in Jutland, which is part of the "Triangle area." Even though the population of Middelfart has a long tradition of being affiliated with Funen (the island where Middelfart is situated), speaks the Funen dialect, and often commutes to the big city of the island, Odense, for jobs and education, the mayor made an important strategic choice in the early 1990s: to loosen the bonds to Funen and to make tighter connections to Jutland. The choice was taken as a consequence of the then economic development on each side of the bridge connecting the two regions. On the eastern side of the bridge, the Island of Funen, there was hardly any economic growth and business development. On the western side of the bridge, in Jutland, all kinds of new industrial and technological enterprises were springing up like mushrooms and the economy was booming.

In 1993, Dahlstrøm, together with seven mayors from the neighboring municipalities in Jutland, took the initiative to establish a formal network of eight cooperating municipalities. The network that has now been operating for more than ten years is working strategically together on areas such as business, urban development, culture, and education. It is organized as an independent institution and led by a general manager. Each of the eight participating municipalities is represented by its own mayor and they take turns as chair of the network.

The alliance with the seven other mayors is not without difficulties. The mayors represent different parties and municipalities of various sizes, and all have different views as to how to develop the region. However, over the years, they have come to realize that their economic growth is closely associated with their cooperation across traditionally municipal borders. Also, Dahlstrøm finds the alliance to be an important explanation of the economic success of Middelfart.

> From the beginning, the mayor has understood the importance of making connections to the "Triangle area," just as we (the local bank) have done .... Today all development on Funen goes to Middelfart and leaves behind the big city of Odense—nothing happens there to be frank.

CEO of the local bank

One of the mayor's closest partners from the local business community is the local bank. Over the years, the bank has made many contributions to support the development of Middelfart, among the most recent is the so-called "Culture island." The Culture island is the community center and new landmark of Middelfart. It is situated at the waterfront of the city, has a view over the sea and holds the public library, the tourist office, a restaurant, a cinema, etc. The first turf was cut in August 2003 and the community center opened two years later. The political process that occurred before construction could begin took several years. This process was characterized by a close cooperation between the mayor, the council, the CEO, the administration, the local bank, and other local private investors. The process started back in the 1990s when the municipality arranged an architect competition concerning the development of the waterfront. At the same time, the Social Democratic party, under Dahlstrøm's leadership, decided to put forward a proposal for a new public library in Middelfart. This proposal was later connected to the gradual development of the waterfront as a whole. The project expanded from a public library to a community center, including a marina, and it became clear to Dahlstrøm that this project could not be carried out with public funds alone. In a joint partnership, the mayor and the municipal CEO contacted many potential local investors, yet they did not succeed until the mayor involved the local bank. The managing director of the bank stressed that the cooperation with the mayor and the municipality was taking place on strictly business terms; they would never invest in a project that would not pay off. However, he makes no secret of the fact that the mayor's facilitative leadership of the council was important for the bank and its partnership with the municipality.

> I think we are privileged to have a mayor as Steen Dahlstrøm. He is a pragmatic person, all he does is meant to benefit our city, not to create

an image of his person ... Even with the majority in the council, he has managed it sober-minded. I feel there is a great harmony in the political line at city hall. He has taken the opposition on board, and I really don't feel that he has abused the power that he actually has.

CEO of the local bank

Sticking to consensus and sharing his power in the political arena clearly seems to be an advantage for Dahlstrøm in the external arena as well. Whereas the support of a ideological and high-handed Social Democratic mayor would be inappropriate for the local bank and other members of the business community in Middelfart, the support of a consensus-oriented mayor serving a unified whole is truly another story. In that case, the support of the mayor is not only appropriate, but also aims at legitimating the business community at large (for a similar argument, see Gissendanner 2004). Apparently the positive outcome of facilitative leadership in one arena, i.e., the political arena, spills over to other arenas as well; in this case, it is even self-perpetuating. The leader of the Liberal party, part of the potential opposition to Dahlstrøm in the council, is only willing to cooperate and take part in the political leadership of the council as long as the mayor is able to control the "real socialists" in the Social Democratic Party group and continues to emphasize and support the private sector firms in the municipality.

3.2.3 Partnerships in the Administrative Arena

The spillover effect from the consensus climate in the council and external arena is also evident in the administrative arena. The formal functions of the Danish mayor vis-à-vis the administration are anything but clear. On the one hand, the mayor is head of the council and, thus, supposed to lay down rules and regulations according to the values of the council while leaving the implementation to the administration. On the other hand, the mayor as the head of the administration is responsible for the implementation of the council's decisions and, thus, has to control the administrators in more detail. In principle, the somewhat unclear functions leave room for various kinds of mayoral behavior toward the administration—from a strong authoritarian role to a more cooperative one. However, several empirical studies have characterized the relationship between the Danish mayors and the administration as very cooperative. In fact, it is seen as a partnership, where both actors cooperate on common goals and, thus, are dependent on each other in order to reach these goals (Mouritzen and Svara 2002; Berg and Kjaer 2005). Consequently, the administration has incentive to support and strengthen the mayor, and the mayor has incentive to empower the administration.

In the case of Steen Dahlstrøm, his partnership with the CEO is well developed as well. They have been working close together since the very beginning of Dahlstrøm's administration. However, the mayor combines two forms of leadership style in the administration. On the one hand, he gives very detailed instructions and controls the administration in a rather authoritarian way. On the other hand, he carefully listens to advice and the "sparring" he receives from the CEO and the lower level managers of the administration and supports their autonomy from the council. An important point is that this autonomy is established by virtue of the mayor's effort in the political arena. By communicating with and involving the council in many of the matters that have not yet reached the political agenda, but are still under way in the administrative process, Dahlstrøm provides the councilors with an administrative insight that is critical to maintaining their confidence in the administration. Consequently, the administration has peace and room for maneuvering:

> I get them involved (the councilors), they are a part of the basis for decision making and it's to their benefit. Yet it is also to the benefit of the administration. It gives confidence to the administration knowing that they are a part of the process. No one will grumble about things they didn't know, the administration will not be questioned all the time and formalities are put straight.

> **Mayor Steen Dahlstrøm**

At the time when the Social Democrats did not have the absolute majority in the council, it was crucial for Dahlstrøm to have the council's support in order to have an effective impact on the administration. Without the broad support of the council, the administration would be forced to consider the various political minorities in the day-to-day administration and more carefully balance their loyalty between the mayor and the council. With the absolute majority in the council, this balance is obviously not as urgent, as the council's support of the mayor is most obvious. However, there is also another purpose behind Dahlstrøm's continuously ensuring the administration's autonomy vis-à-vis the council, which is revealed in the mayor's conclusion regarding these considerations:

> It's to the benefit of them (the councilors), to the benefit of the administration, and also to the benefit of me ... It gives me an excuse to get things done more quickly than else, when they (the councilors) are already informed.

> **Mayor Steen Dahlstrøm**

The facilitative leadership model practiced in the political arena does not only prove to have a positive spillover effect into the external arena, it also has a positive effect in the administrative arena. And last, but not least, it has a positive effect on the mayor's energy and influence in general.

3.3 Facilitative Leadership in Denmark: An Appropriate, Yet Powerful Model of Leadership

The facilitative leadership model as practiced by Steen Dahlstrøm in Middelfart is a model supported by various local government institutions in Denmark.

Even when voters give an absolute majority to one single party in the council, consequently empowering the mayor to use an authoritative style of leadership, the facilitative leadership model continues to be in use. Dahlstrøm's refusal to take advantage of the opportunity to base his leadership on power is probably typical rather than exceptional for cultural and rational reasons. The cultural reason is the appropriateness of the model, which induced the mayor to continue to communicate with the council, involve the councilors in the decision-making process, and to some extent share his political leadership. In other words, the mayor is expected to support the local government institutions whatever happens, even at the expense of the political party program. And he does so. Not only because he is under the influence of strong norms of consensus, which induce him to behave according to the facilitative leadership model, but also it has proved to be rational to stick to the model, as it is a powerful source of leadership. By sharing his leadership in the political arena, there are positive spillover effects in both the external and the administrative arenas, which contribute to the overall empowering of the mayor.

The political leadership as performed by the Danish mayor can be modeled as circulation of political capital (Berg and Kjaer, 2007). Scholars from different schools of social studies use the concept of political capital, although there is not a general agreement about a common definition of the concept. However, within studies of local political leadership, the concept has been particularly referenced to Banfield's study of political leadership and power in Chicago (Banfield 1961), in which he uses the concept of political capital to describe the power of different actors within a political system. According to Banfield, political capital can be perceived as an actor's stock of power, i.e., a limited resource that can be invested in order to obtain control over other actors and, therefore, reach the desired objectives. Like a broker in the stock market, the political leader will invest his political capital in the areas where he expects the largest return. The idea is that reaching the desired objectives will pay off in terms of new power exceeding the amount of power originally invested.

Although our model of political leadership uses Banfield's notion of political capital as a starting point, our definition of the concept is somewhat different. Defined as potential power earned by participating in the political process, the concept of political capital does not only include "power over" other actors, but also "power to" reach objectives in cooperation with other actors (Stone 1989). Further, political capital in our definition is not a part of an exchange model where the political leader exchanges political services (jobs, money, decisions, etc.) for political power. On the contrary, political capital is part of a circulation model where the political leader exercises, yields, and receives power. As a consequence, the investment of political capital is not to be seen as part of a zero-sum game, but rather as a contribution to increase the total amount of power in the political system.

By bringing the potential political power into play and investing it in leadership tasks, such as formulation of policies, controlling the agenda, implementing the political program, making alliances, representing the citizens, communicating, etc.; and, even more importantly, doing so by complying with the norms and demands associated with each of the tasks and their order of priorities, the mayor will receive various forms of rewards from the elected and appointed officials, the citizens, and others. Whether in the form of acknowledgment, accept and, support, confidence, trust, respect, and/or autonomy, the rewards will altogether increase the mayor's potential power, i.e., political capital, and ultimately the mayor's success will feed back into the process of political leadership.

As illustrated in the case of Steen Dahlstrøm, the returns of the leadership investments made in the Danish municipalities seem to be particularly high in tasks concerning alliances. The mayor is not only rewarded for the policies formulated or the implementation of the political program, but also for reaching these objectives through the involvement of other actors, internal as well as external. In fact, the very act of involving these actors pays off in itself.

Thus, the cooperation and consensus in the council provide a cover for powerful, and to some extent autonomous, mayoral leadership. The facilitative leadership model has without a doubt been demonstrated to be powerful in the Dahlstrøm case. The remaining question is whether it is also successful. The short answer to that question is "yes." Dahlstrøm has managed to take advantage of the economic growth in the "Triangle area" and has been able to transform Middelfart from a traditional provincial town into a modern city. As a consequence, the municipality of Middelfart is doing more than well compared to other municipalities in Denmark.

The facilitative leadership model has also shown to be successful in terms of the mayor's personal political career. This can be illustrated by the outcome of one of the latest and biggest challenges the mayor has faced since 2001: The Danish amalgamation reform.* Here Dahlstrøm faced the major task of supporting the reform locally by seeking to merge the city of Middelfart with two smaller municipalities in the countryside, Ejby and Nr. Aaby, creating a new municipality with 36,100 inhabitants. The process was challenging in several ways. First, in the beginning of the national reform process, the amalgamation was optional, leaving a strategic choice for the mayor to make. Second, the decision of merging the city of Middelfart with the two small municipalities challenged the political leadership, as the two mayors from the smaller municipalities became his competitors in the election in 2005. Dahlstrøm managed to easily overcome both challenges. At the first election after the amalgamation, as many as 38 percent of the voters in the city of Middelfart voted for Dahlstrøm and, in the election at-large, more than one out of five of the voters in the new municipality voted for Dahlstrøm.† It was not enough to give him the absolute majority of seats in the new council; however, with many

---

* Effective January 1, 2007, the 275 Danish municipalities, which had been in existence since the latest municipal amalgamations in 1970, were merged into ninety-eight new municipalities. The amalgamations were a result of national legislation passed in 2005 (after an intense political debate begun in 2002), stating that municipalities could no longer have a size of less than 20,000 inhabitants, which was very common before the reformation.

† At Danish local elections, the voters can choose if they will cast their vote on the party or if they will cast it as a preferential vote on one of the party's candidates (almost three-quarters of the votes are preferential votes).

friends and no enemies in the council, it was enough to give him yet another term as mayor and to start up a brand new municipality of Middelfart. The institutionally and culturally appropriate choice he had made to be a facilitator in 2001 was once again the politically necessary choice as well, as it had been for him in his initial twenty years in office.

References

Banfield, E.C. 1961. *Political Influence: A New Theory Of Urban Politics*. New York: The Free Press.

Berg, R. 2005. From cabinets to committees: The Danish experience. In *Transforming Political Leadership in Local Government*, eds. R. Berg and N. Rao. London: Palgrave Macmillan, 85–100.

Berg, R., and U. Kjaer. 2005. *Den danske borgmester* (*The Danish Mayor*). Odense: Syddansk Universitetsforlag.

Berg, R., and U. Kjaer. 2007. *Lokalt politisk lederskab* (*Local Political Leadership*). Odense: Syddansk Universitetsforlag.

Berg, R., and N. Rao (eds.). 2005. *Transforming Political Leadership in Local Government*. London: Palgrave Macmillan.

Ejersbo, N., M.B. Hansen, and P.E. Mouritzen. 1998. The Danish local government CEO: From town clerk to city manager. In *The Anonymous Leader*, eds. K.K. Klausen and A. Magnier. Odense: Odense University Press, 97–112.

Elcock, H. 2001. *Political Leadership*. Cheltenham, U.K.: Edward Elgar.

Elklit, J., and M.N. Pedersen (eds.). 1995. *Kampen om kommunen. Ni fortællinger om kommunalvalget i 1993*. Odense: Odense Universitetsforlag.

Gissendanner, S. 2004. Mayors, governance coalitions, and strategic capacity—Drawing lessons from Germany for theories of urban governance. *Urban Affairs Review* 40: 44–77.

Le Maire, E., and N. Preisler. 2000. *Lov om kommunernes styrelse*. København: Jurist- og Økonomforbundets Forlag.

Leach, S., and D. Wilson. 2000. *Local Political Leadership*. Bristol, U.K.: The Policy Press.

Mouritzen, P.E., and J.H. Svara. 2002. *Leadership at the Apex — Politicians and Administrators in Western Local Governments*. Pittsburgh, PA: University of Pittsburgh Press.

O'Leary, B., B. Grofman, and J. Elklit. 2005. Divisor methods for sequential portfolio allocation in multi-parti executive bodies: Evidence from Northern Ireland and Denmark. *American Journal of Political Science* 49: 198–211.

Peters, B.G. 1999. *Institutional Theory in Political Science. The 'New Institutionalism.'* London: Continuum.

Serritzlew, S., A. Skjæveland, and J. Blom-Hansen (2005). *Explaining Oversized Coalitions: Empirical Evidence from Local Governments*. Aarhus, Denmark: Department of Political Science, University of Aarhus.

Stone, C.N. 1989. *Regime Politics—Governing Atlanta 1946–1988*. Lawrence, KS: University Press of Kansas.

Stone, C.N. 1995. Political leadership in urban politics. In *Theories of Urban Politics*, eds. D. Judge, G. Stoker, and H. Wolman. London: Sage, 96–116.

Svara, J.H. 1994. *Facilitative Leadership in Local Government*. San Francisco: Jossey-Bass.

Chapter 4

Mixing Models of Leadership in a Mayor–Council City: A Study of Yorkville, Illinois

Curtis Wood, Gerald Gabris, and Bart Olson

Contents

4.1 Introduction

In this chapter, the authors examine the proposition of whether a mayor operating in a mayor–council city and possessing statutory executive authority can consistently behave as a facilitative leader (Svara 1990). This is an important question because the dominant thread in urban government theory suggests that the mayor in a mayor–council form of government has the incentive to rely heavily on a "power-based" style of leadership vis-à-vis the city council and administrative staff to advance his/her political and mayoral agenda (Svara 2002; Wheeland 2002; Mullin, Peele, and Cain 2004). As Wheeland suggests, this "provides the foundation for a conflict pattern of interaction among officials who have incentives to compete with one another to accomplish their agendas" (2002). In the power-based model of leadership, leadership is competitive and is focused on individual goals, and relationships are conflictual (Svara 2002). In their study of three California cities, Mullin, Peele, and Cain (2004) discovered that "mayors who do not sit on the council have more flexibility to act in opposition to the council and establish a separate base of power" by going directly to the public or media, "can shift blame for unpopular decisions and unsuccessful programs," or conversely take credit for council policies that go well, and pose a greater obstacle in sustaining a working majority on the council in support of the mayor's legislative agenda.

Alternatively, Svara asserts that mayors in a council–manager form of government are inclined to practice a facilitative leadership strategy (1990). Here, the mayor serves as a liaison between groups, strives to communicate from multiple vantage points, works with the professional manager as a partner, and emphasizes a culture of collaboration and cooperation. Svara's facilitative mayor is also an ideal type in the normative sense. There is evidence of facilitative mayors in mayor–council cities (Thompson and Brodsky 1994; Svara 1994). The implicit argument, however, is that that form of government strongly influences mayoral leadership behavior, and that mayors who practice facilitation are better leaders than those who rely on power.

In this chapter, we make the case that the depiction of a mayor as either using a power or facilitative style of leadership in any form of government is an oversimplification. One reason for this, which will become clear as we develop our case, derives from the fact that many mayors govern in adapted (hybrid) cities that are neither purely "mayor–council" nor "council–manager," but somewhere in between. Furthermore, we hope to show that the wielding of mayoral power may be a natural and legitimate activity of mayors who serve as legal chief executives. Whether this power wielding leads to dysfunctional conflict rather that facilitative cooperation may derive from leadership strategies heretofore not typically described or studied in the literature of mayoral leadership.

Our analysis delves into the dynamics of the governance process during Art Prochaska's tenure (1999–2006) as mayor of the United City of Yorkville, Illinois. Yorkville typifies the rapidly growing community in the western

Chicago suburbs with an adapted mayor–council form of government.* This case also provides an opportunity to examine the governing process from a microanalysis standpoint, where the researchers have had access to query the central decision makers that govern within the "black box." Not much is known about interaction patterns between mayors, council members, and professional administrators in adapted mayor–council governments. The case study approach that we employ may be the most effective methodology for obtaining the kind of objective information from key actors necessary to understand how they perceive the governance process in an adapted mayor–council city. What we have learned should prove useful to academicians, elected officials, and administrative practitioners.

Data for this study were obtained from interviews conducted during the summer of 2005 by Gabris and Wood with the eight alderpersons, the mayor, and the city administrator (see Appendix 1 for a list of interviewees and the interview questions), and follow-up interviews conducted by Wood, Gabris, and Olson during the summer of 2006 with Mayor Prochaska, seven of the eight alderpersons, a former alderperson who recently relocated, and the interim city administrator (see Appendix 2 for a list of interviewees and interview questions). Minutes of city council meetings were also reviewed regarding policy issues discussed by the mayor and council over the previous year, along with several official city documents and newspaper articles.

We wish to acknowledge that we have been participant–observers in Yorkville. We are mindful of the absolute need to maintain objectivity and detachment when analyzing and evaluating the mayor, council, and city staff.

4.2 The Governmental and Community Context

The Village of Yorkville, Illinois was incorporated on July 8, 1873. In April 1957, the residents of Yorkville and Bristol voted to unify the two cities into one city to be called The United City of Yorkville. The United City of Yorkville is located about 50 miles southwest of Chicago and is the county seat of Kendall County, the third fastest growing county in the nation and the fastest growing county in Illinois (U.S. Census Bureau, found in *Beacon News* June 23, 2006, by Matthew DeFour). Kendall County's population more than doubled from 1990 to 2005, from 39,413 to 79,514 (The U.S. Census Bureau, found in *The Chicago Tribune*, by Russell Working on August 29, 2006, Section 1). The 2000 census reported an estimated population of 6,189 persons in Yorkville, a 58 percent increase over 1990

---

* Frederickson, Johnson, and Wood (2004) call adapted mayor–council cities "adapted political" cities. In adapted political cities, the mayor is legally the chief executive officer, but there is a professional city administrator who is accountable to the mayor *and* the council, and the city administrator has been delegated administrative and management responsibilities.

(Center for Governmental Studies 2003). Between 2004 and 2005, the United City of Yorkville was the fifteenth fastest growing city in Illinois, and between 2000 and 2005 the population of Yorkville grew by over 74 percent (U.S. Census Bureau, Matthew DeFour, *Beacon News*, June 23, 2006). The 2006 Special Census indicated a population of about 11,000 persons, a 78 percent increase over the 2000 census count (Olson e-mail, August 18, 2006). The population is predicted to climb to 35,000 persons by 2010, and the geographic size of the city is predicted to double from 8.5 square miles today to about 16 square miles in 2010 (Center for Governmental Studies 2003). By 2015, city staff estimates that the population will rise to 79,450 persons, a seven-fold increase over the next nine years (Bart Olson e-mail to Curtis Wood on August 18, 2006).

Due to its growing population, Yorkville is transitioning from a semirural, relatively isolated river town to a suburban city interconnected by regional and national commerce. The intersections of Illinois highways 34, 47, 71, and 126, and access to Interstate 88 to the north, Interstate 80 to the south, Interstate 55 to the east, and the proposed Prairie Parkway to the west and south have made Yorkville an excellent location for development (Center for Governmental Studies 2003). Yorkville is primarily a residential community, where large residential developments with moderate to high-end homes have recently been completed with more in the planning stage (Center for Governmental Studies 2003). At the end of July 2006, nearly sixty residential projects were under construction, with 21,841 residential units remaining to be constructed (Russell Working, *The Chicago Tribune* August 29, 2006). There are two industry clusters, one located at the north end and the other at the south end of the community. Major employers include Wrigley manufacturing, Newlywed Foods, and F.E. Wheaton. Land is available for more commercial and industrial development in the current industrial and commercial clusters, as well planned clusters along the Prairie Parkway corridor. The city also has the potential for tourism in the downtown area that is located next to the picturesque albeit floodable Fox River.

Rapid population growth in Yorkville has placed tremendous pressures on the city to provide for and expand the necessary infrastructure, facilities, and services that citizens expect from a full-service municipality. According to one alderperson, the exponential growth in the Yorkville population has led to a situation where the mayor and city administrator are so busy with growth-related issues that they have not properly kept the city council informed, leading to tensions between the legislative and executive branches. Tremendous growth pressures have also triggered a need for both a bigger and more technically professional government. In 1999, when Art Prochaska became mayor, there were thirty-four full-time city employees. In 2006, there were seventy-five employees (http://www.yorkville.il.us/faq.htm), and the 2007 Yorkville budget includes fourteen new employees over the 2006 level (Gillers 2006). The general fund budget has gone from $3.3 million in 1999 to $15 million in 2006, and the total assessed valuation has climbed from about $110 million in 1999 to over $400 million in 2006. At present, the city provides a full range of conventional services and has intergovernmental agreements to provide additional services in fire protection and emergency management. Economic development functions are the responsibility of the Yorkville Economic Development Corporation, a public/private partnership.

Since incorporation, Yorkville has retained the mayor–council form of government. A directly elected mayor and eight alderpersons elected from four wards (two alderpersons are elected from each ward) govern Yorkville. Elections are on a nonpartisan ballot. The mayor is officially a part-time employee who serves as the chief executive officer, presides over the council meetings, monitors the conduct of all subordinate officers, and appoints all city officers with the consent of the alderpersons. The mayor may remove city officers and then report the reason for the removal to the city council. If the council disapproves of the action, they can then reinstate the officer with a two-thirds vote. The mayor presides over city council meetings; however, the mayor can only vote in a tie. The mayor has veto authority over council ordinances, subject to a council override. The mayor also has the opportunity to review and make changes to the proposed city budget prior to its going to the city council for review, and the mayor presents the proposed budget to the city council for their approval. In the state of Illinois, the mayor is expected to confer with the council on all important personnel decisions, and this form of government is not classified as having a "strong" mayor. Nonetheless, the political skill and philosophy of a mayor has a crucial impact on how much power (formal and informal) a mayor actually wields.

The United City of Yorkville has incrementally embraced the professional city administrator as an executive. Around 1972, the mayor hired an assistant to the mayor. At that point in time, the United City of Yorkville functioned as a political city because the assistant was accountable only to the mayor, and the assistant was not chosen on the basis of professional experience or qualifications (Frederickson, Johnson, and Wood 2004). In 1978, the mayor hired a city engineer as the assistant. Then, in 1991, the United City of Yorkville became an adapted political city when it hired the first city administrator. Until January 2006, however, when the city administrator position was codified in the city code of ordinances, the city functioned in practice as a political city because the mayor treated the city administrator as his assistant, and the city administrator perceived himself to be solely accountable to the mayor.

The city administrator ordinance approved in January 2006 provides that the mayor, with the advice and consent of the city council, shall hire and terminate the city administrator who shall be accountable to both the mayor *and* the city council. The city administrator, acting on behalf of the mayor, directs, supervises, and coordinates the administration of all departments, offices, and agencies of the city except the police department, the parks and recreation department, and the community relations' manager, which are under the jurisdiction and control of the mayor. The city administrator also has the responsibility to advise and inform the elected officials on any and all policy issues.

In November 2005, the mayor and city council unanimously appointed John Crois as the interim city administrator to serve until a permanent city administrator was hired. Crois has been the first Yorkville city administrator to be accountable to the mayor *and* council. John Crois has a master's of science degree in economics from the University of Notre Dame, and was the assistant administrator in Oaklawn, Illinois, for 10 years and the village manager in Westchester, Illinois, for almost 20 years.

Since 2000, the city has created key top-level professional management and administrative positions to provide the expertise and leadership necessary to respond to and plan for growth. These include the positions of assistant city administrator, director of finance, community development director, parks and recreation director, and community relations manager. Also, the city regularly hires administrative interns and graduates from the Northern Illinois University master's in public administration program.

Although the Yorkville mayor has considerable authority and influence as the only at-large elected official and the chief executive officer, the mayor must share political and executive authority with the city council. While the mayor is officially the chief executive officer, the increasingly complex, technical, and changing external environment necessitates that he/she delegate administrative authority to a professional city administrator and city staff to govern efficiently and effectively. The political and administrative checks and balances found in an adapted political city constrain the powers of the mayor by making the mayor partially accountable to the council, and partially dependent upon a professional city administrator and staff. Given these constraints, one might expect the mayor would be motivated to use a facilitative style of leadership that emphasizes collaboration, cooperation, mutual trust, and respect between elected officials and appointed staff (Svara 2002), rather than a power-based leadership style tethered to control, competition, and positional authority.

While the Yorkville mayor and council may have granted some administrative and management authority via local ordinance to an appointed "city administrator," in practice, the city administrator is still subordinate and answerable to the executive mayor on a day-to-day basis. The city administrator may, in the mayor's view, serve more as the assistant to the mayor rather than as the chief administrative officer who is accountable to the mayor *and* council. As such, there are still incentives for the mayor to act as an executive leader who uses the power-based style of leadership.

A major purpose of this study is to examine under what conditions and circumstances a mayor in a mayor–council city (whether political or adapted political) will use a facilitative or power style of leadership with the city council. In this analysis, we consider factors influencing mayoral leadership strategy beyond form of government, by also including such variables as growth pressures, mayoral personality and life experiences, citizen issues, and mayor–council expectations. If mayors in mayor–council cities are predisposed toward a "power" leadership model as a means for retaining control over the policy process and administrative staff, then when might personal, interpersonal, and environmental conditions favor a shift in leadership strategies? If a mayor cannot nimbly transform his or her leadership style when specific situations suggest such a shift is necessary, such mayors are likely to become ineffective in their broader roles. Thus, investigating whether and under what circumstances mayors predisposed toward a power leadership model can adapt is a worthy research question.

4.2.1 Yorkville: The Context

Over the past several years, a major governance challenge facing the City of Yorkville has been how to effectively manage conflict through civility, collaboration, and compromise. During the 1990s when Yorkville was a smaller, simpler, and slower-paced community, former mayor Bob Johnson did not have the growth pressures or issues that necessitated a hands-on leadership approach. According to several alderpersons, during two four-year terms, Mayor Johnson practiced a facilitative approach to leadership where he would try to "keep peace in the family." Johnson was not a micromanager and he did not attend committee meetings. Today, Yorkville is a bigger and more complex municipal system. Increasing urbanization has led Mayor Art Prochaska to become much more attentive and intimately involved in shaping and responding to the internal and external environment that affects the city. As such, the mayor "is everywhere." Three alderpersons who served with the mayor during his first two terms feel that the mayor has transitioned from a leadership style emphasizing facilitation to one that depends much more on authoritative power, especially in how he relates to some council members and administrative staff. The reasons for this shift vary, however. One alderperson states the mayor has let power go to his head; another says the mayor has become more single-minded and less communicatively open due to the increasing workload from growth pressures; while a third claims that the former city administrator was responsible for creating ill-will between the mayor and some on the council. This last alderperson has also noticed an improvement in the relationship between the council and the mayor since the departure of the former city administrator and the arrival of the interim city administrator.

Mayor Prochaska and the city council have been acutely aware and concerned about the difficulty they have had in forging a functional governance process amidst their changing urban environment. During the summer of 2005, the mayor and council hired two of the authors of this chapter, Gerald Gabris and Curtis Wood, who are both public administration professors at Northern Illinois University, to examine the governance process and recommend ways the mayor, city council, and city administrator could build a more collaborative and cooperative governance process between the mayor, city council, and city administrator/staff. Interview data indicated that although the council was usually able to achieve consensus on the big ticket items, a minority of elected officials were dissatisfied with the conflict and mistrust created within the city council between the council and the mayor, and between the council and the city administrator/staff, attributed in part to the mayor's power-based style of leadership. Gabris and Wood found the council was evenly split in their perception of the mayor's leadership effectiveness. In the summer of 2005, Gabris and Wood also found discontent with some council members regarding the city administrator's lack of respect for some council members and his belief that he worked for the mayor only and not the council. As a result of the interviews, the consultants made recommendations to build a more collaborative and inclusive governance process by clarifying roles for the mayor, council, and administrator; formalizing a policy on appropriate group behavior of the mayor and governing body; and implementing improved communication, interpersonal relationships, and decision-making mechanisms.

In keeping with an organizational development (OD) spirit regarding our involvement with the City of Yorkville (Burke 1982; Golembiewski 1985), Gabris and Wood utilized several basic OD assumptions. First, we recommended that any change in the governance process reflect a collaborative approach based on a felt need by the mayor and council. Second, they felt that the most useful initial changes would be structural rather than interpersonal or cultural. Finally, they felt that the mayor and council would benefit from additional onsite advice from one of the authors as a means of more efficiently facilitating the change process.

The mayor and city council responded positively to the recommendations. After considerable debate, the city council unanimously (5–0) approved a governance ordinance that established ethical standards, rules of conduct at council meetings for elected officials, and reformed the standing committee system. The council also approved a city administrator ordinance establishing and clarifying the role of the city administrator vis-à-vis the mayor, council, and city staff. The mayor and council also held a goal-setting session. Council members were very positive about the way the mayor facilitated this meeting; however, several alderpersons expressed disappointment that some of their priorities had been put on the back burner in favor of the mayor's goals (authors' 2006 interviews).

To keep the council apprised on important issues and happenings, the interim city administrator established a regular written informational memorandum called the "City Administrator Newsletter." To improve city administrator accountability and responsiveness to the city council, the mayor and city council revised the performance evaluation process for the city administrator. The job description of the city administrator also was revised to conform to the intent of the city administrator ordinance. The city administrator's performance evaluation now includes criteria for evaluating the city administrator's management of departments, leadership style, and council relations, as well as general performance. Finally, the process includes a semiannual performance review and goal-setting session with the city administrator. The new evaluation process was implemented with the hiring of a permanent city administrator in 2007.

4.2.2 The Mayor of Yorkville: Art Prochaska

Mayor Art Prochaska moved to Yorkville with his wife, Andrea, and three children in 1990, and began his political career in 1993 when he was elected alderperson for Ward 3. He had never served in government prior to his being an alderperson, and was only involved in politics in a few campaigns. He first became interested in serving as an alderperson when a former alderperson and neighbor encouraged him to run for a council seat. He ran for alderperson and mayor because he saw the potential in Yorkville, and he believed he could make a contribution in building a better city.

In 1999 and then again in 2003, Prochaska was elected mayor of Yorkville. His term expired in April 2007, and he ran unsuccessfully for a third term. In his first try for mayor he ran against two other opponents and garnered a majority of the votes. In his 2003 reelection campaign, he garnered almost 78 percent of the vote against one opponent (information from the Kendall County Clerk's Office). In his four electoral campaigns, he campaigned door-to-door, meeting as many citizens as possible.

As mayor, Prochaska has continued his connection with the citizens by initiating "Coffee with the Mayor," a roundtable discussion with citizens every other Saturday at different locations throughout the community. He constantly reminds citizens, "Government is you." He has faith in citizens, always tries to follow the "general will," and works to demonstrate that government can work for the people.

Mayor Prochaska indicated he uses a contingency style of leadership with the city council in that his behavior and leadership style will vary based on the situation, the person, and issue. He looks at different situations, people, and issues differently, and he asks himself what he needs to do to get support to achieve his goals. He shared with the researchers a story about how moving back and forth between his father's second family and his mother's second family as he was growing up taught him that different rules, expectations, culture, and personalities required a different set of behaviors and responses on his part.

When asked to talk about his accomplishments, the mayor was adamant that he has not accomplished much alone because everything he has accomplished has been due to the involvement and partnership with the city council, citizens, city staff, and community groups. "Sometimes I led the charge, and sometimes I sat back and others led the charge." When asked to tell us what his legacy might be, he indicated that he would forever be known as the mayor who governed during the time of major commercial and residential growth by bringing in new developments and jobs to the community through public–private partnerships, and by involving citizens in the policy-making process. Also, as mayor, he has tried to think outside the box and take advantage of opportunities, such as the idea of public ownership of the land previously owned by the Boy Scouts for use as a forest preserve.

4.3 Mayoral Leadership Style, Roles, and Relationships

The eight alderpersons and the interim city administrator were asked to rate from one (1) to five (5) the extent to which Prochaska uses a facilitative leadership style with regard to (1) the kind of interactions fostered among city council, (2) his approach to goal setting with the city council, and (3) his attitude toward other officials in other governments, the media, and citizens. The mayor was not asked to rate himself. A score of "1" indicates the mayor never uses a facilitative leadership style, and a score of "5" indicates the mayor always uses a facilitative leadership style. A score of "3" is the mid-point. The respondents' average scores were 2.6 for interactions among the council, 3.5 for the approach to goal setting, and 3.7 for his attitude toward other officials. There is a consensus among council members that the mayor more often uses a facilitative leadership strategy when setting goals or dealing with other officials than when interacting with the city council. With regard to mayoral–council relationships, the respondents are considerably more divided about his leadership strategy, exemplified by the wide range in scores. One person gave the mayor the highest score, but two persons gave the mayor the lowest score. Four persons perceived the mayor as putting the interest of the community ahead of his own agenda, with three of those respondents stating he uses a facilitative style of leadership with the council to achieve the community interest. Another alderperson contended that although the mayor prefers to do things by himself, he has seen an improvement in shared leadership and decision making during the past year. Four respondents perceived the mayor as rather controlling. In the latter instance, a sizeable minority felt he forms partnerships with his allies, but not his opponents, and pursues his own agenda rather than a shared vision. The ninth respondent who rated the mayor fairly low on the facilitative leadership scale (rating of 2) did not offer specific comments. The divergent perceptual differences in mayoral leadership style could be indicative of the fact that the mayor uses a different leadership style with different persons, and/or in different situations and issues.

The idea that an executive can change leadership styles by adapting his or her behavior to fit specific situations or conditions is not new (Hersey and Blanchard, 1969). Along with contingency leadership theory (Fiedler 1964, 1967, 1993), the situational approach (Hersey and Blanchard 1969) contends there is no one best approach to leadership for all situations—it just depends. Hence, Prochaska may be adapting his leadership strategy based on council members' understanding and support of his policy positions. With supportive and empathetic council members, the mayor is likely to resort to a facilitative approach, thus reinforcing the council member's impression that the mayor is an inclusive leader. With unsupportive and nonempathetic council members, the mayor may likely resort to a power-based style of leadership, thus reinforcing the council member's impression that the mayor is not an inclusive leader. Leader-member exchange (LMX) theory postulates several interesting insights about leader behavior that may be applicable to municipal government (Graen and Uhl-Bien 1995). LMX argues that leaders within an organization develop special relationships with their followers. Some are perceived and known as the "in-group," while others are perceived and labeled the "out-group." LMX hypothesizes that leaders develop dyadic relationships with specific group members, and once they become familiar with each other they develop self-reinforcing reciprocity patterns. Members of the in-group receive more information, influence, confidence, and trust from their leaders than do out-group members. As such, in-group members are more highly involved, more motivated, more dependable, and more communicative than their out-group counterparts. Predictably, out-group members are less compatible with the leader and tend to become critical of both the leader and the organization. As the relationships mature, there is more reciprocation between the leader and in-group members. The in-group members become highly supportive and the leader reciprocates his/her support. Conversely, there is less reciprocation between the leader and the out-group members. Consequently, the out-group members become even more critical. The upshot of LMX is that wise leaders strive to become as inclusive as possible by conveying in-group status to all members.

These theories may help explain why Yorkville council members are so polarized in their assessment on whether Prochaska is perceived as a facilitative mayor. To the in-group he is viewed as a facilitative mayor, but to the out-group he is not perceived as being a facilitative mayor. Both groups may, in fact, be correct because the mayor is adapting his behavior accordingly.

Respondents were also asked to rate the extent to which the mayor used traditional mayoral roles, active coordination and communication roles, and policy and organizing roles. In addition, respondents were asked to identify strengths and gaps in performance in each of the three areas. The mayor was not asked to rate himself. A score of "1" indicates the mayor never uses a particular role or strategy, and a score of "5" indicates the mayor always uses that role or strategy. Table 4.1 illustrates the mean scores of the respondents for the three mayoral roles.

Regarding traditional roles, the mayor received consistently high marks for how he represents the city to external stakeholders, but lower marks for how he presides over meetings. Several council members believed he interjects his opinions and rebuts council members too often at council meetings; however, there was optimism among the council that the standards of mayoral and aldermanic conduct at council meetings included in the new governance ordinance would improve this situation. The mayor received high marks for initiating policy and facilitating goal-setting sessions, but lower marks on being able to implement policy and goals through delegation.

The majority of the council perceived gaps in mayoral performance in promoting coordination and communication. For example, the mayor is considered "a weak articulator except during an emergency," "he is not forthcoming," "there is little interaction with the mayor," "we are not kept informed," and "he doesn't educate us or the public." The interim city administrator observed that the mayor uses a contingent leadership style. "If battlegrounds are taken already and opinions solidified, he doesn't reach out to opposition, but if positions are not taken yet and

Table 4.1 Average Scores for the Mayoral Roles

Mayoral Role	Mean Score for Alderpersons
Traditional	4.7
Coordination and communication	2.9
Policy	3.2

the issue is open to debate, then he (the mayor) has more flexibility to reach out and develop consensus." However, a mayoral supporter contended that poor relations and the inability to build a team are caused by the inability of some council members to compromise. With regard to the mayor's relationship with the city administrator, most council members noted that the relationship between the mayor and the interim city administrator appears solid and mutually respectful, although the mayor still clearly perceives himself as the chief executive.

The respondents were asked to describe the mayor's relationship with the city council and how the relationship affects council performance. Only one alderperson unequivocally stated that relations between the mayor and council are good. Paraphrasing this alderperson, "the mayor's communication with the city council has been open, two-way, and positive, and he keeps the council informed. However, the relationship can become adversarial quickly, but the mayor makes every effort to not make that happen." Two alderpersons indicated that relationships between the mayor and council have improved slightly, albeit there was a long way to go. Another indicated that during his first year on the council, relations between the mayor and alderpersons have improved. Specific improvements include giving alderpersons a voice in department head selection, the mayor's willingness to listen to alderpersons without becoming emotional or angry, more civil council meetings, and the interim city administrator's respectful, responsive, and cooperative attitude toward the city council members. Another alderperson also indicated improved and more frequent communication with the mayor, although the alderperson was quick to point out that there is still an imbalance of power in favor of the mayor. According to this alderperson, the mayor is inclined to chastise if one is doing something he doesn't like, and the mayor doesn't want alderpersons to hold ward meetings.* Finally, two council members noted poor and unchanged relations between the mayor and council in that the mayor is so busy with growth-related issues that he cannot keep the council properly informed. However, these alderpersons also noted that since the interim administrator arrived, the council tone has improved because the city administrator and staff are more respectful of the council, and that the mayor's earlier proclivity to debate and rebut the council at every council

---

* It should be noted that the new governance ordinance permits ward meetings.

meeting has improved, but periodically resurfaces. Finally, most council members agreed that the new codes of conduct in the governance ordinance would result in more civility and mutual respect.

The interim city administrator observed that agreement or disagreement between the mayor and council depended heavily on the type of issue. Crois noted that with big strategic issues there is little disagreement, while small tactical concerns are more likely to generate division. As more than one sage has remarked, "Councils will approve a $20 million budget in a heartbeat, but spend hours debating where to plant trees on Elm Street." Crois did observe, however, that since the adoption of the governance ordinance the mayor has resorted more often to a facilitative style of leadership with all of the council.

There is little support from the council interviews for the notion that the mayor routinely mobilizes a power base outside city hall, such as the media or public, to oppose or circumvent the council. Three alderpersons argued that the mayor is more inclined to use his allies on the city council to help him win council support for a policy or program. One alderperson claimed the mayor has used a citizen group to persuade other citizens to support an issue, but not to circumvent or oppose the city council. Conversely, three alderpersons argued the mayor does periodically circumvent the city council by going directly to citizens or citizen groups, but only under certain conditions or situations. During an overnight parking ban debate, for example, the mayor supported the citizens who wanted to overturn the parking ban ordinance that had been approved unanimously just two months earlier. The mayor's stance caused resentment among some alderpersons.

There was also little support for the propositions that the mayor routinely shifts blame to the council for unpopular decisions and unsuccessful programs, or takes credit for council policies that go well. Four alderpersons said the mayor "never" shifts blame to the council and four alderpersons said he "generally did not" shift the blame. Yet, three of the latter four alderpersons indicated the parking ban issue was an example of mayoral scapegoating when he criticized the public safety committee, chaired by an alderperson, for recommending the overnight parking ban, and the city council for approving an across-the-board ban. According to the three alderpersons, the mayor never took a position prior to citizen opposition.

Four alderpersons felt the mayor "never" takes credit for the good work performed by council. One alderperson, stated that the mayor is "good at giving credit to other alderpersons." Two alderpersons, however, stated the transfer of the senior citizen programs to Beecher Community Center is one example where the mayor did not give credit to the council. One alderperson stated she worked hard to find other locations for the programs that were displaced from the Beecher Community Center, but was not given credit privately or publicly by the mayor.

Based on the above example, there appears to be evidence that various council members question the mayor's motivation regarding specific issues. Some feel the mayor is an extremely hard worker dedicated to the broader community interest in a selfless context, while others perceive him as taking credit for policy decisions when the credit actually belongs elsewhere. These perceptual differences also underscore the view of a majority of alderpersons that the Yorkville city council reflects identifiable factions that periodically shift in composition based on the issue. The most durable faction, and the one with the most consistent member composition, consists of several alderpersons who frequently impugn the motives of the mayor to a point where the differences have become personalized. This group (which can sometimes shift in composition) is more likely to perceive itself as an "out-group" by not sharing a common vision with the mayor and, instead, is more likely to perceive the mayor as more controlling, unilateral, and power-oriented.

Dysfunctional conflict may not be all that uncommon on municipal boards (Gabris and Davis, 2005). Because city councils consist of a small number of members, they are very familiar with each other and strive to not rock the boat in order to maintain internal group civility. Factional voting disrupts group stability, and if the factionalism is persistent, it is likely to damage interpersonal relationships (Golembiewksi 1985). Factional voting leads to lower trust, lower openness, higher risk, and lower owning (public officials who do not take personal responsibility for their actions, positions, or beliefs. Thus their relationships with others is not honest or authentic). Lower trust, lower openness, higher risk, and lower owning create dysfunctional conflict that make it more difficult for a city council to effectively address complex issues. The key is dealing with complex and controversial issues in a functional rather than a dysfunctional manner. Table 4.2 highlights the characteristics of dysfunctional and functional conflict.

Using the terminology in Table 4.2, factionalism on the Yorkville city council is likely to precipitate dysfunctional conflict that is centered on personalities, win–lose factional outcomes, the perception of an autocratic leadership style, and the creation of insiders and outsiders. The challenge for Yorkville, or any city, is to operate as much as is feasible in the functional conflict arena. Over the past year, Yorkville has made progress in moving toward functional conflict. As noted by one alderperson, "The council was getting tired of duking it out and we are now beginning to realize

Table 4.2 Characteristics of Functional and Dysfunctional Conflict

Factor	Functional Conflict	Dysfunctional Conflict
Decision outcome	win-win consensus	win-lose factional
Focus	issue-oriented	personality-oriented
Purpose	means-to-an-end	end-in-itself
Locus	the group	the individual
Self-perception	insider	outsider
Culture	team-oriented	ruler-oriented
Executive leadership	facilitative, empowering	power-based, dominance/ compliance

that we are not accomplishing anything without consensus. Now meetings are more productive and shorter with no internal conflict. We are streamlining the governance process that should improve productivity and civility at council meetings."

Alderpersons generally describe the relationship between the mayor and the interim city administrator as "professional." They believe the mayor's relationship with the interim city administrator to be better than with the previous city administrator. A majority of alderpersons are convinced that the interim administrator's less assertive personality, his cooperative approach, and his respect for each council member has created a climate of cooperation, trust, and mutual respect between the council, city administrator, and city staff. The interim administrator also commented that his relationship with the mayor has improved over time "as he (the mayor) involves me more." However, the interim administrator also said he still finds it "strange" that the Chief of Police goes to the mayor rather than the city administrator.

Two alderpersons, however, consider the interim administrator a "lame duck" who is not an active partner with the mayor in policy design and implementation.

4.4 Accomplishments and Impacts of Mayor Prochaska

Unanimous consent exists on the city council that the mayor "eats, sleeps, and breathes the city and that his heart is in pursuing the citywide long-term interests as he sees them." All the alderpersons mentioned that Yorkville is a better place to live, work, and play as a result of Art Prochaska's leadership in shaping and responding to the unprecedented growth of the city. The mayor has taken a personal interest in managing and directing the commercial growth of the city, particularly the new shopping center, by serving as a mediator between developers and property owners. He has also worked hard to build public–private partnerships, and is creative in finding ways to put in infrastructure improvements and financing developments through sales tax rebates. One alderperson stated that, as a result of mayoral leadership, "Yorkville is becoming a place people can be proud of."

However, a few alderpersons question whether the ends justify the means and whether the long-term results will be positive. One alderperson argues that the mayor pursues a "growth by defense" strategy that has led to competition on occasion with surrounding communities regarding boundary agreements and excessive subsidies to developers. Others claim, "Because of the mayor, we give developers everything based on his philosophy that if we deny them anything, they will take their business elsewhere," and that "the mayor is not always consistent in giving concessions to smaller businesses in contrast to what he does with larger ones." Yet another alderperson makes the argument that the mayor only gives the council limited information to facilitate their understanding of growth issues and expects the council to rubber stamp many of his decisions. Still another alderperson hears criticisms from citizens about the excessively fast growth and its effects, such as a loss of community and more traffic congestion.

Most alderpersons were complimentary about how well the mayor connects with citizens. They see the mayor as successfully involving and engaging citizens in city government, and in using citizen involvement for uniting the community around common values. According to some, growth pressures have resulted in the influx of more citizens from different places who are vocal about services and new ways of doing things. Consequently, elected officials must be able to respond to citizen demands by delivering better government services. The mayor has been able to lead effective governmental action in response to citizen concerns and needs. One alderperson characterizes the connection between the mayor and citizens this way, "Many people feel he is the sun. He is hard working and pleasant. People like him and his personality. When he does something wrong, citizens let him get away with it because they do not want to hurt his feelings. There is an aura around him and he is a likeable person. Those who show up to meetings tend to like him." Two alderpersons also noted that at times it seems like the mayor's relationship with citizens is akin to a father and his children, as "he corrects citizens when they speak out of turn, as if he is scolding his children."

Every alderperson thought the "Coffee with the Mayor" was highly successful. The mayor of Plano, Illinois, a nearby community, thought that "Coffee with the Mayor" was such a good idea that he has adopted it for his city. One alderperson, a frequent critic of the mayor's leadership style, is complimentary of the mayor's accomplishments when it comes to developing citizenship and citizen engagement. "The mayor has created a lot of volunteerism in city affairs in terms of increased citizen participation on boards and commissions." Due to the mayor's leadership, citizens now sit on the Senior Facility Committee, and citizens have been invited to serve on the Technology Committee. So, once again, how the mayor is perceived as a leader partially depends on the issue.

4.5 The Nature and Sources of Mayoral Leadership

One school of leadership emphasizes the transformational perspective (Tichy and Devanna 1986; Kouzes and Posner 1987, 1995), and suggests that these kinds of leaders need credibility in order to be effective (Kouzes and Posner 1995; Gabris 2004). Credibility is fundamentally built around a leader's vision. Effective leaders are skillful communicators of their vision in a way that ensures follower buy-in. They accomplish this by showing followers how their vision will take the organization or system to a new level that is better than the existing one. Such leaders also practice what they preach, willingly delegate power to others, trust others, and take risks (Kouzes and Posner 1987). Another hallmark of credible leaders is that they follow through on promises (Kouzes and Posner 1987). Finally, credible leaders recognize the accomplishments of others and celebrate success.

A facilitative mayor fosters the creation of a shared vision incorporating his or her goals and the goals of others, promotes commitment to the shared vision, and focuses the attention and efforts of officials on accomplishing the shared vision (Svara 2002). Members of the Yorkville city council are divided in how effective they perceive the mayor to be in crafting a credible vision and in communicating it to them in a manner that ensures their buy-in. All but one of the interviewees stated the mayor was a visionary leader, but only two council members felt the mayor used a facilitative approach with the council when trying to implement his vision. Several council members feel that the mayor has never articulated a clear vision nor endeavored to facilitate council buy-in of his visionary goals. The interim administrator suggested that perhaps the mayor's vision regarding how the quality of life could be improved in Yorkville hinged on the type of development in question. Regarding residential development, the council must participate more intensively because these decisions directly involve the implementation of the city's comprehensive plan. Commercial development, however, involves more staff involvement and interaction. In commercial development situations, the delicacy of the negotiations and potential risk to the community make the mayor more hesitant to release proprietary information to the council and public.

Whether alderpersons perceive the mayor as a facilitative leader regarding how he implements his community vision may also hinge on whether a specific alderperson is in the "in" or "out" group. The out-group alderpersons were more likely to complain that the mayor provided incomplete and one-sided information. The downside for the mayor is that such leadership behavior likely reduces his credibility with the out-group, making it more difficult for these alderpersons to trust the mayor's motives in the future.

Alderpersons contend the mayor did collaborate with the council in setting goals during the 2006 goal-setting session; however, some alderpersons question the value and legitimacy of the goal-setting sessions because the mayor sometimes places council goals subordinate to his goals and may not implement the council goals. Not following through in terms of implementing high priority council goals undermines the mayor's credibility and the use of strategic planning as a policy, planning, and management tool.

Yorkville alderpersons and the interim administrator were asked to rate the mayor on several variables that may contribute to his source of leadership. As in the previous cases, the mayor was rated on a 5-point scale with a "1" the lowest and a "5" the highest. Four sources of mayoral leadership were considered: (1) formal positional authority (resources derived from the position); (2) informal authority (support from key groups; contacts and connections; media support); (3) personal resources and attributes (clear conception of the office, clear sense of purpose, an understanding on how to use coordinating/communication roles, time to devote to the office, personal energy, resourcefulness, integrity, fairness, and respect for others); and (4) personal skills (ability to communicate, listening skills, ability to set goals and priorities, ability to motivate others, ability to resolve conflicts, and flexibility). In addition, alderpersons and the interim city administrator were asked to explain which specific resources, attributes, or skills within each of the four categories they

Table 4.3 Average Scores for the Sources of Mayoral Authority

Mayoral Sources of Authority	Mean Score for Alderpersons
Formal	3.8
Informal	3.9
Personal Resources and Attributes	3.9
Personal Skills	3.4

considered more or less important sources of authority. Table 4.3 illustrates the respondents' average score for the four sources of mayoral leadership.

The most important sources of formal authority mentioned by alderpersons were access to information, linkage to the public as the city's primary representative, and staff support for carrying out ceremonial duties. The interim city administrator perceived the mayor's greatest source of formal authority as emanating from mayoral powers under the state statute and city ordinances, and with the technical support provided by the city staff.

The most important sources of informal mayoral authority reported by alderpersons were the high level of political capital earned by the mayor from citizens through "Coffee with the Mayor," support of community groups such as seniors and senior citizen groups, and the media attention after each city council meeting and between council meetings.

All respondents reported that the mayor's personal resources and attributes are reflected in his pursuit of the public interest, as demonstrated by the huge amount of personal energy and time devoted to fulfilling his mayoral duties and responsibilities.

The respondents rated personal skills as the lowest of the four sources of leadership. The mayor was rated high on the ability to set goals and priorities through strategic planning, but lower on communication skills with the council members and the ability to resolve conflicts with the council.

Interviewees were asked to describe how the mayor handles opposition or adversity, and how the mayor overcomes obstacles to change. Council members were divided, as in earlier cases, as to whether the mayor uses a facilitative or power-based strategy of leadership when overcoming obstacles to change. Two interviewees suggested that he uses a contingent style of leadership. Three alderpersons described the mayor as a peacemaker. They observed the mayor talking with each council member individually, tiptoeing around his political adversaries, and using a make-up approach when needed. Alternatively, three alderpersons describe the mayor's leadership approach as power-based. According to one alderperson, "With the city council, he is getting better as the screaming and personal attacks have subsided, but he can be short with citizens." According to another alderperson, the mayor "doesn't like to be challenged inside or outside of city hall. He's chauvinistic and he talks down to staff members and women." A third alderperson expressed similar sentiments by saying "the mayor is vindictive. He gets his feelings hurt. If you don't agree on something that's important to him, one can expect retribution, such as what happened with the parking ban issue."

All interviewees were asked how the government structure found in Yorkville enhances or impedes mayoral leadership. Interviewees were in agreement that structure and institutions were important influencers of mayoral leadership and governance relationships, but there was disagreement between the mayor and council as to the preferred structures and institutions. According to the mayor, the committee system whereby council members serve on administrative committees impedes his ability to manage the executive branch and implement policy.

A majority of alderpersons was supportive of the proposition that even in a separated system where the mayor serves as the chief executive officer, mayoral effectiveness and a facilitative mayoral leadership style were positively interconnected. According to these alderpersons, a facilitative mayoral leadership style enhances collaboration, mayoral authority, and legitimacy; checks and balances between the chief executive officer and the legislative branch promotes mutual accountability; and city administrator /staff professionalism can overcome the shortcomings of a separated system by leading to more cooperative and trusting governance relationships. Most alderpersons were optimistic that the new governance ordinance recently approved by the council would improve the quality of governance by restoring the balance of power between the mayor and council and establishing the rules and expectations for shared governance in the pursuit of a common vision and goals.

4.6 Toward a Theory of Governance Relationships in Mayor–Council Cities

The council–manager form of government was introduced in the early part of the twentieth century and took hold throughout the last century to combat corruption and political patronage. Few doubt that professional administration in both council–manager and mayor–council cities have successfully accomplished that goal. There is evidence from this case study that accelerating urbanization and the resulting internal and external complexity and community growth pressures inexorably force institutional changes toward more professionalism and alter the governance dynamics between the mayor, city council, and city administrator. A study by Brian Caputo (2006), finance director of Aurora, Illinois, corroborates our finding that mayor–council cities become more professional as they adapt to the pressures of urban growth. Caputo interviewed the chief administrative officer (CAO) in eight mayor–council cities in Illinois ranging in population from 8,967 to 150,115 to find out why mayor–council cities add the CAO position. He found that cities added a CAO to their structure because they wanted to have a professional with appropriate technical knowledge and management training running their day-to-day operations. Some cities were prompted to add a CAO when they began to grow at a pace so fast that only a full-time, trained professional could oversee it.* Caputo found that all of the cities have achieved the benefits from adding a CAO that they were seeking.

The interviews of the major actors in the United City of Yorkville also demonstrate there is support for the theory that the dominant leadership style used by the mayor is a power-based leadership style, albeit interspersed with facilitative leadership with certain council members and under certain situations, and that the mayor has difficulty sustaining majority support on the city council.

Our findings make it possible to postulate a major proposition about mayoral leadership and governance relationships in one mayor–council city, and perhaps to generalize these findings to other mayor–council cities in municipalities that are rapidly becoming urbanized and incrementally becoming more professional.

> Proposition # 1: Mayor–council cities move through four governance stages, categorized as simple, early complex, middle complex, and mature, that reflect the evolution of mayoral leadership styles vis-à-vis the city council and the city administrator (Table 4.4).

Table 4.4 presents the governance stages that we predict will unfold at different periods of time within mayor–council cities, in large part due to increasing system complexity. Invariably, municipalities will mature but at varying rates of speed. In simple systems, the population of a municipality is small and there is stable or slow population growth. In many of these municipalities, the mayor–council form of government flourishes as the system of choice, in part because a part-time council and mayor and a handful of city staff overseeing specific services can get the job done for a reasonable cost. There is no chief administrative officer, and department heads report directly to the mayor. The executive mayor role is actually prescribed by law and most mayors expect to behave as "executive mayors." The mayor is the dominant political and executive leader who has considerable formal powers. However, like Johnson and Prochaska, the mayor may resort to a facilitative style of leadership to keep peace in the family.

Typically, in large metropolitan areas, small rural outer-ring communities can become targets for urban growth due to such factors as cheaper land, looser zoning restrictions, or proximity to transportation corridors, and/or some combination. Urban growth is a powerful force that can quickly cause increasing complexity for affected municipalities. As the population increases, the part-time mayors and councils, even though well intentioned, do not normally have the training, time, or expertise to effectively manage and adapt to a rapidly changing urban environment.

---

* The CAO positions in the eight cities in Brian Caputo's study were added between 1973 and 1995.

Table 4.4   Governance Stages in Mayor–Council Cities

Phase	Environmental Conditions	Mayor Political/ Executive Leadership	Administrator Executive Leadership
1. Simple (Political City)	Stable, slow growth; Small population	Power-based or facilitative leadership; Part-time	No CAO
2. Early Complex (Political or Adapted Political City)	Increased growth; Expanding population	Dominant Power-based or facilitative; Full time	Chief of staff or assistant to mayor
3. Middle Complex (Adapted Political City)	Rapid growth; Much larger population; Increasing development	Competition *and* cooperation; Facilitative *and* Power-based;	CAO; Awkward sharing; Incomplete administrative authority; Council factions
4. Mature (Conciliated City)	Increasing but controlled growth; Complex service	Cooperation; Facilitative leadership; Part-time	CAO is CEO

These cities are in transition from needing relatively little administrative expertise to a condition of depending on technical administrative systems as a survival and adaptive strategy. When the mayor cannot adequately handle the day-to-day complexities of city administration stemming from increased growth and the panoply of cognate issues associated with greater than normal development, the mayor incrementally adapts by making internal organizational changes, such as hiring a chief of staff or assistant (without the consent of the city council) and/or becoming a "full-time" mayor. For the assistant to acquire administrative/management authority, the mayor must agree to delegate such authority, either informally or formally. This does not mean, however, that the mayor enthusiastically enjoys relinquishing power and authority to a new kid on the block. As long as the mayor serves as the "dominant full-time executive," the relationship remains tolerable for the mayor because he or she is still calling the shots.

The more accentuated and rapid urban growth becomes, the greater the environmental complexity. The greater the environmental complexity, the faster most municipalities are pressured to move through the executive leadership transition cycle. Sustained punctuated environmental change and increasing complexity create a realization among the council and mayor that additional managerial expertise and professionalism are necessary to adapt to and shape environmental forces. The governing body and mayor, out of necessity, formally delegate to a professional chief administrative officer broad administrative and management authority over some departments, although the mayor still serves as the chief executive officer. In the middle complex governance stage (stage 3), the political city becomes an adapted political city. The adapted political city allows the city to professionally manage the increased environmental complexity induced by rapid urban growth, yet also retain vestiges of the earlier, more politically nuanced structures.

The middle complex phase is not a precise measure, but a transitional state that may exist in different communities for different lengths of time. Yorkville is a shining example of a new urbanized outer-ring suburb that has recently adapted by delegating to the city administrator formal authority over most departments, and delegating to the city council shared oversight (alongside the mayor) over the city administrator. However, the city has not shed vestiges of its political institutions and culture; namely, the mayor still continues to serve as the chief executive officer and there continues to be the separation of powers between the mayor and council.

Sustained punctuated growth is likely to lead to a situation where the mayor, city administrator, and the city staff are so overwhelmed they cannot sufficiently consult with or keep the city council properly informed, resulting in the perception by some council members that the mayor uses a power-based form of leadership. There is ample evidence that this scenario has occurred in Yorkville. However, the Yorkville mayor and council have attempted to respond to the external and internal growth-related pressures by (1) codifying a city administrator ordinance making the city administrator formally accountable to the mayor and council and in charge of supervising most departments, (2) streamlining the committee process, (3) developing council meeting rules, and (4) clarifying mayoral and council roles. Consequently, the key political and managerial leaders have been able to build a more effective governance process.

However, governance relationships between the mayor, city council, and city administrator in the middle complex governance stage can be spotty and unstable because the mayor and city administrator share executive duties. In addition, the city administrator is also legally accountable to the city council, which shares oversight responsibilities with the mayor. When an executive leader transition cycle enters the middle complex stage, the greatest variation in mayoral behavior is likely to occur because the mayor perceives him/herself as competing with the city administrator for executive power and influence and also with the council for political and policy leadership. Shared executive authority between the mayor and city administrator and shared policy leadership between the mayor and the council creates an uneasy tension that can fluctuate between equilibrium and disequilibria during the middle complex governance stage.

It is during the middle complex stage that city council members are most likely to simultaneously perceive both displays of mayoral power and facilitative-based leadership strategies. To protect his/her policy-making leadership position and achieve his/her political agenda, the mayor is likely to nurture a majority faction on the city council. Such mayors may become quite active and involved in community affairs as a validation of their value and role as the primary and dominant policy leader and executive. Because they often are well connected with community business leaders, contractors, and developers, they may, in fact, have insight into growth issues that is deeper and broader than most city council members or even professional staff. The staff in these rapidly growing communities is unlikely to be long tenured or experienced, compelling them to defer to the more experienced and expert mayor. Council members comfortable with the dominant mayoral executive will probably see the mayor as performing as a true community leader, and as one who helps facilitate growth and expansion. Thus, the mayor is perceived as a champion. On the dark side, the mayor may step on the toes of other council members who question him/her. These council members may feel mayoral strategies aimed at retaining political and executive power and authority, as demonstrated by the mayor's dominant role in growth-related issues, purposefully excludes a minority of the council from having a meaningful policy-making and administrative voice in the community. Thus, those in the out-group perceive the mayor as a unilateral decision maker. The fact that the out-group does not accept the dominant mayoral role may be partially due to the mayor's treatment of members in the out-group, which further reinforces their negative view of the mayor.

The mayor may also engage in other predictable behaviors. First, the mayor will strive to limit the reporting relationships to the office of city administrator. Most of the arguments for this are not administratively rational but make political sense. For instance, the mayor may continue to push for keeping the police chief out of the chain of command of the administrator on the pretext that a police chief cannot work for an appointed administrator. Second, transitional mayors typically spend more time at work doing mayoral business of various kinds. The one area that they generally shine in involves community relations where they portray themselves as full-time workers. Because they are full-time, they are presumably valuable persons whose executive authority should be respected, and allowed to dominate. Such mayors may spend much time on development issues; so much so that the amount of time they devote to political leadership on the city council suffers. The ensuing political vacuum may create or exacerbate council factions. To shore up or reclaim political power, the mayor may choose to create council factions as a tool for solidifying his/her power. In this situation, the mayor may strategically alter his/her leadership style depending on the group he/she is working with. He/she may be a facilitator to some and play a power role with others.

What we do not know is exactly when (or whether) the adapted political city will be catapulted from the middle complex to the mature stage of governance relationships. Once system complexity has reached a tipping point where sophisticated administrative expertise must be routinely applied, or there is a crisis situation, the dominant mayoral executive model will no longer be acceptable to the citizens, and the city administrator will become the chief executive officer. In the mature stage of governance, the adapted political city becomes a conciliated city* that usually uses the council–manager plan as the legal framework (Frederickson, Johnson, and Wood 2004).

Centralizing the executive authority in the office of a professional manager will further enhance organizational efficiency and effectiveness. Furthermore, the transfer of much of the executive authority and responsibilities from the mayor to the city administrator is likely to result in improved governance relationships between the mayor and council and the mayor and city administrator because the mayor is no longer perceived as the unilateral executive by the council, and is no longer in direct competition with the city administrator for executive supremacy.

As a result of the constrained formal mayoral executive powers found in the conciliated city relative to the adapted political city, we would predict that the mayor more consistently uses a facilitative style of leadership with the city council and the city administrator in order to maximize effectiveness (Wheeland 2002). In the best scenario, the mayor, city council, and city administration form a "team" focused on what is best for the community. This proposition will need to be tested in cities that have evolved from the middle complex to the mature stage. It will also be important to examine whether the movement through stages produced by structural and environmental changes is stable, or if cities will move back and forth between the middle complex and the mature stage depending in part on the leadership characteristics of the mayor.

4.7 Conclusion

We believe that our findings indicate that the United City of Yorkville, instead of being unusual in mayoral leadership strategies, may actually be displaying rather predictable and comprehensible system patterns. Yorkville is presently in the pangs of transition from an early complex stage municipality to a middle complex stage. This transition is characterized by the lack of mayoral credibility due to the mixed signals created when the mayor uses a facilitative style of leadership with political friends in certain situations, and a power-based style of leadership with political opponents

---

* Conciliated means to assemble, to unite, or to make compatible, and describes a municipality that is no longer exclusively based on either the separation of powers model or a unity of powers model, but both. Embedded in the conciliated city are the unification of mayoral political leadership, political representation, and professional competence (Frederickson, Johnson, and Wood 2004). As in the adapted political city, there is still a separation of powers between the mayor and council in the conciliated city; however, the city administrator now becomes the chief executive officer and is legally responsible for managing all city departments (Frederickson, Johnson, and Wood 2004). However, the mayor still may be "empowered" in that the he/she may nominate the city administrator, subject to the approval of the city council, and may submit the budget to the council.

when under attack, or on the defensive. Should growth pressures continue, and the evidence suggests that it will, the mayor and council will likely need to evolve into the mature stage of governance relationships by further adapting into a conciliated city. This proposition will need to be tested in other case studies.

Our study and findings suggest that the transition process within mayor–council cities is difficult and stressful for the key players involved. It is not easy. Nonetheless, executive mayors demonstrate a rather amazing ability to adapt and change as environmental conditions dictate. The role of the mayor will likely remain a crucial one in municipal government as municipalities evolve in response to growth complexity. In our view, this evolution will continue to be reflected in the generation of new adapted cities where the mayor and professional administrator will share executive authority and leadership, and the mayor and council will share policy making and oversight of the executive branch. Like any type of administrative system, the shared executive model will at times be problematic. Yet it is nonetheless an administrative reality and fact that students and practitioners of local government will have to learn to live with and work in.

This chapter sheds some light on how one can better understand the evolving role of the mayor, council, and city administrator from the experience of one mayor–council city. The United City of Yorkville represents an excellent case showing how an external organization development intervention (Gabris and Golembiewski 1997), can make a positive difference in the resolution of municipal governance conflict. Two of the authors served as external consultants to the city with the charge of helping smooth out its governing process. The authors utilized the standard action research model of OD (Burke 1982), beginning with identification of perceived need, followed by data collection and diagnosis, which subsequently resulted in a collaborative intervention. The intervention led to several products including a new city administrator ordinance, clarifying this position's role and responsibilities, and also, a new city governance ordinance aimed at reframing the city's committee structure and defining rules of conduct and roles. Both reforms required the mayor to delegate more authority to the city administrator and to the city council. During the intervention, the author/interveners also worked closely with the mayor, the administrator, and members of the city council as process consultants, coaching them on how to be more effective within their small group.

Finally, this case study also demonstrates the need for more research regarding the nature and determinants of mayor–council–administrator governance formal and informal relationships in mayor–council cities to better comprehend and predict the trends and future of urban governmental systems.

4.8 Postscript

On April 17, 2007, Valerie Burd, a two-term alderperson, defeated two-term mayor Art Prochaska to become the next mayor of Yorkville. Burd garnered a little over

58 percent of the vote while Prochaska captured 41 percent of the vote. The turnout was about 34 percent of the registered Yorkville voters, about twice the turnout across Kendall County (data from the Kendall County Clerk's Office). In addition, two aldermen who were supportive of and loyal to Prochaska were not reelected. In 2003, Prochaska garnered 78 percent of the vote against one candidate, much greater than in 2007, and the voter turnout in 2007 was about 34 percent, the same as in 2003 (data from the Kendall County Clerk's Office).

In order to learn why Prochaska was not reelected, Curtis Wood (an author of this chapter) interviewed Prochaska, Valerie Burd, four alderpersons (includes one alderman that was not reelected, one who was reelected, and two not up for reelection), and Bart Olson, the new interim administrator and an author of this chapter. (See Appendix 3 for a list of the questions.) In addition, Wood examined *The Beacon News* articles from August 2006 until the end of May 2007 to better understand the major electoral campaign issues.

During the election campaign, Prochaska focused on his accomplishments and effectiveness in getting things done, such as improving the image of Yorkville, ushering in several commercial developments and a mega-mall, enlisting developers in paving new city roads, and helping to save the Hoover Boy Scout Camp (Yeagle 2007; Gillers 2007). Valerie Burd promised to focus on nuts and bolts issues, such as saving the downtown, improving existing streets, creating a pedestrian friendly place, and moving toward a greener city. However, she also stressed governance issues, such as improved communication between the mayor and alderpersons, and she presented herself as a new leader trying to open local government to more public involvement and public scrutiny through stricter enforcement of the Illinois Freedom of Information Act (Yeagle 2007; Gillers 2007). Burd also stressed the need for an administrative assistant to the city council and she called for a permanent city administrator to help preserve recent progress (Yeagle 2007).

Based on the interviews and *The Beacon News* articles, the mayoral Yorkville election outcome can be mainly attributed to the discontent, disappointment, and dissatisfaction created among citizens by the decision-making process followed by city officials to annex a tract of land for the possible use as a landfill, the decision to annex this land, *and* the subsequent application by a development company to site the landfill on the annexed property. One alderman described the landfill issue as Prochaska's "Achilles heel." Specifically, many citizens came to believe that the mayor and aldermen who were in favor of the annexation were not being honest or open with the citizens, residential developers, and county about the intent to site a landfill on the annexed property—strategies not reflective of a facilitative governance approach.

Many citizens, right or wrong, came to this conclusion for four reasons: (1) the mayor and council fast-tracked the annexation process; (2) citizens learned, after the fact, that the property owner and landfill developer met with one or two aldermen at a time in private "informational meetings"; (3) a confidential memo from the city attorney became public that advised the mayor and aldermen not to inform six prospective residential developers or the county that the city was looking at the possibility of annexing land for a possible landfill; and (4) another confidential memo from the city attorney became public that advised the mayor and aldermen to abide by state case law directing elected officials to remain objective by "not engaging in discussion about the specifics of the (landfill-siting) process with anyone". In the first instance, the citizens perceived they were being marginalized when it took only nineteen days between the time the annexation petition was submitted and when the annexation vote took place. In the second instance, there was the public perception that the mayor and aldermen who favored the annexation were deliberately circumventing the open meetings act and making deals in private. In the third instance, the mayor and aldermen who favored the annexation were perceived by many citizens as not being above board with citizens, residential developers, and the county about the status of the annexation and the possibility of siting a landfill on the annexed property. In the fourth instance, there was a public perception that the mayor and two aldermen up for reelection favored the siting of the landfill on the annexed property. This perception was heightened when they chose to remain silent during the landfill siting public process rather than defend themselves against the arguments and talking points made by the Friends of Greater Yorkville, a group of city and county residents opposed to the landfill, and their electoral opponents who challenged the idea that the landfill was inevitable and who criticized a lack of public discourse in the months leading up to the vote on the annexation.

On May 24, 2007, one month and one week after the Yorkville election, the new city council that included three new alderpersons critical of the proposed landfill voted 7–1 to deny the landfill application. In the resolution denying the application, the city council attested that the application did not meet all nine statutory criteria for siting a landfill. Mayor Burd did not vote as the mayor votes only in a tie. The city council decision has been appealed by the development company to the Illinois Pollution Control Board that can affirm the city's decision, overturn it, or remand the application back to the city council for reconsideration. It could take up to one year for a decision by the state Pollution Control Board.

At this writing, Valerie Burd has been the Yorkville mayor for two months. During the interview, she indicated she is committed to improving relations and restoring trust with the city council, city staff, the public, and neighboring governmental entities by using an inclusive and consensual governance approach, creating a more transparent city government, and ensuring that citizens are more informed and involved. Two of the three alderpersons interviewed contend that Burd has already demonstrated she is more of a facilitative mayor than was Prochaska. According to these two alderpersons, she has already treated them as partners by involving them in creating a community vision and recognizing their strategic priorities and goals, and has empowered alderpersons by keeping them fully informed, involving them in groundbreakings in their respective districts, and encouraging alderpersons to hold district meetings. One alderperson also indicated Burd has already held a town hall meeting on how to achieve a greener city and established contact with a surrounding governmental jurisdiction to fashion an annexation agreement.

However, one alderperson noted that the citizens may have voted for a facilitative mayor, but what they got instead was a power-oriented mayor. According to this alderperson, the new mayor uses a power-based governance style vis-à-vis the council as much if not more so than did Prochaska in that she only follows the governance ordinance when it is convenient and rewards her friends. This alderperson indicated she has super-majority support on the council as a result of the election, and she does not need to use a facilitative approach with the minority.

After the April 17 election, Burd and the city council extended City Administrator John Crois's contract until May 31. However, Burd did not reappoint Crois when the contract extension period lapsed. Instead, the new mayor nominated and the city council confirmed Bart Olson as the interim administrator who would serve until the mayor and council hired a permanent city administrator.

The city has hired a consultant who is facilitating the hiring process of a permanent city administrator. An assessment center made up of four alderpersons, the interim city administrator, a school board member, a chamber of commerce representative, and the city administrator of an adjacent community will conduct the interviews of the five finalists. The assessment center members will recommend to the mayor the most qualified candidate. The mayor, in turn, will take into consideration the advice of the assessment center, and then nominate one candidate to the city council, who will then confirm or deny the mayor's choice by majority vote.

All the elected officials that were interviewed, including the new mayor, voiced their strong desire that the next city administrator should have (1) considerable city administrator experience, (2) the courage and integrity to do the right thing rather than blindly obey the mayor and council, (3) the authority to manage the day-to-day operations of the executive branch in conformance with the local ordinance and governing policies, and (4) be held accountable to the mayor *and* city council.

Yorkville continues to incrementally move toward the mature governance phase (conciliated city) in that the new mayor is committed to using a cooperative facilitative style of leadership in relation to the council, city staff, the public, and neighboring jurisdictions, and the mayor and council are committed to a more professionally managed city. However, it is too early to know for sure whether the movement toward the conciliated city will and can be sustained. There are still too many unknowns. As such, it will be necessary to revisit Yorkville officials to learn whether or not Yorkville has been able to live the vision.

References

Burke, W. Warner. 1982. *Organization Development: Principles and Practices.* Boston: Little, Brown Publishers.

Caputo, Brian. 2006. City administrators in mayor–council governments. Unpublished paper submitted in partial fulfillment of an MPA degree, Northern Illinois University.

Center for Governmental Studies. 2003. *Municipal Assistance Program: Governance and Municipal Practices Assessment for the United City of Yorkville.* DeKalb, IL: Center for Governmental Studies.

Defour, Matthew. 2006. Kendall County towns fastest-growing in state. The Beacon News, Aurora, IL, June 23.

Fiedler, Frederick. 1964. A contingency theory of leadership effectiveness. In *Advances in Experimental Social Psychology*, ed. L. Berkowitz. New York: Academic Press, 149–190.

Fiedler, Frederick. 1967. *A Theory of Leadership Effectiveness.* New York: McGraw Hill.

Fiedler, Frederick. 1993. The leadership situation and the black box in contingency theories. In *Leadership Theory and Research: Perspectives and Directions*, eds. M.M. Chemmers and R. Ayman. New York: Academic Press, 1–28.

Frederickson, H. George, Gary Johnson, and Curtis Wood. 2004. *The Adapted City: Institutional Dynamics and Structural Change.* Armonk, NY: M.E. Sharpe, Inc.

Gabris, Gerald. 2004. Developing public managers into credible leaders: Theory and practical implications. *International Journal of Organization Theory and Behavior* 7: 209–230.

Gabris, Gerald and Trenton Davis. 2005. Suburban city councils and small group behavior: Rethinking the design of political decision-making groups in a democratic system. Paper presented at the annual meeting of the Midwest Political Science Conference, Chicago, IL.

Gabris, Gerald and Robert Golembiewski. 1997. The practical application of organizational development to local government. In *Handbook on Local Government Administration*, ed. Jack Gargan. New York: Marcel-Dekker, 71–100.

Gillers, Heather. 2007. Election 07: Mayoral race centers on landfill. *The Beacon News*, Aurora, IL, April 11, A1.

Golembiewski, Robert. 1985. *Humanizing Public Organizations.* Mt. Airy, MD: Lomond Publications, Inc.

Graen, G.B. and M. Uhl-Bien. 1995. Relationship-based approach to leadership: Development of leader-member exchange (LMX) theory of leadership over 25 years: Applying a multi-level multi-domain perspective. *Leadership Quarterly* 6: 219–247.

Hersey, Paul and Kenneth Blanchard. 1969. *Management of Organization Behavior: Utilizing Human Resources.* Englewood Cliffs, NJ: Prentice-Hall.

Kouzes, John and Barry Posner. 1987. *The Leadership Challenge.* San Francisco: Jossey-Bass.

Kouzes, John and Barry Posner. 1995. *Credibility.* San Francisco: Jossey-Bass.

Mullin, Megan, Gillian Peele, and Bruce E. Cain. 2004. City Caesars? Institutional structure and mayoral success in three California cities. *Urban Affairs Review*, 40: 19–43.

Svara, James H. 1990. *Official Leadership in the City: Patterns of Conflict and Cooperation.* New York: Oxford University Press.

Svara, James H. 1994. Key leadership issues and the future of council–manager government. In *Facilitative Leadership in Local Government*, eds. James H. Svara and Associates. San Francisco: Jossey-Bass, Chap. 11.

Svara, James H. 2002. Mayors in the unity of powers context: Effective leadership in council–manager governments, in *The Future of Local Government Administration: The Hansell*

Symposium, eds. H. George Frederickson, and John Nalbandian. Washington, DC: International City and County Management Association, 43–54.

Thompson, Edward, III and David M. Brodsky. 1994. A mayor in commission and mayor–council government: Mayor Gene Roberts in Chattanooga, Tennessee. In *Facilitative Leadership in Local Government*, eds. James H. Svara and Associates. San Francisco: Jossey-Bass, Chap. 10.

Tichy, Noel and Mary Anne Devanna. 1986. *The Transformational Leader*. New York: John Wiley & Sons.

Wheeland, Craig M. 2002. Mayoral leadership in the context of variations in city structure. In *The Future of Local Government Administration: The Hansell Symposium*, eds. H. George Frederickson and John Nalbandian. Washington, DC: International City and County Management Association.

Working, Russell. 2006. Just 8 years old, Kendall courthouse too small. *The Chicago Tribune*, August 29, Section 1, p. 3.

Yeagle, Patrick. 2007. Mayoral hopefuls square off. *The Chicago Tribune*, April 6, Section 2, p. 5.

Appendix 1: Interview Questions (Summer 2005)

1. What does the council do well?
2. What does the council not do so well?
   a. How can the council's performance in these areas be improved?
3. What does the mayor do well?
4. What does the mayor not do so well?
   a. How can the mayor's performance in these areas be improved?
5. What is the appropriate role of the city administrator?
6. What is the appropriate role of the mayor?
7. What is the appropriate role of the city council?
8. What changes, if any, have you seen during the past year or two in the quality of the relationship between council members and between the mayor and the council?
   a. If the relationship has changed, what caused this change?
   b. How can this problem be solved?
9. Would you support an ordinance that clarifies the role and responsibilities of the city administrator?
10. Would you favor a review of the committee system?
    a. If so, what changes, if any, to the current system would you recommend?
11. What would you like to accomplish from this governance session?
12. Is there anything else you would like to add?

Appendix 2: Summer 2006 Interview Questions

1. Questions for the Mayor only:
   a. What is your background and career in government and your motivation for seeking and retaining the mayor's position?

    b. What have been your election campaign methods and election outcomes when you ran for the mayor's position in 1999 and 2003?

    c. Are you part of a slate or have you worked to elect a slate of like-minded candidates?

2. To what extent does the mayor use a facilitative leadership style? (See Attachment 1*) Please rate the mayor from 1 to 5 for each of the three (3) categories below, using **Attachment 1** that describes the specific leadership behaviors/traits within each of the three categories. A score of "5" signifies the mayor always uses the leadership styles or demonstrates the leadership traits within a particular category, a score of "1" indicates the mayor never uses the leadership styles or demonstrates the leadership traits within a particular category. Use the comments section to explain which of the leadership behaviors/traits within a category the mayor uses less or more often.

    a. Kind of interactions fostered among city officials: 1 2 3 4 5
- Comments

    b. Approach to goal setting with city officials: 1 2 3 4 5
- Comments:

    c. Attitude toward and relationship with elected and administrative officials in other governments, the media, and citizens: 1 2 3 4 5
- Comments:

3. Describe any changes in mayoral leadership style since 1999 when Mayor Prochaska was elected Yorkville mayor?

4. How has Mayor Prochaska's leadership style been the same or different than his predecessor(s)?

5. Describe the mayor's relationship with the city council and how the relationship affects council performance?

6. Does the mayor establish a power base separate from the council and pursue his policy agenda by going directly to the media, the public, or other governments to circumvent council approval? If so, give an example.

7. Does the mayor shift blame for unpopular decisions and unsuccessful programs to the council? If so, give an example.

8. Does the mayor take credit for popular decisions or successful policies made by the council? If so, give an example.

9. Does the mayor use the veto as an assertion of authority and independence from the council, and thereby strengthen his negotiating position? If so, give an example.

10. Describe the mayor's relationship with the city administrator and how the relationship affects the administrator's performance?

11. Describe the mayor's relationship with outside government officials (elected and appointed) and how that relationship has helped or hindered effective governance.

---

* All attachments are available from the authors at the Division of Public Administration, Northern Illinois University.

12. Describe the mayor's relationship with citizens and how that relationship has affected trust in and support for city government.
13. Describe the mayor's relationship with the media and in what ways and how effectively the mayor has used the mass media?
14. What are the accomplishments that can be attributed to the mayor's leadership and how did the mayor make a difference in his community?
15. How were these accomplishments achieved? (Relate the mayor's role/leadership style to the accomplishments.)
16. What are the major roles performed by the mayor and how are they handled? (**See Attachment 2.**) For each of the three (3) categories below, rank the mayor from 1 to 5 with a rating of "5" signifying the mayor plays the role very frequently and a rating of "1" signifying the mayor plays the role very infrequently. When scoring each of the three roles, use **Attachment 2** that describes the specific roles/tasks within each of the three general categories. Use the comment section to explain mayoral strengths and gaps in performance for the specific roles/tasks within the three general categories.
    a. Traditional roles: 1 2 3 4 5
       • Comments:
    b. Active Coordination and Communication: 1 2 3 4 5
       • Comments:
    c. Policy and organizing roles: 1 2 3 4 5
       • Comments
17. Is the mayor a visionary leader?
18. How has the mayor secured support for his vision?
19. To what extent does the mayor's vision include the goals of others?
20. What is the level and nature of support that the mayor has from members of the city council?
21. How has the mayor handled opposition or adversity within or outside city government?
22. When there were obstacles to change, how did the mayor overcome them?
23. What are the sources from which mayoral leadership is derived? (**See Attachment 3**) For each of the four (4) categories below, rank the mayor from 1 to 5 with a rating of "5" signifying that you consider the source of leadership authority for Mayor Prochaska as very important and a score of "1" that you consider the source of mayoral leadership authority as very insignificant. When scoring each of the four general sources of leadership authority, use **Attachment 3** that describes the specific resources, attributes, or skills within each of the four categories. Use the comment section to explain which specific resources, attributes, or skills within each of the four categories are more or less important.
    a. Formal authority: 1 2 3 4 5
       • Comments:

b. Informal authority: 1 2 3 4 5
   • Comments:
c. Personal resources, attributes, and characteristics: 1 2 3 4 5
   • Comments:
d. Personal Skills: 1 2 3 4 5
   • Comments
24. How does the government structure enhance or impede mayoral leadership?

Appendix 3: Postscript Interview Questions

1. Was the mayoral election outcome a surprise? Why or why not?
2. Why did Mayor Prochaska not get re-elected?
   a. Did the mayor's leadership style with the council, staff, public, or other civic and governmental leaders have anything to do with his defeat?
3. Why did Valerie Burd win the mayoral election?
   a. Did it have to do with Prochaska's lack of facilitative mayoral leadership or Burd's promise to provide more facilitative mayoral leadership?
4. Why did P.J. not win reelection?
   a. Did it have anything to do with his loyalty to Prochaska?
5. Why did J.B. not win reelection?
   a. Did it have anything to do with the fact he was appointed by and loyal to Prochaska?
6. What role do you envision for the permanent CAO and what qualities are you looking for in the permanent CAO?
7. (For Valerie Burd) What are your plans for changing governance relationships between the mayor and the city council?
8. (For Valerie Burd) What are your plans for changing governance relationships between the mayor and the public?
9. (For Valerie Burd) What are your plans for changing governance relationships between the mayor and civic leaders/other governmental officials?

FACILITATION IN THE COUNCIL-MANAGER FORM

A. Classic Situations: When Leadership Looks Easy (Even Though It's Not)

Chapter 5

Switching Roles from Administrator to Mayor: Winston-Salem, North Carolina

Kenneth A. Klase

Contents

5.1 Introduction

This case study examines the leadership style and resources of Mayor Allen Joines of Winston-Salem, North Carolina, a mayor who epitomizes the facilitative leadership model as a council–manager mayor. Mayor Joines exercises leadership despite possessing the limited authority of a mayor in a council–manager city. His leadership is clearly different, and the nature of both his style and approach is colored by his unique background and ability to marshal a range of resources. Allen Joines spent his career as a city administrator, rising to the position of Deputy City Manager of Winston-Salem, North Carolina, before retiring in 2000 and being elected mayor in 2001 and, subsequently, reelected in 2005. Based on interviews with him and other leaders in Winston-Salem, the nature of his leadership style and the resources he utilizes in exercising that leadership can be evaluated for what they contribute to a greater understanding of the facilitative leadership model.

5.2 Government and Community Context

Winston-Salem, the county seat for Forsyth County in North Carolina, had an estimated population in 2007 of 227,600 after completion of a recent large annexation, on a land area of over 110 square miles. Winston-Salem is the fourth largest city in North Carolina. In 2000, the population was 55.6 percent white and 37.2 percent African American. Winston-Salem has experienced a declining downtown area and economic development issues relating to the downturn of the traditional industries in the area (textiles, tobacco, and furniture). While these industries have undergone reductions in employment in recent years, the area continues to depend economically on tobacco and textile, and there have been some recent economic bright spots in these areas. For example, R.J. Reynolds Tobacco Holdings and Brown & Williamson Tobacco merged into Reynolds American and brought new jobs with the reopening of a local manufacturing plant; and Sara Lee spun off its apparel business, which has located the new company's headquarters in Winston-Salem. The city has undertaken significant downtown redevelopment efforts in recent years and has pursued economic development strategies to diversify and expand the city's economic base, particularly in health sciences, biotechnology, and computer technology. The city assisted Wake Forest University Health Sciences in development of the Piedmont Triad Research Park, which when fully developed will represent more than thirty thousand jobs. The North Carolina Biotechnology Center opened its first regional office in the Piedmont Triad Research Park in 2003, and since then, the research park has begun to attract biotechnology research companies in this expanding field. Most recently, city incentives helped to attract, in 2005, a new Dell computer assembly plant to Winston-Salem, which added seventeen hundred jobs. The plant is beginning to attract other major Dell suppliers to locate in Winston-Salem.

The city operates under a council–manager form of government. The council consists of eight members elected by ward. The mayor is directly elected at large and presides at all meetings of the council, votes in case of ties, provides leadership on policy issues, recommends appointments to city boards and commissions, carries out special responsibilities during emergencies and represents the city at official functions. The council appoints the city manager who oversees the day-to-day administration of city services

5.3 Background and Career

Allen Joines grew up in Moravian Falls, a tiny Wilkes County, North Carolina, community, in a family of modest income. He received his undergraduate degree in political science from Appalachian State University, and subsequently earned a master's degree in public administration from the University of Georgia. In 1971, he began his career in Winston-Salem as assistant to the city manager. He recalls, "At the time, the city manager was John Gold. He had a national reputation, and it was the only place I applied for a job. I really wanted to work there, pestering people until, in '71, I got a job." (Adams 2006) Subsequent promotions with the city were to positions of director of evaluation, public safety coordinator, director of development, and deputy city manager.

During his thirty-five years in Winston-Salem, Joines has held numerous positions in professional, civic, and community organizations, including the North Carolina Development Association, serving as president; the Triad March of Dimes as chairman and vice chairman; the board of directors of the Salvation Army Boys' Club; and program chair of Leadership Winston-Salem. He has also served as chairman of the Winston-Salem Arts Council, member of the Tourism Development Authority, and as a member of the board of the Housing Authority of Winston-Salem. He is currently serving on the board and executive committee of the United Way, the board of directors for the Children's Museum, The North Carolina League of Municipalities, and chairman of the North Carolina Metropolitan Coalition. Governor Easley also appointed him to serve on the North Carolina Local Government Commission (City of Winston-Salem 2006).

After a distinguished career in city administration, he retired from his position as deputy city manager for the City of Winston-Salem in 2000 to become the president of the Winston-Salem Alliance, a nonprofit economic development corporation established to improve economic vitality and create additional employment opportunities in Winston-Salem. It was during this period that some in the business community perceived that the city was in a downward spiral and encouraged Joines to consider running for mayor. Although he had never thought about running for public office, Joines said he thought that he should consider public service as mayor because he felt he could bring to the position his knowledge of city government and economic development, while also bringing the community together. Consistent with that view, Joines is considered "a genuinely nice guy who entered political life to help his community"

(Sexton 2006). Jack Cavanagh, the Republican who was running for reelection as mayor in 2001, verbally attacked Joines, who was running as a Democrat, during the campaign, "calling him a political pawn for the city's powerful and elite" even though Cavanagh and Joines had worked together amicably only the year before when Joines was deputy city manager (Hamilton 2001). Joines claimed there was a simple reason he had attracted so many of Cavanagh's former backers: "I think it's just an indication of the lack of his (Cavanagh's) effectiveness and lack of leadership" (Hamilton 2001). Joines was elected mayor of the City of Winston-Salem in November 2001 by a margin of 78% to 22%. The local media remarked that Joines took to the job of mayor "like a natural." "From his experience working as an executive for the city and leading the Winston-Salem Alliance …, (they felt) he brought a keen knowledge of key issues, such as downtown revitalization and economic development" (*Winston-Salem Journal* Editorial 2005).

In looking at the city's circumstances as he finished his first term in 2005, Joines said, "There is a positive spirit in Winston-Salem that was not here four years ago. There is an optimism about our future replacing the doubt of the past" (*Winston-Salem Journal* Editorial, 2005). His first four-year term as mayor was generally considered successful, and his reelection in 2005 went uncontested as he rode a wave of popularity that "spooked would-be GOP candidates from even mounting a challenge …" in the election (Guitierrez 2005). "For the first time since 1966, a Winston-Salem mayor had run unopposed for reelection… . The last mayor to have run unopposed was Democrat M.C. Benton, who was first elected to a two-year term in 1963… . Benton won reelection in 1965 and in 1966, when the term was changed to four years, both times running without opposition" (Hewlett 2005). Joines enjoyed so much bipartisan support that even the Forsyth County Republican Party Chairman said, "I have a lot of respect for Allen … I think he could be a better mayor if he were a Republican" (Hewlett 2005).

Joines was briefly considered in such a strong political position after his reelection in 2005 that he considered running as the Democratic candidate for the 5th Congressional District, a strongly Republican district held by incumbent Republican Virginia Fox. He eventually decided not to run for the Congressional seat. He said, "It'd be a betrayal of the people who had just voted for me as mayor" (Adams 2006). This was partly because he had just been reelected as mayor, where he campaigned claiming that there were still unfinished city projects he wanted to see completed in his second term. But political research at the time indicated he may have lacked political support outside the local area, and he also said that "the need to raise lots of money and to campaign until November became critical factors in his decision" (Gutierrez 2006). "I just couldn't do it," Joines said. "Campaigning is one of my least favorite things to do …I don't mind asking for money for things like the United Way, but I really don't like asking for money for myself" (Sexton 2006).

He continues to serve as mayor of Winston-Salem and says he continues to enjoy his mayoral job. According to Joines, the city is better off than it was four years ago, but not where it needs to be. "I think our economy is starting to turn around,"

Joines said. "We're certainly not where we need to be, but most importantly, we've learned how to work together as a community" (Gutierrez 2006). He gives credit for the success of the city thus far during his tenure in office to the city manager, Bill Stuart, and to the city council, and Joines continues to push for unity: "I would hope that I would be viewed as a person who brought the city together — kind of created a vision for where the economy should be going" (Gutierrez, 2006).

5.4 Leadership Style, Roles, and Relationships

As mayor, Joines has been a model of the council–manager mayor as facilitative leader. Mayor Joines functions within the basic features of the classic council–manager government structure and is successful in creating cooperative patterns of interaction among officials. As an elected mayor within the council–manager structure, he exercises effective facilitative leadership by applying the unique qualities of his position and the resources and skills he brings to the position to full effect. He strengthens other participants in the governing process by collaborating and developing shared commitment toward common goals (Svara 1994).

Joines has been effective in creating groups to work on problems in Winston-Salem. He has not been able to operate from a position of power because the position of mayor in the council–manager structure does not exercise specific power that could coerce participants in the governing process. Joines says, "To be effective, you have to look at each situation. In a mayor–council form, the mayor has more power, and the mayor has to be more political. In a council–manager form of government where the mayor has little power (and, in Winston, the county government plays a large role), you have to cooperate with everyone, and you have to keep that in mind." Council–manager mayors like Joines have to actually get participants to buy into joint action and cajole them into getting something accomplished. Joines is noted for his willingness to listen to differing points of view and to be persistent in encouraging the development of consensus.

Joines' style of leadership is epitomized by inclusiveness. He tries to ensure that groups that have a stake, or think they have a stake, in what is being decided are included in the process of deciding what should be done. He tries to act as a "bridge that brings everyone together." In describing the impact of this style of leadership on interactions among stakeholders, Joines says, "People appreciate the fact that you have included them in what is going on, and, in the long run, it will be easier to get a resolution to a problem. People just want to be included in what is going on."

Joines likes to think that he is able to bring together individuals who are needed to make a project or program happen. This requires the ability to articulate a clear objective about what the group wants to accomplish and to rally support around that. Joines feels he is viewed as someone who is open to different approaches to accomplishing an objective and willing to change the approach if needed. Joines believes that being successful in this type of endeavor requires persistence and the ability to persuade participants why it is important. He says, "The approach I have taken is that there is always a way to do it if you just keep thinking about it."

From the broader perspective of long-range planning, Joines was an advocate of having the city council create a strategic vision for the city's future from the very beginning of his tenure in office. When he was first elected, Joines convened a working session of the council and staff to develop a strategic plan focusing on salient issues and defining goals and objectives within each major area. Through this process, the council and staff came together on a common vision and action plans. Then the staff was asked to report to the council on a regular basis on the progress of each one of the actions within the larger strategic plan, thus creating regular council oversight. The council created the first strategic plan at the beginning of Mayor Joines' first term in 2001. That plan had about eighty action items, of which about 97 percent were accomplished by staff during his first term. After the beginning of his second term as mayor, the council enacted a second four-year plan, which has about sixty action items. The council is regularly updated by the mayor on the overall status of all the action items through a color-coded report for quick reference. The city manager and staff regularly communicate the status of all action items. In this manner, Joines has fostered the creation of a shared vision by incorporating goals from council, staff, and himself into a jointly developed strategic plan. Furthermore, he has promoted a commitment to that shared vision by focusing attention on it through a process of continuing oversight to assess accomplishment of action items by staff.

As Joines is quick to point out, the office of mayor in a council–manager government structure like Winston-Salem's has very little power. He does perform the traditional ceremonial duties and presides at council meetings, voting only in the case of ties. Nonetheless, as mayor, he has found an automatic role as a link to the public and as a representative and promoter of the city. Joines prides himself on the degree to which he is accessible to the public through speaking engagements and attendance at meetings and events in the community. He says, "I didn't realize when I became mayor how important it is to people to have the mayor attend a function. It makes them feel that the function is important that the city really cares about them and what they are doing." He believes the mayor can do a lot to promote entrepreneurial activity as a key part of the city's economic development strategy, as well as to promote a good economic environment in the city.

Joines has taken on other roles that are not strictly a part of the traditional role of a council–manager mayor. He has clearly assumed a coordination role in articulating issues, promoting an understanding of problems, and building support for projects and programs. His strategic planning initiatives reflect this role, as well as his actions in bringing groups together to work on city problems. Joines is an excellent communicator, developing support for community efforts through a wide-ranging network of contacts within and outside of government, especially in the local business community. His team-building efforts and promotion of a positive tone for council has enabled the council to better accomplish their goals for the city.

His professional experience in city administration enabled him to understand the policy role of council and to assume an organizing role in helping council in goal setting to address problems, shaping the policy agenda, and building a consensus for change. As a former career city administrator, Joines is very sympathetic to the need for the city manager to refrain from crossing over the line into policy direction. He also recognizes that elected officials should not cross over the line and try to get into management. Nonetheless, he readily admits that the lines are often blurred in the real world and that managers, if they are doing their job, might easily influence policy by providing professional advice. He has assumed a role as liaison between the council and the manager and meets regularly with the manager to keep lines of communication open. Beyond the boundaries of Winston-Salem, Joines represents the city's interests by maintaining good relationships with the county commissioners and state legislators, an essential element in an urban county environment like Winston-Salem's.

Prior to his retirement as a city administrator and subsequent election as mayor, Joines served as deputy city manager under City Manager Bill Stuart. The relationship Mayor Joines had with Bill Stuart could have been problematic, but never was in Joines' view. Joines seems to have maintained a reasonable balance in his relationship with the manager. He never was overly sympathetic to the manager, nor was the manager anything but professional in his relationship with Joines as mayor. From Joines's perspective, Stuart "made it very easy to have an appropriate balance. He (Stuart) is such a consummate professional that he made extraordinary efforts to keep past relationships out of the mixture." While Joines clearly "had an understanding of the issues of being a manager," and as such was sympathetic in trying to be cooperative rather than a hindrance in getting the manager's agenda accomplished, Joines has always felt that the manager (his former boss) respected what Joines wanted to accomplish as mayor and helped him accomplish it. In Joines's view, he and the manager essentially had "a good collaborative working relationship."

The relationships that Joines has cultivated with the city council, the city manager, leaders outside government, and the general public have been instrumental in the effectiveness of his leadership. Before he became mayor, Joines says, "Council meetings were viewed as a circus." He told the story about his experience when he was in city administration and a council member was filibustering the budget. He described how another council member wrote a note on a piece of paper and held it up behind the other council member's head. The sign said, "Shut up!" Joines said, "What would happen if a potential (economic development) client would have been in town and happened to turn the channel and see that. They would have rethought their decision to bring their business to Winston." Joines says that "council members were hungry to bring some control to meetings." As the presiding officer at council meetings, he worked with council members to establish procedural rules for how council meetings should be run that allowed for time limits for each member on an individual subject and an extension if requested. Joines said, "I do try to maintain a good relationship with each one of the other council members." Thus, his personality and style have served him well in building relationships with council members that allow him to lead effectively.

In a similar fashion, Joines has established "a strong solid working relationship" with the city manager that is driven by an approved strategic plan that council adopted working with staff. Having that strategic plan in place helps to protect the manager from requests from individuals or elected officials that deviate from the plan. Joines and the manager meet weekly to discuss initiatives that are underway and problems that have cropped up during the past week, but they also talk on a daily basis if issues arise. Thus, the close relationship that Joines has developed with the city manager has enhanced the manager's performance by focusing the efforts of staff on the shared vision embodied in the strategic plan.

When Bill Stuart recently retired, Joines was a part of the selection process for the new city manager. His role was to facilitate the process, and he did so by suggesting the use of a search firm and assisting in the negotiation and approval of a contract. The council as a whole developed selection criteria and participated in initial screening and final interviews. Joines presided over discussion as a decision was made and "helped move the process along." In the end, the council hired the new manager from within by hiring one of the assistant city managers, Lee Garrity. Consequently, Joines already had a good working relationship with the newly selected manager and has developed "a similar collaborative relationship with certain differences," which is understandable because the relationship with Bill Stuart was a longstanding one.

Over the years, Joines has also developed a good working relationship with the business community. This came from his background as the city's staff person for economic development and work as the president of the Winston-Salem Alliance nonprofit. He has maintained regular weekly contacts with leaders in the business community and holds bimonthly meetings to provide an opportunity for direct communication to get their feedback and to provide information on what is going on in the city. He has the kind of relationship with business leaders in which he doesn't hesitate to ask for their help if resources are needed to address a particular issue.

The mayor is well regarded in the community by the general public. He actively cultivates that relationship by trying to make himself highly accessible and visible in the community. He attends or speaks almost every day of the week at some event, and has logged over thirteen hundred meetings of various types in the last year. One of his initiatives in furthering accessibility to city government (a joint goal with the council that was incorporated into the strategic plan for the city) was the idea of holding a series of town hall-type meetings, called "Talk of the Town" meetings, in each ward once a year, including the member of the councilperson of that ward. The meetings are widely advertised, city staff are present, and the mayor makes a presentation on the state of the city. Then the council member talks about what is going on in his/her ward, followed by questions and an opportunity for dialogue. Attendance has varied from ward to ward, but generally citizens have liked the meetings and so have council members. In this way, the mayor has solidified his relationship, not only with the general public, but also with council members while enhancing the public trust and support for city government.

5.5 Accomplishments and Impacts

Most of Joines accomplishments are detailed in the summary report he provided to citizens upon completion of his first term, which covered 2001 to 2005 (Office of the Mayor 2005). This section summarizes many of the accomplishments he included in that report and that represent tangible evidence of the mayor's leadership, particularly in a number of highlighted areas. The mayor concentrated his efforts in his first term as mayor on three areas that he viewed as critical to the future success of Winston-Salem: (1) economic revitalization and job development, (2) helping to build the city's neighborhoods and make them safe, and (3) fostering community unity. The strategic plan that was jointly adopted by the mayor and the council included thirty-three specific strategies and seventy-two action plans for implementing these strategies. By the beginning of his second term, over seventy of the action plans were completed or on schedule, representing a 97 percent success rate.

Joines continued ongoing revitalization efforts in the downtown area. A number of major projects were successes in this area. The conversion of the historic Nissen Building into luxury apartments fulfilled a long-time goal that city leaders had pursued for more than ten years. New restaurants and clubs relocated to downtown, hotel properties were refurbished and upgraded, additional retail space and condominiums were added to the downtown area, and the historic Goler neighborhood saw conversion of a Brown & Williamson tobacco factory into luxury condominiums. Perhaps the most forward-looking development in the downtown revitalization is the $85 million Biotechnology Research Facility constructed in the Piedmont Triad Research Park. Anchored in Winston-Salem's historic downtown business district, the Piedmont Triad Research Park's downtown location makes it easily accessible from US I-40. The Park reclaims over two hundred acres of the city's central core. In addition, a significant investment in computer technology enabled the city to be ranked as one of the top 10 digital cities in the country. WiFi on Fourth, the city's free wireless Internet hotspot, made Winston-Salem the first city in North Carolina and one of the first nationally to offer public wireless Internet access.

In economic development, the city made significant progress in diversifying its economy by assisting Wake Forest University Health Sciences in the development of the Piedmont Triad Research Park; the opening of the North Carolina Biotechnology Center in the Piedmont Triad Research Park; attracting a major Dell Corporation computer assembly plant; and a number of other job increases, such as tobacco and apparel-related business consolidations or expansions in Winston-Salem. The city has also acquired federal funding for a couple of significant Housing and Urban Development (HUD) Hope VI housing projects that advance the city's community development.

The efforts of the mayor in fostering community unity are noteworthy. He has made community unity and racial healing one of his highest priorities. One significant example is the case of the exoneration of Daryl Hunt, an African American who had been convicted of a murder that took place in Winston-Salem in 1984. After serving 20 years in prison, it turned out upon later analysis that he was not guilty of the crime. Following Hunt's release, the mayor formed a Racial Healing Task Force to address lingering issues in the community. The task force eventually went beyond the Sykes case to address issues raised by the growing Hispanic population in Winston-Salem. The mayor also promoted the city's Race Equality Week. He has sought opportunities to respond to citizen complaints and suggestions and to hold forums for citizens to discuss issues with him and council members.

These accomplishments have occurred in large measure because of the leadership style of Mayor Joines. His approach to interactions with other officials has not been controlling, but rather empowering in focusing them on accomplishing a shared vision. This is clearly evident in the strategic planning effort he has fostered during his tenure as mayor. He has promoted open communication among officials and with various constituencies in the community and has actively sought partnerships to get problems solved. His management of conflictual situations has been masterful, whether in calming and organizing raucous council meetings or defusing the potential for racial discord and fostering community unity. His background and experience as an administrator has given him a unique relationship with his city manager that recognizes distinct roles, but allows him to function in an ongoing coordinative role with the manager on the accomplishment of goals established jointly by council and staff.

Not only his style, but also the leadership roles he has assumed have ensured that the goals mutually envisioned by council and staff have been accomplished. He has gone well beyond merely the traditional or automatic roles that a council–manager mayor assumes, such as ceremonial or presiding officer roles; Joines has been an active coordinator and communicator. He has articulated the shared vision of council across the community and built a working partnership with the city manager in focusing staff's efforts on accomplishing that vision. In his coordinative role with the manager, he has maintained the appropriate role distinctions between council and the manager, permitting the manager to advise and letting the manager manage. In terms of setting the tone for administrative oversight and evaluation of the manager, Joines works very closely with the council on the city manager's evaluation, so that there is "a clear check and balance in place." Joines really sees his role as mayor as initiating the development of actions, policies, or programs that address city problems in a proactive manner. The willingness of Joines to actively assume these diverse roles has been critical to his capacity to be an effective facilitative mayor.

5.6 Nature and Sources of Leadership

Joines says he wants Winston-Salem to be viewed as "a very fertile entrepreneurial environment," and one of the key factors in accomplishing that vision is "for the city government to recognize entrepreneurship as a key part of the economic development strategy to create a good economic environment for the city." Perhaps Joines does not see himself as a visionary leader in promoting this vision for the city, but his efforts have taken on that character as he has secured support for bringing it and other progressive goals to fruition. Within this larger vision, he has worked with council and city staff to create a shared vision in the city's strategic plan he has championed. He has secured the support of council by being open and inclusive in his dealings with other council members and developing a shared vision that enfolded their goals into the strategic planning process. Joines has tried to maintain cordial relationships with all the council members, and he has actively sought to be a "bridge" that brings everyone together.

His leadership is supported by a range of resources, which depend primarily on his personal attributes, characteristics, and skills. His position as mayor does not come with any formal authority, other than presiding at council meetings and voting in the case of a tie. Nonetheless, his direct election and some limited appointment authority, along with his ceremonial responsibilities do enhance his visibility, and he does use his position to build relationships. But, it is really his personal resources that he brings to the position of mayor and his willingness to expand on the potential of the position, which have enabled him to exercise leadership. He came into office with a clear sense of purpose and perhaps a clearer sense of what the position of mayor could accomplish with initiative and enthusiasm for getting things done. At the same time, he was very cognizant from his own background and experience of the appropriate role of the city manager versus elected officials, and he has been very respectful of the manager's prerogatives in administration. He believes one of his principal attributes in being a successful mayor is his resourcefulness in bringing together those who need to be involved in solving a problem and in being persistent in seeing things through to the end. Joines is known for his integrity and fairness and his commitment to inclusiveness in his dealings with officials and the public alike. These personal attributes are enhanced by strong skills in communication and negotiating. Joines has been good at getting officials and staff to focus on goal setting and in getting his colleagues to coalesce around a shared vision encompassed in the strategic planning process.

Joines has been strongly supported by the business community, especially regarding his focus on economic development. He has this support because of his background in economic development when he was a city administrator. He has solidified that support since he retired from that position by his work as president of the Winston-Salem Alliance, a nonprofit development corporation established to improve economic vitality and create employment opportunities in the city. His vision for the city matches that of the business community, and he makes a significant effort to meet with groups of business leaders regularly and to include them in his network of resources and supporters. Although his opponent in his first mayoral election accused him of having too close a relationship with "the city's powerful and elite" (presumably including the business community), the public has spoken clearly in overwhelmingly electing Joines, and by reelecting him in 2005, in an election in which he ran unopposed with bipartisan support. Apparently the public does not share the view that he is too close to the business community, but instead likes Joines' ability to marshal the resources of the business community in pursuit of economic development for the city, perceiving the relationship to be a strength, not a liability.

He has also been very strongly supported by the general public. In large part, this is because of his focus on community unity. His visibility has been enhanced by the degree of his involvement and participation in community events. His support has been further enhanced by his efforts at communication and inclusiveness, for example, his "Town Hall Meetings," which have made city government and its officials more accessible to the general public. Joines believes that his general support in the community is attributable to his nonpartisan approach to issues. He says he tries not to be a lightening rod or stay polarized on a particular position and, thus avoids alienating groups. It is important to him to be viewed as truly doing something for the right reasons rather than to the advantage of particular groups.

Joines' skill in communicating with the public has been an essential resource in his leadership in building community unity. His efforts at outreach and his accessibility have enabled him to build bridges within the community, and have earned him praise and respect for building networks for community support and understanding and for keeping the lines of communication open.

Joines believes it is extremely important that a mayor is visible. In addition to his participation in a large number of public meetings, he gains visibility through the media. He believes an effective leader needs to be able to work with the media fairly and honestly, giving them the information they need in a timely manner for the news cycle. If the mayor doesn't work with the media in this manner, Joines feels it can only encourage an adversarial relationship, which he has successfully avoided during his tenure in office.

In his second term as mayor, Joines has dealt with the problem of developing a new baseball stadium downtown as an element of downtown revitalization. Mayor Joines was elected mayor in part because of his perceived knowledge of economic development and his focus on promoting downtown revitalization. Winston-Salem had experienced a declining downtown for a number of years prior to Joines's election as mayor. One of the areas on which the mayor concentrated his efforts in his first term as mayor was economic revitalization of Winston-Salem, including continued ongoing revitalization efforts in the downtown area. Under the mayor's leadership in his first term, the city had undertaken significant revitalization efforts in the downtown area, including the development of the Piedmont Triad Research Park with its Biotechnology Research Facility. The construction of a downtown baseball stadium in nearby Greensboro had recently demonstrated the potential for a downtown stadium to foster significant downtown revitalization. Winston-Salem already had a minor league baseball team like Greensboro's, but the team did not play in a new downtown stadium, which might attract further downtown development. Mayor Joines and some economic boosters in the business community wanted Winston-Salem to gain the benefits of such a stadium project for furthering the already burgeoning downtown revitalization efforts in their city. This was a new idea for downtown revitalization in Winston-Salem that had not been thought of before, and it was ready-made for Jones' leadership talents. He overcame the obstacles he encountered utilizing the same resources that have served him well in his leadership role as mayor – his resourcefulness, persistence, openness, and communication skills. He quickly realized that the stadium project would need to be a larger mixed-use project in order for it to be something the city would really want to do. The city needed to acquire the property and the mayor's role became one of finding the mechanism to obtain and hold the land for development. Fortunately, the Winston-Salem Alliance, as an economic development nonprofit, was the ideal vehicle to do that. While the mechanism for land acquisition was being formulated, the mayor went to each council member on an individual basis to see what they thought about the idea and what issues would need to be addressed. He had to sell the idea to the council and to the business community as an investment in expanding mixed-use business development that would occur in the surrounding downtown area as a result of the stadium development. Aspects of financing proved controversial, and the mayor negotiated a phased development that shared the risk and made some aspects of future development, like expanded parking, contingent on future support from the developer. Once he had the financing details worked out, Joines went back to the council to get their feedback on what he believed was a solid deal.

Because of the Mayor's position as president of the Winston-Salem Alliance, the involvement of the organization in the stadium development and other economic development projects has raised questions about conflict of interest. The question is whether Joines exerts undue influence as mayor in pushing for projects supported by the Alliance. Joines says, "My primary way to be sure that there is never a conflict of interest or perception is to be very transparent with the council and the public about each project that is being worked on."

In recent years, the Alliance has been involved in a supportive role in a number of joint economic development projects with the city. For instance, the Alliance secured options on the land where the new Dell Computer manufacturing facility is located. In addition, the Alliance, through the Millennium Fund, contributed $3 million to the effort to recruit Dell to locate their plant near Winston-Salem. The Alliance was also a partner with the city in the renovation of the 1926 Nissen Building and made a $3.5 million loan while taking a subordinate role to the city in the project. In every case, the Alliance has always been a contributor to economic development projects in the city, but has been very circumspect in never asking the city for support. The fact that the Alliance is a nonprofit corporation tends to insulate it, and Joines as its president, from conflict of interest concerns. As a nonprofit organization, there is no possibility that the Alliance is involved in projects to make a profit because the Alliance was set up and is supported by the community to counteract negative trends in the local economy.

A potential obstacle to the stadium project was neighborhood opposition, and there were some council members who were worried about the impact on their neighborhoods. The mayor and council members met with neighborhood leaders so that they would be involved from the very beginning and fully understand the project. In addition, the mayor took a personal interest in seeing that the few families that would actually be displaced by the stadium development got moved into decent new housing. The manner in which the project progressed illustrates how Joines overcame the obstacles associated with the stadium project development. He had to convince the city council and the business community of the need for the project in order to continue downtown revitalization efforts. The mayor secured support for the stadium project by individually consulting with each council member about the concept of a stadium project and his proposed mechanism for land acquisition to accomplish it. He solicited their input about possible issues they perceived with the project and sought their advice on how the issues should be addressed. Although there was some controversy about certain aspects of financing for the project, his negotiations between the constituencies involved enabled issues to be resolved through shared risk and additional assumption of costs by the developer. In the end, the mayor's efforts at facilitating the planning of the project and negotiating the resolution of impediments convinced both council members and the business community to agree to a plan for a downtown stadium. His efforts involved orchestrating interactions with a number of constituencies. The mayor's ability to communicate enabled him to get information about the project out to all those constituencies in a very positive manner. Being knowledgeable about the financing, he was able to explain how it was going to work and to elevate the conversation above the rhetoric about excessive tax incentives. In garnering support, it didn't hurt that the mayor retained a measure of trust, particularly among the African-American community. When he said he would help those displaced, virtually all African Americans in the community believed he would, in fact, do just that. When it comes down to it, the critical element in overcoming obstacles is the mayor's ability to communicate effectively with the constituencies involved. Mayor Joines says, "A lot of communication is like keeping frogs in a bucket." He perceives that he is good at keeping a lot of activities going at the same time and getting them to fall in the right place. Overall, he concludes: "Try not to drop the ball."

Joines sees his position as mayor in a positive light, primarily because of the resources that can be brought to bear through effective facilitative leadership. Although he says he might sometimes wish for a little more formal power for the position of mayor, probably in the long run it is better that the position doesn't have this power. He says, "If you get things done because of a collaborative approach, an approach where you convince people of the right thing to do, and you are able to point them in the right direction, then probably it's a more healthy situation than just kind of forcing something." Thus, Joines sees the position of mayor in the council–manager structure as enhancing leadership when done in a facilitative manner.

5.7 Conclusion and Implications for Understanding Facilitative Leadership

Joines clearly represents a council–manager mayor who has used the attributes of the position to improve government performance and make his community better. He realizes that the position of mayor is a unique position that requires the occupant to use the opportunities it presents to coordinate and communicate to make things happen, not by forcing them to happen. He understands that by empowering other participants in the governance process and providing the persistence and sense of purpose needed, things get accomplished. Joines is a good example of the facilitative mayor who exercises leadership through "keeping the frogs in the bucket."

Allen Joines was a successful city administrator before becoming mayor. He has continued to be successful as mayor because of many of the same attributes, characteristics, and skills that served him well as a city administrator. His clear sense of purpose, positive attitude, resourcefulness, ability to communicate, and integrity and fairness have ensured his success. His understanding of the council–manager structure and the appropriate roles of the council and manager have been instrumental in enabling him to focus council and staff on a strategic planning process that has been largely responsible for their successes in improving government performance and accessibility, and achieving their vision of enhanced economic development in Winston-Salem. He understands the position of mayor fulfills an essential role in the council–manager structure by assisting the council and the manager in identifying and realizing a shared vision and helping them to achieve it. Allen Joines has demonstrated that type of facilitative leadership.

References

Adams, J. 2006. Who is Allen Joines? *Winston-Salem Monthly*, June.

City of Winston-Salem. 2006. Allen Joines, Mayor of the City of Winston-Salem, NC, online biography. http://www.cityofws.org/Mayor/meet_the_mayor.html

Guitierrez, B. 2005. In strong position, Joines may run for congress: Mayor says he will push for unity, a growing economy for city. *Winston-Salem Journal*, November 13.

Guitierrez, B. 2006. Study aided Joines' decision not to run: Winning 5th district would be tough, research group found. *Winston-Salem Journal*, January 11, A1.

Hamilton, C. 2001. Winner of the mayor's race will have a tough row to hoe, *Winston-Salem Journal*, October 28, sec. A.

Hewett, M. 2005. Joines to run solo for mayor: 7 of 8 council members to be challenged for seats. *Winston-Salem Journal*, August 6, sec. B.

Office of the Mayor, 2005. Moving ahead: A report to the citizens of Winston-Salem on Mayor Allen Joines' first term 2001-2005, City of Winston-Salem, NC.

Sexton, S. 2006. Nasty battle against Foxx didn't suit Joines' style, *Winston-Salem Journal*, January 12, sec. B.

Svara, James H. 1994. Key leadership issues and the future of council–manager government. In *Facilitative Leadership in Local Government*, eds. James H. Svara and Associates. San Francisco: Jossey-Bass, chapter 11.

Winston-Salem Journal. 2005. Joines' second bid. April 3, sec. A, Editorial.

Chapter 6

Guiding Change in a First Ring Suburb: Plano, Texas

Douglas J. Watson and Alicia C. Schortgen

Contents

6.1 Introduction

The City of Plano, Texas, has an interesting one hundred fifty-year history transitioning from a small farming community on the outpost of the frontier to a vibrant, prosperous, diverse first ring suburb of Dallas. When settlers arrived from Kentucky

125

and Tennessee in 1841, they saw the rich black soil of the Texas prairie on which they would establish their homes and farms. Dr. Henry Dye, the town's first medical doctor, mistakenly thought that "plano" was the Spanish word for plains and began calling the new town by that name. Postal authorities accepted Plano as the town's official name in 1851 (City of Plano 2006a). Plano was incorporated in 1873 when it elected its first mayor and council. By the turn of the twentieth century, Plano's population was only 1,304, but it was the economic center of Collin County because of the railroad that had been extended through Plano in the late nineteenth century.

In 1950, Plano had grown only to a population of 2,126, but was beginning to be thought of as a good small town to raise a family in suburban Dallas. A major development that changed Plano significantly was the construction of the North Central Expressway from downtown Dallas on the south to the town of McKinney on the north. The expressway went through Plano not far from the downtown and served as a direct pipeline from Dallas to the suburbs. No longer was it an inconvenient drive for residents to work in Dallas and commute from their suburban homes in Plano. By 1970, the former sleepy little town's population increased to 17,600 because of the explosive growth in housing based in part on the developing reputation of its fine public school system.

Community leaders in the 1950s and 1960s realized the critical importance of having excellent schools and the necessary infrastructure to support a growing population. In the early 1950s, eight area rural school districts consolidated and became the Plano Independent School District that eventually earned a national reputation for excellence. Similarly, Plano and eight neighboring cities formed the North Texas Municipal Water District to provide for the water, wastewater, and solid waste disposal needs of the region. In addition, in 1961, Plano was granted a home rule charter, which increased its ability to annex adjoining property and to have more flexibility in how it governed itself (Turner 2004).

These forward-looking measures placed Plano in a position to handle the explosive growth that it faced over the next three decades as thousands of people fled the inner city of Dallas. In addition to residential growth, Plano attracted major retail and industrial developments. From the opening of the first mall and first major medical facility in the mid-1970s to 2000, Plano became the headquarters to numerous national corporations, such as Electronic Data Systems (EDS), JC Penney, Frito-Lay, and Countrywide Home Loans. Plano also benefited from the growth of the telecom industry in neighboring Richardson, where many of its new residents worked. Plano's many upscale shopping centers reflect the prosperity of most of its residents who live in well-kept neighborhoods with homes of high value.

6.2 Entering a New Phase of Growth and Development

By 2006, Plano's estimated population was 254,000 and most of its seventy-two square miles had been developed. The new growth in the eastern portion of the burgeoning Dallas–Fort Worth Metropolitan Statistical Area (MSA) was taking place in the suburbs north of Plano: Frisco and McKinney. Frisco and McKinney were considered two of the fastest growing cities in the United States due to the availability of cheaper and newer homes in the outer-ring suburban area of the metroplex. Additional disparities between the inner- and outer-ring suburbs existed due to the provision that cities in North Texas can either dedicate a penny of sales tax to the urban mass transit system or to economic development. Unlike Plano, Richardson, and Dallas that chose to dedicate their share to the region's burgeoning light rail, the cities of Frisco and McKinney chose to use one cent of sales tax for economic development. As a result, the outer-ring cities were in positions to offer incentives to commercial ventures to move from the first ring suburbs of Richardson and Plano to locations in their cities.

While Plano was still prosperous with a median family income of approximately $80,000 in 2000, its neighborhoods (built in the boom period thirty years earlier) were now aging, and its commercial centers were not as grand as some of the new ones built in the suburbs to the north. In addition, Plano's population was no longer overwhelmingly Caucasian and middle class. Its minority communities grew considerably in a short period of time, so that approximately 10 percent of Plano residents were Hispanic, 5 percent African American, 10 percent Asian American, and 5 percent classified as other races by the 2000 Census (Greater Dallas Planning Council 2004). Community leaders believe that the percentages of minority residents have continued to grow quickly in the years since the census so that nearly 40 percent of the population is now nonwhite (Muehlenbeck interview 2006).

In 2004, the Greater Dallas Planning Council held a series of symposia to address the new problems faced by Plano and the other "first ring suburbs" that had developed so dramatically in the last three decades of the twentieth century. The first ring suburbs were defined as the fifteen cities that were contiguous to Dallas, landlocked by suburban cities with most of their land developed (Greater Dallas Planning Council 2004). The report stated clearly the challenge faced by Plano and the other first ring suburbs:

> Following World War II, American cities began a great suburban expansion that continues today.... . The suburbs that surround Dallas today were then small farming communities. After fifty years of dramatic growth, the first ring suburbs surrounding Dallas (and including parts of Dallas) are no longer the focus of new residential development and are facing problems of aging infrastructure, housing, and commercial centers. The future of first ring suburbs is unclear. Lacking the amenities of the urban core or land resources of the outer-ring cities, the first ring suburbs are increasingly at risk of disinvestment and decay. How can these communities remain vital and successful? What planning and design issues must they address (Greater Dallas Planning Council 2004, 3)? Fortunately for the residents of Plano, the city's leadership

understood the changes that it was facing and has carefully adjusted its plans to address the new reality.

6.3 Plano City Government

Since 1961, Plano, like most of the other cities in the North Texas region, has been a council–manager city with a proud tradition of outstanding and dedicated elected officials, top notch city managers, and a very capable professional staff. The council consists of eight members, including the mayor. Four of the eight members are elected at-large while the other four, also elected at-large, must reside within designated geographic districts. Recently, there has been an effort in the community to move to single-member districts, but the city council has resisted the move out of a belief that service on the city council requires people to have the entire city's interest in mind when decisions are made and not the narrow interests of districts.

In 1987, Plano hired Thomas H. Muehlenbeck as its sixth city manager. Muehlenbeck had served as city manager in several other cities, including Virginia Beach, Virginia, and Galveston, Texas, prior to arriving in Plano. At the time of his hiring, Muehlenbeck had a national reputation as one of the top city managers in the country. In the nearly twenty years that he has been the Plano city manager, his reputation locally and nationally has grown even greater. Although Plano has one of the nation's few triple A bond ratings, a Class 1 fire department, an All-America City award, and several accredited city departments, it has not rested on its laurels. Muehlenbeck, with the support of the mayor and council members, has developed one of the country's best-trained municipal workforces. Plano's residents recognize that their city is unique and consistently reward city administrators with high satisfaction ratings in citizen surveys.

The mayor and city council operate as the governing body of the city with the mayor as the presiding officer of the council. None of the council members have administrative authority, which is vested in the city manager. The council appoints three officials: the city manager, the city attorney, and the city judge. All other employees are hired by the city manager, although the council approves the appointments of the police chief and fire chief. There are four operating centers of the city with three executive directors reporting to the city manager. They include the Development Business Center, the Public Safety Services and Technology Business Center, and the Public Services and Operations Business Center. The fourth is the Administrative Services Business Center with the directors of budget and research, finance, internal audit, and city secretary reporting directly to the city manager.

Demographic changes in population have not been reflected in membership on Plano's city council. To date, only two minority community members have been elected to serve on the city council. David Perry, the city's first African American councilperson, served from May 1990 to January 1996 (Muehlenbeck interview

2006). From the end of Perry's term, the city council was devoid of minority repre-sentation until May 2005, when the second African American, Harry LaRosiliere, was elected. Currently, of the eight members of the city council, LaRosiliere is the only minority.

6.4 Mayor Pat Evans: The Right Leader for Plano's New Challenges

Plano has been fortunate over the years to have capable citizens serve as mayor. During the preboom growth period, Plano's mayors recognized the need to have excellent schools and adequate infrastructure to handle the tens of thousands of new residents. During the growth years, Plano's mayors led the efforts to build roads, parks, and other amenities that accommodated the quickly expanding popu-lation. Each mayor partnered with the city manager to create a leadership team that served Plano well. Mayor and city manager leadership partnerships have been especially well utilized since city manager Muehlenbeck has been in office. In the tradition of effective mayors who have fit well with the dynamic changes faced by Plano is its current mayor, Pat Evans.

Evans is a magna cum laude graduate of the University of Texas and an alumna of Southern Methodist University School of Law. As a practicing attorney, she spe-cializes in child advocacy, family law, and mediation. However, her commitment to the Plano community as a volunteer and public official throughout her profes-sional life often overshadows her good work as an attorney. Her commitment to civic service prior to her appointment as a city councilor in 1996 included active involvement with numerous groups dedicated to improving life in Plano includ-ing presidency of the Junior League, founding member of the Youth Intervention Services, a member of the board of Hope's Door Women's Shelter, and chair of the Collin County Planning Board's Land Use Committee. In addition, for the City of Plano, Evans served on the Planning and Zoning Commission for six years and was a member of the Plano Horizon Commission responsible for the development of the Comprehensive Plan.

It is not surprising that this Plano Civic Volunteer of the Year was chosen to fill an unexpired seat on the city council in 1996. Two years later, Evans was elected to a two-year term on the city council, and in 2000 was chosen by her fellow councilors as deputy mayor pro tem. In 2002, Evans decided to run for the position of mayor and was elected with over 54 percent of the vote. She was reelected in 2004 without opposition after being named Citizen of the Year for her tireless efforts to promote Plano and to face its challenges. In 2006, Mayor Evans was reelected for a third term against an incumbent member of city council, who was also a former Plano city manager. Announcing her victory, the *Dallas Morning News* reported: "Ms. Evans touted her coalition-building skills during a campaign that often focused on Plano's growing economic and ethnic diversity" (Housewright and Batsell 2006).

Muehlenbeck stated that Evans is a strong supporter of professional management in local government generally, and of him and his management staff specifically. Evans views her role as a partner with the city manager in the leadership of the city. She is the facilitative leader of the council and the spokesperson for the city with dozens of different community groups and with the press. The city manager is the administrative leader of the city government and, in that role, he keeps the mayor and other elected officials informed of major issues facing the city. Evans is quick to note that she does not get involved in the day-to-day management or personnel issues of the city. Publicly and privately, Evans praises others, especially city employees, and gives them credit for the city's considerable achievements (Muehlenbeck interview 2006).

The numerous people interviewed for this chapter were unanimous in describing Evans as a tireless promoter of Plano, "out of a sincere love for the community" (Wright interview 2006). She has a clear idea of the major issues facing Plano and has worked closely with the other elected officials and the professional staff in developing solutions to them. Once a consensus is reached on goals and strategies, Evans spends hours meeting with key constituencies to convince them to support the city's efforts to reach their goals. The *Dallas Morning News* described her leadership style:

> In her tenure as mayor, she has helped the city age gracefully while carefully working to attract young professionals with new urbanist, sustainable development. Ms. Evans, an attorney who specializes in mediation, often helps solve problems that never even require action from the City Council. For example, her leadership was key to turning the Thornton House into a museum in the city's historically black Douglas Community. She not only embraces the city's increasing diversity, she has championed Sister City relationships and minority outreach. She is a sophisticated realist … who engages Plano's corporate citizen to help keep them in Plano, and she represents the City's interests on the regional level. It was her steady leadership that helped deliver a victory at the polls that showed once and for all that Plano stood behind the shared arts hall project. Ms. Evans oozes Junior League charm and grace, but she can also be tough as nails.

Dallas Morning News **Suburban Editorial Board 2006**

Pat Evans has been involved with most of the major issues facing Plano over the past decade and, even more intimately, during the six years of her mayoralty. There are three major policy areas in which she has shouldered a large share of the responsibility for ensuring that the city is successful. In the next sections, we will describe the challenges faced in downtown development, the tri-city arts center, and the increasing diversity of the city's population. In each case, Evans has been the facilitative leader of the city's efforts.

6.5 Promoting the Redevelopment of the Downtown

Downtown Plano has the appearance of a downtown of a much smaller city. In fact, when Plano's growth spurt began in the 1970s, the downtown remained isolated east of the North Central Expressway while commercial and residential development took place to the west. The expressway was the impetus for the city's residential growth and resulted in the construction of the first mall in Collin County as well as numerous "big box" retailers. The downtown property owners and merchants were not in a position to compete with these large, modern retailers and their businesses suffered. By the early 1980s, the traditional downtown began a quick conversion to a "specialty retail district composed of antique stores and gift boutiques ..." (Turner 2004). There was a high rate of turnover in the small downtown buildings, but generally the vacancies did not last long. The stores often opened in mid-morning and closed by mid-afternoon and few improvements were made to the buildings beyond minimal cosmetics.

City leaders maintained a strong commitment to the downtown area even though most of the Council members were residents of the subdivisions west of North Central Expressway. In 1980, the first evidence of this commitment was locating the 38,000-square-foot municipal building (city hall) one block from the downtown. Several years later, the city purchased an abandoned bank building in downtown and placed the Parks and Recreation headquarters in it. Following serious discussion about moving the center of city government closer to the new population centers in 1990, the Council reaffirmed its commitment to downtown by expanding the Plano Municipal Center by 100,000 square feet (Turner 2004). Other facilities of the city, such as the law enforcement offices and jail, were also built near the downtown area and have been expanded in recent years.

In 1984, Plano voters approved a referendum for funds to refurbish the bricks on the main downtown street, to build brick sidewalks, and to install ornamental lighting and benches. In addition, a plaza was installed at one end of the street and a downtown park was upgraded at the same time. The latter improvements helped to remove unsightly old buildings and to draw attention to the historic interurban electric rail station that was converted into a museum. The park provides open space in the downtown and serves as a magnet for social and civic events throughout the year. "The design of the park complements the historic character of downtown and surrounding neighborhoods ... making Haggard Park the city's ceremonial heart" (Turner 2004).

6.5.1 New Urbanism Project

By the mid-1990s, despite the commitment of the city government to save the downtown, it was still riddled with older, single-story commercial buildings from an earlier era, unattractive overhead power lines, and exposed railroad tracks. The catalyst for major change in the downtown came as a result of Plano's involvement with the Dallas Area Rapid Transit Authority (DART). DART was committed to extending its light rail north from downtown Dallas to Plano because Plano was contributing one cent of sales tax to support DART. Numerous issues involving the specific location of the station site were resolved by the mayor and city council, and by the professional staff during the concept development stage. For example, some downtown merchants doubted the value of a light rail system near their businesses and believed that commuters would take the valued parking spaces reserved for customers.

The opportunity for a DART station inspired city leaders to consider promoting another dream that they had had for a few years — to build a new urbanism village in place of some of the older, worn-out downtown buildings. Frank Turner, Plano's executive director in charge of planning and development, explained the process:

> Inspired by new urbanism projects in the Uptown area of Dallas, the redevelopment concept was to create a high-density, mixed-use project directly connected to the DART LRT platform. Council approved the redevelopment concept on May 11, 1998. Following a period of extended negotiations, the city and DART approved an inter-local agreement on August 10, 1998 (Turner 2004, 7).

Coincidentally, in 1998, the Urban Land Institute (ULI) held its annual conference in Dallas and invited developers to submit their projects for review by a panel of experts. Plano took advantage of this offer and submitted its plan for a new urbanism village in downtown. The ULI panel concluded that it was a workable plan, especially with the DART station as a central component. One of the council members who participated in the ULI review was Pat Evans. She emerged from the meeting with an even greater commitment to make the project work. Soon after the ULI meetings, Evans played a key role in convincing fellow councilors that a request for qualifications (RFQ) should be issued to build what the city was now calling "Eastside Village." The proposed project contained three- and four-story buildings with 234 dwelling units and 15,000 square feet of commercial space on the sidewalk level (Turner 2004).

Over the next several years, Eastside Village and the DART station were constructed. Because of their success, the city contracted with the same developer to build a second phase of the Eastside Village four hundred feet south of the original. The new project removed older structures on the 3.3-acre site that was assembled by the city in partnership with the developer. Eastside Village II with 229 apartments and 25,000 square feet of commercial space was completed by the end of 2002. Within several months, 62 percent of the units had been leased, which gave the downtown a strong residential base, something it had not had even when it was the downtown to a sleepy little farm village.

In order for projects of this magnitude to become reality, they need a champion. The champion for the downtown was Mayor Pat Evans. From the time of the ULI review session, Evans became a convincing proponent of the new urbanism development in downtown. She realized the importance of DART to the future of the downtown, but also to all of Plano and the entire region, and became a strong, supporter of light rail as an alternative to the automobile. The Dallas metro area's rapid growth brought about a significant increase in the number of vehicles on local roadways, which continually taxed highway infrastructure as well as contributed to the area's steadily decreasing air quality. Evans, along with other farsighted regional leaders, knew that light rail provided the opportunity to move thousands of commuters efficiently and effectively throughout the region. This position was especially farsighted in light of the fact that the suburbs to the north of Plano were not members of DART. Instead, the suburbs to the north use the extra cent of sales tax for economic development projects. In some cases, they are enticing businesses out of Plano and Richardson with the economic development funds they have.

As the champion of the downtown project, Mayor Evans never wavered in her belief that it was necessary for the future of Plano to have a viable downtown. In a complicated project like this one with numerous partners, including a private developer, DART, and property owners, there are many opportunities for roadblocks to appear that can derail the deal. Evans joked to staff that this was a "faith-based exercise," but one that everyone needed to support. She was the person who "held people together" on the project, according to Turner (Turner interview 2006). Her enthusiastic commitment to the project convinced the members of the council that the city was making the right decisions in its investment in the old downtown, even if most of the city's residents lived on the west side of the North Central Expressway.

6.5.2 Cox High School Building

In 1994, the Plano Independent School District (PISD) moved its headquarters from the Cox High School building near the downtown to a new facility several miles to the west, closer to the center of Plano's population. The Cox High School building, built in 1924, was the oldest public building in the city and had been used as an administrative building by the PISD since 1962 when a new high school was opened. Because the city viewed the downtown as the government center of the community, some city leaders were unhappy that the PISD left the Cox site. However, others realized that PISD needed more property for expansion than it could assemble in the neighborhood where Cox was located. Nonetheless, some hard feelings developed between the city and the PISD over this issue.

During the past decade, the City of Plano developed a strong interest in the arts. Mayor Evans realized that for Plano to be more than a bedroom community with excellent public schools, it needed to have a vibrant arts community (see the next section for more discussion on the arts in Plano). One of the opportunities to accomplish several goals toward this end involved the Cox High School building, which lay unused near the downtown. Not only could the fine old building be used for a cultural center, but the activities that it would also generate would bring businesses to the downtown. In addition, the city and the school district had an opportunity to partner on a project that would be favorable for both organizations in the eyes of the taxpayers.

In 2001, representatives of the city, the PISD, and Collin County Community College met to explore ideas for use of the building. The three entities agreed to finance both a possible uses study and a feasibility study. Once the studies were complete, the city and the PISD agreed on the use of the building and engaged an architectural firm to design the rehabilitation of the former school. Following the design phase, the project was placed out to bid and the successful bidder was named in December 2004. Construction was completed in early 2006, with the old building upgraded to meet code, but still retaining the charm of the 1920s. On the second floor, a museum of school district history was created in the area that once housed the superintendent's office. The first floor was converted into offices for the City's Creative Arts Division of the Parks and Recreation Department, as well as a one hundred-seat performance space, a classroom, and storage areas.

Behind the scenes, Mayor Evans played a central role in developing the partnership with the PISD to use tax increment financing to give the Cox school building a new lease on life. In addition, she encouraged the city council to financially support the project, partly out of the knowledge of its synergistic effect on the other arts and recreation projects in and near the downtown. In her speech at the dedication of the Cox Building, Evans explained the connection between this project and downtown:

> We are most excited about the synergy with this facility and the rest of Downtown. One can imagine the energy that will fill the air on evenings when audiences arrive in Downtown to enjoy a comedy at the Cox Building, or murder mystery at the Courtyard Theater. They'll come on foot, by car, or DART train, to be greeted by music on the street. After a casual stroll, they may do a bit of shopping, take in one of the many art galleries, and enjoy a meal in one of the wonderful restaurants. Afterward, they will enjoy a show in one of three theaters or a concert in the park. It is a lovely scene to contemplate, and the rebirth of the Cox Building is a big part of the picture.

For those who knew the Mayor's passion for downtown Plano, her description of the downtown demonstrated her vision, leadership, and hard work over many years. Her speech reflected the vision she had years earlier to make the downtown a viable place once again, even if the center of the city's population had grown away from it. The public space, the arts facilities, DART, large-scale residential projects, new businesses, and modern infrastructure were coming together to the satisfaction of the mayor and other leaders of the city. While she would be quick to give others credit for the rejuvenation of the downtown, Evans deserves significant recognition for her important role.

6.6 The Arts in Plano

The City of Plano maintains a vibrant cultural arts community. Its increasingly diverse population requires the city to provide venues appropriate for cultural festivals and theatrical productions year-round. Even prior to Evans' mayoralty, the City of Plano began expanding its arts infrastructure. Originally chartered in 1981, the nonprofit Cultural Arts Council of Plano promotes the development of community arts programs in the area. The council was credited with the development of such facilities as the ArtsCentre of Plano. The Plano Art Association (PAA) is an active nonprofit membership organization that promotes art education and cultural enhancement in the city. Other organizations and capital projects such as The Classics and the Plano Courtyard Theater contribute to Plano's thriving arts community.

Cultural development in Plano remains a priority to Evans. In August 2005, the PAA recognized her support of the arts by donating a large abstract painting to the City of Plano. In pursuit of Evans' quest to urbanize Plano, she proposed funding a public art project that included the painting of a mural in the Douglass Community Center and the construction of a children's themed sculpture in the city's Haggard Park. In 2005, the city council approved the Public Art Funding Ordinance in support of the city's Public Art Program, whereby 2 percent of the city's bond program goes directly to "enhancing the community by beautifying local spaces" (Plano Public Art Program 2006). The use of public funds for art proliferation sparked a similar interest in nearby first ring suburbs, such as Allen, Texas (City of Allen 2006). Evans is credited with recognizing the economic impact of the arts and making its development a priority for the City of Plano (Bane interview 2006).

Plano's close geographic proximity to multiple arts venues makes competition inevitable. Dallas, Plano's closest major urban center, touts several successful arts centers, including the Myerson Symphony Center, the Fair Park Music Hall, and the Majestic Theatre. Additionally, the City of Dallas is currently involved in a multimillion dollar expansion of its downtown Arts District that will include an opera venue and improvements to the city's performing arts high school. Even closer to Plano's borders, the Eisemann Center for Performing Arts and Corporate Presentations in Richardson hosts cultural presentations by most of the area's community arts groups and attracts major traveling productions to the northern suburbs of Dallas.

Despite local competition, Evans sought to develop a performing arts center that Plano's residents could directly utilize. The performing arts center became a contentious issue when the city began to search for the appropriate location for the project. Multiple years passed as the project began to take shape, and several potential sites were examined. When Evans proposed to build the center on Plano's west side, residents and representatives from the east side of the city mounted strong opposition to the project claiming the city favored the west side (LaRosiliere interview 2006). Recognizing the geographic constraints of her own city and the regional impact of a large-scale cultural development, Evans reached out to surrounding cities to partner in the development of the arts center.

After the mayor led a series of discussions on the issue, regional representatives agreed to the location and plan for the facilities. The Plano city council approved the city's participation in the development of the Performing Arts Center in May 2005, and authorized a bond election to fund the city's portion of the construction and operating expenses. In her December 13, 2005, State of the City Address, Evans (Mayor Evans 2005) highlighted the city's solid partnership with neighboring cities Allen and Frisco for the development of the area's Performing Arts Center and Arts Park. Plans for the 124-acre venue, located outside of Plano city limits, include a gallery, sculpture garden, and amphitheatre.

Pat Evans' work on the tri-city Performing Arts Center was indicative of her overall leadership style. Uncharacteristic of many city officials in North Texas, Mayor Evans expanded her concern beyond her own city's residents to include the constituents of the surrounding area. The mayor promoted her arts agenda in Plano while advocating the importance of regional participation in cultural development. Throughout the arts center planning process, Evans facilitated discussions among competing cities and encouraged a mutually beneficial resolution. Her devotion to the broader scope of the project was paramount to its success, and, as a result, Evans earned the respect of Plano's citizens and those of surrounding cities.

6.7 Multicultural Interests

As city officials worked to improve infrastructure and broaden community appeal in Plano, the face of the city began to evolve. The most significant demographic changes in North Texas have occurred over the past two decades. In 1990, Plano's population was 15 percent minority. Since then, Hispanics, African Americans and Asian Americans have moved to Plano in greater numbers, further diversifying the city's demographics. According to the 2000 U.S. Census, the city's population of all minority groups increased to 25 percent that year. The African-American population saw the smallest growth from 4.1 percent in 1990 to just under 5 percent in 2000. The Hispanic population in Plano grew from 6.3 percent in 1990 to slightly more than 10 percent in 2000, a 169 percent increase over ten years. Most noteworthy in their population increase, Asians comprised only 3.9 percent of the city's population in 1990. By 2000, more than 10 percent of the city's residents were Asian, a 300 percent increase over a decade. The city's demographic base has continued to diversify this decade at an accelerated rate. According to City Manager Muehlenbeck, the minority population continues to grow in Plano. As mentioned earlier, Muehlenbeck estimates that the city's population now consists of nearly 40 percent minority citizens, a considerable increase over just five years (Muehlenbeck interview 2006).

The city of Plano is plagued by a notorious "east side/west side" rivalry that extends well beyond high school football. The city is geographically divided by the North Central Expressway. As mentioned earlier in the chapter, west Plano contains most of the city's commercial development as well as the majority of the city's population. The far-western areas of Plano are least diverse, and more of the minority population resides in the eastern sections of Plano. The 2000 U.S. Census indicates that the African-American population on the east side of the city is twice as large as on the west. While there are concentrated populations of Hispanics throughout Plano, the Hispanic communities are more densely populated on the city's east side (U.S. Census Bureau 2000a). The Asian population is also evenly distributed across the city. In contrast to Hispanics, however, Asians are more likely to reside west of North Central Expressway. In addition to demographic dispropor-tion, economic differences abound between east and west Plano. As of 1999, the highest percent of families below poverty level in the city lived on Plano's east side. Accordingly, east Plano's average per capita income was $11,000 lower than for west side residents (U.S. Census Bureau 2000b). In September 2002, Evans formed the Multicultural Outreach Roundtable (MCOR) in an effort to create partner-ships between the city council and the diverse communities of Plano, as well as to encourage understanding and participation in the governing process. Accordingly, MCOR seeks to "fulfill the needs and desires of its diverse citizens" (City of Plano 2006c). Voluntary members of the roundtable are responsible for maintaining an open dialogue between city officials and minority citizens. The relationship is symbiotic. MCOR members represent the needs and interests of their respective communities to city government while concurrently relaying the intentions of city officials to people within their cultural network.

MCOR meets monthly to discuss the city's emerging issues. The roundtable's membership is fluid, but the group maintains consistent leadership with two gen-eral committee co-chairs. Members are encouraged to get involved with one of the many subcommittees formed under the MCOR umbrella. Subcommittees include Recreation/Facilities/Services, Diversity and Cultural Affairs, Provision of Direct Services to New Residents, Homeland Security, and City Government Participation. After appointing roundtable members, Mayor Evans participates indirectly in MCOR by encouraging involvement by others and attending meet-ings and events sponsored by the group and its members.

In addition to recognizing the need for minority representation in governance, Evans has encouraged city council members to invest in expanding community activities to include cultural events and festivals. With the Mayor's leadership and support, the MCOR held the city's first-ever International Festival in Fall 2005. The one-day event was funded primarily by the city council and attracted 5,000 visitors. Now in its second year, the Plano International Festival promises to "showcase the rich tapestry of cultures represented by the residents of Plano through ethnic food, music and dance performances, children's workshops, cultural displays, and other events and activities" (City of Plano 2006b).

Celebrating the influence of Asian culture in the Plano community, the Asian Heritage Festival began in 2003. Similar to the International Festival, the Asian Heritage Festival began during Evans' tenure and is partially funded by the city of Plano. As part of the most recent festival, Evans declared the week of the event "Asian American Heritage Week" to celebrate the contributions of the local Asian community. The festival is typically held over Mother's Day weekend in Plano's Haggard Park, located in the city's downtown district. The event is free of charge in an effort to encourage all citizens to attend. In 2006, more than 4,000 people participated in the Asian Heritage Festival, more than double the prior year's attendance.

Evans, in recognition of Plano's increasing diversity, has sought to involve minority communities in city government. She has made clear her position that the city has a responsibility to involve all of its citizens and to make sure that minorities understand that they have a role to play in the governance of Plano (Pat Evans interview 2006). According to her campaign supporters, Evans desires to have minority citizens involved in the process of city government, not removed from its decision making (Charles Evans interview 2006). As we have documented, she was instrumental in opening dialogue with the Asian, African-American, and Hispanic communities shortly after taking office in 2002. Prior to Evans' tenure, no other Plano mayor attempted to reach out to minority constituents. Those interviewed for this research described her multicultural outreach as profoundly important to the city and distinctive to her mayoral legacy.

Specifically, Evans is also credited with recruiting minorities to vie for elected office in Plano. Harry LaRosiliere, currently the city's only minority councilperson, was criticized by his opponent during their campaign for being Pat Evans' "pawn" (LaRosiliere interview 2006). LaRosiliere and Evans met while serving on a nonprofit board and worked together on several community projects before his run for city council. Evans encouraged LaRosiliere to become involved in city leadership, but never formally endorsed his candidacy. While the councilman acknowledges Evans' role as a mentor in public service, LaRosiliere stands on his own established record of civic involvement and demonstrated competency in leadership (LaRosiliere interview 2006).

Evans' success in leadership is derived from her ability to empower others, especially members of minority communities in Plano. When faced with staunch opposition during her last reelection campaign, constituents praised Evans for bringing Asian Americans, African Americans, and Hispanics into a dialogue with city government. A May 2006 opinion letter to the *Dallas Morning News* touted: "Pat Evans embraces the increasing diversity in our community, and she encourages our acceptance and our involvement in every aspect of cultural diversity.... She demonstrates her belief that we all have a stake in our community" (Hightower 2006).

Evans remains dedicated to enhancing Plano's responsiveness to the city's growing minority populations and to their involvement in the city government. Evans is undiscriminating in her time spent with constituents and will agree to meet with any constituent that expresses an interest in meeting with her (Wright interview 2006). Her formation and promotion of the MCOR, as well as her general presence throughout the city, have earned her the respect of Plano's diverse communities.

6.8 Conclusion

Constrained in her position on the city council, Pat Evans sought out the position of mayor in an effort to provide leadership to the city she loved (Charles Evans interview, 2006). Evans recognized the potential of the mayoral role in Plano, and capitalized on her leadership skills to navigate relationships with citizens, council, and the city manager. Mayor Evans has demonstrated during her tenure that council–manager mayors can be leaders in government and affect positive change in their communities. According to Svara, successful mayors in council–manager governments are unique in their ability to empower others to accomplish policy objectives (Svara 1994). The untraditional use of power in facilitative leadership requires increased communication among officials and constituents. According to the interviews we conducted on the leadership of Mayor Pat Evans, we believe that she continually exhibits behavior that makes her a successful facilitative leader.

Council–manager government mayors are challenged to rise above the ceremonial roles typically assigned to them. Facilitative leaders capitalize on their frequent audiences with constituents to maintain communication with them. Over the years, Evans' professional experience and charitable endeavors provided ample opportunity to interact with the community. As a result, Evans was uniquely positioned to represent Plano's citizens to business executives. The mayor's gentle style of persuasion was pivotal to her success in multiple projects, including the development of Plano's downtown, the promulgation of the arts throughout the north Texas community, and the involvement of minority citizens in city government.

Plano's steady growth and diversification continue to present challenges for the city's government. Evans has been challenged to balance economic interests of her city with the social interests of its citizens. While extremely important to Evans, downtown revitalization and corporate recruitment efforts have not been pursued to the exclusion of other goals. Interviews indicate that she is mindful of the city's need for an integrative leader. Recognizing the geographic and socioeconomic division that results from economic growth, Evans instituted mechanisms through which the new, diverse citizenry could exercise control over the changes in their community. Instead of attempting simply to represent the interests of minority constituents in Plano, Evans facilitated the direct involvement of minority citizens in government, thereby providing a new, important voice to discussions of Plano's major issues. The most prominent example of this initiative was the mayor's encouragement and support of Harry LaRosiliere's city council candidacy. LaRosiliere remains the only minority member of Plano's representative body and has been successful in championing the interests of diverse groups in the city.

"For council–manager mayors," writes Svara, "effective leadership is built on strengthening the other participants in the governing process, rather than controlling or supplanting them" (1994). In addition to strengthening the position of community groups that had not been previously involved in the governing process, Evans expanded the city's focus to encourage diversity in participation. Recognizing their absence from governance, Evans actively engaged Plano's minority populations in city government through the formation of the Multicultural Outreach Roundtable. Her success and popularity are partly attributed to her inclusive approach to leadership.

While those interviewed alluded to a few contentious issues that Plano has faced over the past few years, everyone agreed that the political climate in Plano has been generally cooperative. To a large degree, the stable political environment is due to the contributions of elected leadership over the years. Pat Evans became mayor at a critical time in the city's history when it faced the challenges of making the transition from a prosperous bedroom community to a city that had to change its development patterns and offer expanded amenities. She also recognized the need to be inclusive of the growing minority communities and demonstrated by her example that everyone is welcome to participate in the governance of Plano. Because of her progressive stand, the city's increasing diversity is considered an asset and not a matter of contention.

Mayor Evans readily acknowledges that she is fortunate to work with a long-serving city manager whose foresight and vision for the city is consistent with her own. The city of Plano's cooperative pattern of interaction among officials (Wheeland 2002) existed before Evans was elected mayor, but Evans has become an independent and dominant actor in government by utilizing political capital without crossing the boundaries established by the position she holds. She is the facilitative leader of the community, while the city manager is the administrative leader of the city's outstanding workforce.

Evans is tough-minded in that once she concludes that a course of action is the right one, she takes the steps necessary to achieve the goal. As an effective facilitative mayor, she is proactive in seeking out people who might oppose her position in an effort to co-opt them. We saw examples of that in the downtown and in the multicultural roundtable cases. She works hard to develop consensus on key issues before a decision has been made. Evans does not jump to conclusions, but studies issues before deciding what she thinks are the best answers for Plano.

The successful programs described throughout this chapter demonstrate Evans' ability to use her position for positive change in Plano. Successful facilitative leaders re-allocate their power in the direction of consensus building, empowerment of others, and enhanced communication. Mayor Evans close working relationship with City Manager Tom Muehlenbeck, as well as her dynamic interaction with various city council members, creates an environment suitable for the mayor to act as Plano's "guiding force in city government who helps ensure that all other officials are performing as well as possible and that all are moving in the right direction" (Svara 1990).

References

Bane, Sally. 2006. Personal interview by the authors. September 26.

City of Allen. 2006. *City Council Ordinances and Resolutions.* http://www.cityofallen.org/councilresord_05.htm (accessed October 21, 2006).

City of Plano. 2006a. *Discover Plano: The Plano, Texas Visitor and Community Guide.* Plano, TX.

City of Plano. 2006b. Preparations Underway for Second International Festival. http://www.plano.gov/News/Press+Releases/2006/pr080806.htm. Released August 3.

City of Plano. 2006c. Multicultural Outreach Roundtable Statement and Committees. http://www.plano.gov/Departments/Community+Outreach/MulticulturalOutreach/statement.htm (accessed October 16).

Dallas Morning News. 2006. She's a Flexible Leader who Handles Change and Diversity Well. Suburban Editorial Board, April 23, B12.

Evans, Charles. 2006. Personal interview by the authors, September 21.

Evans, Mayor Patricia. 2006. Personal interview by the authors, April 5.

Evans, Mayor Patricia. 2005. State of the City Address. www.plano.gov/News/Top+Stories/2005/nb121505_stateofcity.htm (posted December 15, 2005).

Greater Dallas Planning Council. 2004. Dallas' first ring suburbs. Paper presented at the Dallas' First Ring Suburbs Symposium, Fall 2004, Dallas, TX.

Hightower, Myrtle N. 2006. Letters from Plano. *Dallas Morning News,* May 11, B12.

Housewright, Ed and Jake Batsell. 2006. Plano Mayor Evans Wins Third Term. *Dallas Morning News,* May 14, A19.

LaRosiliere, Harry. 2006. Personal interview by the authors, September 26.

Muehlenbeck, Thomas. 2006. Personal interview by the authors, September 21.

Plano Public Art Program. http://www.plano.gov/Departments/Arts/Public+Art+Program.htm (accessed October 21, 2006).

Svara, James H., et al. 1994. *Facilitative Leadership in Local Government: Lessons from Successful Mayors and Chairpersons.* San Francisco: Jossey-Bass.

Svara, James H. 1990. *Official Leadership in the City: Patterns of Conflict and Cooperation.* New York: Oxford University Press.

Turner, Frank. 2006. Personal interview by the authors, September 19.

Turner, Frank. 2004. *Downtown Plano: Creating a Transit Village.*

U.S. Census Bureau. 2000a. American Fact Finder. *5-Digit Zip Code Tabulation Area 750 - Race.* http://factfinder.census.gov (accessed October 21, 2006).

U.S. Census Bureau. 2000b. American Fact Finder. *5-Digit Zip Code Tabulation Area 750 – Income and Poverty in 1999.* http://factfinder.census.gov (accessed October 21, 2006).

Wheeland, Craig M. 2002. Mayoral leadership in the context of variations in city structure. In *The Future of Local Government Administration: The Hansell Symposium,* eds. H. George Frederickson and John Nalbandian. Washington, DC: International City/County Management Association, 59–65.

Wright, Sharon. 2006. Personal interview by the authors, September 21.

Chapter 7

Commitment to Engagement: Chapel Hill, North Carolina

Vaughn Mamlin Upshaw

Contents

7.1 Chapel Hill: Background and Context

The town of Chapel Hill is centrally located in Orange County, North Carolina, and is part of the Research Triangle area. Chapel Hill is best known as the home of the University of North Carolina (UNC) at Chapel Hill, which was established before the town itself was founded. In 1793, Chapel Hill was selected as the site of North Carolina's first publicly funded university.[*] The doors of the university were opened in 1795 and the town of Chapel Hill was founded in 1819 specifically to serve the university, though the town was not formally chartered until 1851.[†] Once a university town, Chapel Hill has evolved into an independent town coexisting with a university.

At its founding, the town covered 820 acres and it retained these boundaries for almost a century, with the first modern annexation taking place in 1950.[‡] The town now covers approximately 21 square miles and has a population of 51,485, of which 15,000 are university students with a Chapel Hill address. Regional growth is contributing to a population spike of nonuniversity related residents in Chapel Hill (Planning Department 2005). Half of the town's population falls into the 15 to 29 age group, but the population is increasing fastest among those 65 and older. Racially, Caucasians make up the majority of Chapel Hill residents. A little over a tenth of the population is African American, but the largest population increase has occurred among Asian and Pacific Islanders.

Managing growth is a continuing challenge for the town and the university. Chapel Hill established an Urban Services Area boundary policy in 1986 to plan for expected growth and determine how to extend urban services to areas within the boundary, but not outside it. As a result, two areas, northwest and southeast of the city limits, were annexed by Chapel Hill in 2003 and 2004. These two annexations alone accounted for 62 percent of growth in the town.[§] Residential development dominates land use in Chapel Hill, followed by institutions, including UNC, and privately owned commercial and industrial businesses. Chapel Hill's local economy is dominated by the university and UNC hospitals, which together employed 17,788

---

[*] Carolina—A Brief History. Adapted from an article by William S. Powell, Professor Emeritus, Department of History. http://www.unc.edu/about/history.html (accessed March 29, 2006) Article I.

[†] Chapel Hill, North Carolina, http://en.wikipedia.org/wiki/Chapel_Hill%2-C_North_Carolina# History (accessed January 31, 2007).

[‡] History of Chapel Hill. http://www.ci.chapel-hill.nc.us/index.asp?NID=6 (accessed January 31, 2007).

[§] Town of Chapel Hill, Annexation. http://www.ci.chapel-hill.nc.us/index.asp?nid=342 (accessed January 31, 2007).

people in 2005 (Planning Department 2005). The university's development plan seeks to add 6.2 million gross square feet by 2010 on top of its existing 13.7 million square feet. From 1992 to 2004, privately owned land use increased by 35 percent, while the housing rate of about 200 to 400 new units per year remained steady.

Transportation services are central to Chapel Hill's long-term plan. In January 2002, the town went to a fare-free transit service and in the next four years had a 192 percent increase in riders. Both the town and university built park-and-ride lots to address parking shortages in town and on campus, which increased transit riders. The town credits the transit system with reducing traffic near the center of town and on the UNC campus. Transit remains important as more UNC employees and students live outside of Chapel Hill. The university and town of Chapel Hill continue to seek alternative options for off-site parking and are working to enhance safe corridors for pedestrians and bicyclists.

7.1.1 Chapel Hill City Government

Chapel Hill operates under a council–manager form of government. The nine-member, nonpartisan council and the mayor are elected at-large. Elections are staggered every four years with four seats up for election every two years. The mayor, elected for a two-year term, is a voting member of the council, but has no veto over council actions and no executive authority.* The council's responsibilities include things, such as approving council operating procedures; adopting rules, ordinances, resolutions and budgets; appointing boards and commissions; evaluating the town manager and attorney; and conducting public hearings. The mayor presides over council meetings and is recognized as "the official head of the town by the courts for the purpose of serving civil processes, and by the public for all ceremonial purposes, and has the power to administer oaths."† The mayor represents the council with federal, state, and other local governments.

The Chapel Hill town manager is appointed by the council and responsible for "[t]he overall management of town services under the direction of the mayor and council, and for various support services to the mayor and council. In accord with policy direction by the council, the manager's office directs, coordinates, and evaluates the performance of town services; and provides staff support to the council."‡.

---

* Town of Chapel Hill, *Council Procedures Manual*. http://www.ci.chapel-hill.nc.us/index. asp?NID=23 (accessed January 31, 2007).
† Town of Chapel Hill, Mayor Kevin Foy. http://www.ci.chapel-hill.nc.us/index.asp?NID=11 (accessed January 31, 2007).
‡ Town of Chapel Hill, Town Manager. http://www.ci.chapel-hill.nc.us/index.asp?NID=50 (accessed September 4, 2008).

7.2 Becoming Chapel Hill's Mayor

"As long as I can remember, I've been interested in politics," said Kevin Foy (present mayor of Chapel Hill) (Foy interviews 2006, 2007). After graduating from Kenyon College in 1979, he worked for two senators in the Democratic caucus of the Ohio state legislature. Because he worked on policies, he was able to watch how politics influenced what happened in districts. This experience provided Foy with a good overview of the house and senate process, exposure to lobbyists and the "political" side of law making.

After a few years in the workforce, Foy attended North Carolina Central University Law School where he pursued his interest in environmental law and learned how much authority local government had over land use decisions. During and following his law school experience, Foy began to pay closer attention to Chapel Hill's land use decisions. His impression of Chapel Hill in 1995 was that it was a "really nice place that was going to be exploited by people selling it out." Foy and his neighbors ended up suing the town to protect open space in their neighborhood. This experience led Foy to run for local office, and he was elected mayor in 2003.

7.2.1 Crisis Creates Opportunity

Foy's neighborhood included three to four acres of open space near a creek. This open land, owned by the original developer's widow, was being sought by a developer proposing to construct fifteen houses. Neighborhood residents knew the land flooded and were frustrated that the town had originally approved building sites. In 1995, the neighbors sued the town to prevent the developer from building in the flood plain, lost the case in district court, appealed and lost again.* Kevin Foy and his wife, Nancy Feder, were among the core group that took the town to court, with Foy doing much of the legal work himself to save on neighbor costs. This process enabled Foy to learn that legal proceedings, even unsuccessful ones, can delay construction. His impression was that the town did not want construction in the flood plain either, but was bound by its own rules (because the lots had been previously surveyed and approved). The neighborhood's legal action gave the town time to renegotiate with the developer, buy the land and retain the open space, eliminating further law suits. This experience also confirmed Foy's fears that the town was unprepared for rapid growth and showed him how a motivated group could coalesce around a common goal.

Working with others to identify key issues, aligning neighbors around the law suit, and maintaining direction despite disappointment are behaviors consistent with those of a facilitative leader (Svara and Associates 1994). Foy said that "someone had to step up and take a leadership role." His neighborhood's lawsuits helped him understand each person's responsibility in learning to ask the right questions.

---

* *Lloyd v. Town of Chapel Hill and the Town of Chapel Hill Board of Adjustment*, 127 N.C. App. 347, 489 S.E. 2nd 989. September 2, 1997.

Affecting change in his community captured his interest and he realized that "the town may not be making all the right decisions, but 'the town is us.' If the town is making the wrong decisions, then we can change it." The mayor reflected on this experience saying that it "helped him see that local government was made up of real people like me, interacting daily." He also said this experience was what prompted him to run for local office.

In Chapel Hill, neighborhoods are the primary vehicle for political action. Around the same time Foy was involved in suing the town over the proposed development in his neighborhood, plans for another large subdivision, Meadowmont, were attracting public attention. An extended network of neighborhood groups began working to oppose Meadowmont, giving Foy an opportunity to learn more about city planning. "Things, such as traffic counts, parking requirements, density levels, and commercial properties' proximity to major thoroughfares became important. These were things I hadn't learned about in law school." During this period, Foy said he learned that "you have to know something to even ask the right questions."

7.2.2 An Unsuccessful Run for Mayor

In 1995, at the age of 39, Kevin Foy ran for mayor of Chapel Hill. This occurred right after he and his neighborhood had lost their lawsuit against the town. He learned that a council member was running for mayor, not the incumbent, and thought the public should have an alternate choice. "I thought I had something different to say and wanted to say it." He asked a neighbor to serve as his treasurer and formed a committee of neighbors to help him run for mayor.

Because Meadowmont was on the council's agenda, the media labeled Foy the "antigrowth" candidate. Foy said retrospectively that this was an inaccurate portrayal because he supports thoughtfully managed growth, but the label made a rough distinction between him and the other candidate for the public and brought attention to his campaign. People started contacting candidate Foy to come talk, and he went everywhere he could to gain introductions to people around town. As an unknown, people were reluctant to trust him at first. "Understandably," he said, because he was new to the political scene and had limited professional experience. Although he had lived in Chapel Hill for six years, he was still perceived as a newcomer and was described as such in the local media.

As a mayoral candidate, Foy used informal resources—seeking the support of key community groups, talking to a wide range of organizations and increasing his visibility in the public. "I was oblivious to political cliques and even spoke to groups already committed to my opponent," Foy explained. His campaign gained media attention; endorsements came from the Sierra Club and the *Independent Weekly* (a free, regional paper), and with these endorsements his public support grew. He said he "learned to think on his feet and to come prepared to talk on any issue, not just environment and land use." In his 1995 mayoral campaign, Foy spent $3,000 and lost the election. However, he received 46 percent of the vote (*Herald Sun* 2001).

7.2.3 A Successful Run for Town Council

In 1997, Foy decided to run for town council. Having run for mayor two years earlier, he said he had become a savvier campaigner: he followed local issues closely, was better prepared for his interactions with the public, felt more confident, and was better known in the community. He acknowledged that running for council was less "high profile" than running for mayor because he had no single opponent, but rather was one of eight candidates seeking to be selected for one of four open seats (*Chapel Hill Herald* 1995). Foy described the council as "highly factionalized" in 1997, and a lot of people wanted him elected to strengthen or shift the minority votes into the majority on the council. Once again, he won endorsements of the Sierra Club and the *Independent Weekly* and he had support from sitting members of the council. In his 1997 campaign, Foy received the second highest number of votes among the eight candidates.

Council member Foy decided not to run for mayor in 1999 because he was only two years into his four-year term as a member of the council and, in his view, Mayor Rosemary Waldorf was doing a good job with a council that was already factionalized. When, in 2001, Waldorf chose not to run for reelection, council member Foy decided to jump into the race, as did the mayor pro-tem.

The council was split on the proposed Meadowmont subdivision. The town's previous mayor and three members of the council supported the development, while four other members of the council opposed it. One council member was considered a "swing vote." The Meadowmont controversy got council member Foy interested in running for mayor. By the time Foy was elected, Town Manager Cal Horton explained, "Meadowmont had been approved and, though the mayor opposed the development as a council member, as mayor he accepted it as a fact … The mayor is a realist and this is a hallmark of his working style. Once something is decided, the mayor accepts it and never revisits what has already been done. He works hard to make things happen or prevent certain things from occurring, but once they are done, he accepts the outcome" (Horton interviews 2006).

7.2.4 Successfully Running for Mayor

Foy described the 2001 mayoral race as a "different level of campaigning." For one thing, he realized by spending more money he could increase his recognition among voters. A key factor in the 2001 mayoral race was a policy limiting candidates to donations of $200 or less from individuals and requiring names of all campaign contributors. Council member Foy knew his opponent had access to a lot of cash, but under the new policy was required to follow the fundraising rules. Mayoral candidate Foy spent $25,000 on the 2001 mayoral campaign and had more than 100 volunteers working for him. He said, "I was surprised by all the volunteers and the passion they had. They gave their time, took walking lists and literature and walked neighborhoods for *me*! It was just amazing!"

As a mayoral candidate, council member Foy worked to clearly articulate a message for his campaign and mobilize volunteers ready to take action on his behalf. Though he had not planned or expected much volunteer support in 2001, he and his wife understood from the 1995 campaign that "people want something to do." So, they were well organized in 2001. With a campaign plan and e-mail distribution list, they invited people to an organizational meeting. Twenty-five people attended and councilman Foy laid out his campaign plan. He demonstrated to this core group his readiness for the race, shared a calendar of events, and established roles and responsibilities among his supporters.

His experience as a member of the council, a previous mayoral candidate, and a community leader enabled candidate Foy to articulate positions that were consistent with the priorities and values of Chapel Hill. In the 2001 mayoral race, candidate Foy understood that if his message was wrong, it would not matter how much money he spent on the campaign. He said, "I believed that if the voters heard what I had to say they would vote for me." He worked hard to focus his message and campaign literature on three things: (1) protecting the natural environment, (2) focusing on inclusiveness, particularly with affordable housing, and (3) improving relations between the university and the town. Foy said the 2001 campaign was challenging because he was doing three jobs simultaneously. He kept his law practice to pay bills, was a member of the town council, and a candidate for mayor. He and everyone else thought the 2001 mayoral race was going to be close, but Foy was elected with 63 percent of the vote. He said his organizational structure paid off because he was able to "penetrate the consciousness of voters and articulate something people could connect with."

In 2003, Mayor Foy was reelected to a second term with only write-in candidates opposing him. In 2005, he ran a third time for mayor against a "stealth candidate." His opponent filed on the last filing day having moved to town only a week before. The candidate never attended public events, though he had supporters at every local polling station on the day of the election. The mayor laughed about this, saying the myth of *his* being a newcomer persisted. During the 2005 election, local news reporters called seeking Foy's reaction to his opponent's moving to town and filing to run on the last possible day, saying "didn't you do the same thing in 1995?"

7.3 Mountains or Mole Hills

When asked about his major accomplishments, Foy prefaced his remarks saying some things appear "small" on the surface, but turn out to be "big" on examination. The mayor focused on two achievements: (1) rewriting the town's land use ordinance, which sets in place how Chapel Hill will develop over the next ten years; and (2) renaming a major thoroughfare in honor of Martin Luther King, Jr.

The mayor campaigned on environmental protection, opposing developments already approved by the town. Town Manager Horton, reflecting on the mayor's handling of the land use ordinance, described Foy as an exceptional moderator for a highly complex process. As a facilitative leader, Foy understood the importance of engaging the community around the town's land use plan and knew multiple actors and complex actions had to be coordinated for the effort to succeed (Svara and Associates 1994). The manager recommended an elaborate, multilevel approach for gaining citizen input into the revision of the land use ordinance, which took a lot of time. As the process unfolded, some council members became tired and disenchanted, but the mayor kept the ultimate goals in front of the council, helped the council understand its responsibilities and the role of staff, and was instrumental in sustaining energy necessary for the public process to be completed.

His second accomplishment, renaming a road to honor Martin Luther King, Jr., seemed "small" at first, but the name change evoked big, underlying, and historic racial tensions with which the community had to grapple.* The manager agreed that this issue was a challenging one for the community and for the mayor, but the manager said, "The mayor handles himself well in difficult situations and stays focused on goals while demonstrating consideration and respect for others." In this situation, Foy demonstrated how facilitative leaders bring people together from inside and outside government, engage the community in government initiatives, and set the tone for council and public conversations—even when things did not go as originally planned.

The council's Naming Committee proposed changing the name of a major thoroughfare, Airport Road, to Martin Luther King Boulevard. Residents and business owners on Airport Road expressed concerns about financial problems and headaches associated with changing addresses on everything from bills to company letterhead. Long-time residents resisted the change because it meant giving up an address they had had for many years. Supporters of the change accused those opposed of being resistant for racial reasons. At town meetings, people expressed anger that lower income residents, many of whom were African American, could no longer afford to live in Chapel Hill (Dees 2004). Despite these concerns, the council voted to change the name to Martin Luther King Boulevard.

Describing the decision to support the change, the mayor said, "You're elected to make decisions and you can't always ask everyone how they feel. Chapel Hill has a history of public input and many of the ways we get input are informal. Our council is relatively young. I'm among the older members of the council and I was about 48 years old when the road renaming issue was brought to us. Also, most of the council members were not raised in this community or even in the south, so we weren't experienced with the history of racial turmoil. We quickly learned the issue was relevant to the entire community even though the majority (i.e., white) population didn't realize it."

---

* Town of Chapel Hill. Renaming Airport Road to Martin Luther King Boulevard. http://townhall.townofchapelhill.org/news/events/mlk/ (accessed November 14, 2006).

Once the council was on record supporting changing the road name to Martin Luther King Boulevard, the mayor said it was hard to go back and do background work to engage and regain the trust of community stakeholders. Foy said his own perception was that the council was "in tune with what people wanted and our staff was in the community on a daily basis, yet all of us failed to see the significance when the name change for Airport Road to Martin Luther King Boulevard was proposed." Because the council easily reached agreement on the name change, the level of controversy in the community came as a surprise.* The mayor said this was a "*big* mistake. We should not have agreed to act without testing the water and engaging concerned citizens and key stakeholders."[†]

Foy understood he and the council must respond to the public, and, in this situation, he thought he knew what the community wanted. As it turned out, there were voices out there that had not been heard and, when they expressed frustration, the mayor and council took action. The council hired an external, neutral facilitator and held a series of community meetings to sort out the issues. The mayor and council found themselves listening to how African Americans in the community felt about race, not just historically, but in today's environment. "These conversations changed people like me," said the Mayor, "not people who are 'racists,' but people for whom race is outside their experience and awareness." The mayor acknowledged that it is unusual to have African Americans tell elected officials about how it feels to live in the community. The naming of the road was symbolic, yet African Americans in town still experienced racism on a daily basis. For example, Foy was surprised to hear African-American professionals describe going into local stores and being monitored because they were thought to be shoplifting. "I would be angry, humiliated, and frustrated if I was treated this way and my white friends never had the same experience," the mayor said. Giving people a chance to share their stories helped raise awareness of racial issues in the community, and, according to the mayor, "It was cathartic."

The road renaming helped Foy and the council learn to ask first before entering into controversial issues. For example, before deciding to offer benefits to domestic partners, the council and Mayor asked a consultant to "work with our staff to survey residents about their attitudes and experiences regarding sexual orientation, race, and gender. We have used this information to raise awareness about the nature of employment in the town, such as domestic partner benefits, and as a tool for other decision making."

---

* Excerpt of the minutes from the May 24, 2004 business meeting, Item 6: Continuation of Public Forum on a Proposal to Rename Airport Road in Honor of Dr. Martin Luther King Jr. http://townhall.townofchapelhill.org/agendas/airportrdrenaming/Excerpt%20of%20the%20 Minutes%20from%20the%20May%2024%202004.htm (accessed November 15, 2006).
† Ibid.

7.4 Shaping the Future

Foy described three continuing areas where he is having a positive impact. First, the Mayor has set a positive tone for ongoing work with the University of North Carolina, the town's largest landowner and employer. Secondly, he builds community consensus about the future identity of Chapel Hill. And last, the mayor has been instrumental in creating a sustainable downtown development effort emphasizing principles contained within the town's comprehensive plan. The mayor's ability to work across boundaries, promote cooperation and foster a positive image for the town and university are highlighted in the first of the following examples. The second illustration shows how, as a policy initiator, the mayor uses his position to identify issues, engage key partners, and shape conversations about long-term challenges facing the town, such as how it will retain its unique identity in a rapidly expanding region. Finally, the third example demonstrates how the mayor mobilized downtown business leaders, gained council support for the group's efforts, and focused on creating a sustainable downtown, retaining its character while improving economic opportunities.

Foy is a liaison for Chapel Hill with other governments, the business community, and the university. The university is a formidable institution empowered as a creature of the state, making the relationship challenging for town officials to manage. The mayor understands the university's perspective and acknowledges that it must be frustrating for a nationally and internationally recognized academic institution to be regulated by the town's zoning ordinances. Tensions between the town and university increased in 2000 when the newly appointed chancellor went to North Carolina's General Assembly seeking an exemption from the town's zoning authority over the university's planned expansion.

Under Chapel Hill's zoning regulations established in the 1980s, the university could do almost anything it wanted on its main campus property as long as it stayed below an agreed maximum square footage. As the university approached the square footage cap, the town took the opportunity to renegotiate zoning on campus, seeking to increase its regulation over things such as storm water, lighting, traffic, and noise. Under the leadership of the previous mayor, councilman Foy had served as a member of the negotiating committee involved in developing the new zoning guidelines.

Four to five months of negotiation had gone on and the town thought things were nearing agreement when the new chancellor surprised the town by going to the General Assembly and asking for the university to be exempt from the town's zoning requirements. Eventually, the town and university reached agreement, eliminating the cap on square footage and setting criteria related to "off-site impacts," such as traffic congestion, noise, and light pollution, by which new construction would be judged. Even with the new zoning agreement some council members and citizens thought UNC had been a bully, and that the town had cowered in response to university demands. The mayor said the new agreement actually "retained the town's responsibility to make sure the university doesn't grow too quickly or inconsistently with the surrounding area while giving the university more flexibility in how it decides to expand."

The need for positive relations with the university became important again in 2003 when the university proposed to build a chiller plant creating new public tensions. Foy remarked, "UNC was oblivious to the controversy the new chiller plant unintentionally created for the town." On its own, the university decided it needed to build a parking deck and chiller plant behind an old cemetery on campus. This proposal raised concerns for nearby neighbors who feared members of the town council would "cave in" to the university's plans. Months of negotiation ensued, leading to modifications in the design to minimize noise and improve appearance, and ultimately to the council's approving the permit for the parking deck/chiller plant. This issue was particularly difficult for the mayor because it was mid-campaign in his run for another term. Neighborhoods had banded together to oppose the university's request. The mayor saw improvements and modifications to the university's plan for the chiller plant and thought the proposal met the town's zoning criteria (i.e., storm-water management, traffic, noise, light impacts). The council heard people's concerns, but agreed to the permit. "It is not the council's job to make decisions for the university," the mayor said. "As long as the decisions the university proposes meet the criteria set out by the town, the town has to support their requests." The mayor told the council that "this is how I look at the issue. What do you think about it? Is this really inappropriate for the university to do? As long as the plan meets our criteria, UNC should be able to proceed."

The mayor acknowledges UNC continues to create challenges for the council. The university has no more room to build on the main campus and is shifting its focus to a new site called "Carolina North." Located on 250 acres two miles north of the main campus, Carolina North is planned as a state of the art research and mixed-use educational facility (University of North Carolina 2008). The council was split for several years over how to proceed with the development of Carolina North. The mayor advocated early engagement with UNC during the "preplanning" phase of the process. Others on the council expressed reservations about negotiating with UNC at all, wanting to "wait and see" what the university proposed. The mayor worked with council members to articulate the key issues and clarify goals developing an approach that involved conducting a long-range transit study and a fiscal equity study prior to establishing new zoning classifications to ensure environmental protections for Carolina North.

Foy's facilitative leadership skills are evident in how he and the council are guiding Chapel Hill, a town in transition, toward its next identity. The university owned and operated the town's power station and water system until the 1960s. In the past thirty years, both the town and university have changed. Many people who now live in Chapel Hill are not connected with UNC. "You can't disconnect the town and university," the mayor said, "but a lot of Chapel Hill residents never go on campus and this is driven by the growth of regionalism in the area." An example of the town's evolving identity appears in Figure 7.1. In 1989, the town's seal included dates for the founding of the town and the university (see the seal on the left). The seal was updated in 2005 to focus on the Town of Chapel Hill, showing only a university tower in the graphics (the seal on the right).

1989   2005

Figure 7.1   Changes to the Chapel Hill town seal. Available online at: www. ci.chapel-hill.nc.us/ (accessed Janurary 31, 2007).

For years the town's population was smaller than the university's student population. When students left in the summer, the town became quiet and traffic was light for a few months. Now, Chapel Hill is emerging as a city in its own right and the mayor is helping to shape a policy agenda to define the nature of the town and figure out how to transition from being a small town to an urban, sophisticated city without turning Chapel Hill into a series of sprawling housing developments and shopping malls. The mayor has worked strategically as a spokesperson for the town, engaging the council on "the right issues at the right time," said the City Manager Horton.

A third example illustrates how Mayor Foy took it upon himself to bring downtown business leaders together to create a need for action. He had downtown leaders identify common downtown problems, ranging from image to parking to panhandling. The mayor then independently convened members of the business community and revised an approach to downtown development. By establishing relationships with the business community and gaining business and university support for creating a sustainable downtown up front, the mayor was able to present the council with a coalition plan for downtown development. As a result, the council agreed to fund the downtown partnership group.

Getting the business community to push for a sustainable downtown initiative "avoided the taint of having the partnership controlled by the town," said Horton. The mayor helps keep the council focused on trying to revitalize the downtown using a model consisting of small stores combined with residential buildings. The downtown partnership fits within the town's comprehensive plan, which calls for increasing the number of people living in town and providing denser development with a mix of residential and commercial services to support this shift. Tangible evidence of the town's philosophy and goals for sustainable development continues to shape council decisions. The council unanimously approved plans for an eco-friendly condominium complex downtown that "will set a new standard in this state," said Larry Shirley, director of the NC State Energy Office. In addition to being a model for sustainable construction, the complex developers "agreed to subsidize fifteen of ninety-nine condominiums making them affordable for households earning between $30,000 and $50,000 a year" (DeConto 2007).

7.5 Dealing with Adversity

While the examples in this case study paint a picture of a mayor who fosters a common sense of purpose and rarely takes a stand apart from the community's stated interests, Foy also understands people sometimes need an authority figure to take a position. When Apple Chill, an annual street festival sponsored by the town, started attracting an "After Chill" street gathering not sponsored by the town, the postfestival event became increasingly difficult for the town to manage. First, a shooting and then gang activity became problems. The mayor recognized the public had an interest in how these issues would be resolved and, at his suggestion, the council appointed a review committee and convened multiple public conversations. The council's goal was to find ways to engage some of the young African Americans and motorcyclists in festival events to minimize the "after event" gatherings, which tended to become violent. When there was a second shooting, the mayor simply and directly made a pronouncement that "Apple Chill is over." Horton recalled, "The mayor did not consult anyone on this decision as far as I know. He just knew his council and his audience and had good timing. The difference between a good and a great mayor," said Horton, "is knowing when to take the risk."

7.6 Working with Others

Foy effectively manages relationships with key partners outside Chapel Hill, among members of the council itself, and with the town manager and town employees.

7.6.1 Engaging External Partners

In mid-1980, the town's Comprehensive Plan included a loop around Chapel Hill. Part of it called for turning two-lane Weaver Dairy Road into a five-lane road with center turn lane and sidewalks. Over the years, pieces of the plan were used to guide construction along Weaver Dairy, but other portions of the loop road never will be completed because the loop plan was abandoned in early 1990s. The previous mayor wanted Weaver Dairy to be a four-lane road with a median and sidewalks, and she pushed the North Carolina Department of Transportation (DOT) on this during her last term as mayor. When Mayor Foy assumed office, he advocated for Weaver Dairy to be more pedestrian friendly, seeking to narrow the road and reduce the number of lanes. Horton said Foy skillfully managed the dialogue with the DOT helping them understand the shifting politics of the town and illustrated how the town's interests differed from state and regional preferences. "The mayor also engaged the community during this process," said the manager, "and he was always respectful and developed positive relationships with key stakeholders in the community and with the DOT."

The town's history of working with the DOT had, at times, been difficult. For years, the town, DOT, and UNC Hospital officials disagreed about how a major road, South Columbia, would be upgraded. In 1989, the town asked DOT to identify options for the road and DOT came back with multiple proposals; most involved widening the road and adding sidewalks. The town, nearby residents, and UNC Hospitals could not agree on a single option. Several years passed and the council eventually settled on a proposal to upgrade to a two lane with turn-lane, sidewalks, and bike path, but the DOT declined to pursue this option. When Mayor Foy took office, he wanted the issue settled so property owners would know what was going to happen. UNC Hospitals wanted at least four lanes. The chancellor of UNC and the chief executive officer of UNC Hospitals wanted two lanes in each direction with a center turn lane and sidewalks. Foy used the university's desire for town approval of the new chiller plant as leverage, and succeeded in getting agreement from the chancellor and UNC Hospital CEO to support the South Columbia plan calling for two travel lanes with turn lanes at intersections. Once the chancellor and the UNC Hospital CEO were in agreement, the mayor and manager still had to work with DOT to get their buy-in to move ahead. "Mayor Foy's positive relationship with the regional DOT representative was instrumental in reaching a final agreement," said Horton. "Mayor Foy quickly figured out who had power in the process and was persistent in seeking a common goal that everyone (including the council) could support."

Foy said the council is connected to the community and, as its leaders, they are responsible to call for action on citizens' behalf when national legislators are thought to be overlooking perceived abuses. "There aren't clear boundaries," the mayor acknowledged. "We don't necessarily want to step into national issues, but we are the voice for the community." The mayor and council do not bring national issues to the table. "Citizens bring issues forward and ask for the council to respond. As local officials, we give people a sense that someone's speaking out." The mayor understands that what occurs in Chapel Hill would not be possible everywhere. The mayor takes seriously the responsibility to be a link for the public letting national representatives and senators know the community's concerns. In doing so, the mayor noted the council's willingness to take strong positions and this "lets other residents of North Carolina know local government is willing to speak out and raise awareness."

The mayor and town council sought to raise public awareness on gay rights by asking the NC General Assembly to repeal the Defense of Marriage Act. Chapel Hill provides domestic partner benefits. "You have to be willing to go against the dominant public opinion if needed. You can't just stick your finger in the wind and see which way to go," Foy said. He knew that people had been bussed in to intimidate the council when it considered the domestic partnership issue, and understood a packed chamber did not reflect the broader community sentiment. Even if "no one ever said, 'I support domestic partner benefits,' I have a sense of people's positions just by being out in the community and listening."

Acting in support of national or state issues has been relatively straightforward for the current council, but "regional relationships are harder to manage," explains Foy. This is because "regional issues are often out of our control, but affect our future." Though the mayor meets regularly with mayors from cities and towns in the region, these meetings help improve communication among municipalities but have yet to lead to substantive collaboration on regional issues. Specifically, Foy explained how a major link among triangle governments is transportation. In 2006, the defeat of Triangle Transit Authority's (TTA) proposal for regional rail was a real setback for local governments in the region. "This didn't reflect a problem with local governments' ability to work together," the mayor explained, "but there was lack of leadership (broadly) in the community and lack of stable funding to support it." Part of the failure the mayor attributed to the fact that federal money was not available for regional rail. In addition, the triangle local governments were unable to demonstrate necessary financial commitment because revenue options are limited by the general assembly. Under the original proposal, the TTA was able to generate an estimated $18 million from rental car sales taxes, an amount insufficient to support the project. The failure of the original proposal led the local governments to establish a new group to take a fresh look at transit that would support a regional approach. The mayor said, "I support the new look, but recognize western triangle needs are different from eastern triangle needs. The eastern triangle historically has not been interested and we cannot impose our ideas on them. Chapel Hill and Durham are poised to move, but the eastern triangle is not. We're ready to listen to what they want and when they are ready, we're positioned to act."

7.6.2 Working with the Council

Pulling together the right people on the right issues is one of Foy's strengths. "The mayor figures out what the problems are then figures out who can help solve them," says Horton. The mayor recognizes and capitalizes on individual talents and interests, drawing individual council members out on particular issues or bringing together unlikely partners in the community, such as developers and environmental groups, to resolve local problems. He uses members of the council, town employees, and people in the community to keep issues moving.

"I use all members of the council and focus on their interests to get them engaged" the mayor said. "I've served on five different councils with at least two people changing in each election cycle. Even when two of nine members change, it affects the total dynamic of the council." Until he has more experience with his current council, the mayor is not sure what to expect. He has served on previous councils with splits, he said, but "not consistent voting blocks of aligned members." In the mayor's experience, "All councils are friendly. Although each member is autonomous, we are a group of equals."

The mayor said he is careful not to overplay his role vis-à-vis the council. "It is delicate to be a leader and not take credit for everything. You also must 'learn to count.'" He said that "to get anything done, I acknowledge the 'council did it' or 'led it,' not the mayor." He is careful to acknowledge the council's shared role while knowing each person is individually elected. "When I need to do something, I need to be credible and not tell the council what to do. I never tell the council what to do, but use persuasion and lobby for my position when necessary. I remind people of times I supported them on their issues and ask them to support me in return."

Foy engages others in open and honest communication, understands how to combine different people's talents to arrive at common solutions, fosters leadership in others, and appeals to members of the council as both individuals and as a group. Horton described Foy as someone who ably leads the council, using process and relational skills to resolve issues and reach conclusions. "The mayor," he says, "avoids having a fixed view on any issue. Without promoting any particular agenda, the mayor engages others and gains input from a broad cross section of the community." Horton describes Foy's leadership style as "very public and transparent."

"You don't get elected without having an agenda," Foy explained. "You advocate for specific things and have a general philosophy." The mayor highly values natural resource protection, but he also helps others promote their agendas. "Sometimes I actively help them, other times I remain neutral or discourage the agenda issue all together," he said. "For example, there have been efforts to change the development proposal process to improve efficiency in permitting. I support efficiency, but sometimes the process requires tools and legitimate hurdles to maintain standards." In addition, the mayor is reluctant to support proposals to "study something," because he says studies are usually ploys to eliminate the initiative. "I rarely make studies a priority," he acknowledged. "I try not to stifle any issue because that's not good practice for me and not my style."

Foy takes the lead on a variety of different issues and serves a critical role in developing and maintaining positive relationships with the community and other local governments. Each mayor adds roles and responsibilities as they assume office, according to Horton. The manager said that over time, Chapel Hill has evolved in such a way that it has created a place for facilitative mayoral leadership. "I have heard stories about previous mayors who were not as consultative, who viewed themselves as an authority on issues, and who were at odds with the council," he noted. "Each individual makes a big difference by how they behave in the role."

7.6.3 Mayor, Manager, and Employee Relations

Cal Horton retired as Chapel Hill's town manager in September 2006. The selection of his replacement became Foy's role. Appointed in July 1990, Horton was the longest serving manager in the history of the town. As he talked about preparing for the transition to a new manager, Foy said, "I didn't realize my leadership role with the staff at first." He knew the manager was leaving in September, but the council breaks in July and August, so it quickly became clear that the real date for the manager's departure—as far as the council was concerned—was June 30, 2006. "I came to understand that I was going to have a different job," Foy explained. "The metaphor I use is that the current manager is carrying a 'suitcase' and he is going to pass it off to the new manager, but I will have to help the new manager carry the suitcase for a while until it's clear that I can let go." The mayor described Horton as a "wise, experienced leader who offers good counsel to me and the other elected officials. I've not always followed his advice, to my own detriment. The new manager will not have the historical perspective, so I'll have to provide a lot of context for the new manager as he or she takes over."

Foy realized that it was his job to "step forward, be the leader and take the reins" of the recruitment process. He knew it was necessary to envision the process from start to finish and set forward the steps so others would know where the process was progressing. "This was the first time any of us were in a situation where we did not have managerial experience to guide us." The mayor spoke with Jonathan Howes, the former mayor of Chapel Hill, who had hired Horton, recognizing there were significant differences in time and place. He also called Nick Tennyson and Bill Bell, former and current mayors of Durham, both of whom had gone through manager selection processes, as well as Carl Stenberg from the UNC School of Government. Foy noted that the other mayors offered political advice while Stenberg offered information about the nuts and bolts of recruiting and hiring a new manager.

Chapel Hill's council rejected idea of using a "national consultant" model and went instead with a local human resource company experienced with placing personnel in large companies, and Tim Dempsey, a former director of human resources at Nortel, an international corporation located in the Research Triangle Park. Dempsey had prior relationships with Foy and Mayor Pro Tem Bill Strom, with whom he had served on the Planning Board for four years. "The mayor and mayor pro tem invited me to have lunch with them and Anita Badrock, a professional recruiter with whom, by coincidence, I also had a professional relationship," Dempsey said. "We discussed what an organization effectiveness approach to hiring a town manager would look like. I outlined a basic process: needs analysis, future vision, gap analysis. They had, predictably, asked for a defined set of capabilities to be developed and I, politely, suggested that it might not be the starting point. Instead, I suggested a vision as to what they wanted Chapel Hill to become. What are the opportunities and obstacles? What will the 'work' be, for the new town manager? Only out of this approach can you define capabilities in the best context." Following the lunch meeting, Badrock and Dempsey agreed to partner on the project. Dempsey's experience was instrumental on the front end (needs analysis, process development, etc.) and Badrock contributed to the back end (recruiting, screening, interviewing, reference checking). Together they brought complementary skills to the process (Dempsey interview).

A council subcommittee consisting of the mayor and three others worked with the consultants to develop a process. The council supported Dempsey's "Appreciative Inquiry" approach. Dempsey said, "When I interviewed all the council members, all the department heads, some university and community leaders and held a public workshop, my presenting questions were: 'What works well in Chapel Hill? What are you most proud of?' Out of that data, we developed a profile and recruited nationwide. The consultants and subcommittee members checked in regularly with other members of the council regarding their work, but everyone agreed the full council did not need to review the pool of one hundred candidates. Using agreed upon criteria, we narrowed over a hundred applications to fifteen applicants who were separately interviewed by at least two members of the subcommittee. This group of fifteen was then narrowed to three finalists." Foy remarked, "It was hard to get the numbers down to five or six, and really hard to get to three because there was not an obvious candidate." Once the subcommittee had agreed to the three finalists, they had a full council, full-day meeting facilitated by the consultants.

The three finalists were brought in for face-to-face interviews in Chapel Hill. The interviews were designed as a "pressure cooker," according to Dempsey, beginning with a dinner with all candidates and council the evening before a day of interviews, an assessment center with managers using an ice storm simulation, and a meeting with the full council followed by a public forum with a citizen question and answer session. The following day, the consultants asked senior managers for their opinions.

After the interviews were completed, Dempsey facilitated a day-long conversation with the town council members, starting in appreciative inquiry mode, listing the strengths of each finalist. "I made sure that the council stayed with the process that we had agreed to: discovering which candidate had demonstrated the best capabilities to deliver the Council's vision. We met all day and at the end of the meeting I called one finalist—Roger Stancil—and asked him to come to Chapel Hill to meet with the council the next day. Because he was in Fayetteville, he was able to drive up and agreed to do so. We had one more round of very focused and specific conversations. At the end of that day, after Roger left, the council had about an hour-long discussion during which they agreed to make him the offer and discussed the terms of the offer in great detail. On Monday, they worked with the town's attorney to finalize the offer."

Dempsey noted an important aspect of the process was that the objective was not just to hire the right person, but also to assure that he or she would be successful and the inclusion of a lot of involvement from the staff worked toward that purpose. Only after the process was over did Foy learn that senior managers initially perceived that the council did not want their input and that they would be left out of the process. The senior managers were, in retrospect, pleased to have been involved and felt their opinions were valued in the final selection of the new manager.

The council timed the recruitment process to make sure the new manager was hired before the previous manager retired. The mayor offered the new manager the position in June, but the previous manager did not retire until the end of August. This gave the new and retiring managers a chance to talk, share information, and assure a smooth transition. The council was prepared with two alternatives in the event they did not fill the manager's position: (1) although the retiring manager was firm about his retirement date, they also knew that he would be willing to stay on in a contractual relationship if it became necessary; and (2) the senior staff included a deputy manager who was considered to be well qualified to keep the organization running.

Foy expressed satisfaction with the process. "It took less than a year from the time the previous manager announced his retirement to having a new manager hired. The process was well thought out and planned and had integrity. I was determined to have a unanimous vote and have council completely united in the hiring process. I wanted to address everyone's concerns. It was a unanimous vote and, as a result, we have a strong underpinning for Roger Stancil."

Stancil, the new manager, also thought the recruitment and hiring process was well managed. "The process reflected the town and sold me on the openness of Chapel Hill. The listening sessions with citizens about 'what goes well, what changes they want, and what advice they have for the new manager' illustrated town services are at a high level and citizens think the quality of service they receive is excellent. I realized my job was to 'do no harm' to basic services while we managed change" (Stancil interview).

Foy is credited with helping the council understand the manager's perspective. By communicating regularly with the council and the manager, the mayor serves as a conduit between the two. The manager and staff expect the mayor to be the point-person for the council. The mayor works most closely with the manager and is expected to have current and relevant information. During the transition process with the new manager, Foy said that he and Stancil did not have a formal orientation session because both of them understood the fundamentals of the council–manager form of government in North Carolina. Rather, they have weekly lunch meetings where they are getting to know one another, identify issues, and clarify expectations for how they will address priorities for the town.

Chapel Hill has a tradition of giving mayors a lot of autonomy. Foy has his own assistant and that individual does not report to the manager, only to the mayor. The manager explained that this arrangement started when Chapel Hill elected the first African American mayor since reconstruction, Howard Lee, and calls started coming in from all over asking Lee to speak at various events. The demands on the mayor's time were such that a personal assistant was assigned to manage his schedule. This arrangement continues today. In addition to having his assistant help manage his own activities, Foy uses his personal assistant to also help with council issues.

From the mayor's perspective, the council wants the talents of town employees to be freed from bureaucracy, more vibrant, and empowered. This requires plans, methods, ideas, and ways to institute such thinking. His vision, in part, is to "energize the organization." For instance, the council has asked town employees to suggest

- How to innovate, get money, and other resources
- How to get public buy-in
- How to institutionalize ethics of empowerment, learning, and innovation

Foy went on to say, "We need town employees to be empowered to think. We need to capitalize on the staff and get their light bulbs to go off."

7.7 Getting the Message Out

As the primary spokesperson for the council, Foy is regularly called on to perform ceremonial functions. For example, the mayor is accustomed to speaking to community and business groups, representing the council and town at regional and state meetings, and responding to media requests. To keep himself informed about what is happening in the town, the Mayor said, "I use every available source of information on a daily basis." He gets information from

- Local newspapers
- Local letters to the editor
- Local newsletters (League of Women Voters, advocacy organizations, community publications)
- Talking to people at events

For more than 30 years, Chapel Hill has televised its council meetings on a local access channel, but no regional television stations routinely cover town issues. Foy understands regional media outlets want sensational stories, but he believes important issues are covered by local sources. For example, two recent articles illustrate how different media outlets portray the mayor and the town. The *Raleigh News and Observer* reported that Mayor Foy and another council member had accepted campaign donations from a local HR consultant ($50 each) and then the consultant was granted a contract for $50,000 to work with the town employees on organizational development. From a regional perspective, the potential conflict of interest was considered newsworthy.[*] The same day, a front page article appeared in the *Chapel Hill Herald* that focused on Foy's work to get the General Assembly to approve Chapel Hill's proposed requirement to have developers include plans for

---

[*] http://www.newsobserver.com/161/v-print/story/461681.html (accessed July 19, 2006).

incorporating local bus lines in any new development (Margolis 2006). Foy said the *Chapel Hill Herald* article was relevant to residents of Chapel Hill because the town's transportation system is its "crown jewel." The bus system is a convergence of community values and priorities around protecting the environment, reducing use of single occupancy vehicles and being egalitarian (all town buses are free to ride). The council and community have coalesced behind the transit system. "We have eighty buses and need thirty more" said the mayor. "Ridership continues to increase—we had three million riders in 2001 and six million in 2005." The mayor explained that since the town built the transit system it has become imbedded in how the town operates. "Having it free makes it easy—you just walk on, sit down, then get up and walk off," he said.

7.8 Kevin Foy: An Example of a Facilitative Leader

When asked about his leadership style, Foy talked about how he helps keep the council on track as it moves forward with its implementation of the town's comprehensive plan. The mayor said, "Anyone can say 'here's my vision for the future,' but that's not what people are asking. Rather they want to know: 'What avenues are we taking to achieve our goals? And How are going to get where we're going?'" The mayor said his understanding has evolved regarding the limits of determining paths to the future. Although the town's comprehensive plan was developed through a rigorous public process, making it viable depends, in part, on good will and the ability to influence regional neighbors. "We can't do what we need to do without involving and gaining support from Raleigh, Durham, Chatham, the Department of Transportation, and people who work for the town," the mayor explained. The council has limited authority and time, he said, so "our job is to prioritize and select things that fit our long term goals and regional vision."

Chapel Hill's Mayor Foy is praised for his ability to listen to people, build trust, convene key groups of concerned citizens, learn from others and increase community and organizational awareness of significant issues. As this case study illustrates, Foy's leadership parallels attributes and behaviors associated with extraordinary leaders and facilitative mayoral leadership. He keeps the council focused on the town's long-term vision, helps people see how issues before the council relate to the town's long-term agenda, and brings new partners together to work toward common goals.

Like other successful leaders, Foy understands the complexity of public problems and is not afraid to expose conflicts (Heifetz 1994). The mayor cited as an example the current homeless shelter issue. He said, "About four years ago, I helped convene, with the Inter Faith Council (IFC), a meeting of local governments and university officials to find a location for a men's homeless shelter that would be long term and stable. IFC currently leases a former municipal building downtown not intended for homeless men, but residency is limited to about thirty beds and IFC serves approximately 95,000 meals annually. Because the building is on the historic register, limited changes are allowed in its renovation. A task force was established about two years ago that created a blueprint; adopted by the IFC board, it included recommendations to (1) move the kitchen to new location, and (2) establish a separate new men's homeless shelter.

"Pressure has been growing due to increased homelessness caused by a growing population and state mental health reform. The current space is insufficient for IFC and they are unable to offer additional services such as transitional help. Also, the shelter is closed during the day and people have no place to go, so they hang out on streets downtown. We have considered many possible locations and all have been rejected. Recently, a retiring county commissioner suggested IFC consider putting a new shelter at the county's human services complex, which houses the health department and division of social services, but there is also a new senior center on the campus."

Foy said he was "correctly quoted in paper saying, 'This is a community problem not an IFC problem,' but the scuttlebutt has turned things around. I encouraged citizens to contact the county because the human service complex is county property, so now the county commissioners and representatives from the senior center are mad at me. I agreed to visit with a group of citizens at a community meeting (a meeting not organized by me or the town), but now I'm being accused by elected officials from other towns and the county of operating with ulterior motives. For instance, some are saying that I'm trying to put the food kitchen in Carrboro."

Every six months the Assembly of Governments meets, which includes elected officials from Orange County, Chapel Hill, Carrboro, and Hillsborough. Chapel Hill hosted the last meeting and as mayor, Foy set the agenda. "I decided to put the issue of IFC and the men's homeless shelter on the agenda. I asked IFC to present options for the men's shelter, kitchen, and food pantry. We established a committee to review the issue and were able to make public an issue that had been below the radar. Some say I was naïve presenting the issue this way and things could have been settled without such public attention. My goal is to make people aware that homelessness and poverty are all of our problems not just IFC's. Similarly, at monthly meetings Chapel Hill leaders discuss issues of common interest. I asked that panhandling be put on the agenda and this set off gripes about panhandlers. Homeless issues are not the same as panhandling, but these are ways I put forward difficult issues that can only be addressed as common problems."

Mayor Foy's leadership style is supported by his strong interpersonal skills. Using language similar to other effective leaders he downplays his personal role in town or council accomplishments, preferring to talk about what "we" accomplished, rather than what "he" has done (Zenger and Folkman 2002). Others point to his ability to bring the right people together, foster collaboration, and to seek consensus on common goals—again, characteristics associated with strong leaders (Kouzes and Posner 2002). Even as he continues to promote a vision for Chapel

Hill that encompasses environmental protection, affordability, and sustainability, Foy remains noncommittal about his political future. He will only say that as long as he enjoys what he is doing, he will continue to do it; that is, as long as the community wants him to.

References

Chapel Hill Herald. 1995. Candidate, neighbors take stand against plan council to step back, let courts solve fight over houses on stilts. August 10. http://archives.newsbank.com/ar-search/we/Archives?p_action=list&p_topdoc=21 (accessed November 14, 2006).

DeConto, Jesse James. 2007. Green light for green condos: Chapel Hill approves project. *The News and Observer*, February 27, p. 1A, 7A.

Dees, Matt. 2004. MLK road debate stirs up racial tensions. *The Chapel Hill News*. June 16, p. A1.

Dempsey, Tim. 2007. Personal interview with the author, June 22.

Foy, Kevin. 2006/2007. Personal interviews with the author, March 23, July 6, and July 18 (2006) and June 7 (2007).

Heifetz, Ronald A. 1994. *Leadership Without Easy Answers*. Cambridge, MA: Belknap Press of Harvard University Press.

Herald-Sun, The (Durham, NC). 2001. Foy wins Chapel Hill mayor race controlled-growth candidate is landslide victor; 3 new members elected to council. November 7. http://nl.newsbank.com/nl-search/we/Archives (accessed February 28, 2006).

Horton, Cal. 2006. Personal interviews with the author, April 6, August 15,, and September 7, and September 21.

Kouzes, James M. and Posner, Barry Z. 2002. *The Leadership Challenge*, 3rd ed. San Francisco: Jossey-Bass.

Margolis, Greg. 2006 Town can seek transit funds from builders — General Assembly measure allows council to enact new law. *Chapel Hill Herald* (NC), July 18, p. 1A.

Planning Department. 2005. *Data Book*. Town of Chapel Hill, NC.

Stancil, R. 2007. Personal interview with the author, June 7.

Svara, J. H. & Associates. 1994. *Facilitative Leadership in Local Government: Lessons from Successful Mayors and Chairpersons*. San Francisco: Jossey-Bass.

University of North Carolina. 2008. Carolina North Design Framework. http://research.unc.edu/cn/index.php (accessed September 2, 2008).

Zenger, John H. and Joseph, Folkman. 2002. *The Extraordinary Leader: Turning Good Managers into Great Leaders*. New York: McGraw Hill.

FACILITATION IN THE COUNCIL-MANAGER FORM

B. Council-Manager Communities with Adversity and Conflict

Chapter 8

Building a Town and Its Institutions: Midway, Florida

Yahong Zhang and Kaifeng Yang

Contents

8.1 Introduction

This chapter investigates the mayoral leadership in a small council–manager city. Some scholars have argued that the major weakness of council–manager governments, in comparison to mayor–council models, is the lack of clearly established institutional arrangements for formal policy leadership (Adrian and Press 1977; Morgan, England, and Pelissero 2007). However, the lack of formal leadership based on legitimate reward or coercive power does not mean that effective leadership is unlikely to occur in council–manager governments. Rather, these governments may require a different type of policy leadership. For example, James Svara (1994) advocates for a facilitative model of mayoral leadership in council–manager cities. His model suggests that mayors lead by "enhancing and influencing the performance of other officials, promoting information exchange among the council members, the manager, the public, and other organizations, and providing a sense of purpose and direction" (1994).

We support this general model, but we also believe that facilitative leadership can take place in different ways in varying situations. In other words, while cooperation, partnership, and communication are essential for effective governance in council–manager governments, the manner in which these strategies are exercised may differ depending on contextual factors. In this respect, detailed case studies can reveal the rich nuances inherent in this model of mayoral leadership. We provide such a case study in this chapter and demonstrate how facilitative leadership developed in a particular city during a particular period of time.

8.2 The Case and Data

The subject of this chapter is Delores Madison, the mayor of Midway, Florida. The city of Midway is located in Gadsden County, about ten miles west of Tallahassee. Incorporated in 1987, the city now has 200,000 acres of land and a population of 1,500, of which 94 percent are African American. The education level in the community is very low, with only 59.5 percent of the residents of 25 years of age or above having a high school diploma and only 5.5 percent having a bachelor's degree. Midway has a council–manager form of government. The council has seven seats, two elected at large and five from districts, with each member serving a four-year term in office. The council elects one of its members to be mayor and one to be mayor pro-tem.

Delores Madison was elected to the council in April 2000 and to the office of mayor pro-tem in October 2001. She became mayor in June 2002 when her predecessor, Morris Thomas, resigned. In 2005, Mayor Madison was named the "Municipal Official of the Year" by the Northwest Florida League of Cities and the "Florida Mayor of the Year" by the Florida League of Cities. The award entry of the Florida League of Cities lists some of Midway's accomplishments under Madison's leadership, including:

- Passed FY 2002/2003, 2003/2004, and 2004/2005 budgets in time or on time.
- Completed 2001/2002, 2002/2003, and 2003/2004 audits successfully on time.
- Completed and filed all state-mandated financial reports on time.
- Updated the Department of Revenue Communication Services Tax database.
- Purchased property insurance, general liability insurance, workers compensation insurance, and vehicle insurance coverage.
- Adopted all state-mandated building codes.
- Provided health insurance for all city employees.

These accomplishments may look like routine tasks that a normal city government performs, but they were treated as important successes because the city of Midway did not function normally. According to City Manager Paul Piller, the city area was "a dumping ground of Gadsden County." It was incorporated in 1987 because "a group of citizens decided that they would be better off if they incorporated and got control of the area" (Piller interview 2006). Before Madison's election, Midway had been providing virtually none of the municipal services taken for granted in many cities. There were no municipal fire stations, police force, or parks, and the county did not locate a school or library in Midway. Further, most of the roads in the city were dirt because of a lack of money for paving. The city had a complete lack of commercial services and establishments with no clinics, drug stores, grocery stores, restaurants, or banks. "We did not have a lot of what a normal city would have. But yet, we were a city, but the city had dirt roads; we had problems with school buses going down to pick up the children, and when it was in a very rainy season, the school bus couldn't get down to get the children" (Madison interview 2006a).

In addition, the city of Midway faced such serious financial problems that Governor Jeb Bush attempted to dissolve the city. As documented in Florida's Outstanding Rural Community of the Year Detailed Project Report, by August 2002, the city

- Was in a "state of financial emergency" as defined by Florida Statutes, and had been in financial emergency virtually every year since its incorporation
- Owed approximately $110,000 to more than one hundred creditors in past due bills dating back to 1999
- Owed the U.S. Department of Justice, Office of Community Oriented Policing Services (COPS) $140,000 for alleged misuse of a COPS Grant
- Had failed to pass budgets on time, and audits and reports to state agencies had either not been filed at all or were filed in an untimely fashion

- Had no general liability, property, vehicle, or workers compensation insurance coverage
- Had no records retention/disposal system in place and, consequently, the city council chambers was full of boxes of records dating back to 1987
- Had an outdated Comprehensive Plan with most of the goals and objectives unachieved and amendments unimplemented
- Had an outdated City Charter due to changes in state law
- Lacked the financial capacity to keep city government functioning. The city had no money to purchase any goods and services and was even unable to get a credit card

In short, the city government was in a state of total chaos and fiscal downward spiral when Mayor Madison came on board in 2002.

Under Madison's leadership, Midway experienced a dramatic revitalization. More than twenty new businesses have located in the city. The tax base increased from approximately $13 million in 2001 to almost $39 million in 2005 and $65 million in 2007. Now, the city is in good financial shape: it has paid off all debts, has money in the bank, and is paying bills on time. Given these results, the city successfully prevented the governor from dissolving it. Although it still has no school, library*, or police force, Midway is moving toward becoming an independent city in which these facilities or public services are provided.

Because of the dramatic progress in Midway within a few years, Madison has garnered a highly positive reputation in Florida despite being from a very small community and having a relatively short political career. In order to fully review and analyze Madison's mayoral leadership, we collected data from the following sources:

1. Interviews with Madison, Piller, Community Services Director/Growth Director Roosevelt Morris, and several council members.
2. E-mail conversations with Madison and Piller.
3. Electronic documents on Midway's Web site, including council meeting agendas and minutes, city newsletters, the City Charter, and the Comprehensive Plan.
4. News and archives from the local newspaper, *The Gadsden County Times (GCT)*.
5. Other archived documents, such as letters, agreements, grants and awards applications, and council meeting minutes that are not available online.
6. Field observations of regular council meetings. We made field notes to record observations of the interactions among council members, the city manager, and the citizens.

---

* The Gadsden County School District has not placed a school in Midway. Students are bused to the city of Quincy ten miles away. The county library system has not built a library in Midway and citizens have to travel ten miles to get library services. Mayor Madison does not think Midway is an independent city without these services.

8.3 Toward Effective Mayoral Leadership

Effective leadership is a product of both individual and situational characteristics. Great leadership often emerges due to dramatic events, disasters, or crises. Indeed, the dire situation in Midway forced the city to search for a strong leader with a clear vision and the capacity to bring it to reality.

8.3.1 Collapse of Previous Leadership

While no written records or documentation on the activities and performance of previous officials were kept by the city, the leadership crisis was apparent in various news articles. In February 2001, the city government of Midway started to appear in the regular coverage of the county newspaper, the *Gadsden County Times (GCT)*. Between then and August 2002 (Madison took the mayoral position in June 2002), almost all the stories about Midway were negative, with titles such as: "Midway to dissolve?" (07/27/01), "Problems continue in Midway" (11/09/01), "Who is the legal mayor of Midway?" (03/14/02), "Midway stumbles over agenda" (05/10/02), "Midway fires attorney" (05/17/02), "Does Midway have a mayor?" (06/14/02), "Midway Mayor resigns" (06/20/02), "Midway city manager ousted" (07/11/02). Phrases such as "in violation of the city charter," "tempers flared and words flew in council meeting," "financial downward spiral," "serving illegally," "again in a heated debate," "stalemate," "adjourned the meeting," and "resigned" filled out the newspaper. These news stories stand in stark contrast with later *GCT* coverage, between April 2003 and June 2006, that concentrated exclusively on Midway's annexations, economic growth, awarded grants, and honors.

At the time, city officials recognized the crisis and knew that strong leadership was necessary to revitalize their community. In interviews with the mayor, city manager, and council members, all were very careful in choosing words to talk about the former leadership. Nevertheless, they repeatedly used words such as "shame," "negative," "harsh," "arguing," "pointing finger," and so forth. To them, the leadership vacuum was obvious in council meetings that were uncivil and ineffective, as members argued with, shouted at, and blamed one another while accomplishing very little. "As you heard in the community about how they were conducting their meetings, really you didn't want to waste your time coming out here and listening to them because nothing was going to be accomplished" (Madison interview 2006b).

The unproductive council meetings were related to the lack of rules governing members' behavior. The city charter was fragmented and the institutional procedures were either unspecified or ignored. For example, when former mayor Verda Bennett resigned in October 2001, the council immediately voted Delores Madison in as the new mayor. However, the council reversed this decision two months later, deciding that then Mayor Pro Tem Thomas should assume the mayoral position, with Madison becoming the new mayor pro tem. But Madison would become the mayor again in June 2002, when Thomas resigned. In addition, there were several times when a majority of the council members did not attend regular council meetings, and meetings were often cancelled for lack of a quorum.

The leadership deficit was evident in the high turnover of city positions. Between January 2000 and July 2002, three consecutive mayors resigned; and two city managers and one city attorney were fired. Behind the unpleasant and frequent turnover were great tension and conflict between the mayors and council members, between the council members and appointed officials, and among the council members themselves. Distrust and hostility were a serious problem in city government.

Citizens felt desperate with the leadership and fiscal crisis. In July 2001, an affidavit, signed and notarized by the Affidavit Petition Committee (consisting of a council member and four citizens) proposed to dissolve the city.

8.3.2 Rise of the New Leadership

Collapse and crisis created opportunity for new leaders to arise. When Madison became mayor in June 2002, Governor Bush was planning to close the city. As Madison recalled, "When I was running for my seat, the first thing that citizens wanted to know was if I was going to dissolve the city. I said no." Madison emphasized, "I was for making the city financially stable ... People here have suffered for a long time. They liked to see something different." In order to save the city from totally collapsing, it was a natural reaction for the new mayor, the majority of the council members, and ordinary citizens to work closely together in striving for changes. Madison saw solving the financial problem as the number one priority. "We had to convince the governor that we can stand on our own feet ... The city had to be solvent before it could begin providing municipal police protection, update its fire department equipment, or begin construction on roads, parks, and other capital improvement projects" (Madison interview 2006a).

With this vision in mind, Madison immediately began to take steps to bring it to fruition. She understood that she needed help from professional experts, so she went to the Florida League of Cities and asked them to recommend a city manager. In August 2002, the new city manager, Paul Piller, was hired and Madison has worked closely with him since then in making changes. After analyzing the economic situation of Midway, Madison and Piller decided to enlarge the tax base via annexation. The city had only four businesses that paid a combined 25 percent of all tax revenue. In the meantime, a number of large commercial and residential properties were located near the city limit, but were governed by Gadsden County. Madison and Piller promptly initiated a series of meetings with the landowners to discuss annexation into Midway. The landowners were dissatisfied with Gadsden County because of long waiting times in obtaining building permits. "It was neither a money issue nor an incentive issue," Piller remarked. "What the landowners truly desired was to streamline the permit process" (Piller interview 2006). The council rapidly agreed on this agenda and reduced the review time for building permits to within three weeks. Compared with the approximately two-year cycle of Gadsden County, this offer persuaded the commercial owners of the merits of annexation by the city.

Having succeeded in the annexation of commercial properties, the city decided to annex some residential areas as well. Madison went directly to homeowners— often with Piller, the growth director, and the city attorney—and gave them reasons why they should support annexation. Several large parcels of residential land were annexed shortly thereafter. With these annexations, the taxable property value in the city increased by almost $50,000 (about 40 percent) during the 2004/2005 fiscal year. Developers started to build more homes in the city, which attracted commercial investment in the form of restaurants, grocery stores, and retail shops.

At the same time, Madison encouraged Piller and the city attorney to make efforts to negotiate with state agencies for grant extensions and new grants. Midway had been awarded three state grants to be used for park improvements in 1999, 2000, and 2001. But the city had been unable to take advantage of the grants due to a lack of financial management capacity. Piller successfully negotiated an extension for two of the three grants. Then the administrative team worked closely with the Florida Department of Environmental Protection (DEP) to get the park improvements done. As the city began to accumulate small amounts of money, they bid out portions of the grants, paid for the work in a piecemeal fashion, and submitted invoices to DEP. Recognizing the city's problems, DEP turned the money around promptly. As a result, Midway finished the park improvements before the deadline established by the extension. In addition, Midway applied for and received from the state a $650,000 Community Development Block Grant to pave roads and provide drainage.

While annexation and grant extension were in process, Piller and other staff worked hard with the city's various creditors in setting up payment schedules, going over every bill and every service the city was receiving from vendors. At the end of fiscal year 2003, the city had a positive balance of $127,460 and received a perfect audit. Finally, Madison and Piller were able to successfully convince the governor of the turnaround, preventing him from closing the city. In order to get support throughout this long process, Madison and the city council actively communicated with the citizenry. For example, they mailed newsletters to residents explaining the city's problems and asking for their help and patience.

Midway's resurgence, growth, and expansion were quickly recognized in northern Florida, especially in Gadsden County. Since April 2003, the local newspaper *Gadsden County Times* has changed its tone in reporting on Midway, with positive articles, such as "City of Midway on the move" (10/09/03), "Midway is awarded Rural Community of the Year" (11/12/04), "Midway gets grant" (01/21/05), "Midway Mayor Madison is 'City Official of the Year'" (06/17/05), etc. Following are excerpts from a few of these news stories from the *Gadsden County Times* to illustrate the newly established reputation of Midway.

A good example of what happens in a community when people put their heads together is the City of Midway. That's right, the City of Midway. Over the past two years it has annexed over 800 acres of land, most of it industrial property (Spires 2004a).

The City of Midway has gone from a city of "doom and despair" to winning Florida's Rural Community of the Year award for 2004. The metamorphosis has occurred over the past two years as the city has moved from a cloud of debt and unrest, to the poster child for annexation (Spires 2004b).

Growth and annexation were topics of concern for Quincy* commissioners Tuesday night. "I'm envious. What is it they have (Midway)?" Mayor Derrick Elias asked, referring to the tremendous growth that has been occurring in the City of Midway over the past two years. … Elias wanted to set up a meeting with Midway's city manager and council to discuss ways Quincy could take advantage of some of their ideas (Spires 2005a).

It was recognized that Midway's accomplishments were closely associated with Madison's effective leadership. As Jeff Hendry, executive director of the Northwest Florida League of Cities (NWFLC), appraised in the ceremony for the "Municipal Official of the Year":

> Madison had been responsible for and provided the leadership to rewrite, promote and overwhelmingly pass a new city charter. Madison had been instrumental in obtaining nearly $1.7 million in state and federal funds for the City of Midway. Madison had helped convince property owners of over 3,000 vacant acres of residential and commercial land to voluntarily annex that property into the City of Midway. Madison had been at the helm of the city when Midway was recognized by the Governor's Office with the 2004 Florida Rural Community of the Year award (Spires 2005b).

8.4 Strategies of the Facilitative Mayoral Leadership

In mayor–council cities, it is assumed that mayors provide strong leadership because they have greater institutional authority than other city officials. Further, mayors can enhance their leadership capacity by reconstructing the city government with various strategies such as creating a new political order, promoting civil service reform, or building up multiracial coalitions (Flanagan 2004; Thompson 2006). By way of contrast, mayors in council–manager cities usually

---

* Quincy is the largest city in Gadsden County and sits ten miles northwest from Midway.

do not have such formal institutional power. Yet, they can still enhance their leadership capacity given their special position in the council, their superior policy knowledge, their coordination with other officials, and their individual characteristics (Svara 1994).

According to the city charter of Midway, the mayor is elected from among the council members. The office has the same level of institutional authority as that of other council members, although the mayor is the head of city government for all ceremonial purposes. Thus, having only a central position in the city government and lacking superior formal authority, Madison built and enhanced her leadership by self-education, networking in regional organizations, and most importantly, cooperating with appointed officials, particularly the city manager and the city attorney.

8.4.1 Self-Education and Networking

Delores Madison is a Tallahassee native and a graduate of Florida A&M University. She had a career as a federal bank examiner in the state of Washington for twelve years before returning to Florida to work as a research assistant for the Agency for Workforce Innovation. She had little political experience before running for the city council. As such, she made some mistakes in the beginning period of her mayoralty, partially due to her lack of political knowledge. One of the mistakes took place during a board meeting of the Gadsden School District (each county is a single school district in Florida) in which Superintendent DuPont was requesting permission from the school board to transfer approximately twenty-five acres of land owned by the district to the city of Midway. Madison was puzzled by the transfer process and regulations of land use, so she kept asking questions in the meeting until the superintendent was exasperated. DuPont finally asked the board to pull the item from the agenda: "I am not willing to give someone something they don't flat out want." The board voted 4 to 0 to keep the property. Later in the meeting, Madison realized her mistake, apologized to the board, and asked them to reconsider the decision, but they did not revisit the issue (O'Halloran 2003).

Madison admitted that "I knew little about the position and policy when I became the mayor. I had to learn. So I joined the League of Cities, which has become my best friend. Almost every weekend I was in workshops. I learned in the workshops" (Madison interview 2006a). City Manager Piller and other council members confirmed her diligence and persistence to learn about the dynamics of local government policy.

Madison has been very active in the Florida League of Cities and its branch, the Northwest Florida League of Cities (NWFLC), for both workshops and networking opportunities. Her deep involvement in the professional networks helps establish her reputation in a large social setting. She was awarded "Mayor of the Year" and "City Official of the Year" by these organizations, respectively. The NWFLC even elected her as second vice president in 2005 and president in 2007. Madison's reputation in the networks is an invisible resource for her, yet it has helped her to earn support in a larger political context and to obtain additional resources, such as grants, for her community.

Both self-education and networking have enhanced Madison's leadership capacity relative to the other council members. As one of the council members comments, "When I was attending a meeting with Florida League of Cities, you mentioned Madison, everybody knows her. In any state commissions, you mention Madison, everybody knows her. She is representing the city of Midway very well" (Council Member Hinson interview 2006b). In the council meetings we attended in 2006 and 2007, we noticed that Madison tended to be much more knowledgeable than other council members about regulations, financial matters, and city management.

8.4.2 Partnering with a Strong City Manager in Policy Making

In contrast to the politics–administration dichotomy model, extensive leadership by a city manager can be consistent with democratic accountability and professional responsibility. The assertive manager is not necessarily a replacement or competitor for the mayoral leadership. When strong mayoral leadership is supported by the manager, and the communication between the mayor and the city manager is effective, the city manager may serve a mayor's vision and become an important resource for him or her. "Strong facilitative leadership can be provided by the mayor, along with that provided by the city manager … mayors and managers offer team leadership rather than competing with each other" (Svara 1994; also see Boynton and Wright 1971). But it cannot be a two-way relationship alone. A city manager can be dismissed at the will of the elected officials, and must win and maintain the support of the council to be effective.

Piller actually was the first city manager of Midway in 1987 for a period of two months when the city was formed. He had served other Florida cities for many years, and was running his own local government management consulting business when Madison invited him to Midway. Besides his city management experience, Piller is an active lobbyist "who knows how to talk the language on the Capitol Hill" (Madison interview 2006a). His lobbying skills were greatly utilized by the city in negotiations with federal and state agencies.

Piller's technical, informational, and managerial expertise in local government administration led him to play a very important role in shaping policy via proposals and agenda setting. In reviewing the council meeting agendas and minutes, we find that Piller advised on many important initiatives, such as annexing properties into the city, negotiation with the federal and state agencies on grants, amendment of city charters, and economic development plans.

Madison works closely with the city manager on policy making. "I talk a lot with Paul. Two, three, or four phone calls a day," said Madison. Because of their frequent communication, they can openly exchange thoughts and, as such, usually agree on policy issues. In comparison, other council members have far fewer contacts with the manager and, thus, are less likely to understand each other on policy issues. "I try to call him (Piller) once a week to learn what is going on," said a councilperson.

Piller's expertise on policy issues is one impetus for Madison to share policy leadership with him. But another fundamental factor is that they trust each other, and both have a strong commitment to serving the public interest. Piller appreciates Madison's frequent communication with the citizens, as well as her persistent efforts at self-development to become a better mayor. Madison praises Piller's extended willingness to serve for Midway, as he did not initially plan to be a long-term city manager. "I thought I was going to work here for about two or three months and then back to my own business," Piller recalled. But he eventually served for almost five years. "Paul's pay is very, very low because we cannot afford a high salary. He is here not for money. He wants to help us" (Madison 2006a).

The political and the administrative leadership in Midway are not separate nor are they completely intermixed; they are coordinated and complementary. The mayor understands the real needs of the community and possesses a promising vision for the way forward. But this vision needs to be actualized with someone's help. For example, Madison had the goal to save the city from collapsing, but she also realized that the city would not be saved unless the financial crisis could be overcome. Unlike her predecessor, who looked for a city manager from within the community for help, Madison believed that they really needed an administrative professional with economic growth expertise. That is why she went to the Florida League of Cities for recommendations. When she understood that expanding the tax base was the surest means for growth, she accepted the ideas of property annexation from the manager, discussed the process with him, and went out to communicate and persuade the property owners. When she had ideas about city infrastructure priorities, she talked with the manager for technical and financial feasibility.

Madison makes policy with the city manager's help. It is not the case that the mayor contributes policy ideas and directs the manager in implementation, nor is it the case that the mayor simply agrees with the manager's proposals. Rather, the mayor and the city manager share policy leadership through frequent communication and coordination. It is this coordination that facilitated many positive changes in the city of Midway.

8.4.3 Protecting and Assisting Administrative Operation

Piller was appointed city manager during Midway's fiscal emergency. In the beginning period of his tenure, the council and citizens were quite supportive, and his interactions with the council members were constructive. The process of negotiation with COPS over grants illustrates the healthy interactions between the council and the city manager. By 2002, Midway owed the U.S. Department of Justice, Office of Community Oriented Policing Services (COPS) more than $140,000 for alleged misuse of a COPS Grant. Midway had no ability to pay off this amount of money at that time. The city manager decided to negotiate with COPS.

> He (Piller) found out who was the person that we needed to talk to. The council gave him the direction of going on to talk to that person, and tried to see how we can help and work it out. In every council meeting that we had, he was giving us updates on the progress that had been made. It was like, okay, I am here with this (the amount of money that was negotiated with COPS). But they (the council members) said that it is still huge. He then went back to bargain and bargain, piece by piece, and, finally, he got to the point that we were able to pay it off. That point was about $1,700 (Madison interview 2006b).

Madison added, "If it has not been for Paul, talking for hours and hours to the federal government in reference to our COPS grants, this city would not have been here today." She emphasized, "It was the process that the council needed the patience, and we needed Paul for the persistency."

However, as the city became increasingly solvent, disagreements over municipal service priorities occurred among council members. These disagreements eventually affected how to evaluate the manager's performance. Some council members began to criticize the city manager for not following their directions, while some citizens blamed the manager for not addressing their needs, even when it was not the city manager's fault or responsibility.

When this happened, Madison defended Piller. "The city manager did whatever the council has directed him to do. If we have problems of working together, then we have problems in the council." Madison does not think the complaints from citizens are always right and fair, especially because the city has so much to do with its limited resources. So she decided to take action to help Piller by talking with citizens directly: "When they come in, let them call me. And I talk to them. When I talk to these individuals, I always try to make them understand that there are always two sides of a coin; ... nobody is perfect. I told them, if we had done something wrong, give us an opportunity to correct it. If you can give us the opportunity to correct it, then we can work together. If you think that I should be doing something differently than what we are currently doing, let me know what it is."

Madison thinks that administrative operations should be insulated from unnecessary distractions, and that the conflicts among council members should not extend to the manager. She emphasized "we should accomplish something, not just sit there arguing and arguing."

8.4.4 *Monitoring and Guiding Council Meetings*

The Florida Sunshine Law (Chapter 286 of the Florida Statutes) prohibits elected officials from exchanging policy ideas behind closed doors.* Being effectively constrained in her ability to build consensus on policy issues and to create coalitions among council members, Madison largely relies on cooperation with the city manager in order to accomplish public business. But having experienced a dysfunctional council in the past, Madison knew she needed to discipline the institution.

Madison read and distributed a letter labeled "directions and instructions" in the first council meeting she presided over as mayor. She advised the council members on how they should conduct themselves and how they should respect each other. With emphasis that the only purpose of the council meetings is to conduct the business of the city, she guides the council with the following directions.

First of all, she advises that time should be spent in an efficient and productive way, and that the meetings should strictly follow the agenda with set time limits on discussions. "Only items on the agenda would be addressed," she stressed. "We don't really have time to listen to one council person go on and on and on about something that you are not going to accomplish. We need to get something accomplished." When the council members cannot agree on an issue, she normally lets them go home, do more research, and then come back to a subsequent meeting and vote again. "Research is very important. We do not need to argue very much in the city hall."

Secondly, she prohibits any finger pointing in the meeting. "Pointing fingers never accomplishes anything," she explained. "If we are all going to be here as the council, cutting each other's throat, and fighting the citizens, then what kind of picture is shown to the citizens? It is a picture that they do not work together and I don't trust them. This is the thing that we should try very hard not to let happen" (Madison interview 2006b).

Thirdly, Madison requests that council members adopt a more collectivist sense in lieu of articulating individualistic concerns in the meetings. "We, as a city, a community, cannot work and accomplish anything unless we work together." She told the council members, "When you came to this council, you became a part of this council." She stressed, "WE are responsible, WE are the reason why you have this problem; WE are the ones that need to get out of here and do something to correct it" (Madison interview 2006b).

---

* Florida Sunshine Law requires that meetings of any public decision-making body must be open to the public, and reasonable notice of such meetings must be given and minutes of the meeting must be taken. The law applies to any gathering where two or more members of a public board or commission discuss some matter on which foreseeable action will be taken by that board or commission. Anyone who carries messages about public business from one public official to another in an attempt to resolve an issue outside of the Sunshine statute violates the law. This would apply even if two members of a commission were having a casual dinner, or chatting on phone, and public business came up in the course of conversation.

In addition, Madison encourages council members to educate themselves in order to develop as legislators. Compared to regular citizens in Midway, the council members are relatively well educated. Yet, they generally lack formal policy-making experience. Some of them are unable to understand the issues and problems that confront the community. Madison feels that many arguments in the council meetings are due to a lack of relevant knowledge. As discussed in the previous section, Madison is deeply dedicated to self-education via diverse workshops offered by the Florida League of Cities. She often brings handouts and materials back to Midway in an attempt to instruct other council members.

8.4.5 Gaining Support from City Attorneys

Effective mayoral leadership needs technical and managerial support from the city manager, in addition to legal support from the city attorney. This is especially the case when amateur politicians distract council meetings with their personal conflicts. The city attorney, John Williams, was appointed in June 2002, after the council fired his predecessor. Assistant attorney Larry White was hired shortly thereafter. Their professional knowledge and commitment has protected the mayoral leadership from unnecessary distraction and kept the council meetings from becoming unproductive stalemates. We describe here two scenarios from Midway monthly council meetings to illustrate the attorneys' strong support of the mayoral leadership and city administration.

> *Scenario #1*: While Madison and Piller were engaged in efforts to annex properties into the city limit, they needed council's prompt permission in the council meeting. However, a council member tried to postpone the decision, "I need time to do investigations on the annexation." When a stalemate was about to occur, City Attorney Williams confirmed the legality of the annexation and praised the city manager on developing the process for annexation. He said the process might become a model for other cities to use in their annexation process. After his explanation, the motion of the annexation was passed (Spires 2003).
>
> *Scenario #2*: Prior to the city's election in April 2007, the city attorney and city manager had been trying to convince the council to put the residents in new subdivisions into a city district. They failed because two council members and a group of citizens strongly opposed the proposal. The election proceeded as scheduled and a candidate from a new subdivision was elected, which led to a lawsuit against the election result. The monthly council meeting in May 2007 was held while the lawsuit was pending. Prior to the invocation, the mayor pro tem suggested the regular council meeting be adjourned until June and no council member be sworn in. Madison consulted with Assistant Attorney White. He suggested that there be no public discussion of any pending lawsuits per Florida Statutes. White further advised that

the meeting must continue because the council is bound to take care of the business of the city. With his persistence, the new elected council members were sworn in. The mayor pro tem and a council member then went away discontented. Madison presided over this meeting and the council worked through the agenda (Piller e-mail 06/06/07; council meeting minutes 05/03/07).

8.5 Challenges and Dynamics of Mayoral Leadership

Madison regrets being unable to advance some policy issues that she thinks are extremely important to Midway. One such issue is public education. For years, Midway has suffered from having no schools and their students have to be bused to other cities four to ten miles away.

According to Piller, if Midway continues to grow and expand rapidly in the next decade, it will eventually surpass Quincy and become the largest municipality in the county in both area and population. However, Midway is the only municipality without a school, which may hamper its future growth and development. Madison and Piller have advocated for building a school in the community since early 2005. "We don't want people looking around for a school and then moving out because their young children have to be bussed to Havana or Quincy," said Madison (*GCT*, 07/15/05). After many discussions, the district board eventually approved Midway's request for a new school. However, Midway was confronted with another problem.

Considering financial constraints and legal procedures, Madison and Piller agreed that a charter school was the most realistic option. They discussed this idea with local developers and education providers. A developer was willing to donate one hundred acres of land in the center of a new subdivision, and Academies of Excellence, an educational institute that has run charter schools in other districts in Florida, was interested in operating the school. It submitted a Midway Charter School application to the Gasdsen School Board in September 2005. However, two council members and a group of citizens became strong opponents of the proposal. Jerry Range, director of the Midway Chamber of Commerce, presented the school board with a petition of two hundred signatures opposing the charter school. He suggested that the push for the charter school was tied to the developer's desire to sell homes quickly in the subdivisions sprouting up all over the city. But he believed that "it will do nothing for the children of people who already live in Midway." The mayor pro tem insisted that a charter school is not a public school and that she preferred not to have one. Due to this strong opposition, the charter school application had to be withdrawn (DuPont 2005).

The charter school issue uncovers a considerable political split among council members and citizens. This split has been demonstrated on many other issues as well, including annexation, election, and garbage collection. There has been an interesting pattern in the council demonstrated by the many decisions that are passed by votes of 3 to 2, 4 to 2, or 5 to 2. Generally, the same two council members often criticize and oppose the mayor and the manager's proposals, while two other council members usually show them support. The remaining two members swing depending on the issue.

The biggest split broke out on the issue of the city manager's continuation in office. In the July 2006 council meeting, two members expressed their concerns about the city manager's power relative to other institutions. "Too many powers are put in one man's hands and more powers should be placed with the mayor and council." Because of these concerns, they unsuccessfully attempted to remove the city manager from office. Piller was criticized again by a member in a January 2007 meeting for awarding the city's garbage collection contract to a "white" company without giving a fair chance to "minority" firms. "We minorities in Midway want to give minorities a chance to apply and bid for those jobs like everyone else," the council member said (*GCT*, 01/12/07). Along with another member, he attempted once again to remove the city manager.*

The political split in Midway may reflect the fear and repulsion of the long-time, low-income African-American residents, many of whom live in mobile homes, toward the new residents in the subdivisions. The new residents are typically young professionals, perhaps not minorities, working in Tallahassee while enjoying the less expensive homes in Midway. The split may also be interpreted as the extension of conflicts between progrowth and antigrowth forces. The antigrowth residents may think that growth and expansion will diminish their influence. Alternatively, the split may involve the inherent tension between government efficiency and social equity. Studies have shown that conflicts between a city council and manager may occur because council members are more oriented to address constituents' special needs and demands, while city managers tend to be more oriented by their professional norms to promote consistent treatment for all residents, economic growth, and efficiency issues (Svara 2005; Zhang 2007). It is also possible that the split was related to the city election in April 2007, during which some council members tried to draw the attention of the long-time residents in order to earn their political support.

Nevertheless, divisiveness among the council has been ruinous to city government in the recent past and it may have the same impact again if not appropriately addressed. The problem is becoming increasingly severe as evidenced by familiar signals in council meetings, such as heated arguments without accomplishments. The *Gadsden County Times* sees the problem and presents an example, "heated squabbling among council members, frequent interruptions and lengthy tangents off the agenda, but little productive official business discussion, highlighted Thursday's Midway Charter Workshop. The two-hour workshop ended with no clear recommendations for official action, and recommendation for further review on only one of five agenda items" (07/06/06).

Due to excessive pressure from the council, Piller tendered his resignation as city manager and left Midway in early May 2007. The successful mayor–manager

---

* The *Gadsden County Times* was unable to locate a regional garbage collection company that was owned and operated by a minority proprietor (Gadsden County Times 2007).

leadership team thus collapsed, and the city is attempting to find a new manager. For Madison, it may be necessary to develop new partnerships, not only with a new city manager, but also with new council members and other segments of the community. As the environment changes, the strategies that constitute effective mayoral leadership are likely to change as well.

8.6 Conclusion

The council–manager form of government assigns no substantial formal authority to the mayors, which makes their exercise of leadership a challenging issue. In order to effectively lead, mayors in council–manager governments have to take strategic actions to enhance their capacity. Such actions include networking with political organizations, building coalitions among council members, and/or forming a mayor–manager leadership team (Boynton and Wright 1971; Svara 1994; Whitaker and DeHoog 1991).

In the case of Midway, Florida, the mayor's informal communication with other council members is considerably constrained by the Sunshine Law. This has the practical effect of rendering coalition building a strategy that the mayor cannot explicitly pursue. But the mayor has still provided strong leadership with a clear vision and a strong desire to save the city from financial crisis. She has contributed much greater effort to the overall conduct of city business than her council colleagues. She has been actively involved in local municipal organizations, sitting in workshops, educating herself, and networking to obtain more political resources. Notably, she enhanced her leadership with help from a strong city manager. This case illustrates that mayoral leadership and administrative leadership can work synergistically together to enhance the effectiveness of both. This empowered mayor–manager leadership team can better overcome obstacles and distractions and make positive changes for the community.

However, the mayor–manager leadership team may also be unstable. In the case of Midway, instability came from conflicts among the council members, some of whom considered Madison a political opponent and the city manager her agent. The observed facts in this study are consistent with Whitaker and DeHoog's (1991) finding that a city manager is more likely to be forced to leave office when the council is divided by conflict, which in turn is more likely to occur during council election campaigns. Alternatively, the political conflict may be an expression of differing attitudes over growth. It may also reflect two distinct orientations in that council members are inclined to represent the concerns of their constituents, while city managers are oriented toward administrative efficiency and other professional norms (Svara 2005).

In addition, this study implies that the effectiveness of the mayor–manager leadership team may be temporary in nature and highly dependent on timing. When the city was in a severe financial crisis, the basic consensus among the mayor, council members, and citizens was to save the city by stimulating economic growth. Therefore, a city manager with experiential skill in economic growth policy and lobbying was favored by all parties. But when the city has moved to a different developmental stage, when it has a fiscal surplus and distributional justice becomes a focal issue, it may need a city manager with different interests and skills. From this perspective, Piller's resignation is not necessarily a disaster. It may provide the city with an opportunity to think about the change in overall direction for the city and the change in leadership strategies that necessarily accompany development. We suggest that Midway consider hiring a new city manager that, rather than being exclusively focused on economic growth and fiscal health, can communicate effectively with citizens and council members and be sensitive to their local needs.

References

Adrian, Charles R. and Charles Press. 1977. *Governing Urban America*, 5th ed. New York: McGraw-Hill.

Boynton, R.P. and D.S. Wright. 1971. Mayor–manager relationships in large council–manager cities: A reinterpretation. *Public Administration Review* 31: 28–36.

DuPont, Alice, 2005. School for Midway? *Gadsden County Times.* October 14. http://news.mywebpal.com/news_tool_v2.cfm?pnpid=582&show=archivedetails&ArchiveID=1145831&om=1 (Accessed July 17, 2007).

Flanagan, Richard M. 2004. *Mayors and the Challenge of Urban Leadership.* Lanham, MD: University Press of America.

Hinson, James. 2006. Interview with the authors, November 10.

Madison, Delores. 2006a. Interview with the authors, October 17.

Madison, Delores. 2006b. Interview with the authors. November 10.

Morgan, David, Robert England, and John Pelissero. 2007. *Managing Urban American*, 6th ed. Moline, IL: CQ Press.

O'Halloran, Michael, 2003. Midway mayor talks board out of gift. *Gadsden County Times.* November 1.

Piller, Paul. 2006. Interview with the authors, October 17.

Spires, Byron. 2003. City of Midway on the move. *Gadsden County Times.* October 9. http://news.mywebpal.com/news_tool_v2.cfm?pnpid=582&show=archivedetails&ArchiveID=990628&om=1 (Accessed July 17, 2007).

Spires, Byron. 2004a. It is already here. *Gadsden County Times.* September 3. http://news.mywebpal.com/news_tool_v2.cfm?pnpid=582&show=archivedetails&ArchiveID=985580&om=1 (Accessed July 17, 2007).

Spires, Byron. 2004b. Midway is awarded Rural Community of the Year. *Gadsden County Times.* November 12. http://news.mywebpal.com/news_tool_v2.cfm?pnpid=582&show=archivedetails&ArchiveID=1069847&om=1 (Accessed July 17, 2007).

Spires, Byron. 2005a. Commissioners look at growth. *Gadsden County Times.* April 15. http://news.mywebpal.com/news_tool_v2.cfm?pnpid=582&show=archivedetails&ArchiveID=1101953&om=1 (Accessed July 17, 2007).

Spires, Byron. 2005b. Midway mayor Madison is "City Official of the Year." *Gadsden County Times.* June 17. http://news.mywebpal.com/news_tool_v2.cfm?pnpid=582&show=archivedetails&ArchiveID=1118433&om=1 (Accessed July 17, 2007).

Svara, James H. 1994. Redefining leadership in local government: The facilitative model. In *Facilitative Leadership in Local Government*, eds. James H. Svara and Associates. San Francisco: Jossey-Bass, 1–36.

Svara, James H. 2005. Institutional form and political leadership in American city government. In *Transforming Local Political Leadership*, eds. R. Berg, and N. Rao. Singapore: Blackwell Publishing, 131–49.

Thompson, J. Philip. 2006. *Double Trouble: Black Mayors, Black Communities, and the Call for a Deep Democracy*. New York: Oxford University Press.

Whitaker, G. and R.H. DeHoog. 1991. City managers under fire: How conflict leads to turnover. *Public Administration Review* 51: 156–65.

Zhang, Y. 2007. Local official's incentives and policy-making: Through a lens of the politics–administration relationship. PhD diss., Florida State Univ.

Chapter 9

Expanding the Scope of Policy Leadership Through Networks: Grand Rapids, Michigan

Eric S. Zeemering and Roger J. Durham

Contents

9.1 Introduction

Michigan's second largest city has undergone a quiet renewal since the early 1990s. While Michigan's economy has suffered from losses in the automotive and manufacturing industries, public and private sector actors in Grand Rapids have pushed the city forward to the new information and service economies (Nasser 2006). Presiding over much of the Grand Rapids renaissance was Mayor John Logie (1992 to 2003), the longest serving mayor in the city's history. Upon departing from City Hall, Logie's contribution was recognized by *The Grand Rapids Press:*

> The mayor's unwavering advocacy for "his" city made Grand Rapids a better place to live and do business. The results can be seen everywhere … He fought with purpose and vigor. He used his considerable gifts for the public good at a crucial time in the life of Grand Rapids. For that, he deserves heartfelt thanks and a large place in the city's memory (Grand Rapids Press 2003).

George Heartwell assumed the duties of mayor in January 2004, after a lightly contested election. Although many may view him as a mayor committed to continuing the goals of traditional downtown development and renewal, he offers a contrast to Logie in both style and vision for public policy in the greater Grand Rapids area. Heartwell is challenged to live up to the high standards of public engagement and downtown boosterism set by John Logie, while also making his own distinct contributions to policy and the public character of city government.

Heartwell exemplifies facilitative mayoral leadership. His style can be summarized as policy-based facilitation, employing extensive intergovernmental and intersectoral policy networks. In addition to the formal structures of city government, Heartwell successfully draws in additional public, nonprofit, and business actors to pursue specific policies. His efforts move Grand Rapids toward a sustainable model for business and government, while also investing in human capital through support of education and community programs. Heartwell exercises this leadership while constrained by the time and resource limitations of the city's part-time structure for the office of mayor.

Both Logie and Heartwell acknowledge the important role Grand Rapids holds as the urban center anchoring the metropolitan area. Heartwell's leadership during his short time as mayor embodies a facilitative approach in addressing challenges that impact the city and the entire metropolitan area. In his effort to address problems facing Grand Rapids, Heartwell helps link government and community actors in a dialogue about the future of the metropolitan area. He articulates a vision that includes goals that stretch beyond the municipal boundaries of the city of Grand Rapids. H. George Frederickson (1999) argues that public administrators have become critical actors in recognizing problems that span traditional municipal boundaries and developing strategies that focus the efforts of a network of actors for the public good. Facilitative leaders like Heartwell demonstrate that elected leaders also play an important role in facilitating problem solving through networks. Heartwell has rallied the city government and the community to address key challenges in Grand Rapids. Yet, the institutional structure of the mayor's office and the challenge of crafting cooperation in the metropolitan community may limit the effectiveness of his facilitative leadership.

9.2 Methodology

The case study research design is commonly used in the study of mayoral leadership and local governance. Detailed process tracing within a case allows for the examination of specific relationships or causal processes (George and Bennett 2005; Munck 2004). This analysis can help further refine the understanding of how facilitative mayoral leadership contributes to the performance of local government. Grand Rapids provides an ideal case for the study of facilitative leadership due to its long-established history of council–manager government and its status as Michigan's second largest city. In developing this case study, the authors conducted a series of in-depth interviews with elected and administrative government officials, community leaders, leaders in the business community, and practitioners in targeted policy areas (Dexter 1970; Leech 2002). These interviews were digitally recorded for accuracy in reporting of the research. Subjects were offered the option of speaking anonymously and not for attribution, and several interviews were conducted in this manner. A list of those interviewed on record for this research can be found at the end of the chapter.

Additionally, a content analysis of articles from *The Grand Rapids Press,* the metropolitan area's largest daily newspaper, was conducted for 2003, the final year of the Logie administration, and 2004, the first year of the Heartwell administration (Krippendorff 1980). All articles mentioning the Grand Rapids mayor were coded to identify the primary policy area discussed in the article. A sample of articles was coded by both authors independently for an intercoder reliability check.*
These newspaper stories and *Grand Rapids Press* coverage from additional years also contributed to the development of the case study.

---

* The coding protocol is available from the authors.

9.3 Grand Rapids, Michigan

The city of Grand Rapids expanded with the vibrant logging and furniture industries of the nineteenth century. The city now serves as the commercial, entertainment, and service center of West Michigan. The 2000 U.S. Census reported a city population of 197,846, ranking only second in Michigan to Detroit. The multi-county metropolitan area spans to the Lake Michigan shoreline with a population over 1,088,000.

The natural development of the furniture industry, based on a supply of timber from northern Michigan, provided the foundation for Grand Rapids' economic growth. By 1890, Grand Rapids was known as the "Furniture Capital of America" (Olson 1981). This industrial base contributed to a diverse local economy. Currently, industries ranging from office furniture (Steelcase) to consumer products (Amway) anchor West Michigan. Despite the history of strong locally owned business, deindustrialization and globalization has, as in many other industrial cities of North America, negatively affected the West Michigan manufacturing economy.

Recent economic progress has been made in other fields. Grand Rapids has experienced major investment and development in the medical and healthcare industry. The creation of the Van Andel Institute for medical research, the merger of two large local hospitals into the Spectrum Health system, and increases in healthcare employment have helped the economy (Longcore 2004). The healthcare sector continues to grow as Michigan State University's medical school plans operations in the city; existing hospitals are engaged in expansion; and the Van Andel Institute also expands (Radigan 2006).

At the same time, investment in downtown has drawn area residents to city offices and entertainment venues (Knape 2006). Downtown office space and condominium development has expanded largely through the renovation of older buildings; however, this growth is challenged by Michigan's struggling economy (Czurak 2001; Grand Rapids Press 2006). Still, the city's cultural and recreation infrastructure continues to improve. Since its opening in 1996, the Van Andel Arena has served as an important regional entertainment venue for concerts and sporting events, like Grand Rapids Griffins hockey. The recently expanded convention center draws more guests to town and has fueled new hotel construction. Construction of a new art museum demonstrates interest and support for artistic and cultural events in the city.

City government has responded to these economic changes by encouraging private and public cooperation in the revitalization efforts. Private investment and philanthropy have been critical for Grand Rapids' success, but the city government has also been an active participant in economic development. The city forged a strong link with The Right Place, Inc., a nonprofit organization for economic development led by a board of directors representing community and business leaders. The city government's participation in economic development is exemplified by Grand Rapids City Manager Kurt Kimball's membership on The Right Place board of directors. One of the roles played by the Right Place Inc. is as liaison between private economic interests and local government.

The current city charter was approved in 1916, following lengthy urban reform debates shaped in part by a 1911 strike in the city's furniture industry (Kleiman 2006). The charter provides for a city council, called a *city commission*, with six members plus a mayor. Two commissioners are elected from each of three wards. The mayor is the only member of the city commission elected at-large, and serves as chair of the commission. The city comptroller is also elected at-large. The city commission appoints a manager, attorney, clerk, and treasurer. The Charter specifies the organization of the city's administrative departments and states that "the administrative services of the city shall be under the supervision and direction of the city manager." Kimball has served as city manager since 1987 and is the longest serving manager in the city's history.

The Grand Rapids metropolitan area exhibits the characteristics of urban sprawl and jurisdictional fragmentation common in the United States. As Grand Rapids expanded, township residents threatened by annexation opted to incorporate their own municipalities, resulting in neighboring governments that blocked expansion of the central city. Michigan's tradition of strong township government provides area residents with many options for suburban and rural living, attracting mobile citizen-consumers to jurisdictions with lower property tax burdens and different bundles of public services (Browne and VerBurg 1995; Stephens 1989; Tiebout 1956). The metropolitan area exhibits disparities in tax base, fiscal stress, employment, and poverty (Orfield 1999). However, local governments engage in dialogue over metropolitan problems through the Grand Valley Metropolitan Council (GVMC), the region's council of governments. Through GVMC and voluntary interlocal cooperation, the region exhibits a level of voluntary cooperation consistent with the view that policy coordination can occur in the absence of centralized metropolitan government (Oakerson 1999; Thurmaier and Wood 2004; Visser 2004). Mayors of Grand Rapids and the city manager have been important participants in metropolitan dialogue at the GVMC.

John Logie's activism as mayor contributes to high expectations for his successor. In a case study discussing Logie's role in intergovernmental relations, Rex LaMore and Faron Supanich-Goldner (2000) identify Logie as a "director" under Svara's classification of mayoral leadership. They argue that Logie exercised "a rational approach to decisionmaking [sic] with an optimistic leadership style intent on achieving mutually beneficial results" (LaMore and Supanich-Goldner 2000). Logie describes himself as a hands-on participant in urban affairs, being ever-present in policy discussions, just as he was active in the ceremonial functions of the office. Serving on twenty-three boards and commissions, *The Grand Rapids Press* (2003) explains, "… he made frequent use of the bully pulpit and was a dominant presence at meetings." City commissioners who served with Logie note his efficiency. Logie's use of a three-minute egg timer during public comment time exemplifies his orderly approach to public business. The timers limited the verbose and allowed for a greater number to have the opportunity to speak. Logie will be remembered as a vocal advocate for downtown development, and an energetic participant in city governance (Harger 2003). His style of working with private investors illustrates his commitment to market-oriented growth and the belief that private investment will have lasting positive effects for the city.

Heartwell may not exhibit the same Logie efficiency at the commission table, but he has sought to expand participation in local affairs by developing policy networks with participants from every sector of the community. While attentive to continuing investment in downtown, his policy focus is oriented to sustainability and human investment. Before assessing Heartwell's leadership style, the structural constraints on his performance must be considered. Logie and Heartwell are more active policy leaders than previous Grand Rapids mayors. Both articulate that the structural support for mayor and the public expectations for the mayor's performance diverge.

9.4 Keeping the Mayor's Office Part-Time

Grand Rapids voters have demonstrated a reluctance to modify the city charter to expand mayoral power. This was demonstrated most recently when voters rejected a proposed amendment to make the position of mayor "full time" by increasing compensation and modifying some powers associated with the office. Hybrid power structures melding council–manager systems with greater mayoral power have become increasingly common (Frederickson, Johnson, and Wood 2004), but Grand Rapids voters turned down a series of proposed charter amendments in the 1970s that would have expanded mayoral power, and their opinions changed little over the intervening thirty years (Harger 2002a). Voters rejected a 2002 charter amendment proposal by a vote of 29,714 (60.3%) to 19,550 (39.7%).

Logie brought forward the proposed changes to the charter in his 2002 State of the City Address (Harger 2002d). During his time in office, Logie committed almost a full-time schedule to the work of being mayor. Logie was able to manage this schedule because of his own energy for the job, and because he was able to negotiate with his law firm to gain flexibility. Current compensation for the mayor is just over $39,000 per year. Historically, Grand Rapids mayors have maintained their preelection professions. Logie significantly expanded the time the mayor committed to city business, and considered an active mayor critical to the advancement of the city. Upon introducing the proposal in 2002, Logie stated:

> My motivation is, and must be, that mayors in the future will need more structure and a greater opportunity than the current charter creates in order to provide effective leadership that meets the demands and needs of our dynamic community (Harger 2002c).

The proposal was premised on the view that the City of Grand Rapids has grown to the point at which the elected mayor should be compensated at a full-time pay rate, similar to the city manager, in order to fulfill the community's expectations for appearances in the traditional mayoral roles, while also maintaining involvement in public policy and planning.

However, the charter amendment proposed by Logie was more expansive than a recommendation for full-time pay. Rather than acting as commissioner-at-large, chairing meetings of the city commission and voting on all resolutions, Logie's proposal would require the mayor to vote only in the case of a tie-vote by the commission. The mayor would have veto power, which could only be overridden by a vote of five commissioners. Further, the mayor would exercise appointment power for the city manager, clerk, attorney, and treasurer, with commission approval. The mayor would also participate in a review of the manager's budget before the document reached the full commission. The proposed amendment was significantly scaled back by the city commission before it was approved for the ballot. Commissioners rejected additional mayoral veto and appointment power, but favored increased compensation and full-time work expectations for the mayor (Harger and Deiters 2002). The modified proposal that went onto the ballot would have expanded the capacity of the mayor to engage in traditional ceremonial functions, but would not have altered mayoral power in commission voting. Logie's commitment to expanding the office of mayor led him to announce in July of 2002 that he would not seek reelection in 2003. Addressing the city commission, Logie explained, "I'm willing to give up another term to convince you and the citizens that [the charter amendment] is the right thing for the City of Grand Rapids" (Harger 2002e). Logie rallied support for his plan among the city commissioners who witnessed the extensive time he committed to the position.

Logie's surprise announcement about his intention not to seek reelection helped secure ballot access for the charter amendment, and *The Grand Rapids Press* editorialized on the importance of having a discussion about electoral leadership in the city (Grand Rapids Press 2002). As the election neared, voices supporting council–manager government and a part-time mayor increased their participation in the debate. Opposition to the amendment came from former mayors, former administrators, the Grand Rapids Chamber of Commerce, the Michigan Local Government Management Association, unions, and Kimball, the city manager (Harger 2002b; Harger 2002f; Renando 2002).

Former city manager, Joe Zainea, wrote in *The Grand Rapids Press* that the modification of the mayor's budgetary input and mayoral control of the manager's salary were particularly "dangerous." The former manager argued that the proposed charter amendment might slowly lead the city toward a strong mayor system (Zainea 2002). The "No Charter Amendment Committee" offered counter-arguments to the proposal, primarily emphasizing the limited justification for change and the threat to professional city administration. The organization of opposition, in addition to city voters' historic aversion to modifying mayoral power, resulted in a poor showing at the polls for Logie's plan.

While the electorate rejected the 2002 charter amendment, the debate on the role of the mayor in Grand Rapids politics will continue. Jim Rinck, an early entrant into the 2007 mayoral campaign, voiced support for a strong mayor system. City Commissioner Rick Tormala has also advocated for a strong mayor system. He suggests an elected executive would be more accountable to the public, particularly when making budgetary decisions. Several interviewees noted the possibility that low compensation and high time requirements may limit the pool of candidates who seek the office, a concern for the quality of local democracy.

Kimball also recognizes the limitation. The manager explains that after watching Logie and Heartwell in the job, he can envision a system in which an active mayor can work full time, but "not upset the apple cart in terms of basically how we operate." Kimball notes,

> If the mayor could convince the Local Officers Compensation Commission that they're putting in full time and it warrants that, then that would be fine …

> Both the former mayor and the current one could easily spend additional time beyond what they were able to do in the service of the city without tripping over my responsibilities or messing with the executive powers. Just the requirements for the role of the mayor to be in the community, the double, triple booking on many nights, [requires] a lot of time. And I am not fretful about having a political figure in the office next door to me full time. There is enough work here for both of us to do.

Paying for a "full-time" mayor without expanding executive power would be possible; however, the Local Officers Compensation Commission may be unwilling to take such a step during a time of budgetary austerity, following the electoral defeat of the "full-time" mayor plan in 2002.*

Grand Rapids voters or the Local Officers Compensation Commission may opt to provide the mayor with greater support in the future. Until then, elected leaders like Logie and Heartwell craft careful time management strategies to attend myriad community events and engage in meetings, research, and advocacy to advance their policy priorities.† The facilitative leadership style allows Heartwell to share his vision for Grand Rapids with others and network the city government with community actors to achieve his goals. While the institutional structure of City Hall does not

---

* The Local Officers Compensation Commission is a board composed of seven Grand Rapids residents appointed by the mayor and approved by the city commission. The board meets in odd numbered years to set the salary for the mayor, city commissioners and the comptroller (Grand Rapids City Code, Part 2, Chapter 8, Article 7; Section 1.360).

† From 2002 to 2005, Heartwell was director of the Community Leadership Institute at Aquinas College in Grand Rapids, where he worked with students and contributed to community initiatives on lead abatement and other issues. In addition to serving as mayor, Heartwell currently works as president and CEO of Pilgrim Manor Retirement Community.

grant the mayor time to address all of the issues that might call for his attention, Heartwell has drawn from his background as a businessman, pastor, and city commissioner to mobilize diverse constituencies in the community around new goals.

9.5 Mayor George Heartwell

George Heartwell formally entered politics in 1992 when was elected to the Grand Rapids city commission from the city's third ward. However, his political activity can be traced to a mission trip to Haiti over twenty-five years ago, where he saw and experienced deep poverty (Schellenbarger 2005). This prompted him to dramatically change professions. He left the family mortgage business and enrolled in Western Theological Seminary. He was ordained as a minister "and went to work at Heartside Ministry, helping the poor, the addicted, the homeless, and the mentally ill in the low-income neighborhoods" (Schellenbarger 2005). This theologically based entrance into public affairs in Grand Rapids began Heartwell's political career as a spokesperson for the disenfranchised in society. Through his work at Heartside Ministries, he regularly came into contact with local public policy, especially at City Hall.

These interests motivated Heartwell to run for the city commission in 1991, where he served two terms. He explains, "The impulse to do so was really a concern for the poor and a desire to be involved in public office in a way that I could influence their lives for the better." His political activity expanded as he participated in a variety of agencies and boards, such as Habitat for Humanity, Grand Rapids Urban League, the Interurban Transit Partnership, and the Women's Resource Center. Heartwell explains that he began thinking about a run for mayor shortly after his 1995 city commission reelection. When John Logie announced he would seek a third term as mayor in 1999, Heartwell opted to forgo a challenge to the mayor he considered a friend and political ally on a number of key issues. But, Heartwell began planning his 2003 run for the office very early, lining up a lengthy list of supporters that was published in a *Grand Rapids Press* advertisement to launch his campaign. Heartwell's early entry into the race provided a tactical position from which the former commissioner prevented stronger opponents from entering the field.* Two opponents with little experience vied for the position, but Heartwell collected over 83 percent of the vote in the August primary election, forgoing the need for a November run-off election.† Heartwell collected over 50 percent of the vote in his August 2007 reelection bid.

---

* Term-limited Republican State Senator Glenn Steil briefly flirted with a bid for the office, but declined to run. City Commissioner Scott Bowen was another potentially strong opponent, but Bowen's interest in a judicial appointment from the governor kept him from entering the race.
† The uncompetitive campaign mustered a turnout of less than 13 percent of registered voters.

9.5.1 Policy Network-Based Facilitative Leadership

Heartwell engages the job of mayor by exercising both traditional and policy-oriented roles. Logie's visible public profile set high community expectations for the mayor's participation in traditional public mayoral roles. Heartwell fills traditional mayoral roles, but his interests and efforts are oriented to being a mayoral "director" for city policy (Svara and Associates 1994; Svara 2003). One of his greatest strengths is discerning unaddressed challenges in the community, articulating these problems publicly, and coordinating community resources to respond to these challenges. To achieve this, Heartwell sets out visible goals, initiates new policy, and incorporates community actors in goal setting and policy development.

The mayor explains his role in city policy making:

> As mayor, I understand my role, and I think others see me … as the vision bearer for the city. Because of the office, I represent and have the opportunity to speak to the direction that the city is going. Then my job, really, is to engage people around that vision, to fall in line, to follow, to work, to accomplish that vision …

Heartwell advances problems on the public agenda by building networks of participants to dialogue and problem solve. His efforts to bring together government and community resources around specific problems is consistent with collaborative management and metropolitan cooperation research that has identified significant collaboration and horizontal bargaining activity in metropolitan communities, with local officials working to establish partnerships with public and private-sector actors (cf. Agranoff and McGuire 1998; Thurmaier and Wood 2002; Visser 2002; Wood 2006). While Frederickson (1999) emphasizes the administrative role in multijurisdictional problem solving, mayors and elected officials have consistently been identified as participants in intergovernmental networks, though to varying degrees (Keller 1989; Sørensen 2006; Wright 1973). The council–manager system of government does not limit an elected official's capacity to act as a public entrepreneur or policy leader (Schneider, Teske, and Mintrom 1995; Wikstrom 1979).

In contrast to those who conceive of "regionalism" as a comprehensive agenda for metropolitan reform, Heartwell works to form networks and coalitions around specific issues. These networks draw a broader range of participants into city policy making and push the mayor's goals beyond the city's boarders and into private sector dialogue. For example, Heartwell discusses transportation policy goals in the context of the metropolitan area. In his second* 2004 State of the City address, he argued, "… the health of our economy, the well-being of our county's citizens, and the strength of the core city are integrally linked to quality public transportation services." His rhetoric on sustainability and education chime a similar note. On an

---

* Heartwell delivered two State of the City addresses in 2004.

issue-by-issue basis, Heartwell draws participants into coalitions to address policies that have implications for the core city, for the private sector, and for governments and residents in the wider metropolitan area.

Heartwell's effort to build participatory teams around the city's problems is exemplified by the transformation of the State of the City Address into a conference in which community members and stakeholders in specific problems participate in day-long conferences with working groups and policy discussion in addition to the mayor's address. In his first four years in office, Heartwell used these sessions to emphasize education, and environmental, economic, and social sustainability. While the mayor has limited time to address his priorities alone, he uses these conferences, as well as working groups, roundtables, special committees, and conferences to share ownership of public problems, expanding the number and diversity of participants in the policy formation and implementation process. By locating problems outside of the city government's traditional institutional structure, this model may also provide organizational resources and support that the city would not be able to muster alone in a time of budgetary stress.

The mayor's ability to forge inclusive policy links has limits. In conservative West Michigan, Heartwell's liberalism and social agenda may be consistent with a growing Democratic base in the city, but contributes to tensions in relations with the county government and conservative Republicans in the larger community. Logie was known for acting as a true nonpartisan in the nonpartisan office of mayor. Logie explains, "… local issues are just that, local issues." The former mayor backed both Republicans and Democrats for the state legislature, and worked with both parties when advocating for policy with state government. In contrast, Heartwell's Democratic Party loyalties are more transparent. As a candidate, Heartwell drew support from community leaders affiliated with both political parties; however, several observers suggest Heartwell's ideological positions may stand in the way of forging the countywide consensus he seeks on some issues. For example, before the 2006 election, the non-partisan mayor and city commissioners publicly endorsed a Democratic political newcomer for a seat on the Kent County board of commissioners against the incumbent Republican and Board Vice-Chair Dan Koorndyk. Some observers suggest this endorsement was a political gaffe for Heartwell, as city politicians deepened the fissure with the Republican-dominated county board. Heartwell will be challenged to foster bipartisan participation as he continues to advance his policy agenda.

9.5.2 Heartwell and Internal City Politics

The development of robust policy networks outside of City Hall is not fully mirrored by cohesive policy networks within City Hall. Heartwell emphasizes his responsibility to develop a vision for the city. The policy priorities he articulates are generated from his own study and through interaction with the public, not from city staff. "My priorities are my priorities. The city staff has more or less come together around those priorities," he explains. City manager Kimball and the mayor meet on a regular basis, including "big picture" lunches in which they take time to discuss the long-term threats and opportunities to the city. However, to advance policy priorities, Heartwell makes heavier use of the informal networks he creates outside of City Hall, rather than amassing more leadership capacity within City Hall. Kimball explains, "George likes to be on the forefront with important ideas that he wants to bring the public along with in terms of their thinking process." Heartwell engages the public in policy dialogue through task forces and citizen deliberation, which results in an "inclusive and participatory approach." At times this creates challenges for city staff. "It requires us to be nimble. We feel often like we're chasing twenty objectives at the same time."

Current and former city commissioners explain that Heartwell seeks their input and works to incorporate their priorities and concerns in policy. Kimball notes the mayor has also worked hard to share information about his priorities with the commission, citing sustainability goals as an example. However, some commissioners have been surprised by mayoral initiatives that receive attention from community members before consultation with the city commission. Policy advocacy in networks may lead to neglect of the traditional institutions of democratic representation (cf. Bogason and Musso 2004; Sørensen 2006). This theoretical observation directs us to critically inquire about the implications of facilitative mayoral leadership through external policy networks for mayoral interaction with the city commission. Heartwell recognizes that chairing the City Commission is "an important function." This is his principal duty under the city charter; however, he explains "I was surprised when I took office at how much is done, at how much I can get done, outside of the commission process. There's a lot that gets done that doesn't have to come to the commission that I can simply do." Heartwell's interest in developing participatory citizen coalitions around policy problems may direct his policymaking attention away from the city commission table.

At the same time, Heartwell's activist policy agenda is limited by the city's austere budgetary conditions. Kimball explains:

> Over the last several years, the debate has gotten a lot more vociferous and acrimonious. Part of it has to do with the changing nature of elected officials and their demand to be more involved. Part of it has to do with the last five years we have had a shrinking pie. So, you don't have resources to add new programs, which frustrates our current mayor a lot, too.

Heartwell's approach can result in a unique configuration of costs and benefits. Spawning new policy initiatives and networks of citizens to engage in deliberation stretches a city staff that is already short on resources. At the same time, by expanding interest in a policy problem beyond city hall, Heartwell gains the capacity to have external actors take ownership in his vision for the city, moving the initiatives forward, and diffusing goals like sustainability in the wider community.

9.6 Public Impact of the Heartwell Administration

What are the implications of Heartwell's facilitative style and network development for the development of public policy in Grand Rapids? Analysis of sustainability, education, and wastewater treatment policy help us understand how Heartwell employs a facilitative approach to address issues on his agenda, and problems that arise from the political environment. The case of wastewater treatment also demonstrates that adoption of a facilitative style does not guarantee success.

9.6.1 Sustainability

The concept of *sustainability* underlies many of Heartwell's initiatives. The mayor explains, "I've started largely organizing my thinking around the triple bottom line of environmental sustainability, social equity, and economic sustainability." In his 2007 State of the City Address, Heartwell highlighted the city's gains in all three categories. For example, in the environmental field, Heartwell noted the use of bio-diesel trucks, an 11 percent reduction in energy consumption in city facilities over the last three years, and progress toward goals in the use of renewable energy. The city has incented LEED (Leadership in Energy and Environmental Design) standards in the private sector, and all future municipal buildings will be built to LEED standards.*

How does facilitative leadership contribute to the achievement of sustainability goals in Grand Rapids? Numerous U.S. cities have undertaken sustainability initiatives (Portney 2003). Sustainability efforts can be consistent with the traditional goals of local governance. Organizing public affairs with attention to intergenerational impact, and reducing information asymmetries by incorporating citizen knowledge about the local environment complement traditional principles of public administration like equity and efficiency (Leuenberger 2006). Civic engagement is an important component of sustainability efforts (Agyeman and Angus 2003; Portney 2005). Heartwell and Grand Rapids policymakers recognize the imperative of public participation for sustainability success. City Hall is working to achieve sustainability goals internally. The city incorporated public participation on sustainability through its revised master-planning process. City goals span from diversifying modes of transportation and maintaining city parks and green spaces to reduced crime and support of downtown and neighborhood business (Grand Rapids 2006).

Externally, a network has formed to coordinate private and nonprofit sector efforts. The Community Sustainability Partners—a collaboration involving the

---

* According to the U.S. Green Building Council (www.usgbc.org), "The Leadership in Energy and Environmental Design (LEED) Green Building Rating System™ is the nationally accepted benchmark for the design, construction, and operation of high performance green buildings."

City of Grand Rapids, Grand Rapids Public Schools, Grand Rapids Community College, Grand Valley State University, and Aquinas College—are engaged "in a three-year planning, development, and implementation initiative to imbed sustainability best practices into the policies, procedures, and cultures of [their] respective organizations" (Bleke and Heartwell 2005). The Partnership does not belong to the city or Mayor Heartwell alone. Policy networks require participants to develop common perceptions of policy problems and negotiate collective policy goals (Kickert, Klijn, and Koppenjan 1997; Rhodes 1997). Sustainability has diffused as a goal in Grand Rapids, and the policy network includes an expanding number of actors.

Heartwell's facilitative style has helped to advance sustainability through his work to help structure, develop, and guide the agenda of intergovernmental and multisector networks. He can be credited for firmly imbedding sustainability on the community agenda and contributing to the expansion of the participants in the sustainability collaborative network. Don Stypula, executive director of the GVMC says Heartwell's sustainability goals were received "very positively" by the Metro Council. Heartwell outlined current conditions and goals for sustainability. Stypula explains the involvement of local universities, the private sector, and opinion leaders paved the way for Metro Council support. Heartwell's advocacy for sustainability, and the development of a broad, participatory constituency for sustainability goals, may be his most lasting impact on the city as mayor.

9.6.2 Education

Heartwell used his first State of the City Address in 2004 to foster expanded community support for education and the Grand Rapids Public Schools (GRPS). He explained:

> I have chosen today to speak about the interdependent relationship between the City of Grand Rapids and the Grand Rapids Public Schools, to propose new possibilities for partnership, to challenge citizens to engage individually in supporting a future of excellence for the public schools, and to call on all sectors of the community—business and labor, neighborhoods, colleges and universities—to join city government and a growing number of community partners in realizing a vision for educational excellence for all our children.

GRPS operate independently from city government, and are governed by an elected school board. The GRPS have experienced decreased enrollment and funding. Aging facilities, as well as challenges associated with teacher compensation and program cuts result in concerns about educational quality (Reister 2002). In his 2004 address, Heartwell highlighted that 40 percent of children in Grand Rapids attend private schools, signifying a lack of public support for the public school system. Relationships between the city and the school system have often been strained by disagreements about funding and bond proposals. But, Heartwell argues, "It was my determination that we should move in a different direction, we should try to find ways to work together rather than fight each other."

Setting his education agenda, Heartwell argued that the entire West Michigan region depends on the strength of the "core city being healthy." During our interview, Heartwell explained, "If you don't have a K-12 system that produces kids ready to assume roles and leadership in the economy of the future, then you've short-changed yourself as a community." His 2004 address outlined a three-part process to create new links between the city and the school district. These included a renewed focus on literacy, enhancing formal partnerships between governmental agencies, and the creation of an Education Renewal Zone.

Grand Rapids Community College President Juan Olivarez explains how Heartwell's State of the City set goals for literacy that rallied community participants. Olivarez explains, "… he set out a challenge, and he wanted to increase our literacy rates, he wanted to double that within ten years. So, he was very specific … about how do we close that gap and within what timeframe. So, that was very helpful and that kind of gave us the charge." How did Heartwell arrive at these goals? Olivarez explains that the mayor "is very astute" and has been listening to the community for a long time. "He gets perspectives; he gets ideas about how to move things forward and tries to incorporate them into what he thinks is possible and doable. He is listening." The mayor has rallied Grand Rapids city employees toward these goals as well, encouraging their volunteerism in a reading tutoring program.

One of the mayor's education initiatives has not yet been adopted. Heartwell called for the creation of an Education Renewal Zone, a tax increment authority to divert an increment of local property tax increases to GRPS. This proposal would require authorization by the state legislature. Heartwell has not had city commission support to advance the proposal. Current budgetary conditions for city government make consideration of the proposal difficult. The mayor explains, "Fifty percent of that increment today and redirecting it means fewer dollars available for public safety functions or parks and recreation services." But, the mayor awaits an opportunity to bring a coalition together for the proposal in the future. "It's a good piece of work whose time has not quite yet come."

9.6.3 Wastewater Treatment

The facilitative leadership approach has limitations. Time, political conditions, and the existing organization of public policy constrain and shape the potential for mayoral leadership (Flanagan 2004). The city of Grand Rapids experienced a protracted contract dispute with wastewater customer communities in northern Kent County. LaMore and Supanich-Goldner (2000) identify wastewater as a point of cooperation in the metropolitan area. The city of Grand Rapids successfully renegotiated wastewater treatment agreements with three neighboring cities and several inner-ring townships in the late 1990s. Linked to the wastewater agreement were provisions for growth management, an Urban Cooperation Agreement instituting revenue sharing for metropolitan projects, and a rate structure that resulted in higher costs for fast-growing communities more distant from the urban core. These provisions concerned the representatives of local governments in northern Kent County. These communities had already organized the North Kent Sewer Authority (NKSA) to work with the county government on the maintenance of wastewater treatment lines. This early collective action prepared the North Kent communities to negotiate with the City of Grand Rapids when the new wastewater treatment contract was proposed.

After receiving contract renewal details from the city of Grand Rapids, NKSA members began to study the feasibility of constructing their own wastewater treatment plant (Heibel 1999). Mayor Logie and the city administrators were central participants in contract negotiations between Grand Rapids and the NKSA. The cost formula for wastewater treatment was the primary point of conflict. Grand Rapids had little incentive to change the formula for the NKSA because the new contract had been adopted by other local units in the metropolitan area. GVMC Executive Director Don Stypula explains, "They were ... through the mechanism of pricing of sewage treatment services, trying to impact ... development patterns in the metropolitan area." What were the cost implications for the NKSA? NKSA Chairman Michael Young* explains, "This was an enormous cost shift ... .The cost of their new contract was more than building a $50 million wastewater treatment plant." Grand Rapids' efforts to tie land-use control to sewer rates were problematic. "The cost of wastewater should be the cost of wastewater. You pass that on to your residents as a legitimate cost," Young argues. An Urban Cooperation Agreement (UCA), which Grand Rapids required sewer customers to sign along with the wastewater contract, was one key problem. The UCA created a system of revenue sharing, which the city of Grand Rapids used to fund regional projects. Young notes NKSA members are willing to discuss regional issues, but those conversations should occur at the GVMC, not through a new Urban Cooperation Board created by the city of Grand Rapids.

After taking office as mayor, Heartwell pursued a new approach to deal with the NKSA. Several people interviewed for this project noted the significance of a meeting shortly after Heartwell's election in which he met with Young in his Rockford office, in contrast to previous meetings, which had been held in Grand Rapids. Heartwell made efforts to reach out, but the long-running conflict and the NKSA's process of planning their own wastewater treatment plant made the success of a last-minute facilitative intervention unlikely. Young explains:

> Mayor Heartwell is a gentleman; he listens; he went out of his way
> to try to work with us. As soon as he was elected he met with me ...
> Mayor Logie damaged the relationship so badly with our communities
> that I do not think anyone could ever get over that, and really created

---

* Young serves as the city manager of Rockford, Michigan, one of the NKSA member communities.

a feeling that we cannot trust Grand Rapids, right or wrong. And, so George Heartwell was saddled with that, and despite his best efforts, he wasn't going to overcome that.

The conjunction of distrust or negative perceptions of intergovernmental partners and negative economic terms for collaboration resulted in the failure of interlocal cooperation (Zeemering 2007). Officials from the NKSA began with concerns about the costs of the new sewer contract, and through extensive negotiation with an unshifting intergovernmental partner, developed skepticism about the potential for a revised contract.

What does this example mean for the practice of facilitative leadership?* Don Stypula explains, "That was an example where we had the best of intentions. George had his heart in the right place. But, just because of old wounds, old personalities, and conflicts, we couldn't bring them together." Experimental research shows that face-to-face communication and repeated interactions improve the potential for cooperation (Ostrom, Gardner, and Walker 1994; Ostrom and Walker 2003). Social networks can contribute to interlocal cooperation (Thurmaier and Wood 2002). This case suggests that an extended period of conflict cannot necessarily be resolved if a facilitative style is introduced late in the decision-making process. Facilitative leadership, with its emphasis on collaboration and sharing the policy-making process with multiple actors, may be important for interlocal cooperation because participants in the policy process feel their involvement is critical for achieving mutual success. Logie's pursuit of a strong Grand Rapids with innovative land-use controls through wastewater treatment rates may have failed because metropolitan partners like the NKSA did not feel included in a dialogue about wastewater and metropolitan land-use policies.

Contrasts exist in the approaches to intergovernmental relations used by Logie and Heartwell. The literature concerning collaborative public management provides some insight. A facilitative leadership approach might seem necessary to achieve success through the development of metropolitan-wide policy networks. However, McGuire (2006; 2003) notes that at times the skills associated with hierarchical management can be employed in network management. We suggest that Logie and Heartwell illustrate these differences. Both have had success in intergovernmental relations using different models of mayoral leadership. Logie was more

---

* For the practice of public policy in Grand Rapids, several local policymakers noted that the failure of cooperation in wastewater should not be belabored, and officials should look toward new areas of common ground. Failed collaboration in wastewater does not mean local governments in the Grand Rapids metropolitan area cannot find common ground on other issues. On a metropolitan-wide basis, the GVMC is a venue for bridging communities and fostering positive interactions. Michael Young reports that the development of the NKSA has led to cooperative interactions in policy areas outside of wastewater treatment for members of the NKSA. The Grand Rapids area exemplifies many areas of active or latent interlocal and metropolitan cooperation.

inclined to bring together peak associations in which the city or mayor exercised a dominant leadership role. Heartwell, in contrast, tends to encourage the formation of networks around policy problems. Additionally, Heartwell is inclined to introduce new problems onto the community's agenda and encourage policy networks outside of the city's direct control to plan and implement solutions. Heartwell's network-building process may take longer to achieve results than more hierarchically formulated plans. His emphasis on and attention to the city's educational needs is one example. He has not achieved his goal of education renewal zones, but has successfully rallied the community around literacy and education goals. A facilitative approach to mayoral leadership and network building may be valuable due to its power to include a broad spectrum of actors in community problem solving.

9.6.4 Contrasting Policy Priorities for Logie and Heartwell

Stylistic differences between John Logie and George Heartwell are apparent, but do differences in two individuals' approach to the job of mayor result in differences in public attention to policy priorities for city government? Wolman, Strate, and Melchior (1996), analyzing city expenditure data, find that changing a mayor can have implications for city policy priorities, even in council–manager systems of government. A content analysis of *Grand Rapids Press* coverage mentioning policy activity by the Grand Rapids mayor allows us to compare Logie's last year in office (2003) and Heartwell's first year in office (2004).* Figure 9.1 shows the number of newspaper articles that mention the mayor in association with ten different policy categories.

The mayor's agenda and activity is shaped both by his own initiatives and by the political context in which he operates. While Logie received more coverage for economic development and planning activities, *The Grand Rapids Press* covers both mayors heavily in this area. Heartwell's education initiative during his first year in office garnered attention at a level significantly different than his predecessor. This indicates Heartwell was successful at directing media and public attention to his policy goals.

During his first year in office, Heartwell and the city commission faced controversy about whether or not to rename a city street after Martin Luther King, Jr. Heartwell supported the initiative, but commission members expressed concern about renaming streets and changing residents' addresses. After the city commission voted against the renaming, Heartwell appointed a Civil Rights Recognition Commission to recommend strategies to heal community divisions (Harger 2004).

---

* For our coding, we excluded editorials, letters to the editor, and community calendar announcements. In 2003, *The Grand Rapids Press* printed 212 articles mentioning Mayor Logie. For an intercoder reliability check, both authors coded just over 30 percent of the articles mentioning Logie. For the policy variable, intercoder reliability is 87.7 percent. In 2004, there were 239 articles mentioning Mayor Heartwell. For an intercoder reliability check, both authors coded just over 28 percent of the articles mentioning Heartwell. For the policy variable, intercoder reliability is 95.8 percent.

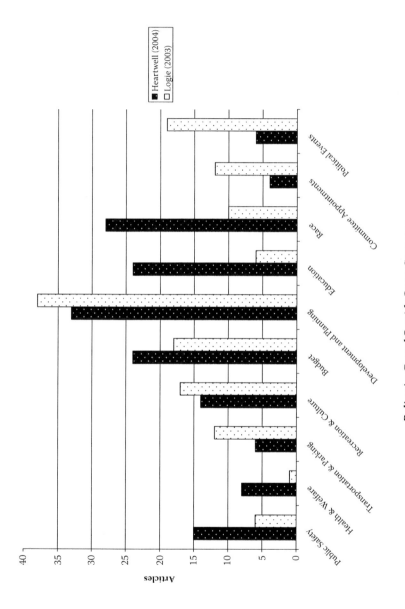

Figure 9.1 Policy in *Grand Rapids Press* coverage.

Confronted with a new challenge in the political environment, the mayor built a new group for policy dialogue and advice, consistent with his network approach to governance. Heartwell engaged the issue and developed a participatory strategy, but did not work extensively with opponents on the city commission. Later in the year, the city commission approved a commemorative designation for King on Division Avenue, one of the city's major roadways.

Adopting a facilitative leadership approach that uses networks of actors across the public and private sector does not grant a mayor greater control over events that develop in a city's political environment; however, these examples suggest developing a network of policy supporters has given Heartwell the opportunity to advance his own initiatives *and* address new challenges. Heartwell pursues somewhat different policy priorities than his predecessor, and he articulates a clear vision for the city and enlists participants inside and outside of government to achieve his goals.

9.7 Facilitative Leadership and Policy-Based Intergovernmental Relations

"I recognize that on my own, I am not going to get as much done as I can get by bringing others to the table," explains Heartwell. The part-time nature of the mayor's office in Grand Rapids limits the time that Heartwell can contribute to public policy, but the development of active policy networks around key priorities allows the mayor to exercise policy leadership. Those involved in public affairs in Grand Rapids describe Heartwell as a consensus builder who brings many community voices to the policy-making table. City Manager Kurt Kimball summarizes the mayor's approach to leadership:

> George Heartwell is a very conciliatory man, generally. He is anxious to listen to all voices and to invite all manner of points of view on a subject. By definition, it enables him to receive a broad spectrum of perspective on things. If the audience thinks you're listening, and if you listen first and talk later, as Mayor Heartwell has a tendency to do, I think it makes him a legitimate player and better empowers him to exercise facilitative leadership.

Heartwell relies on the city manager and staff to execute policy, but emphasizes that the mayor is responsible for crafting and sharing a vision for the city. The "bully pulpit" allows Rev. Heartwell to direct the community's attention to some goals, like social sustainability, that had not been high on the agenda before his election. The local political and fiscal context can limit the viability of this strategy in some areas. The city's financial needs trumped Heartwell's Education Renewal Zone proposal to direct resources to the school system. The previously strained relationship with the NKSA could not be redeemed by a new mayor with a new style.

Heartwell and former Mayor John Logie have approached the job of mayor with different leadership skills. Content analysis of *Grand Rapids Press* articles showed coverage of the two leaders emphasizes similar involvement in areas like economic development, but Heartwell directed new energy to education during his first year in office. Both Logie and Heartwell exemplify mayors who work as policy directors to advance Grand Rapids. Heartwell believes that the failures and successes of the city of Grand Rapids are crucial for the rest of West Michigan. "I see Grand Rapids as the strong commercial center for the region—the center that holds the region in some kind of equilibrium. If the center falls apart, then in progressive waves, the region deteriorates..." Described as "trustworthy" and "pastoral," Heartwell draws participants around his vision for the city, advancing social equity, education, and sustainability to build a stronger core city. Heartwell's performance as mayor illustrates the use of policy networks to share mayoral vision and priorities, while expanding our understanding of facilitative leadership.

9.8 List of Interviews Cited in Text[*]

Rev. Robert Dean, former Grand Rapids city commissioner	November 2, 2006
Rev. George Heartwell, mayor, Grand Rapids	September 15, 2006
Kurt Kimball, city manager, Grand Rapids	October 16, 2006
John Logie, former mayor, Grand Rapids	October 17, 2006
Dr. Juan Olivarez, president, Grand Rapids Community College	January 18, 2007
Lynn Rabaut, former Grand Rapids city commissioner	October 18, 2006
Roy Schmidt, Grand Rapids city commissioner	February 28, 2007
Don Stypula, executive director, Grand Valley Metropolitan Council	October 12, 2006
Dr. Bernard Taylor, superintendent, Grand Rapids Public Schools	March 21, 2007
Rick Tormala, city commissioner	January 17, 2007
Michael Young, chairman, North Kent Sewer Authority	October 13, 2006

[*] Additional sources were interviewed anonymously and not for attribution.

References

Agranoff, Robert and Michael McGuire. 1998. A jurisdiction-based model of intergovernmental management in U.S. cities. *Publius: The Journal of Federalism* 28 (4): 1.

Agyeman, Julian and Briony Angus. 2003. The role of civic environmentalism in the pursuit of sustainable communities. *Journal of Environmental Planning and Management* 46 (3): 345–363.

Bleke, Bert and George Heartwell. 2005. Memorandum: Charge and outline for our joint work: Community Sustainability Partnership, City of Grand Rapids.

Bogason, Peter and Juliet A. Musso. 2004. The democratic prospects of network governance. *American Review of Public Administration* 36 (1): 3–18.

Browne, William Paul and Kenneth VerBurg. 1995. *Michigan Politics and Government: Facing Change in a Complex State*. Lincoln, NE: University of Nebraska Press.

Czurak, David. 2001. Amount of downtown office space grows. *Grand Rapids Business Journal*, June 4, 2001, B10.

Dexter, Lewis Anthony. 1970. *Elite and Specialized Interviewing*. Evanston, IL: Northwestern University Press.

Flanagan, Richard M. 2004. Opportunities and constraints on mayoral behavior: A historical-institutional approach. *Journal of Urban Affairs* 26 (1): 43–65.

Frederickson, H. George. 1999. The repositioning of American public administration. *PS: Political Science & Politics* 32 (4): 701–711.

Frederickson, H. George, Gary A. Johnson, and Curtis H. Wood. 2004. *The Adapted City: Institutional Dynamics and Structural Change*. Armonk, NY: M. E. Sharpe.

George, Alexander L. and Andrew Bennett. 2005. *Case Studies and Theory Development in the Social Sciences*. Cambridge, MA: MIT Press.

Grand Rapids, City of. 2006. City of Grand Rapids: Sustainability vision statement, 2006–2010.

Grand Rapids Press. 2002. A full-time debate for city. *The Grand Rapids Press*, July 15, 2002, A8.

Grand Rapids Press. 2003. Honoring hizzoner; Hard work, a downtown rebirth marked Logie's years at the helm. *The Grand Rapids Press*, December 22, 2003, A10.

Grand Rapids Press. 2006. Downtown condo project under way or in the works. *The Grand Rapids Press*, April 7, 2006, C1.

Harger, Jim. 2002a. Beefed-up mayor lacked support first time around. *The Grand Rapids Press*, February 1, 2002, D3.

Harger, Jim. 2002b. Logie cash backs mayor plan;: Opponents of the full-time mayor proposal get a boost when the Chamber of Commerce says no to the amendment. *The Grand Rapids Press*, October 8, 2002, A1.

Harger, Jim. 2002c. Logie lobbies for stronger powers in mayor's office. *The Grand Rapids Press*, January 31, 2002, A21.

Harger, Jim. 2002d. Logie lobbies for stronger powers in mayor's office; He calls for a charter amendment to make the Grand Rapids post a full-time job. *The Grand Rapids Press*, January 31, 2002, A21.

Harger, Jim. 2002e. Logie won't seek re-election. *The Grand Rapids Press*, July 9, 2002, A1.

Harger, Jim. 2002f. Workers' union opposes charter change. *The Grand Rapids Press*, October 14, 2002, D4.

Harger, Jim. 2003. Logie testimonial touts landmarks, starts scholarship. *The Grand Rapids Press*, November 14, 2003, D1.

Harger, Jim. 2004. Heartwell looks for healing with rights panel. *The Grand Rapids Press*, June 2, 2004, B8.

Harger, Jim and Barton Deiters. 2002. Concessions may put mayor's powers on ballot. *The Grand Rapids Press*, July 7, 2002, A19.

Heibel, Lawrence R. 1999. Five communities mull building a sewer treatment plant. *The Grand Rapids Press*, February 11, 1999, 5.

Keller, Lawrence F. 1989. City managers and federalism: Intergovernmental relations in the administrative city. In *Ideal and Practice in Council–Manager Government*, ed. H.G. Frederickson. Washington, DC: International City/County Management Association.

Kickert, Walter J.M., Erik-Hans Klijn, and Joop F.M. Koppenjan, eds. 1997. *Managing Complex Networks: Strategies for the Public Sector*. London: Sage Publications.

Kleiman, Jeffrey D. 2006. *Strike! How the Furniture Workers Strike of 1911 Changed Grand Rapids*. Grand Rapids, MI: Grand Rapids Historical Commission.

Knape, Chris. 2006. Energy, economy roar in shadows; Arena has spurred tens of millions in investment, development downtown. *Grand Rapids Press*, October 3, 2006, A1.

Krippendorff, Klaus. 1980. *Content Analysis: An Introduction to its Methodology*. Newbury Park, CA: Sage Publications.

LaMore, Rex L. and Faron Supanich-Goldner. 2000. John Logie and intergovernmental relations in Grand Rapids, Michigan. In *Governing Middle-Sized Cities: Studies in Mayoral Leadership*, eds. J.R. Bowers and W.C. Rich. Boulder, CO: Lynne Rieneer Publishers.

Leech, Beth L. 2002. Asking questions: Techniques for semistructured interviews. *PS: Political Science & Politics* 35 (4): 665–668.

Leuenberger, Deniz. 2006. Sustainable development in public administration: A match with practice? *Public Works Management & Policy* 10 (3): 195–201.

Longcore, Kathleen. 2004. Spectrum scrambles to fill 1,000 new jobs. *The Grand Rapids Press*, June 15, 2004, D1.

McGuire, Michael. 2003. Is it really so strange? A critical look at the "Network management is different from hierarchical management" perspective. Paper read at the seventh national public management research conference, October 9–11, 2003, Washington, D.C.

McGuire, Michael. 2006. Collaborative public management: Assessing what we know and how we know it. *Public Administration Review* 66 (Special): 33–43.

Munck, Gerardo L. 2004. Tools for qualitative research. In *Rethinking Social Inquiry: Diverse Tools, Shared Standards*, eds. H.E. Brady and D. Collier. Lanham, MD: Rowman & Littlefield.

Nasser, Haya El. 2006. Mich. pulling itself out of slump. *USA Today*, April 25, 2006, A3.

Oakerson, Ronald J. 1999. *Governing Local Public Economies: Creating the Civic Metropolis*. Oakland, CA: ICS Press.

Olson, Gordon. 1981. *Grand Rapids, Past, Present and Future*. Grand Rapids, MI: Urban Concern, Inc.

Orfield, Myron. 1999. *Grand Rapids Area Metropolitics: A West Michigan Agenda for Community and Stability*. Grand Rapids, MI: Grand Valley Metropolitan Council.

Ostrom, Elinor, Roy Gardner, and James Walker. 1994. *Rules, Games, and Common-Pool Resources*. Ann Arbor: University of Michigan Press.

Ostrom, Elinor and James Walker. 2003. *Trust and Reciprocity: Interdisciplinary Lessons from Experimental Research*. New York: Russell Sage Foundation.

Portney, Kent E. 2003. *Taking Sustainable Cities Seriously: Economic Development, the Environment, and Quality of Life in American Cities*. Cambridge, MA: MIT Press.

Portney, Kent E. 2005. Civic engagement and sustainable cities in the United States. *Public Administration Review* 65 (5): 579–591.

Radigan, Mary. 2006. Health-care industry spurs economic growth in area. *The Grand Rapids Press*, January 14, 2006, B1.

Reister, Cami. 2002. City schools get 'C' in poll. *The Grand Rapids Press*, August 16, 2002, A1.

Renando, Warren D. 2002. Don't tinker with mayor-manager setup. *The Grand Rapids Press*, October 17, 2006, A21.

Rhodes, R.A.W. 1997. *Understanding Governance: Policy Networks, Governance, Reflexivity and Accountability.* Buckingham, U.K.: Open University Press.

Schellenbarger, Pat. 2005. The Sunday profile: George and Susan Heartwell, Grand Rapids' first couple; soul mates of the city. *The Grand Rapids Press*, April 10, 2005, J1.

Schneider, Mark, Paul Teske, and Michael Mintrom. 1995. *Public Entrepreneurs: Agents for Change in American Government.* Princeton, NJ: Princeton University Press.

Sørensen, Eva. 2006. Metagovernance: The changing role of politicians in processes of democratic governance. *American Review of Public Administration* 36 (1): 98–114.

Stephens, G. Ross. 1989. The least glorious, most local, most trivial, homely, provincial, and most ignored form of local government. *Urban Affairs Quarterly* 24 (4): 501–512.

Svara, James H. and Associates. 1994. *Facilitative Leadership in Local Government: Lessons from Successful Mayors and Chairpersons.* San Francisco: Jossey-Bass.

Svara, James H. 2003. Effective mayoral leadership in council–manager cities: Reassessing the facilitative model. *National Civic Review* 92 (2): 157–172.

Thurmaier, Kurt and Curtis Wood. 2002. Interlocal agreements as overlapping social network: Picket-fence regionalism in metropolitan Kansas City. *Public Administration Review* 62 (5): 585–598.

Thurmaier, Kurt and Curtis Wood. 2004. Interlocal agreements as an alternative to consolidation. In *City/County Consolidation and Its Alternatives: Reshaping the Local Government Landscape*, eds. J.B. Carr and R.C. Feiock. Armonk, NY: M.E. Sharpe.

Tiebout, Charles M. 1956. A pure theory of local expenditures. *Journal of Political Economy* 64 (5): 416–424.

Visser, James A. 2002. Understanding local government cooperation in urban regions: Toward a cultural model of interlocal relations. *American Review of Public Administration* 32 (1): 40–65.

Visser, James A. 2004. Voluntary regional councils and the new regionalism: Effective governance in the smaller metropolis. *Journal of Planning Education and Research* 24: 51–63.

Wikstrom, Nelson. 1979. The mayor as a policy leader in the council–manager form of government: A view from the field. *Public Administration Review* 39 (3): 270–276.

Wolman, Harold, John Strate, and Alan Melchior. 1996. Does changing mayors matter? *Journal of Politics* 58 (1): 201–223.

Wood, Curtis. 2006. Scope and patterns of metropolitan governance in urban America: Probing the complexities in the Kansas City region. *American Review of Public Administration* 36 (3): 337–353.

Wright, Deil S. 1973. Intergovernmental relations in large council–manager cities. *American Politics Quarterly* 1 (2): 151–188.

Zainea, Joe. 2002. No reason to change city charter. *The Grand Rapids Press*, October 26, 2002, A17.

Zeemering, Eric S. 2007. Who collaborates? Local decisions about intergovernmental relations. PhD diss., Indiana Univ.

Chapter 10

From Conflict to Cooperation: Auburn, Alabama

Wendy L. Hassett

Contents

10.1 Introduction

The year was 1836. Judge John Jackson Harper and his eleven children were among the first to settle in what is now Auburn, Alabama. Those early settlers quickly went to work constructing homes and buildings. In 1839, the Alabama legislature approved the incorporation of Auburn as a town of 1,280 acres (Logue and Simms 1996). Since that time, Auburn has enjoyed a rich history inextricably tied to and influenced by the presence of Auburn University, located in the heart of the city and adjacent to the downtown.

Auburn is located along the Interstate 85 corridor in east central Alabama at the junction of the Piedmont Plateau and the Coastal Plains. It is forty miles southwest of Columbus, Georgia, sixty miles northeast of Montgomery, Alabama, and one hundred fifteen miles southwest of Atlanta, Georgia. Since the 1960 census, Auburn has grown from a population of 16,260 to 42,987 in 2000. The historical growth experienced by the city of Auburn during the 1960s and 1970s was largely attributable to the presence of Auburn University. During this growth period, the city of Auburn was challenged to provide public services and infrastructure to adequately meet the needs of a growing community. This growth brought with it not only an increasingly diverse mix of new residents comprised largely of university faculty, staff, and students, but also an increase in economic diversity. In the mid-1970s, Auburn established an industrial development board to lure the location of industrial manufacturing facilities. Also during the 1970s, Auburn's first shopping mall was constructed, making the city a regional retail destination. Leading a community through these kinds of growing pains is not a simple task. As a result, most elected officials faced with similar potentially divisive issues rarely serve multiple terms. However, that was not the case with the individual featured in this chapter.

Jan Miles Dempsey served as the mayor of Auburn for eighteen years (1980 to 1998).* Throughout that lengthy mayoral term, municipal election results consistently demonstrated strong constituent support, as seen in the following list:

> Won 1980 election—(five candidates) with 46.4 percent of the votes
> Won 1984 election—(five candidates) with 64.5 percent of the votes
> Won 1986 election—(two candidates) with 71.5 percent of the votes
> Won 1990 election—(two candidates) with 70.1 percent of the votes
> Won 1994 election—(three candidates) with 60.2 percent of the votes

While serving as mayor of Auburn, she became as much of a tradition as a politician. For many young Auburn residents, Jan Dempsey was the only mayor they had ever known. The *Auburn-Opelika News* recounted a true story that illustrates this point:

---

* There are no term limits on the Auburn city council. Jan Miles Dempsey chose not to run for mayor in the 1998 election in order to seek a higher public office at the state level.

While explaining the workings of civic government to a group of fourth graders at Dean Road Elementary School, Mayor Dempsey asked a little boy what he wanted to be when he grew up. Just as he began to express his desire to one day run for mayor, a little girl jumped to her feet and proclaimed, "You can't be the mayor! You're a boy!" (Buckner 1998).

In a state that is commonly associated with "good ol' boy" politics, Mayor Jan Dempsey brought with her a new perspective on leadership, good government, and a vision for a promising future for what was, by many accounts, a sleepy college town in the early 1980s.

10.2 The Setting

Jan Dempsey moved to Auburn in 1972 with her husband, a general and vascular surgeon, and three young children. Soon after arriving in Auburn, she joined a local church and became involved in its community ministry programs. She also became active in the PTA, which ignited a deep-seated commitment to the Auburn city school system.

Not long after she became involved in the community, she began to recognize that the local government was not functioning effectively. She was not alone in this perception. Many residents in the community at that time questioned who was in charge at city hall.

By most accounts, conflict characterized most of the workings of the local government, evidenced by 5 to 4 votes on a majority of the issues that came before the council. The general sense among the citizenry was that the local government was a barrier rather than a partner in efforts to improve the city. Ultimately, the city manager became a target for much criticism. Over time, a vocal faction grew that wanted the city manager fired, a desire that surfaced again during the 1976 election. While the mayor elected in 1976 advocated making a personnel change in the city manager position, he was unsuccessful in doing so before the end of his term. As a result, the issue of replacing the city manager resurfaced again as a campaign issue.

During the years prior to the 1980 election, the city manager and the mayor spoke only on very rare occasions and divisive community issues packed large public venues. Long-time resident and former Auburn University professor Gerald Johnson (2006) recalled that during that time of Auburn's past, there was "no vision" and that "turmoil" characterized the local government. Ironically, this was also a time when Auburn University and the city were experiencing significant growth. However, instead of enjoying cooperation and coordination, which are so important during times of growth, the city was a "boiling pot."

Among the Auburn community there was a yearning for something different. The approach the city had used in the past was simply not working and had not worked for years. The political environment at the time was "the perfect storm for new leadership" because there was a general desire on the part of the community to do things differently (Johnson 2006). A new approach to managing the business of the city was needed.

10.3 The Mayoral Race

Organizationally in 1980, the mayor was elected at-large, but was not a member of the city council. A council president presided over the council meetings. Because there was no provision in Alabama law at the time to adopt the pure council–manager plan, Auburn had used a system since 1958 allowed by state law where it hired a city manager who worked for the council president and the other eight members. However, the mayor was not on the council and had no administrative authority. Despite this arrangement, Auburn had a history of influential mayors, including Jim Haygood who served from 1968 to 1976.

In 1980, Jan Dempsey was considered a relative newcomer to the area. She co-owned a local retail business and was mother to three children aged 8, 10, and 12. In spite of these responsibilities, she also cared deeply about the future of Auburn and felt that if elected mayor she would be able to make a positive impact on the city. Former Auburn mayor Jim Haygood (2006) commented on Dempsey's motivation to seek office: "Jan was not beholden to any segment of the community. She was unfettered by influences that could have skewed her judgment and credibility with Auburn citizens."

Retired professor Gerald Johnson did not know Dempsey before she ran for mayor. In fact, he said many at that time did not know her. He supported Dempsey for mayor because he saw in her "the absence of conflict." He said, "She was and remains an energetic woman who has a presence that conveys confidence, stability, and has a no-nonsense approach to things. These characteristics appealed to a vast majority of citizens who had seen a lot of nonsense at city hall" (Johnson 2006). Former councilwoman and Auburn University faculty member Charlotte Ward also supported Dempsey for mayor. Interestingly, Ward favored Dempsey over one of her personal friends who also ran for mayor that year. Ward (2006) said the reason for her choice was that Dempsey could "just get people to do things and had a vision for what Auburn could become."

Auburn native and prominent businessman Ed Lee Spencer (2006) recalled, "Jan was not afraid to enter the fray. She welcomed the challenge of the political arena. She was opinionated, determined, and had good ideas." When Dempsey approached former mayor Jim Haygood and asked his opinion about her running for the office of mayor, he recalled that although he felt that Jan *could* do the job, he did not think Auburn was ready for a female mayor at that time (Haygood 2006). And, at that time, none of the cities the size of Auburn had a female mayor. In fact, for more than a decade of her tenure as mayor, Dempsey was the only female mayor in Alabama in a city with a population of more than 30,000.

Five individuals ran for mayor in the 1980 election, including Dempsey. Prior to her candidacy, she determined that the existing situation at city hall was non-functioning. In response, she devised a number of goals that she shared with anyone who would listen. Dempsey spent about $900 on her campaign, which consisted of going door to door, handing out campaign cards, and introducing herself to the community one person at a time. Her goals were straightforward. First, she wanted to guarantee local financial support of the local school system. Her passion for quality education was one of the key reasons she chose to run for mayor. Second, she felt that long-range planning was essential for Auburn to become the community it could become. Third, she supported an entirely new approach to development. She strongly felt that the development occurring in Auburn at that time was not well-conceived. Fourth, she strongly felt that there needed to be a new atmosphere at city hall that encouraged cooperation instead of the conflict that existed at that time. Finally, she wanted Auburn's city government to be synonymous with "good government" in order for it to serve as a catalyst for positive change as Auburn continued to grow.

Of all the candidates for mayor in the 1980 election, Dempsey received the highest number of votes (46.4 percent). The individual who received the next highest percentage of the vote later withdrew, causing Dempsey to be declared mayor without a run-off. In the months following Dempsey being sworn in as Auburn's mayor, she observed the work of the local government from a new perspective. As mayor, Dempsey deeply felt that she had a mandate from the citizens to make significant changes in how things were being done in city hall. She approached the business of the city as a part of a team, never focusing on what she could not or should not do, but instead serving as a political leader and advocating significant policy changes that were in line with the goals she advocated in her campaign. Dempsey (2006) commented on her approach at that time, "I knew the community was with me. So, it was a matter of strongly believing in what you were proposing and getting it done."

10.4 Serving as Mayor

As mayor, Dempsey held herself to certain standards: she was always well-prepared; she was glad to listen to opposing points of view; she looked for consensus, but realized unanimity was not necessary to move forward; and she was a strong and active communicator. Former mayor Haygood (2006) commented, "Jan certainly brought a new dimension to city government."

Retired professor Gerald Johnson (2006) stated, "It quickly became evident that the newly elected mayor was competent, honest, and committed. Then what emerged was that Jan had ideas and a vision. Her vision had to do with a better Auburn rooted in community values, aesthetic values, and a sense of fairness." Looking back on the Dempsey era, long-time observer of city affairs Ruth Wright (2006) stated, "I never believed she acted on behalf of any personal or financial interest of her own or that of any friends. The concept of 'the common good' is rarely discussed in these polarized days, but I believe she had a vision of what it was and how to achieve it in Auburn."

Even though the position of mayor at that time was not officially a part of the council and carried with it no administrative authority, Dempsey did not let that stop her from influencing the council members to see issues from her perspective and take action. In fact, at that time, the mayor did not physically sit on the dais during the council meeting. Instead, she, like the mayors before her, sat in the audience. There was, however, a place on the council agendas for "Mayor's Communications" where the mayor publicly addressed the council.

One thing Dempsey sought to change immediately was to tap into the talent and education that was present in the community, but was not being used to improve the community. As home to Auburn University, the city was home to educated professors and skilled consultants. Unfortunately, many of these talented professionals did not want to be a part of Auburn's citizen advisory boards and commissions.

According to many long-time residents, there existed a vast town-and-gown divide in the community at that time. As a result, most municipal boards were nonfunctioning. Dempsey was determined to get talented and capable individuals to serve on these boards. Her proactive approach was to identify qualified and talented individuals and simply tell them that she was appointing them to a board. If they did not want to serve, she was known to say that they could tell the local news reporters in the morning why they refused to serve. Her direct approach worked and, as a result, Dempsey quickly enhanced the talent, creativity, and capability of the city's citizen boards and commissions. Gerald Johnson (2006) spoke to Dempsey's approach to attract the active involvement of the community residents who had not been involved in the past: "Jan knows that people are more apt to perform if they know what is expected. She would meet with people and get them to serve on boards. People like to be asked to do something important and be a part of something good. Her style was to bring people in and follow up with them to find out what is going on and stay informed. Jan has personal confidence. She is not threatened by capable people. She *wants* to have capable people around her."

Another of her main priorities was to make changes to how the city was run. She quickly began urging the council to take steps that she felt needed to be taken in regard to the management of the city. Following a meeting she had with the city council where she expressed her dissatisfaction with the approach to the management of the city at that time, the city manager had a heart attack. While he was recovering in the hospital, Dempsey became a permanent fixture at city hall. Johnson (2006) commented that she quickly became the "Margaret Thatcher of Auburn city government." During this period, a number of administrative changes occurred.

Not long after the city manager returned to office in the summer of 1982, he resigned. As a result, the city had the opportunity to hire a new city manager. Thinking back on the search for the new city manager, former councilwoman Charlotte Ward (2006) said that it was "apparent to most on the city council that the city needed new ideas and should look for someone who was receptive to change" in order to be successful with the new city council and mayor.

10.4.1 City Management

A national search began immediately for a new city manager, with approximately one hundred fifty applications being submitted. Three finalists were interviewed. Dempsey was specifically looking for a record of good government, a proactive management style, proven management skills, a creative thinker, an academic background, an overall approach to problem solving that was research-based and thoughtful.

At the end of the interview process, Douglas J. Watson was selected as Auburn's next city manager. Dempsey recalled that she saw in Watson an intellectual and scholarly ability that she appreciated and felt was desperately lacking in the local government of that day. He also had a demeanor that she felt would work well in the civic culture and organizational environment at that time. She said she was not apprehensive at all about hiring Watson. In her words, they just "clicked." Former mayor Jim Haygood (2006) agreed that Watson was the right person for the position. He stated that it was made evident as Watson "assembled a cadre of real professionals to serve as department heads."

Watson began work in August 1982. And, once in place, he immediately began to take control of the inner workings of the city government, freeing Dempsey to operate outside the walls of city hall and advocate the many civic-minded projects she was determined to see come to fruition.

Watson (2006) recalled the situation when he began working as city manager in Auburn:

> When I arrived in 1982, the council with Jan's urging, had forced into retirement my predecessor who had been city manager for eight years. He was a retired army colonel who never quite got over his military approach to city management. He was very unpopular with the business community, which referred to city hall as *Fort Auburn*. He had hired some of his army buddies and placed them in key positions even though they were not qualified. He had been under heavy attack during the four years prior to Jan and had a 5 to 4 majority on council for the whole time.
>
> A local businessman had just been elected as president of the council in August 1982. He had three other councilors elected that year who were in opposition to Jan—one who died in office, one who later came around although he ran against Jan for mayor later, and one who quit the council because he could not control his temper.
>
> There were staggered term elections at that time, so you basically had the five incumbents versus the four newly elected councilors. Jan sided with the five who had been on the council.

Former city manager Watson (2006) commented on the mayor–manager relationship when he worked with Dempsey: "Jan was an effective leader of the council in that she stayed in touch with all of the council members on a regular basis. She and I talked practically every day about what was going on. She was well-informed. Once she was on board with an idea, she was a powerful ally with the council because she was passionate about what she believed in." Looking back on her working relationship with the city manager, Dempsey said, "It really operated as a model council–manager form of government. In many ways, the roles just 'fit' our personalities. Doug didn't need to worry about council and board members intruding on administrative matters because I protected him and the staff from political daggers." This effective relationship was seen by community leaders as well. Former mayor Haygood (2006) commented, "The city council left Doug alone because Jan kept the city council at bay. She was quite protective of Doug's role. If Jan saw someone meddling, she was in your face." Ruth Wright (2006) commented on the form of government while Dempsey was mayor: "The council–manager form of government seems to me to have reached its peak in Auburn when Dempsey and Watson operated almost as co-equals, who both disputed and agreed."

On November 9, 1983, a question was placed on the ballot to accomplish three things in regard to the Auburn city government. First, it proposed to make the city council terms concurrent. (Terms were staggered at that time, but they were concurrent prior to October 1976). Second, it eliminated the position of council president. Third, it made the mayor an official member and the presiding officer of the city council. These changes were approved by the voters and all three changes became effective in October 1986.

During Dempsey's first two years in office, she brought order to the city largely by being a strong advocate for the formalization of the council–manager form of government and creating the environment for Watson's hiring as city manager in 1982. Watson enjoyed an unusually long tenure at the city lasting more than two decades. In her role as mayor, Dempsey understood and appreciated the professionalism, wisdom, and knowledge that the city manager brought to the organization. This appreciation led her to develop a successful and trusting working relationship with Watson and she highly valued his involvement in all aspects of the policy process. For example, in a speech to the Auburn Chamber of Commerce in 1990 updating the members on the city's growth, Dempsey first credited the professional management of the city as a key factor in Auburn's success and growth (Thomaston 1990).

While Dempsey clearly understood (and enjoyed) her ceremonial and political role as mayor in a council–manager city, she spent much more time at city hall than her part-time position required. In addition to closely aligning herself with the city manager, she also invested time in developing relationships with key staff members in order to create a team approach to idea generation and the planning of city projects, all the while honoring the legal limits of council–manager government in terms of administrative intrusion.

The accomplishments of Dempsey in this arena contributed greatly to institutionalizing the effective functioning of council–manager government in Auburn. Subsequently, the stability and credibility of the local government set the stage for securing broad community support for a number of innovative initiatives that would be set in motion during the Dempsey years.

While many significant accomplishments were realized during Dempsey's eighteen years as mayor, three key policy issues were addressed and given a fresh direction under her leadership.

10.4.2 Long-Range Community Visioning

From Dempsey's vantage point, much of what ailed the city of Auburn could be cured with a long-range plan. She realized that a community vision was desperately needed to direct the future of the city. The city was ready for "something"; however, up to that time, no one had proposed what that "something" might be. Early in her term of office, she learned about a large metropolitan city undertaking a long-range plan to lay out the city's future goals through the year 2000. Instinctively she recognized, "This is what Auburn, Alabama, needs to do."

Dempsey had a vision for a better Auburn before she even decided to run for office. She also knew that coming into a contentious situation like Auburn's, she had no choice but to visibly and vigorously gain the trust and support of the community to overcome the status quo. She strongly felt that a long-range planning process was the method by which a common vision could be created. In her mind, only a comprehensive, grassroots approach to improving the community that involved all stakeholders in the community could turn the city around in a new direction and allow Auburn to be the model community that Dempsey knew it could be. Auburn native and prominent businessman Ed Lee Spencer (2006) stated, "Jan is determined, intelligent, and is able to visualize how things should be and ought to be."

Out of her conviction that Auburn needed a collective community vision, *Auburn 2000* was born—a visioning process that outlined the city's long-term goals through the year 2000. Through this process, Dempsey inspired and strongly encouraged the involvement of city council members, all segments of the Auburn community, Auburn University, as well as the city management and staff. The resulting document represented a community consensus about the direction of the city for the next two decades.

In late 1981, *Auburn 2000* began. Former mayor Jim Haygood (2006) recalled that *Auburn 2000* was "well received" and that participation was high. He felt that one reason it was so successful was because the process "corralled the talents that were already in Auburn, but were not being utilized to provide community leadership."

Dempsey used her reputation as being a "novelty" female mayor to her advantage. Requests from civic and nonprofit groups flooded her office, and she was too happy to accept the invitations. During her speeches, she relished the opportunity to promote *Auburn 2000* and advocate this long-range visioning effort, which was so unique at that time. Because she knew that Auburn citizens wanted to be a part of something "good," she used that fact to elicit involvement in the process. She advocated the *Auburn 2000* process as the way that the community's ideas and values could be identified. In her mind, the resulting document would provide the council and city manager with a community consensus on the future actions of the city government.

Just as important as the final *Auburn 2000* report was the *process* of creating *Auburn 2000*. Bringing together a diverse group of citizens and community leaders to talk with each other, work together to identify issues, and arrive at a common vision was a significant accomplishment that resulted in large-scale payoffs for the city.

After numerous public meetings and committee work sessions, the *Auburn 2000* report was produced and distributed. But unlike many studies, *Auburn 2000* was not simply placed on a shelf. It was an active document that was used to guide budget priorities and departmental goals for years to come. The process was repeated as the year 2000 approached, and *Auburn 2020* resulted in a renewed sense of community support and clear direction (Ponds 1997; Scales 1997; McLaughlin 1998). Because the city government was much different at that time, this second process also was much different from the first.

Former city manager Watson (2006) commented on Dempsey's role in *Auburn 2000* and *Auburn 2020*:

> Jan played an essential role in *Auburn 2000*. Since it was primarily a citizen involvement exercise, she appointed the committees and organized the effort. Jan's role in both efforts was one of facilitative leader. I believe that *Auburn 2000* and *Auburn 2020* were unifying efforts in the community.

Ruth Wright (2006) agreed:

> The defining event [of Jan Dempsey's term as Auburn's mayor], I believe, was *Auburn 2000*—an early and inspired version of the kind of "visioning" that is now common elsewhere. Organizing it required a vision of participatory democracy and an ability to convince citizens to commit to hard work over several years. As the results proved, Auburn citizens were uniquely fit to achieve excellence in this project. *Auburn 2020*, in which I participated, was less comprehensive. Both had the merit of promoting a more unified community.

These large-scale, community-involvement efforts are just two examples of Dempsey's skills as a master organizer and motivator (Ham 2006). Dempsey demonstrated her ability to inspire community leaders and average citizens from all segments of the community to such a degree that they agreed to put aside their personal priorities temporarily and dedicate their time to this positive, civic-minded project.

10.4.3 Planning and Zoning

At this same time in Auburn's history, there were, by many accounts, unattractive developments being constructed in and around the downtown, which is adjacent to the campus of Auburn University. These developments generally consisted of apartment buildings that served as off-campus student housing.

Retired professor Johnson (2006) stated that the university's decision to strictly limit student housing options on campus had a direct impact on the housing market of the city. With student demand for off-campus housing increasing, the market responded with construction of a number of apartment buildings that were built with little, if any, landscaping. Instead of greenspace, large asphalt parking lots covered most of the property. Dempsey described the new structures as "barrack-like." Former city manager Watson (2006) commented on the problems with zoning at that time: "One thing is for sure, the zoning ordinance prior to 1984 was a mess. A number of three-story monstrosities with the tiny rooms for student housing came out of that ordinance. There was no landscaping requirement and paving lot line to lot line was common."

Most new developments required variances to begin construction. The business of the local Board of Zoning Adjustment was evidence that the planning ordinance in place at the time was out of date. Further raising public criticism was the fact that a number Auburn's "architectural treasures" were torn down to make room for these new student apartment buildings (Ward 2006). The developments of the day caught the attention of many in the community who, like Dempsey, valued a more attractive and thoughtful approach to community planning and development.

Former city councilwoman Charlotte Ward (2006) remembered that another planning-related issue that received public attention was the increasing number of portable, flashing signs appearing along one of the major thoroughfares in the city. She and others considered these signs a "menace" because they were not only unattractive, but also distracted drivers from watching traffic.

About that time, a planning consultant introduced Dempsey to the concept of performance zoning, which was essentially a different approach to planning that could address many of the planning-related challenges facing the community. In theory, performance zoning states that mixed uses can be compatible if buffered properly. The concept appealed to Dempsey because of the central role of open space, landscaping, greenspace, and setbacks. Since mixed uses were the order of the day in Auburn, this idea hit a chord with Dempsey.

Ward (2006) also supported performance zoning because she saw it as offering the "flexibility" that was needed at the time. However, not all of the Auburn community was onboard with the new approach to planning the future build environment of Auburn. In fact, Ward feels that her strong public posture in support of performance zoning was the reason she lost the next election.

One of the deeply felt fears at the time was the juxtaposition of off-campus students next to families living in Auburn's traditional, older neighborhoods in and near the urban core. Former city manager Watson (2006) recalled the community deliberations regarding performance zoning: "[Performance zoning] was a major controversy in 1984. Every meeting was packed with people who opposed it, many convinced that their neighborhoods were in jeopardy. The intent was the opposite—to protect the existing neighborhoods from encroachment by other uses."

While performance zoning advocated buffer yards to address different housing uses, Dempsey strongly felt that buffers were inadequate to "buffer lifestyles." Therefore, a number of modifications were made to the housing definitions of the "pure" performance zoning ordinance to address the concerns and fears voiced in the public meetings. Specifically, the zoning ordinance adopted in 1984 incorporated "step-down" zones representing different housing densities allowing for more categories. The first draft of the ordinance provided for ten districts; however, three additional districts were added to customize the ordinance to better fit with the unique elements of the Auburn community. Those additional categories were *holding district*, applied to the land owned by the State of Alabama (specifically Auburn University and a state park) and the land that surrounded Lake Ogletree, which was the city's source for drinking water; *university services district* applied to the land that immediately surrounded the campus of Auburn University and that accommodated the residential and service needs associated with the university; and *redevelopment district* designed to encourage redevelopment in certain areas in the central part of the city that were deteriorating or otherwise needed a higher and better use.

The new ordinance also included improvements to the sign ordinance, which was later strengthened to make signs lower and smaller, and remove blinking signs, portable signs, and fluttering banners. Long-time observer of city affairs Ruth Wright supported the new ordinance: "The 1984 zoning ordinance, designed specifically for Auburn by *Auburn 2000*, provided a foundation for productive development." Watson (2006) commented, "Overall, the value of the new ordinance was realized in the subsequent aesthetic improvements to developments in Auburn that occurred following the passage of performance zoning."

Based on her credibility with many community leaders and council members, Dempsey was able to effectively argue for the need for a unique and novel zoning ordinance. While it was unfamiliar to the community, performance zoning was successfully adopted and implemented due in large part to the efforts of Mayor Dempsey who framed the issues and advocated strongly for this special type of zoning control.

10.4.4 Housing Initiatives

Some might consider Dempsey a woman of contrasts. To those who did not know her, her image may have been one of a well-educated, doctor's wife most likely out of touch with the needs of the disadvantaged. This image, however, could not be farther from the truth.

While Dempsey is certainly comfortable among those considered to be influential or prominent, she is just as comfortable with those at the lower end of the economic ladder. She cares deeply about the disadvantaged. With her involvement in the Lee County Council for Neglected and Dependent Children, the White House Conference on Children and Youth in 1960 and 1970, church-related mission work and outreach, and work with foster children, Dempsey became increasingly sensitive to the plight of those in need.

As mayor, Dempsey used her position to better the lives of those in Auburn who, in the past, had been overlooked and ignored. Ward (2006) commented on these efforts: "One of the main things I remember about Jan was her commitment to help Auburn's poor. At a time when no one would speak up for their needs, Jan was a vocal and persuasive force who worked to make things better for them." Ruth Wright (2006) echoed this sentiment: "Jan Dempsey took account of the needs of those who were not powerful and considered the effects of city action on those who did not show up at city hall speaking up for themselves."

For many decades, northwest Auburn was considered the "poor side of town." The housing stock was occupied by low- and moderate-income African-American households. Many of the homes began deteriorating as minor repair needs were neglected due to limited household income. Even before she became mayor, Dempsey's eyes were opened to deplorable housing conditions by the late Neil Davis, founder and editor of *The Auburn Bulletin*, a local newspaper. Dempsey actively worked with the city manager and staff to put together a targeted plan to address Auburn's housing needs. She stated, "This was a hidden problem to so many in Auburn at that time. While these citizens were integrated into the community, they were isolated and unrecognized politically."

She cites the "Broken Window Theory" as one reason why she felt the actions in the area of housing were so important to the future of those neighborhoods and the greater Auburn community. Dempsey believes that if neighborhood decay and degradation remain in place over time, it causes the people who live and work in that area to feel increasingly helpless to improve the conditions or to intervene to maintain public order. A further consequence is that vandalism often increases and residents become increasingly fearful causing them to withdraw from community upkeep and community activism. The theory claims that to keep this kind of neighborhood condition from escalating, certain actions can be undertaken, such as replacing broken windows in buildings and homes, cleaning up graffiti, removing abandoned vehicles and illegally dumped items, and improving deteriorating housing conditions.

Through the housing-related policy initiatives that were enacted during her consecutive mayoral terms, Dempsey's strongly held values in this regard were made clear. In fact, a number of innovative programs and projects addressing low-income housing were set in motion while she was in office.

1. *Housing rehabilitation*: Because Auburn was not an entitlement city during Dempsey's tenure, the city had to compete against other cities for Community Development Block Grant (CDBG) funds. A housing rehabilitation program was a key component of the city's application for these coveted federal funds. This program was built into the funding applications in order to address the serious needs of the houses located in Auburn's low- and moderate-income neighborhoods, which had gradually deteriorated. During Dempsey's tenure, 193 houses were rehabilitated with this program, representing an investment of more than $1.7 million dollars. Furthermore, the city council established a goal, which was later realized, of having water and sewer serving every home in the city limits during the time that Dempsey served as mayor and paving all of the unpaved streets where citizens lived.

2. *Affordable housing*: The city's "match" funding for the CDBG funds described above was aimed at building new homes on in-fill lots in the same low- and moderate-income neighborhoods. It was hoped that new construction might ignite new private investment in the same area and, over time, revitalize these increasingly dilapidated neighborhoods. The program allowed individuals and families to purchase a home for as little as $500. Closing costs were deferred and, through a creative financing arrangement, mortgage payments were often less than what these families were already paying in rent. As a part of this CDBG match program funded through the city's coffers, twenty new homes were built on in-fill lots in northwest Auburn representing a public investment of more than $900,000. These new homes not only provided home ownership opportunities for families who otherwise would have never been able to afford a new home, but also injected a sense of energy into these communities. New housing construction began that was not a part of the city's efforts. New, privately funded houses began to spring up throughout this community. Instead of neighborhoods that were overlooked and avoided, people now wanted to live there and new investment was evident by the construction of new homes.

3. *Habitat for Humanity housing*: Dempsey had been involved with Habitat for Humanity for a number of years. Because of the increasing value of residential property in Auburn, buildable lots for new Habitat homes were unavailable. During the latter part of her service as mayor, Dempsey played a key role in garnering political, administrative, and community support for the development of infrastructure (roads, water lines, and sewer lines) for a new neighborhood consisting of only Habitat for Humanity homes. These newly created lots enabled a number of civic, university, and church groups to come together and build homes for qualified recipients who had desperately desired a home of their own.

When asked how she garnered political support for these programs, she said it was easy. "Once the basic 'good government' items were taken care of, such as police and fire protection, garbage collection, and street conditions, the community was willing and more comfortable stepping out in new directions. Everyone began wanting the city at the table because it now offered talent and credibility. The school board, the chamber of commerce, Auburn University—they all wanted the city as a partner." If anyone challenged her support of spending public dollars on these programs, she simply countered with a series of questions: "I would ask them: 'What are the values of this community? Do they not include decent living conditions for every citizen?' Who could disagree?"

10.5 Dempsey: Leading the Parade

"When Jan Dempsey gets involved in something, she is not content just to be *in* the parade. She *leads* the parade" (Ham 2006). While Dempsey was leading Auburn's parade, the city experienced significant changes. Former mayor Haygood (2006) described Auburn's progress during the Dempsey years as transitioning from "a crawl to a gallop." And, Haygood was not alone in viewing her leadership this way. Dempsey's successful years of civic service in Auburn earned her the Chamber of Commerce's President's Award, the Rotary Club's Citizen of the Year, the League of Women Voters' Service Award, and induction to the Parent–Teacher Association Hall of Fame.

In fact, the Auburn city school system continues to be recognized as one of the top five school systems in Alabama and top one hundred twenty-five school systems in the nation. The 2006 *Washington Post* Challenge Index measuring a public high school's effort to challenge its students ranked Auburn High School seventy-ninth overall. The May 8, 2006, issue of *Newsweek* ranked Auburn High School as number seventy-seven among the top one hundred best public high schools that do the best job of preparing average students for college. In an editorial in the *Opelika-Auburn News* published toward the end of Dempsey's last term as mayor, Paul Davis (1998) asked: "Can Auburn survive without Mayor Dempsey? She's been most active in transforming—for the better—the loveliest city and also for pumping millions into what is regarded as one of the finest school systems in the state."

10.6 Lessons from this Chapter

This chapter brings to light certain environmental, personal, and structural characteristics that are important backdrops for leaders to identify. Only when these components are recognized and understood can one set out a plan to address them in order to succeed as a facilitative leader.

10.6.1 Political Environment

When Jan Dempsey appeared on the political radar in Auburn, Alabama, the city government and its administration were embroiled in conflict in most matters that came before it. There was no vision or common direction for the city. The local government was viewed as a hindrance rather than a help by those who contemplated investing in community-related projects. The manager and mayor did not communicate on most issues, and most city council votes were split 5 to 4. Community meetings to debate civic matters were well attended and cries for "something better" were heard. And while this tumultuous political environment was the order of the day, both the city and Auburn University were expanding. The political environment was referred to as "the perfect storm for new leadership" because of the community's desire to do things differently (Johnson 2006).

10.6.2 Personal Approach

How did Dempsey garner so much community support during a time that was, by so many accounts, embroiled in conflict, controversy, and bickering? Many in the community cite her personality and determination. An article in the *Opelika-Auburn News*, stated, "Disagreements and policy battles are a bitter reality in the political realm. However, Mrs. Dempsey believes that getting Auburn city officials to stop back-biting and start concentrating on the job at hand will be something she's remembered for" (Buckner 1998).

Dempsey was not inclined to give in to those who disagreed with her. Instead, she was of a mind to win over those who were undecided so as to garner a majority on her side. Prominent Auburn businessman Ed Lee Spencer (2006) commented on Dempsey's approach in overcoming opposition: "Jan did a whole lot of pushing and she got things done. She didn't mind confrontation. It quickly became known that if you went against her, it was a waste of time. She'd whip ya. Jan would ask you your opinion and then give you the answer. She could do that because she had researched the issue and had thought it through. She always had the right motives." Her witty, articulate, energetic, and positive approach opened doors for her with key state leaders as well, allowing her to advocate ideas that were critical to the future of Auburn, most of which were conceived in *Auburn 2000*.

Dempsey was able to get people who had never considered being involved in civic matters to take on leadership roles. Former mayor Haygood (2006) described her approach as "intimidating, but engaging." He commented that her direct approach "catches you off-guard." Current Auburn mayor Bill Ham (2006) recounted an experience with Dempsey's direct approach in 1986 when she recruited him to run for a city council seat:

> I was standing in line at Auburn Bank in July of 1986 when Jan walked up to me and said, "I hadn't thought of you for city council, but this city has been good to you. It's your time to pay back the community. You need to sign up to run for city council today." Within thirty minutes, Jim Haygood called to encourage me to run. He told me he'd be by in fifteen minutes to see me. When he arrived, he had Trey Johnston

[another local businessman] in the car as well. He said he was driving us both to city hall to sign up to run for council. I won a seat on council that year and continued serving on the council until Jan stepped down. That was the year I ran for mayor and have been serving as Auburn's mayor ever since.

Bill Ham and Trey Johnston were not the only people who, at Dempsey's urging, ended up serving the city in a formal capacity. She encouraged a number of others to run for city council as well. However, while she actively sought out individuals to become involved with the city government who would prove valuable, she never developed a slate of candidates as many mayors do.

Dempsey also understood how important it was for the city to "put on a good face" so the citizens could be proud of what was occurring in the community. It was this approach that Dempsey used to involve so many citizens in *Auburn 2000* and later *Auburn 2020*. Former councilmember Charlotte Ward (2006) said, "Jan's efforts to organize *Auburn 2000* were well received because it was the first time anyone took a long look at what the community should be." Retired professor Johnson (2006) commented, "Jan understands human nature. She knows that people like to be involved in positive things that are going on in the community."

10.6.3 Organizational Structure

It is important to note that when Dempsey was elected mayor, she stepped into an ambiguous institutional structure. She made it work at the time because she was determined to make it work even without the benefit of executive power or being a voting member of the local elected body. At that point, Dempsey's credibility and persuasiveness were of the utmost importance in order to gain the support of the council.

However, she also played a part in adjusting the institutional arrangement into one that was more workable for the city in the long-term. These structural changes included adopting a true council–manager form of government, reverting back to concurrent council terms, and making the mayor an official member of the city council. An underlying benefit of these institutional changes was strengthening the administrative safety net so Dempsey could focus on doing what she does best. Johnson (2006) commented that Dempsey was a master at being political—in the best sense of political. Once the organizational and administrative matters were addressed, Dempsey was able to "major on the majors" and focus her energy and effort on the big picture and what Auburn was yet to become. Her desire to improve the municipal organization for the long-term enabled her to understand that the city's organizational structure mattered, that a change was needed, and that her support of that change was necessary to make it happen.

10.7 Conclusion

To many long-time Auburn residents, Mayor Jan Dempsey personified the leadership and community vision that was so lacking in the years prior to her election. The strategies she used during those early years were ones she drew on throughout her eighteen year tenure as mayor. This case study suggests that there are a number of things that are key to being a successful mayor and a facilitative leader in a council–manager government:

1. *Having a vision*: The mayor should take the initiative to visualize a better community and then have the determination to make it happen. Former councilmember Charlotte Ward (2006) stated, "Jan has initiative, and she takes the lead. She is forward looking. She sees a need and goes after solving it. Jan is an activist in the best sense." Auburn mayor Bill Ham (2006) agreed, "Jan is a true visionary. She has never been satisfied on how things have been done in the past. She was always looking at how things could be better. The future of Auburn was always at the forefront of her mind."

2. *Being passionate and persuasive*: Dempsey is quick to point out that passion excites people. She ignited a passion within the community for a common vision of what the community of the future could be. Dempsey said, "When there is a sincere passion, it is easy to persuade citizens to become involved." Auburn mayor Bill Ham (2006) commented that Dempsey was a master at garnering support for policy initiatives: "[Jan Dempsey showed me] the importance of selling ideas to the community. She also impressed upon me that every time you vote on an issue, your decision will upset a certain percentage of people and will delight another group. What is important is that you keep your eye on the bigger picture. As long as you have analyzed the issue at hand and can argue in favor of the bigger picture, those who are mad will at least respect you."

3. *Being energetic*: By all accounts, Dempsey brought with her a dynamic positive energy. She worked hard for things she believed in. She devoted a great deal of time and energy to her duties as mayor. Often referred to as a "go-getter," Dempsey is known as an individual who is not afraid of setting challenging goals and persevering until they are achieved. Prominent businessman Ed Lee Spencer (2006) felt that much of Dempsey's mayoral success was her approach to the work at hand: "She gets action and results because she 'bores in' and is determined to see things accomplished."

4. *Acting as a constant communicator*: Dempsey states, "Don't be afraid to articulate what people are (or should be) thinking." Many consider Dempsey to be a master at presiding over council meetings. She conducted an efficient meeting while still listening to citizen input. In terms of speaking engagements, she advocates "preparation and research" as the keys to

composing civic-minded remarks that stick in the minds of those in attendance. Taking full advantage of any and every opportunity to communicate a clearly articulated message will reap large dividends. Ruth Wright (2006), a long-time observer of city affairs, commented on Dempsey's communication skills in the policy arena: "Her major asset was probably her ability to explain clearly the benefits or disadvantages of a course of action, combined with a willingness to continue to explain them until others were convinced."

5. *Being relentless in consensus building*: Dempsey's mayoral successor Bill Ham (2006) commented on Dempsey's consensus building while serving with her on city council: "One of the most important things I learned from Jan that has been invaluable to me as I have served as mayor is the art of consensus building." Ruth Wright (2006) agreed: "She has an ability, unrivaled in my experience, to understand conflicting viewpoints and find common ground. Her excellent judgment on civic matters enabled her to use that consensus to take the city in intelligent directions."

Dempsey's success in implementing the key policy initiatives described in this case does not simply "happen." Using coercion and squabbling over policy direction typically does not bode well for long-term mayoral success. Dempsey's popularity across racial, political, and economic lines enabled her to win support for policies that many viewed as potentially controversial. In the policy areas where she chose to be involved, she played a key leadership role. The key to her success hinged on her willingness to take a high profile role in controversial matters, which was supported by a strong staff working to implement her ideas for change.

While Auburn has experienced a number of contentious policy battles since 1980, the individuals interviewed for this chapter feel that the political climate was generally one of cooperation under Dempsey's leadership. Without question, the city enjoyed a political environment that was a world away from the years prior to Dempsey's election in 1980. For Dempsey, her high level of credibility, political leadership, and personal charisma all contributed to her success in establishing a highly functioning council–manager government that was rooted in citizen involvement, cooperation, partnership, and a shared a vision for the future.

Acknowledgement

I would like to extend my sincere appreciation to Jan Dempsey, Bill Ham, Jr., Jim Haygood, Gerald Johnson, Ed Lee Spencer, Charlotte Ward, Douglas J. Watson, and Ruth L. Wright for their time and efforts in this project. I would also like to thank Earline S. Cobb who provided research assistance with city election documents and news clippings.

References

Buckner, Brett. 1998. Former Auburn mayor reflects on 18 years of service. *Opelika-Auburn News*. November 8, A3.

Davis, Paul. 1998. Jan Dempsey stepping down as mayor? *Opelika-Auburn News*. March 22, A5.

Dempsey, Jan Miles. 2006. Personal interview by the author. September 20.

Ham, Bill, Jr. 2006. Personal interview by the author. September 27.

Haygood, Jim. 2006. Personal interview by the author. September 27.

Johnson, Gerald. 2006. Personal interview by the author. October 6.

Logue, Mickey and Jack Simms. 1996. *Auburn: A Pictorial History of the Loveliest Village*, (Auburn, AL).

McLaughlin, Elliott C. 1998. Into the future. *Auburn Bulletin*. April 22.*

Newsweek. 2006. America's best high schools. http://www.prnewswire.com/cgi-bin/stories.pl?ACCT=104&STORY=/www/story/04-30-2006/0004350747&EDATE (accessed November 13, 2006).

Ponds, Tonya. 1997. Auburn 2020: A plan that will shape the future of our city. *Lee County Eagle*. February 23.*

Scales, Tom. 1997. Auburn has vision for 2020. *Opelika-Auburn News*. February 23, A1-A2.

Spencer, Ed Lee. 2006. Personal interview by the author. November 16.

The Washington Post. 2006. The index challenge. http://www.washingtonpost.com/wp-srv/education/challenge/2006/challengeindex01.html (accessed November 13, 2006).

Thomaston, Carmel. 1990. Mayor Dempsey gives city update. *The Sunday Eagle*. April 1.*

Ward, Charlotte. 2006. Personal interview by the author. September 29.

Watson, Douglas J. 2006. Personal interview by the author. September 12.

Wright, Ruth L. 2006. Personal interview by author. November 13.

---

* Clipping from file in Auburn City Government. No page number was indicated on the clipping.

Chapter 11

Partial Leadership and Alternating Styles: Stockton, California

Robert Benedetti and Shayne Lambuth

Contents

11.1 Introduction

In the past thirty years, both the style and the structure of the office of mayor in Stockton, California, have changed. These shifts reflect a growing desire on the part of the community to take control of the city's destiny in the face of new demographics, economic realities, and political alignments. This ferment has occurred in the context of California's special political culture and complex institutional patterns. It has also been influenced by Stockton's unique history and geography. Stockton, established in 1848, was one of the first cities in California and continues to provide a deep-water gateway to the rich agricultural heartland of the state.

The legacy of Stockton's first two mayors to be elected citywide is the particular subject of this essay. They both took advantage of structural changes proposed and implemented in the wake of a local politics dominated by corruption, neighborhood self-interest, and incivility. Joan Darrah, one of the architects of these structural changes, was first elected in November 1989 and reelected in November 1992. Gary Podesto followed in 1996 and 2000. The city's Charter limits the mayor to two terms.

As pioneers in the reformed office of the mayor, both Darrah and Podesto provided models for future occupants. Their personal styles helped to flesh out the potential of the new structure and to explore its limitations. Their mayoral histories suggest that James Svara is correct when he concludes that facilitative leadership is well suited to the office of the mayor in a council–manager form of government; both of these occupants have assumed this style (Svara and Associates 1994). However, it is clear to all observers that Darrah and Podesto differed dramatically in the way in which they sought to facilitate cooperation among the various constituencies. Each appears to have emphasized a different attribute of the facilitator. Darrah embodied the coordinator, helping "to achieve high levels of shared information, but weak in policy guidance" (Svara and Associates 1994). On the other hand, Podesto "emphasized policy guidance and advocacy, but neglected coordinative activities" (Svara and Associates 1994). The result is that Stockton has come to understand these aspects of facilitative leadership as alternatives rather than aspects of a unified model. Svara's description of the "director" or complete form of the facilitative mayor, an integration of coordination and advocacy, here seems an ideal type, out of reach of mere mortals. In its first cycle since reform, Stockton's experience has been that coordinators and advocates alternate as mayor, each occupant responding to the particular challenges of his or her times.

To describe further the experience of facilitative leadership in Stockton requires attention to the social context of the city, the evolution of the office of the mayor, and the experience which Darrah and Podesto brought to the office. With this background in mind, the impact of their leadership across a series of issues can be assessed. It will become clear that each adopted a mix of leadership roles and crafted a set of networks in accomplishing their goals. The application of these strategies to the challenges at hand reveals the different ways a coordinator and an advocate approach facilitation. An analysis of their activities indicates that this distinction is one of emphasis. Both Darrah and Podesto utilized a wide range of tactics in pursuing their goals. Further, it appears that the styles they adopted were recognized by the public as responsive both to the challenges Stockton faced during their terms in office, and to the governmental structures under which they operated. One indicator of their success in both cases was the support each received as they considered higher office at the end of their mayoral service. Darrah was encouraged to run for Congress, but declined. Podesto ran for State Senate, but was subsequently defeated.

11.2 Setting

Stockton, California, is a city of over 250,000 in a county of 633,000 residents. San Joaquin County is one of the ten most productive agricultural counties in the United States and contains one-third of the San Francisco Bay Delta, which recharges much of California's water. In recent times, residents of the Bay Area counties have crossed the Altamont Pass and the Delta in search of cheaper housing. In addition, the Sacramento metropolitan region has been expanding southward toward Stockton and an increasing number of city residents commute daily to the state's capitol city. The area is bracing for rapid urbanization, competition with overseas agricultural producers, and the environmental challenges of pollution and levee failures. There is much for government to do.

Stockton shares the county with six other cities: Lodi, Escalon, Ripon, Manteca, Lathrop, and Tracy. Lodi to the north is famous for its Zinfandel wine and hometown atmosphere. Escalon and Ripon are small agricultural towns getting their first taste of suburban dwellers. Manteca, Lathrop, and Tracy have absorbed much of the new migration from the Bay Area. However, they lag in industry and urban services; in many ways they are copies of those urban places in the Livermore Valley which were named "edge cities" by Joel Garreau (Garreau 1991).

Though Stockton is by far the largest and the most comprehensive city in the county, its neighbors do not defer to its authority. They conceive themselves as independent rather than suburban; in fact, there continues to be significant agricultural space between them despite the growth of strip mall development along major arteries. There is much competition among cities for retail tax revenue in the wake of Proposition 13, which dramatically reduced the ability of cities and counties to raise property taxes in California. On the other hand, San Joaquin County has come together to support the development of highways under the leadership of its Council of Government (COG). Currently, COG has been successful in getting the ACE (Altamont Commuter Express) commuter train up and running between Stockton and San Jose, as well as providing the capital necessary for dramatic upgrades to Interstate 205 through Tracy and over the Altamont Pass to the Bay Area.

Though California has a tradition of charter cities and "home rule," it is also known for its large number of special districts and its centralized control of state services, particularly after Proposition 13. Critical issues, such as water, are most often special district and state prerogatives. Upgrades to transportation, including Stockton's airport and deep water port, require careful negotiating with state and county agencies. The Delta and the rivers that feed it are monitored by hosts of regulators from Sacramento. Large portions of city and county revenues are in the form of rebates from the state or, alternatively, are withheld to pay state debts.

Stockton has not always done well lobbying for state assistance. Beginning in the 1930s when the car and truck replaced boats as the vehicles of choice to reach inland cities, Stockton was unable to obtain highways linking itself directly to San Francisco and thereafter began a long period of isolation from the coast. Later the city had to wait in line for a cross-town freeway linking the two major highways that define the east and west boundaries of the city. Unfortunately, when this project was finally authorized, it eliminated culturally significant ethnic neighborhoods in the downtown area, a loss that the city is still attempting to overcome.

Recently the political fortunes of the Central Valley have started to improve. It has become a potential mediator between Northern and Southern California. Its politicians are traditionally more conservative, but have experience dealing with ethnically diverse populations. Stockton, for example, has, for more than a decade, been a majority minority community. It is estimated that 75 languages are spoken in the downtown daily and the local schools report that they have tracked 39 spoken in the schools. These diverse communities have played host to the tidal wave of immigrants that have come to Stockton in search of jobs in agriculture and food processing. In recent years, immigrants from Mexico have been most numerous and now comprise over 30 percent of the city's population.

As a port of entry for immigrants and a market for agricultural and industrial labor, the city has experienced high welfare rolls, low family incomes, and crime. The segregation index for the city is low; crime appears to be clustered in areas where drug transactions occur, often along downtown streets. Much of the crime involves youth and, therefore, flows over into the schools.

Since Stockton and its neighbors have conservative political instincts, but increasing numbers of immigrants and poor, both political parties see opportunities to gain supporters. Despite gerrymandering, Assembly and Senate elections in the area are often competitive and the winners have assumed leadership roles in Sacramento. However, because the districts are drawn to please incumbents, meet court-ordered standards of diversity, and adhere to the principle of one person—one vote, cities like Stockton do not have a single representative that they can call their own in the state legislature. For the city to gain state assistance takes careful negotiating even as political power shifts increasingly in the Valley's direction.

Another difficulty Stockton leaders face in attempting to link to state and federal leaders is the nonpartisan tradition of California cities. In fact, the state's constitution continues to follow Progressive Era impulses in banning partisan labels in local races statewide. The result is that local parties are weak and easily manipulated by a few vocal members. On the other hand, this tradition has meant that candidates from both parties can enter politics without the fear of facing a political machine. As if to underscore the open nature of the local political scene, Darrah is a Democrat and Podesto a Republican.

While not favored by political parties or influence at the state level, Stockton has been blessed with voluntary associations serving in a multitude of areas. Significantly, when President George H. W. Bush was awarding Points of Light to exemplary nonprofits, he gave a total of eight in Northern California, four of which came to organizations in Stockton. Voluntary associations have given the city the third oldest symphony in California, an acclaimed art and history museum (The Haggin Museum), and one of the most successful private shelters for the homeless in California. There are three local Chambers of Commerce, differing in their ethnic focus, and a partnership organization of business leaders that seeks to improve the local economic climate. These organizations, in addition to their primary purposes, have served as incubators and recruiters for local political leadership. Darrah talks about her extensive nonprofit experience and the ways in which it provided her fundraising expertise (Darrah 2003). Podesto had the respect of the Chamber of Commerce throughout his public career (Schroeder 2005) and used his association with them to test ideas and strategies.

11.3 Governmental Structure

Currently, Stockton has a city council of seven members, one of which is the mayor. From 1850 through 1989, 139 years, a nine-member council elected its own mayor who, on average served slightly less than two years. In 1923, Stockton adopted the manager–council form of government.

Throughout the 1960s, Stockton resisted pressure to respond governmentally to the Civil Rights Movement. Unlike other cities in the San Francisco Bay Area, Stockton was governed by a business elite during that time period and refused to accept federal assistance from programs such as the War on Poverty for fear that it would impose burdensome regulations on the city (Browning, Marshall, and Tabb 1984, 1990). Instead, Stockton continued to rely on private organizations and agencies to respond to poverty and racism. It attempted to respond to the outward and visible signs of such social ills by urban renewal projects, in part, occasioned by the construction of the cross-town freeway.

In 1986, the city passed a reform package called Measure C that overturned an earlier (1971) experiment in district voting and implemented a hybrid system in which council members face primary elections in a district, but in which run-offs between the top two contestants are citywide. The council was reduced in size from nine to seven members including the mayor who is elected citywide, but limited to two terms of four years each. These term limits were also applied to members of the council; their tenure in office cannot exceed two four-year terms.

This reform was contentious and court action preceded its implementation. Though Stockton has avoided the creation of defined ghetto areas, Mexican

Americans and African Americans were concerned that an at-large system of any sort would work against the electoral fortunes of minorities. Indeed, the reform was occasioned by the behavior of a particular black councilman who some in the community found divisive (Darrah 2003).

Darrah was part of the group that proposed Measure C. She had also been active in opposing legal and political maneuvers aimed at delaying its implementation. When, in the spring of 1989, the courts finally ordered elections under the reformed charter to occur in November, she made her decision to run, thus becoming the first mayor to be elected citywide. However, because of court-ordered delays, her first term in office would only be three years (Darrah 2003).

When Podesto was elected in 1996, he became aware that several California cities had recently reformed the office of the mayor to increase the leadership potential of the position. He worked with supporters to craft a charter revision, which was placed on the ballot and passed in 2000. The revisions increased the mayor's public persona, giving him the power to set the agenda of the council, recommend policy and programs to the council, demand information of departments, appoint boards and commissions with the consent of the council, address the city annually in a State of the City address, recommend budget adjustments, preside at council meetings, and have a modest staff. In addition, the mayor would henceforth be a full-time position.

However, the reform was carefully crafted to emphasize facilitation rather than executive action. For example, the mayor is defined by his role as communicator and assistant to the council:

> It is the intent of this Article that the Mayor shall be the political leader within the community by providing guidance and leadership to the Council, by expressing and communicating to those he or she serves the City's policies and programs and by assisting the Council in the informed, vigorous and effective exercise of its powers. (Stockton City Charter, Section 1101)

The reform was particularly careful to be sure that the powers of the mayor to recommend and publicize did not conflict with the authority of the city manager or the council. Thus, the amended section of the charter ends with the following:

> Nothing in this Section shall be construed in any way as an infringement or limitation on the powers and duties of the City Manager as Chief Administrative Officer and head of the administrative branch of the City government as prescribed in other sections of this Charter. Except as otherwise provided in this Charter, the Mayor shall possess only such authority over the City Manager and the administrative branch as he or she possesses as one member of the Council. (Stockton City Charter, Section 1102)

These reforms took effect in time for Podesto's second and last term in office, 2000 to 2004.

11.4 Profiles of Mayors Darrah and Podesto

Joan Darrah attended a private school in Southern California, college at Radcliff and UC Berkeley, and graduate school at Stanford and the University of the Pacific. She married an attorney from Stockton and they moved to his hometown. Over the years her husband rose to a judgeship and she took her place as a leader of various community groups. After rising in the ranks of the nonprofit world, she realized that she had exhausted those leadership challenges and decided to run for county supervisor. Her opponent won easily, the beneficiary of good press and more money. Following the loss, she assessed her strengths and weaknesses and vowed that she would learn to raise money so that she would never again lose a race by being outspent. She founded a small public relations firm and undertook a variety of local fundraising challenges successfully, waiting for the right political opportunity (Darrah 2003).

The opportunity came when another, more seasoned, member of her reform group decided not to run for mayor under the reformed charter. She jumped at the chance and began to organize and to fundraise in earnest. Her opponent was a well-known African-American politician, but one who had been associated with council members notorious for their incivility. Darrah was vulnerable to accusations that she had never held public office, but defended herself as a leader untainted by the conflicts and incivility of past administrations. When she was able to point to fiscal excesses by her opponent during his time on the city council, this brought her point home; a vote for Darrah was a vote for clean politics, a new beginning. Her major substantive issue was crime, a perennial concern in the city. She blamed drugs and promised to attack the problem zealously.

Gary Podesto had never run for office until he decided to compete for mayor in 1996 when Darrah was term-limited out. Podesto was the owner of a chain of local markets before selling his business. He had undertaken some community service, including membership on the board of regents for the local private university. He had played football at Marquette University and Santa Clara University in his youth and maintained an interest in both education and sport throughout his maturity. However, his passion was for Stockton; he was a native son and wanted to help make the city thrive as his businesses had done. He had an inherent distrust of government and preference for the private sector and business management (Sams 1995, 1996).

He was willing to invest his own money in his campaign and ultimately is reported to have personally funded 80 percent of his first run for mayor. He was running against a long-time city councilman who had a reputation as a political insider. His attack was not against the results of the Darrah administration, but against the bureaucracy and the politics that hamper any administration from reaching its potential. This allowed him to score against his rival without criticizing Darrah directly. Initially, he did not identify major issues that he would resolve, but promised that he would ensure that creative ideas were pursued.

The electoral campaigns that brought Darrah and Podesto to office were markedly different in tone, organization, and financial structure. They built on the concerns of citizens at the time, as well as the failure or accomplishments of predecessors. However, both were blessed by contests without incumbents and with good community reputations before entering office. Neither had held a prior office in the city.

Both Darrah and Podesto won initially by substantial margins. Darrah enjoyed 65 percent of the vote in a two-way race, while Podesto had 70 percent in a five-way race. They were clearly the people's choice. However, neither had clear cues regarding how to be mayor of Stockton, an essentially new office for Darrah and still not fully institutionalized by the time Podesto took the helm. Nor were they beholden to a political party or identifiable clique. Both were members of what could be loosely termed the "Stockton elite." Their families were known and were financially comfortable. They could afford to be their own person in office, and they were. In fact, this independence allowed them to learn on the job as they faced the issues that came their way.

11.5 Defining the Mayor in Law and Practice

The office of the mayor in Stockton has, as related above, undergone significant changes since 1986. Before that time, the office could best be described as inviting traditional or "automatic" mayoral behavior. Mayors were appointed by the council for two-year terms in anticipation of ceremonial behavior and service as a presiding officer. Some mayors extended this definition by undertaking external relations to the public at large and to other governmental or community organizations. Average mayors celebrated and presided; exceptional mayors became community spokespersons.

With the reforms brought by Measure C in 1986, the expectation for the mayor changed. As the only official elected citywide in the primaries and in the general election, it was clear that the reformed office anticipated more energy in regard to both coordination and policy initiation. The further expansion of the office in 2000 emphasized these additional expectations. Stockton mayors today are defined structurally as mobilizers and goal setters as well as ceremonial figures and chairs at council meetings. Today's mayors are to bring Stockton together and rally citizens around common values and worthwhile projects.

As mayors before 1986 exercised some latitude in the degree to which they became community spokespersons, so Darrah and Podesto differed in the degree to which they emphasized coordination or policy initiation. This stylistic difference was reflected in their different attitudes toward others, the kind of interactions they fostered, and the manner in which they set goals. Table 11.1 summarizes the

Table 11.1 Mix of Mayoral Roles

Leadership Roles	Joan Darrah	Gary Podesto
Ceremonial	Strong suit	Strong suit
Spokesperson, link to public	Strong suit	Strong suit
Presiding officer	Strong suit	Strong suit
Educator	Strong suit	Strong suit
Liaison/partner with manager	Strong suit	Strong suit
Team/network builder	Strong suit	Weaker suit
Goal setter	Strong suit	Strong suit
Delegator/organizer	Strong suit	Weaker suit
Advocate/articulator/ mobilizer	Weaker suit	Strong suit
Policy initiator	Weaker suit	Strong suit
Intergovernmental relations	Weaker suit	Weaker suit

particular mix of roles which became their hallmarks. These role definitions are the result of research by Svara on cities in North Carolina, but are fully applicable here (Svara and Associates 1994).

Among this list of roles, the ability of the mayor to work with the city manager is key for a mayor adopting a "facilitative" style: "… mayors build effective leadership by strengthening the other participants in the governing process, rather than controlling or supplanting them" (Svara and Associates 1994). Both Darrah and Podesto found, when they entered office, a city manager with whom they had some difficulty working. The manager Darrah inherited had been supportive of her election, but she found his professional demeanor off-putting. In addition, city employees were fearful of his wrath, and his manner in front of the council was condescending. Though Darrah's style was to avoid conflict, particularly at the beginning of her first term, she went along with the council's desire to conduct an evaluation. During an oral session reviewing his performance, the manager took offense at the attitude of the council and resigned on the spot. In the news coverage that followed, three council members, but not the mayor, were said to have treated him unfairly. This chain of events allowed Darrah to help select and install a new city manager whom she described as "competent, professional, diplomatic"; skills she herself valued most highly (Darrah 2003).

Podesto, however, found the manager selected by Darrah and her colleagues to be too bureaucratic. Even before his election, he indicated that he would want him to change his style and keep the mayor more informed about issues the city faced (*The Record* Editorial 1996). During his first months in office, Podesto kept regular office hours and spent time reading journals on urban governance. He often ran off copies for staff and council members to stimulate new initiatives. He constantly asked for information and held staff responsible to provide it to him (Sams 1997b).

After Podesto's first term and the passage of the charter amendment granting the mayor additional responsibilities, the city manager retired. This gave Podesto the opportunity to work with the council to find someone with a closer fit to his own style. He supported the appointment of an experienced manager who had a reputation for cutting red tape and implementing major projects quickly. Podesto's choice was subsequently known for his brusque style and unwillingness to communicate to either the public or the council once a project had been approved. Many of the renewal projects that Podesto had supported, this new manager was able to bring to conclusion, but with high price tags and serious overruns, and without keeping the city council fully informed.

Five years and several major projects later, when the council and Podesto's successor fired this manager, Podesto wrote a letter to the editor in the local paper concluding that he was "a very talented city manager and deserves credit for his role in the new Stockton ... . Can the community be proud of this progress? You bet. And (our former manager) deserves his share of the credit" (Podesto 2005).

While the type of city manager Darrah and Podesto preferred was different, they both wanted to have a partner with whom they could work, but not necessarily dominate. They were not inclined to take over the executive functions of that office, but to coordinate with a manager to accomplish the city's goals. Significantly, they were also supported by their councils in this regard. While Svara cautions that where mayors dominate in the selection and direction of city managers, a move to a strong mayor form of government cannot be far behind (Svara and Associates 1994), it is also true that facilitative mayors are interested in finding managers with whom they can work collaboratively. While Podesto may have been the more anxious of the two to find a manager who would take his lead, for both mayors, the independence of the manager was assumed. Hence, Podesto, as well as Darrah, were involved in the selection process of the city manager as facilitators rather than CEOs. Reflecting Svara's findings in other cities, it was also true in Stockton that "mayors and managers offer team leadership rather than competing with each other" (Svara and Associates 1994).

While both mayors were able to obtain managers that fit their particular styles, they did not have similar opportunities in regard to the councils with which they served. For example, both mayors had challenges over small issues and committee service; however, they were effective in keeping their colleagues together in regard to more significant issues. As Svara found among other facilitative leaders, Darrah and Podesto focused the attention of the council on goal setting, policy decisions, oversight, and staff performance (Svara and Associates 1994).

Darrah attempted to avoid conflict and talked extensively to her colleagues to find what issues concerned them and how those issues might be pursued. In one case, a councilwoman defied her and the rest of the council, taking her agenda to the press. Darrah had repeated confrontations with her, but arranged for her to have a valued committee assignment. Though this did not satisfy her, Darrah may have succeeded in pacifying some of her constituents. During her reelection campaign, all members of the council except this individual were more than willing to say favorable things about her to the press.

Podesto was viewed by observers as "hard-charging" (Sams 1997a). He was not concerned with briefing council members on his initiatives until they required council action. During periods, particularly in the second term, when major actions were on the agenda, Podesto carefully counted the votes. Whether the issue was the privatization of the water system or the development of an extensive waterfront complex, Podesto could count on the support of a substantial majority of the council. Even those who opposed him respected his prodigious work and his willingness to roll up his sleeves and get to the bottom of an issue. While his style was more that of a business executive than Darrah's, he nevertheless focused on holding the attention of the council rather than on manipulation or dominance. His powers were the powers of persuasion rather than the twisting of arms, and his fellow council members maintained their loyalty to him.

Both Darrah and Podesto were energetic and often met with the public beyond council chambers. They were facilitators of public opinion as well as the actions of the manager and the council. Darrah ruffled feathers by having the office of the mayor redecorated to encourage its use for meetings and greeting constituents and visitors alike. She was proud to be known as "the mayor who was not afraid to make house calls" (Darrah 2003). Darrah also made it a point to make presentations to business as well as women's groups regularly. She notes how her willingness to speak her mind in public swayed business leaders away from a plan to bring large card rooms, which would markedly increase the presence of gambling in Stockton (Darrah 2003).

Podesto made particularly good use of the State of the City address, which was authorized by the charter reforms he had supported. He generated considerable comment when, in his first such speech, he encouraged the community to face its racial and ethnic stereotypes and inaugurated several programs to celebrate and promote diversity. When he had the opportunity to appoint a member to the council, he selected a well-qualified African-American female attorney, further driving home his point.

Of the two, Podesto appears to have mastered the media most effectively, though Darrah certainly appreciated their importance. Stockton is served by one daily newspaper and, less directly, by television stations from Sacramento. There was considerable coverage of Stockton's debate over the privatization of its water system, and throughout the debate Podesto was able to gain attention for his point of view, despite the strength and popular appeal of the opposition's grassroots organization.

When he left office, the local paper concluded, "Podesto helped inspire Stockton and many of its residents to aspire to greatness" (*The Record* Editorial 2004).

Darrah, on the other hand, often complained that she had not understood how the media would reconstruct her comments on a particular event. At the time of her reelection, she reports:

> ... the paper tried to put up a candidate against me. The publisher ... himself paid a visit to a member of my council and, saying that he was a spokesman for the business leadership ... urged him to run against me. The council member declined and later told me the story. Initially, the staff was no more supportive of me than the paper's leadership. However hard I tried to convince the city news reporter that I had been an effective mayor for two years, he began his preelection summary on the candidates with "Joan Darrah is Stockton's feel-good mayor—a former public relations person who often seems more interested in handing out commendations and thanking community volunteers than in the nitty-gritty of local government" (Darrah 2003, 105).

Both Darrah and Podesto had access to decision makers in Stockton and beyond and they used it. Darrah talks about how she enlisted Senator Dianne Feinstein and Senator Barbara Boxer in her efforts to gain attention from the Federal Emergency Management Agency (FEMA).* She mentions with pride her negotiating concessions from developers and business leaders, as well as rallying their support for a redesign of Stockton's waterfront. In fact, one of her supporters who served on the council under Podesto complained that much of what Podesto accomplished had already been agreed to during Darrah's time in office and that his mayoralty simply reaped the benefit. Whether or not this is a fair statement, it demonstrates Darrah's powers as a goal setter.

Podesto, too, was a goal setter, but his greatest strength lay in his ability to get private investors enthusiastic about Stockton's opportunities. He helped the business community seize upon the city's priorities even when they disagreed with some of his policies. As the president of the Chamber of Commerce noted after Podesto stepped down, "... while the Chamber and Podesto haven't always agreed with each other's position, I found Podesto to be a quality person who could, on one hand, disagree with a person's position, while, on the other hand, work with them on other issues" (Schroeder 2005). His leadership in this regard extended beyond his term in office. When the professional hockey franchise opened in Stockton a year after Podesto's last month in office, the new mayor recalled that "Gary Podesto was at the forefront of this ..." (Linesburgh 2005). Podesto was also at the forefront of building the city's reputation nationally, successfully competing twice for the designation of All American City in 1999 and 2004.

---

* The city was locked in a conflict with FEMA over flood plain maps and the safety of the levees.

Though both mayors were courted by their political parties for higher office (in Podesto's case early in his second term), their interaction with state or national leaders were effective, but limited in number and depth. Their communications followed formal lines of authority, as when Podesto wrote to Governor Schwarzenegger to limit the flow of sex offenders to Stockton, or when Darrah was part of a delegation to visit California's Senators to ask their help with FEMA. These leaders had influence because of the size and position of Stockton, but little more.

In sum, Darrah and Podesto shared mastery of many of the roles of both the traditional and the facilitative leader. However, Darrah did not always seem to be forceful in her initiation of policies, preferring them to emerge from the consensus with others. Thus, she was able to hold the loyalty of her council where, at the end, Podesto clearly had two councilmen who actively questioned many of his initiatives. Podesto, however, could claim credit for the dramatic development of downtown Stockton because he articulated this vision clearly and actively recruited from the private sector to make it a reality, even though there is some evidence that Darrah first brought the essential concept forward and developed an early consensus around it. He was rewarded with particular praise in the press at the end of his terms in office because of his advocacy and achievement (*The Record* Editorial 2004).

11.6 Similarities and Differences in Leadership

Both mayors are usually credited with having had a positive impact on the City of Stockton. In the case of Darrah, this assessment usually rests on her ability to bring the community together and to stop the circus atmosphere which prevailed in councils prior to her time in office. She demanded civility and focused the city on issues of crime, neighborhood development, and downtown renewal. Podesto, on the other hand, is most remembered for his efforts to privatize governmental services, particularly the water system, and for his efforts at bringing entertainment, particularly sports, to the downtown area. Darrah built community understanding by sparking dialogue, while Podesto contributed to community pride by providing leadership in the provision of services and by the establishment of professional sports in Stockton. Table 11.2 attempts to summarize and compare their major accomplishments or engagements.

This listing is not exhaustive. In Darrah's case, it tracks her own assessment (Darrah 2004). In Podesto's case, it follows the assessment of the local paper and business leadership, as well as his own State of the City speeches (*The Record* Editorial 2004). What is missing in both cases is the day-to-day managing that a mayor must accomplish. As Podesto noted six months into the job, "You deal with situations and you try to get them on and off your desk as quickly as possible with different solutions" (Sams 1997b).

What is significant here, however, is the fact that most of the contributions Darrah identifies are in terms of interpersonal relationships. During her time in office, she is proud of the way she was able to get people to work together to combat

Table 11.2 Accomplishments/Engagements of Darrah and Podesto by Term

Term	Joan Darrah	Gary Podesto
One	Police funding	Charter change for expanded mayoral role
	Safe Stockton: Safe schools/safe streets	All American City application
	Downtown security and redevelopment	CSU Stockton Initiative, Redevelop state mental hospital
Two	Aftermath of SWAT raid and death of Hispanic	Privatization of water system
	Luncheons for change: Initiative toward ethnic groups	Racial harmony initiative
	Aftermath of death of Cambodian child	Second All America City application
	Unsuccessful attempt to block amendment to general plan for additional housing units	Renovation of Hotel Stockton
	Defeat of Stockton (Card room) casino	New ball park
	World Wildlife Museum lost	New sports arena
	Gun control: Concealed weapons passed	Multiplex theater in downtown
	Code enforcement extended	Renovation of Historic Fox Theater
	FEMA flood plain maps	Weber Point Event Center
	Redesigning Stockton's waterfront	Addition of county acreage to Stockton's sphere of influence as part of its general plan

crime, to better ethnic relations, and to accept or reject plans for future development. Podesto's accomplishments, on the other hand, focus on physical changes and heightened recognition of the city's accomplishments. He was able to implement economic development and market the city nationally.

Relating this analysis to the discussion of roles above, it is clear that the facilitation that Darrah achieved required negotiating skills within the city staff and between the city and average citizens. The strength of her administration was its ability to get neighbors to take charge and people to listen to each other. This required the organizational and networking skills that Darrah had developed in her work in nonprofit organizations.

Podesto, on the other hand, needed to be able to interest investors in Stockton. He believed in privatization, but this required private partners. His understanding of the need to market Stockton to venture capitalists and to sell the wares of the investors to Stockton made him particularly effective. In this, he played the mobilizer and the initiator. He was often out in front of the council, taking the lead with the public, media, and business partners. It was his ability, as one sometime opponent noted, to talk to developers the same way he talked to the average man or woman that allowed him to sell his policies to the public and to businessmen looking to make a profit (Sims 1997b).

In both cases, the mayors appear to have been most effective in their second terms. In order to build the relationships internally as well as externally necessary to move people toward goals as well as to intuit those goals requires time. Darrah notes that she needed to harden herself and to learn how to manage conflict without fearing its consequences (Darrah 2003). Podesto, on the other hand, needed to understand that government was different than business and did require persuasion in place of a more direct exercise of authority. Both mayors appear to have learned their lessons in the first four years and were ready to pursue a more aggressive agenda in their second terms. The pattern does raise questions concerning the practice of limiting terms to two; mayors, at least of the facilitative variety, may need one term simply to understand the right goals to achieve. That leaves them with only a single term in which to accomplish what they have discovered to be in the public interest.

11.7 Resources for Leadership

The success of each of these mayors with different styles and different agendas can be attributed to six dimensions:

1. Both had a vision of what they wished to accomplish, even though that vision expanded over their terms in office.
2. Both mayors were able to maintain the loyalty of the city manager and strong majority support from their councils for their programs. Even when they lost over a particular initiative, they quickly recovered and regained their authority.
3. Both had strong community bases, founded on established local networks and records of accomplishment. They were already recognized as leaders before they accepted the position of mayor, and came into office with strong majority support from the voters. They never experienced organized opposition during their terms in office.
4. They were both extraordinary communicators and took this aspect of the job very seriously.
5. Both had great tolerance for adversity. They were able to listen in the face of abuse. They could learn even under fire.

6. They were supported by an evolving understanding of the structure of the office of the mayor, which increasingly allowed for an expanded role in the areas of coordination and policy initiation. They fully understood that they did not have control over a bureaucracy, a budget, or a party structure. Yet they also understood that they were more than ceremonial heads of their city.

Darrah's vision was to restore dignity to the council and thereby to Stockton. As she says in her summing up of the experience:

> The city council now attracts candidates with a sense of citywide responsibility, people who are respected in the community and who work for the public good. That's a big difference, too, from how things had been before the passage of Measure C and also since the days of my first city council (Darrah 2003, 244).

She admits to not having an agenda to start; one of her first initiatives during her first campaign was to find out what the people wanted. When describing what allowed her to accomplish a plan for restoration of the waterfront, she emphasizes her focus on involving key staff and diverse elements of the city population (Darrah 2004). In sum, she defined success as much in terms of process as result.

Podesto initially brought a vision which emphasized process to the position. He promised to shake up city hall by running it more like a business. He aimed to "restore the proper relationship between the elected, policy-setting council and the hired, policy executive staff." (*The Record* Editorial 1996) Once his service began, however, he sought additional responsibilities in order to undertake significant projects in partnership with the private sector. His vision increasingly was privatization, and his focus was recruiting willing partners.

Darrah and Podesto each had a councilperson that they could not control and rebellion on occasion from others. Otherwise, they were able to hold the loyalty of their colleagues even when they lost a vote or, in the case of Podesto, failed to endorse them for higher office. Both mayors were able to convince those around them that they took the interest of the city seriously. Both brought to the city recognizable leadership styles from the nonprofit or business world. They were open and predictable leaders, willing to accept that others did not agree with them on all things.

Neither mayor had a political base in the traditional sense; the California Constitution denies cities partisan politics. However, both enjoyed organized followings in the community. Darrah often rallied women's groups and regularly organized leadership luncheons. She took seriously her contribution as a role model for other women considering public office. Podesto continued his contacts with the business community where his entrepreneurial skills had been widely respected. He listened to the concerns of local business and was able to get their support in return.

Darrah was sufficiently concerned about her communications skills to have taken lessons in preparation for her second campaign. However, public relations were her profession and she proved skilled in the use of printed materials. She twice was able to get her message across without newspaper endorsement. In office, she learned to stage events that gained positive press coverage, but was never able to command complete respect from the local paper.

Podesto was masterful at public events. His State of the City speeches were printed in the local paper and fully covered. He was skilled in television appearances and knew how to boil down his positions for public consumption. Throughout his two terms in office, he received strong newspaper coverage. Clearly he had the respect and admiration of local reporters and their bosses. Part of his appeal was his ability to express emotion. On two occasions he wept in public; both were widely reported (Siders 2004).

Neither mayor had an easy time interpersonally. While they were able to work well with their managers and council members for the most part, they faced angry citizens all too often. Some were irritants, including a woman who rambled on at too many council meetings. Darrah was called upon to listen to attacks on the city occasioned by the death of an elderly Hispanic man at the hands of the police. She consoled a grieving Cambodian community on the death of a child by drowning in a local river. She opposed developers who had supported her regarding land use regulations, and was seen as unfriendly to those supporting the location of a wild-life museum in Stockton. In every case, she appears to have listened and won praise in the local press for the orderly way she conducted public meetings.

Podesto was widely praised during his first term and was able to avoid difficult confrontations. However, his support of an initiative to increase the responsibilities of the mayor was seen by some as a power grab and as inappropriate for a city of Stockton's size. This controversy was eclipsed, however, by the strength of the opposition to the privatization of the water system. The opposition drew national coverage to Stockton, and the issue became the subject of a significant documentary film and book, entitled *Thirst*, on the management of water internationally (Snitow, Kaufman, and Fox 2007). Though Podesto later regretted some of his rhetoric during that controversy, he actively used letters to the newspaper to circulate his point of view on the matter. He was also able to keep the council together and to approve the contract before it could become the subject of a referendum. The opposition, however, took the city to court and the contract was subsequently overturned. His skillful management of council business also allowed him to expand Stockton's sphere of influence over land north of the city and to authorize dramatic development on the city's waterfront with minimal delay or adverse publicity.

Finally, it was the evolving structure of the mayor's office in Stockton which shaped and encouraged the leadership styles Darrah and Podesto provided. They were limited in the resources available to them in that the office does not control administration, budget, or partisan loyalty. However, they recognized that the office was more than ceremonial. Though Darrah assumed that the position was that of a "weak" mayor, she nonetheless understood the mandate to coordinate and lead. In fact, she appears to have assumed many of the "powers" expressly assigned the major in the charter reform of 2000. Podesto, particularly after the responsibilities of the office were increased, seized the advocacy role with relish. However, he did learn that government service was different from business and came to appreciate the role of the mayor as more facilitative in nature.

11.8 Conclusion: Coordinators and Advocates

The story of these two Stockton mayors suggests that facilitative leadership can come in at least two types, coordinative and advocacy-based. These two alternative styles echo the styles identified in larger cities with mayors more fully resourced. The coordinative style has some attributes in common with the pluralist mayors described by Robert Dahl (1961) and others (Judge 1995). As Edward Banfield observed, mayors often work between groups, bringing segments of the city together for productive purposes (Banfield 1961). Alternatively, advocacy mayors share some of the qualities associated with the regime leadership identified by Clarence Stone, among others (1995, 1989). They attempt to forge external partnerships with business and other community groups to accomplish dramatic goals, particularly related to economic development.

However, these distinctions do not bring into question the reality of facilitative leadership. It is grounded in the structure of the council–manager form of government, particularly when amended to include a mayor elected citywide and provided a modest expansion of responsibility. Structure, of course, does not guarantee that particular styles will emerge. However, even in nonpartisan settings, there are leadership incubators for leadership appropriate to the facilitative role. Specifically, experience in nonprofits appears to prepare mayors for the coordinative aspects of their positions, while business leadership provides useful lessons for policy advocacy.

What Stockton does suggest, however, is that coordination and advocacy may be different talents and not often found in the same person. Each skill set is based on different personality characteristics and life experiences.

In addition, each approach responds to different urban challenges. The coordinator helps to resolve interpersonal conflicts and social pathologies. In fact, the coordinator may help prepare the "culture" of a council for a mayor who emphasizes advocacy. Darrah, for example, did return the council to civility. Under her leadership, serious debate could be held in public without resorting to histrionics. Thereafter, this tradition was available to moderate the high-profile discussions that accompanied the issues for which Podesto advocated. Advocates like Podesto can stimulate economic development and privatization, but only if they have a forum in which restrained discussions that lead to action can be held.

Clusters of such issues, those requiring coordination and those calling out for advocacy, are on urban agendas, but may be undertaken cyclically as was the experience here. Darrah and Podesto both contributed to the quality of life of the community, both helped to bring the city closer together, but each made a unique contribution to the definition of the position of Stockton's mayor. While it is difficult to read the tendency of their successor, Mayor Edward Chavez, he appears to favor a return to an emphasis on coordination, responding to the need of the city to consolidate its activism and reconsider its agendas (Fitzgerald 2007).

References

Banfield, Edward C. 1961. *Political Influence: A New Theory of Urban Politics*. New York: Free Press.

Browning, Rufus P., Dale Rogers Marshall, and David H. Tabb. 1984. *Protest is Not Enough*. Berkeley, CA: University of California.

Browning, Rufus P., Dale Rogers Marshall, and David H. Tabb. 1990. Minority mobilization in ten cities: Failures and successes. In *Racial Politics in American Cities*, eds. Rufus P. Browning, Dale Rogers Marshall, and David H. Tabb. New York: Longman.

Dahl, Robert A. 1961. *Who Governs*. New Haven, CT: Yale University Press.

Darrah, Joan. 2003. *Getting Political: Stories of a Woman Mayor*. Sanger, CA: Quill Driver.

Fitzgerald, Michael. 2007. With condos on hold, downtown Stockton's revival looking dubious. *The Record*, September 14, B1.

Garreau, Joel. 1991. *Edge Cities: Life on the New Frontier*. New York: Doubleday.

Judge, David. 1995. Pluralism. In *Theories of Urban Politics*, eds. David Judge, Gerry Stoker, and Harold Wolman. London: Sage, 13–34.

Linesburg, Scott. 2005. Hockey? In Stockton? Podesto's visions of grandeur. *The Record*, December 8, C1.

Podesto, Gary. 2005. Ex-mayor: Don't be so hasty on Mark Lewis. *The Record*, September 4, R1.

Sams, Jim. 1995. Gary Podesto throws hat in mayoral ring. *The Record*, December 6, Section 2, 1.

Sams, Jim. 1996. Podesto mandate: It'll take power, patience, persuasion to get City Hall. *The Record*, March 28, Section 2, 1.

Sams, Jim. 1997a. Council clashes on panel: Mayor defends solo decision. *The Record*, June 10, Section 2, 1.

Sams, Jim. 1997b. Mayor gets high marks after first 6 months. *The Record*, June 20.

Schroeder, Dan. 2005. Podesto improved city during mayoral reign. *The Record*, January 10, Business, 6.

Siders, David. 2004. His days as mayor done, Gary Podesto leaves Stockton with a window of opportunities, Last day on job is a time for nostalgia. *The Record*, December 31, A1.

Snitow, Alan, Deborah Kaufman, and Michael Fox. 2007. *Thirst: Fighting the Corporate Theft of Our Water*. San Francisco: Jossey-Bass.

Stockton City Charter. 2006. Stockton, CA.

Stone, Clarence. 1989. *Regime Politics: Governing Atlanta, 1946-1988*. Lawrence, KS: University Press of Kansas.

Stone, Clarence. 1995. Political leadership in urban politics. In *Theories of Urban Politics*, eds. David Judge, Gerry Stoker, and Harold Wolman. London: Sage, 96–116.

Svara, James H. and Associates. 1994. *Facilitative Leadership in Local Government: Lessons from Successful Mayors and Chairpersons.* San Francisco: Jossey-Bass.

The Record (Editorial). 1996, Mayor: Gary Podesto offers fresh approach in City Hall. March 24, Section 2.

The Record (Editorial). 2004. A positive legacy, Gary Podesto dared to dream about greatness as Stockton's mayor. December 5, B8.

Chapter 12

Charting Progress of the Empowered Mayor: The 'Stronger Mayor' in Cincinnati, Ohio

John T. Spence

Contents

253

12.1 Introduction

In May of 1999, a mere 18 percent of Cincinnati, Ohio's registered voters set in motion the most dramatic changes in municipal operation since 1926, by changing the city's form of government from what was locally labeled a "weak mayor" to a "stronger mayor" form.*

During the 1990s, there had been considerable dissatisfaction with the way the Cincinnati city council functioned—or failed to function. Council relations were perceived as hostile, performance sluggish, and an apparent lack of productivity frustrated many citizens. With the adoption of a stronger mayor system, expectations rose that beginning in December 2001, both accountability and efficiency in city government would improve. The change to a stronger mayor in Cincinnati was, in the words of one neighborhood activist, "not about who's in charge," but about "who's going to be held accountable"(Wilkinson and Anglen 2001).

Cincinnati's stronger mayor council–manager government was a compromise between those seeking an executive mayor and those protective of the more traditional council–manager form. Cincinnati has a strong adherence to the council–manager form—not supporting direct mayoral election until long after many larger American cities. One reason may be attributable to the historical legacy of the city's reform movement from the 1920s: the Charter Committee, which remains very active in city politics. This group sees the city manager as the linchpin of good government and has strongly opposed efforts to reduce the city manager's administrative freedom, or council's ability to check mayoral power.

Despite the city's support for council–manager government, leaders of Cincinnati's movement to create an executive mayor argued that the current system was unable to deliver effective leadership, and they promoted an executive mayor as a means to clarify lines of authority and increase accountability. Voters, however, rejected this proposal in 1995.† Yet all parties, even those who organized against

---

* According to standard classifications, "weak mayor" refers to a variation of the mayor-council form, and the term used nationally to refer to a substantially expanded mayor's position in a council–manager government is the "empowered" mayor (Hansell 1999).
† Issue 1 called for an executive mayor. It was placed before the voters in a special election in August of 1995 and rejected, with 64 percent against. The measure was funded by the local Republican Party and Cincinnati business interests.

the executive mayor proposal, realized that the argument for some type of change to strengthen mayoral leadership was persuasive and that the "top voter" method of selecting the mayor was contributing to a high level of dissension within the city council. Expectations were that a compromise stronger mayor would now provide leadership to solve some of the stubborn urban problems associated with the city for several decades: population loss, economic flight, and a perception of negative race relations.

Specifically, the change from a weak mayor to a stronger mayor meant that the mayor would be directly elected for a four-year term (with a nonpartisan primary), have the power to appoint the vice mayor, appoint and replace council committee chairs, and assign legislation to council committees. The mayor, although not a member of the council and, therefore, unable to vote, would be able, however, to exercise a legislative veto, and hire and fire the city manager with the consent of a majority of the nine member council. Term limits would allow the mayor a maximum of two consecutive four-year terms. (See Table 12.1 for a more detailed comparison of institutional differences between the prior council–manager and current stronger mayor forms.)

Since the development of council–manager government in Cincinnati, the mayor has been selected using three very different methods. From 1926 to 1987, the mayor was chosen by council. From 1987 to 2001, the city practiced a unique method of selection—the council candidate who received the most votes in the at-large council election became the mayor. This was known as the "top vote getter" form. With the adoption of the stronger mayor form, the mayor is now elected in a separate head-to-head race. Leadership expectations during the "top vote getter" period became complicated; there were high expectations and perceptions of low performance. This situation contributed to a growing frustration with governmental leadership and led to the adoption of "Issue 4," the stronger mayor proposal, albeit by a margin of only 2,277 votes (53 percent "yes"). While the change to stronger mayor has stretched the definition of what constitutes a council–manager form of government, this compromise enabled the community to find a politically acceptable means to reduce political conflict and calm criticism of city hall.

The organization of political units affects the distribution of power, political relationships, and performance expectations. Each form of government and each institutional change has a different set of costs and benefits (Wheeland 1990). To paraphrase political scientist Harold Lasswell (1936), the institutional structure defines who holds control over who gets what, when, and how. Of interest to the researcher is not only the form institutional change takes, but the motivations of those who demand or resist change, the consequences of change, and whether or not the final outcomes of the change meet expectations.

In the case of this research, the primary goal was to determine the impact of recent changes made to Cincinnati's council–manager form of government and whether or not they met expectations.

Table 12.1 Comparison of Differences: Council–Manager to Stronger Mayor Plans*

Previous Council–Manager Plan	Stronger Mayor Plan
The mayor is elected through "top vote getter" method—the council candidate with the highest vote total. Previously, the mayor was chosen by council majority. The election is nonpartisan.	The mayor is directly elected by voters in a head-to-head race between the top two candidates selected in a nonpartisan primary. The General Election is a partisan race.
The mayor has a two-year term. With the introduction of term limits, council members serve a maximum of four terms.	The mayor has a four-year term with term limits allowing two terms. Council member terms do not change.
The mayor is a member of council with no formal powers other than to preside over council meetings. Other formal powers, such as assigning legislation, are granted the mayor by council.	The mayor is not a member of council and, therefore, cannot vote. The mayor's formal powers include hiring and firing of city manager, with consent of council; presiding over council meetings; assigning legislation to committees; naming vice-mayor and committee chairs; and veto of legislation. The mayor is formally recognized as head of the city for purposes of contracts, inter-governmental relations, etc.
Council is composed of nine members who are the top candidates elected at-large in a nonpartisan race. Prior to 1957, council members were elected by proportional voting.	No change
The city manager reports to council, and serves at the pleasure of council.	The city manager reports to the mayor (council cannot initiate hiring or firing).

* Sources: Derived from the Charter of the City of Cincinnati (November 1999) and Fox (1999).

12.2 Cincinnati and Council–Manager Government

Council–manager government in Cincinnati was adopted in 1926, as a result of the political successes of progressive reformers of the post World War I era. At that time, city government was considered by many to be corrupt, inefficient, and poorly managed (Taft 1933, Childs 1965). Through the introduction of scientific management techniques, and as a result of structural changes designed to decrease "cronyism," the reformers reasoned that government would be more efficient, accountable, and ethically managed (Schiesl 1977). A key element of the reform agenda was to separate municipal administration from political interference while bringing expertise to bear on policy making. A professional city manager would advise the council on policy and administer the bureaucracy, while the council would limit itself, at least theoretically, to policy making and general oversight.

The changes the reformers imposed on the structural organization of municipal government resulted in changes (to paraphrase Wilson) in the distribution of power, administrative focus, and in the authority to appoint and dismiss (Wilson 1912). These structural changes remained intact in Cincinnati for almost thirty years, at which time the first change voters made was choosing to drop 'Proportional Voting,' part of the Model City Charter recommended for the council–manager form, but adopted by very few cities. Dynamic partisan conflict and a changing demographic in community leadership caused further modifications to Cincinnati's council–manager form in the latter half of the twentieth century. (See Table 12.1 for a comparison of the former and current council form.)

As a result of the changes wrought by the Progressive Era, some large American cities like Cincinnati adopted the council–manager form, while other smaller municipalities which had adopted the form experienced substantial population growth in the postwar period. Since 1990, several of these larger American municipal governments have experienced the change from council–manager to a strong mayor or "executive mayor" form. Others have only modified the council–manager form and, like Cincinnati, created "stronger mayors." These cities provide some sense of the administrative and political impact that might be expected in Cincinnati as a result of this change.

Sparrow's (1985) study of San Diego, for example, illustrated a case in which a mayor with a strong personality was confronted by an electorate that was not ready for dramatic institutional change. In that case, the mayor responded by developing political strategies that eventually led to the creation of the strong mayor form he sought. Seemingly minor modifications to the council system, and the development of nonelected boards responsible to the mayor, allowed for a significant shift in power from the council to the mayor without a direct voter mandate or official change in form. Ironically, later it was argued that the remnants of these very strategies were responsible for San Diego's inability to meet the challenges of the new century (Michaud 1999). In 2006, San Diego did change its form of government.

San Jose, California; Charlotte, North Carolina; and Kansas City, Missouri, adopted various reforms to empower the mayor in varying degrees in order to increase the capacity for, and speed of, policy initiatives. These cities modified the council–manager form primarily by investing the mayor with enhanced powers. Whether the alterations constituted a new "form" of government (Svara 2001), and whether these changes have enabled these municipalities to meet their challenges more effectively has not yet been determined.

Much has been written in the media about the benefits of the "strong" and "stronger mayor" forms of government, but little has been published in the way of academic comparison. Like the "Hawthorne effect," it may be that the change itself, and not the specific governmental form taken, is the key factor leading to people's perceptions that the negatives of an existing governmental form have been overcome by adopting new structures or a new form (Frederickson, Johnson, and Wood 2004).

As smaller council–manager cities grow into more heterogeneous and complex urban environments, the ability to set policy becomes more difficult and conflicted. Some observers criticize municipal elected officials in this situation for being afraid to make decisions, emasculated by political infighting, and this argument was made repeatedly in Cincinnati. With fragmented power and a slow political reaction to change, bureaucracies may be deemed unaccountable and government decision making too slow. Many reformers declare a need for decisive leadership (Ferman 1985) as a means of reinvigorating their city, although some argue that such leadership can be achieved within the logic of the council–manager form (Svara and Associates 1994).

To municipal analyst Terrell Blodgett, Cincinnati's mayoral powers should be of concern to those who support council–manager government because the current mayor has:

> … the power to set the agenda, and the power to appoint all the council committees. He has a four-year term versus a two-year term for council members, which means he can campaign against at least half the council without being at risk himself because he's in the middle of a term. He can appoint assistants and set their salaries. He has the veto. Only he can initiate hiring a manager. Only he can initiate firing the manager. He holds such power over the council that he can punish them if they don't vote the way he wants them to. He can bury their items and never put them on the agenda. He can put them on useless council committees. … If he wants to exercise the legal powers he has, he could certainly put the council members very much at a disadvantage.*

Often the argument for change in a council–manager government is sparked by a call for improved policy innovation and accountability through the strengthening of the office of mayor. As it has been suggested, the argument is largely related to determining where power ought to reside within the political structure (Ehrenhalt 2004). Conflict often arises between defenders of the current system and those who wish to modify it to overcome perceived community challenges.

---

* Taken from an interview with Terrell Blodgett, Professor Emeritus in Urban Management at the LBJ School of Public Affairs at the University of Texas, in McGrath (2001).

Such conflict about the best way to organize the structure of municipal government appears to be ongoing. In fact, it may well be cyclical, shifting between an emphasis on consolidating power in the mayoralty versus an emphasis on representative democracy and an appointed executive. Cincinnati's urban reformers of the early twentieth century established a council–manager form of government hoping to improve efficiency, and accountability; ironically the same arguments were used at the end of the century to increase the mayor's power over the council. What determines the nature of reform, or which side of the power equation is prioritized at any point in time, may well be determined by what has not been tried recently (Frederickson, Johnson, and Wood 2004).

The terms "efficiency" and "equity" have many meanings. For this study, enhanced policy innovation is regarded as concentrating decision making in one elected office, that of the mayor. Theoretically, concentrating power will result in fewer problems with coordination and reduce conflicting interests; thereby enhancing the speed of policy making (as fewer elected officials are involved in decision making). The variable "efficiency" was used in this study to describe this condition: streamlined policy making.

Another definition of "efficiency" in government is the efficient use of resources for achieving a goal (cost versus benefit). Equity, on the other hand, most often refers to issues of public participation and access, or policies designed to ensure that resources are distributed fairly. A government that rates highly the issue of equity might, for example, give priority to processes that result in maximizing public participation.

Some analysts of municipal government declare that as a result of the "stronger mayor" structural changes, Cincinnati no longer has a council–manager form of government (Blodgett 1998). In a typical strong mayor government, the mayor is the chief executive officer of the city, and manages the day-to-day functions of the city government. Others argue that since the city manager still retains executive responsibilities, the council–manager form is modified but intact (Hansell 1999). As the mayor's powers under the recently adopted government in Cincinnati are somewhat more limited than the casebook definition of the strong mayor form, the new government has been referred to in Cincinnati as a stronger mayor council–manager form. Still, the new governmental form endows the mayor with considerably greater formal institutional power than under the typical council–manager plan. As a result the Cincinnati print media began describing the new form as "strong mayor" almost simultaneously with the adoption of stronger mayor by the voters. There is the possibility that perception can become reality.

12.3 Debate Between Forms of Municipal Government

Each form of government has a different set of costs and benefits. Depending on what values are being stressed by a community at any given time, the government of the day may be considered sufficient or antiquated. In American municipal history, the change from one form to another is usually a result of conflict, which tends to reflect national political trends, and the continuing struggle to frame the content, and control the implementation of public policy (Straayer 1973).

Cincinnati's adoption of the council–manager plan in the 1920s was a result of concerted efforts made by reformers over the course of many years seeking to rid the city of what was considered by many, an antiquated, corrupt, and unaccountable political system (Taft 1933, Miller 1968). Eventually a reform movement called the Charter Committee accomplished the task. They were able to do this by offering a well-defined alternative to the current system, effective elite leadership, support from an increasing number of middle-class voters, and because, after the passing of "Boss Cox," the Boss system in Cincinnati began to lose its political clout.

The council–manager plan remained relatively intact for four decades, with the most important institutional modification perhaps being the change from proportional voting in 1957 to a "9X" system where voters cast ballots for up to nine individual council candidates. In the 1960s, and until the mid-1970s, the Democratic Party and the Charter Committee agreed to split the council-appointed mayoralty, with the mayor representing one group one year, the other the next. This was followed in 1987 (until 2001) by a system where the "top vote getter" in council elections was named mayor.

Cincinnati's "top vote getter" system contributed to institutional conflict that helped drive a growing perception that Cincinnati's social and economic challenges were unsolvable by the current distribution of political power within council. There was no natural coalition to support the council member who had been elected mayor. Even the mayor's nominal leadership roles formed the basis of competition. In 1997, for example, council stripped former mayor Roxanne Qualls of the mayor's traditional role of assigning legislation to committees. As interviews gathered for this study attest, under the "top vote getter" form, collegiality was perceived to be secondary to political "one-upmanship." In this form, in which council members were continually vying for leadership, former city manager John Shirey found that "sometimes there [were] ten city managers" (Goldberg 1996).

Reformers began calling for the adoption of a "strong mayor" plan both, according to one pundit, to "streamline" communication and "put one person in charge" (Radel 1999). This modern reform movement was further energized by a general perception that the "top vote getter" method for electing the mayor from among council candidates was flawed, further exacerbating the lack of accountability and reducing efficient decision making at city hall. Several times in the 1990s, stakeholders representing those supportive of the traditional council–manager form and those pushing for more mayoral powers formally debated the most appropriate institutional arrangement needed to address the twin challenges of economic development and improved race relations. In 1991, term limits were adopted, in part as a result of the perception that council was ineffective (Beaupre 2000).

In 1995, a "strong mayor" ballot initiative was rejected by voters. However, stakeholders agreed that the "top vote getter" election of the mayor should be replaced. A series of meetings between stakeholders resulted in a new ballot initiative calling for the modification of the council–manager form by creating a "stronger mayor." This was approved by voters in 1999, taking effect in 2001. Ironically, months before the first mayoral election under this modified council–manager plan, the city experienced several days of "race riots," and the perception of a slow response by the city's elected officials to this "crisis" seemingly substantiated the voter's support for shifting power from council to a directly elected mayor.

What these changes illustrate is the continuing conflict that revolves around municipal institutional structure between those in the community that perceive that they are benefited best by the status quo and those seeking benefit through change. Because many municipal institutional changes must be approved by voters, the effort to affect voter perceptions is a key strategy for change. In Cincinnati, it took five ballot initiatives before voters replaced proportional voting, and several modifications to council elections and methods of mayoral appointment before the adoption of the stronger mayor proposal. As perceptions of ineptitude on the part of council grew in the 1990s, so did support for supplementing mayoral power. However, Cincinnati has a strong commitment to the council–manager form and, as a result, changes in the basic structure of city government tend to be modified incrementally. While an executive mayor was rejected, a more modest shift in power from council to the mayor was accepted. The debate as to what form of municipal government will provide the best response to perceived community challenges depends on what goals are being prioritized at the time the question is asked, and how well those supporting change make their case.

12.4 Measuring Perceptions of Change

When attempting to determine whether changes made in Cincinnati's council–manager system were significant, examining institutional elements may allow some assumptions to be made; however, interviewing "informed observers" permits a more robust approach. Perceptions provided the basis for the actions taken to modify the existing institutional structure, and it will be perceptions that will eventually determine whether the stronger mayor form has been successful in meeting expectations. Perceptions were, for example, a major factor influencing whether or not voters in Massachusetts adopted prospective structural changes to the town meeting government (Fahy 1998). In El Paso, the impact of voter perceptions regarding the weaknesses of an existing governmental form was the force for structural change, in this case ironically from strong mayor to a council–manager form (Okubo 2005). A perception of racism was suggested as the underlying reason behind the recent failure of St. Louis to change from a weak mayor–council form to the strong mayor form (Cropf and Swanstrom 2005).

For this study, perceptions were obtained from informed observers using a pretest and posttest interview process. "Informed" in this case refers to those members of the public considered to have an intimate knowledge of the preexisting council–manager form and the modified stronger mayor form. The selection criteria were based on three identifying factors. They were: (1) their leadership in the respective movement either for changing or preserving the preexisting governmental structural form, (2) their membership in organizations involved in the community discussion surrounding the proposed change, or (3) their professional experience in the previous council–manager form and their role in the community discussion.

Upon review of ten years' worth of Cincinnati's two daily newspapers, 60 individuals were identified as meeting the criteria for inclusion in the study. Of these, 39 participated in the pretest interview, and 34 of these individuals participated in the posttest interview. Those interviewed included current and former elected officials, interest group leaders, city administrators, business leaders, and media representatives. Demographically, those interviewed represented a cross-section of the community, but selection was not based on an ideal demographic.

Pretest (or prechange) interviews were conducted *two months* prior to the implementation of the stronger mayor form. Posttest (or postchange) interviews were conducted approximately *one year* after the stronger mayor form was implemented. The same questions, using the same closed response set, were used in both interviews. The first round of interviews (prechange) focused on developing an understanding of how the council–manager form was being operated. It also provided a baseline for evaluating whether differences would be seen on key issues in comparison with the stronger mayor form.

Data were collected from a series of questions whose content was based on generally recognized powers, duties, and roles played by elected officials, and issues related to local government. Those interviewed were asked about government performance, current political relationships and the distribution of power, how policy was made, the legislative and political process, elections, and political affiliations. In the second round of interviews, questions previously asked were reexplored to ascertain if, and in what ways, the new stronger mayor governmental form was different.

To examine perceptions from another vantage point, cues were sought from the print media to determine whether they had perceived any shift in power as a result of the structural change. In a traditional council–manager form of government, the council is generally considered the policy leader. Did the change to stronger mayor result in a difference in the way the print media credited policy leadership? Information gathered this way augmented the analysis of data collected from interviewing.*

---

* One area of research that was foregone due to lack of data was the measurement of policy leadership using press conferences and press advisories. These are typical means elected officials use to advise the press and public on issues, gain name recognition, and garner credit as a policy leader. After an exhaustive search of the city clerk's office, it was determined that records of press conferences are not maintained at city hall.

Interview questions were developed to allow research to be focused on four primary category areas of municipal government.* These categories were

- Issues of Performance
- Issues of Structure
- Issues of Power, Policy Making, and the Legislative Process
- Issues of Politics, Elections, and Political Affiliation

12.5 Perceptions of Change

Changes made to Cincinnati's council–manager form of government have had significant impacts in several key areas. Chief among these is the perceived shift of power from council to the mayor, and to a lesser degree, from the city manager to the mayor. These perceptions are based on the adoption of stronger mayor, but also as a result of a change in the composition of the council. The change in council and, therefore, its personality, can be credited primarily to the impact of term limits. Together, institutional changes and term limits have altered dramatically the power-sharing arrangements at city hall, and significantly affected perceptions of Cincinnati's political situation in a number of key ways.

- There has been a significant shift in power from council to the mayor.
- There is significantly less importance given to the mayor's ceremonial roles as a criterion for evaluating mayoral performance.
- Expectations have increased for the mayor to play a more significant role in the areas of policy development and organizing.
- There has been a significant decrease in the relative importance of council's role as appointer, supervisor, and appraiser of the manager.
- There has been a significant shift toward a more positive perception of council collegiality.
- There is a significant decrease in the relative importance of the city manager's role in making recommendations to council.
- There has been a significant shift in opinion regarding the quality of the relationship between council and the city manager, with a substantial majority now having a more positive, although cautious, view of this relationship.

As significant as these changes are, the areas in which there have not been significant shifts in perceptions are equally of interest. Despite arguments that the change to stronger mayor would enhance efficiency and accountability, study findings indicate that has not happened. Further, there has been no change in the level

---

* For a more detailed description of the methodology employed in this study, see the end of the chapter.

of equity; perceptions are that the stronger mayor form provides just the same level of citizen participation as did the previous council–manager form.

Perceptions by the general public of the mayor as the leader at city hall seem to have been enhanced by the addition of a mayoral legislative veto. Yet the informed observers understand that the mayor's power to ensure policy implementation is primarily dependent on the issue involved. Despite the fact that the perception of the quality of the relationship between city hall and the community-at-large remains relatively the same, survey respondents seem to exhibit a cautious optimism about the future of the stronger mayor council–manager form. That optimism may be related to the hope that the institutional and personality changes that have taken place at city hall will result in better relationships among elected officials, and between city hall and the community.

The caution however, is based on the knowledge that Cincinnati is facing several challenges. Key among these is the quality of race relations and the reinvigoration of economic development. Many respondents said that progress toward resolving these issues needs to be evident before they would be optimistic about the future.

Finally, survey respondents saw no significant difference in the way Cincinnati's electoral environment has been affected by the change to stronger mayor. Given that future mayoral elections will be different because of the switch to a "head-to-head" race as opposed to the former "top vote getter" model, respondents understand that council elections will remain the same. Name recognition will continue to be the primary council election strategy. Because candidates are identified by their party label during campaigns, party affiliation will continue to play an important electoral role. However, perceptions are that the importance of the party itself to the success of individual candidates in local elections is generally minimal.

Party affiliation also continues to be seen as playing a minor role in relationships among elected officials at city hall. Collaboration is based more on common issue interests or beliefs than party politics. Yet, informed observers know that party affiliation will still play a role in affecting the committee chair assignments council members receive. In general, though, Cincinnati has a history of cross-party collaboration and this situation is expected to continue.*

12.6 Understanding Perceptions of Change

The basis for the perceptions of change found in this study can be explained in large part by three basic political changes Cincinnati has experienced since 1990:

---

* Candidates for Cincinnati mayor and council are generally Democrats, Republicans, or Charterites. The Charter Committee originated in the reform efforts of the 1920s. Although it does not consider itself a political party, Charter acts as one, recruiting, funding, and supporting candidates who run for city office under the Charter label. Charter members who run for county and state offices run under party labels, primarily Democrat.

1. With Cincinnati's move from council–manager to "stronger mayor," institutional arrangements of power have been modified significantly, thus creating increased expectations for mayoral leadership.
2. The change of the mayoral election system from the "top vote getter" model to a separate "head-to-head" election.
3. The adoption of term limits leading to a significant change in the composition of the council and, thus, its personality.

The first of these changes modified form, while the other two altered election rules. Each of these modifications has contributed to perceptual changes in terms of power arrangements, relationships, and expectations. Exactly how much each of these changes individually has contributed to perceptions found in this study is speculation. Although the structural change to stronger mayor and the electoral change from "top vote getter" garnered most of the public analysis, one cannot discount the impact of a new cast of characters on council due to term limits. While institutional structure remains important, the political skills of the individuals in government may ultimately determine whether it operates economically, efficiently, effectively, and equitably (Blodgett 1998).

12.6.1 Structural Changes Bring Power to the Mayor

The mayor has now become the unquestioned leader of the Cincinnati council–manager government. Perceptions are that the mayor should be evaluated more by his ability to develop policy, set goals, delegate, and organize than by his nominal leadership roles, such as ceremonial head of the city. Perceptions of council indicate a decreasing expectation of performance in the area of appointments, management, supervision, and appraisal. For the city manager there is a lower performance expectation in the making of policy recommendations and preparation of the budget.

With the enhanced powers assigned to the mayor, there are increased performance expectations. The mayor is expected to become more aggressive in developing policy, and showing both political and social leadership. These expectations do not seem unjustified given the mayor's new powers. The new institutional arrangements are such that the mayor now has the ability to do more than coax and cajole. The mayor has been removed from, and elevated above, the council. The mayor presides over council meetings and can introduce and veto legislation. For all practical purposes, he appoints and manages the city manager.* This has the potential to allow the mayor to play a role in setting council's agenda and influencing administrative actors and processes. While council's role in naming the manager is not unimportant, it is generally acknowledged that in the case of Cincinnati's manager, his first allegiance is to the mayor.

---

* Regarding use of the male pronoun when referring to mayor—This is used here because the first two mayors to serve under the new system were male, the second of whom is serving as mayor at the time of this writing.

Naming council committee chairs is a powerful tool for the mayor to use to build policy support within council. Council members generally enjoy public attention and the ability to initiate policy discussions and legislation. This is a carrot. A council member who supports the mayor can receive recognition, special titles, and the opportunity to share in the spotlight of public attention. The mayor's veto power is often seen as a negative authority used to block legislation and enforce adherence to the mayor's agenda, but it can also be used to promote compromise. For council to override the mayor's veto, a super majority of six votes must be formed. This threat gives the mayor the opportunity to initiate legislative compromise and have more than an equal role in the policy making process (Morgan and Watson 1996).

The threat of replacing the committee chairman is, ultimately, the greatest leverage the mayor has to gain legislative adherence. A mayor willing to exercise this power of the stronger mayor can greatly diminish opportunities for political leadership and visibility for council members who do not share the same philosophical orientation, or have an opposing agenda. This is a stick. Like the veto, this power holds greater value as a threat, or when used sparingly. While council has some flexibility to develop leadership on issues, if council perceives that the mayor is not reticent to use his "stronger" powers, it would be critical that the mayor's counsel be sought.

The mayor can exercise a legislative voice by submitting legislation through committees, on the floor at a council meeting, or through a council member. If, during the course of legislative discussions, changes were made to the original legislation that did not require a vote, the mayor could not veto those specific changes. The mayor may only veto a piece of legislation that has received an officially recorded vote, but he does not have a line item veto. Thus, this scenario requires the mayor to rely on a council member to introduce disagreeable changes leading to a council vote before casting a veto.

During the 2003 budget process, for example, several individual changes were made to the budget that were not based on separate votes of council. These changes to the mayor's proposed budget were made during the typical legislative negotiations required to obtain a council majority. The mayor would only be able to veto a specific line item if there was an up or down vote on the matter. In effect, the mayor must rely on his relationship with council to provide this opportunity.

Institutional arrangements have also provided the mayor with the ability to develop a unique relationship with the city manager. Although technically working for the mayor *and* council, the reality is that the city manager is more dependent on the mayor than at any time in the last eighty years. Under the current institutional arrangement, council cannot initiate the manager's removal. Only the mayor may initiate action to have the manager removed. However, the mayor cannot unilaterally remove the city manager. It takes majority support from the council to do so.

The institutional relationship between the mayor and city manager raises serious questions. Is the manager now seen as the mayor's staff that leaves with the mayor at the end of his term in office? How well would city hall function administratively if the manager's relationship were better with council than with the mayor? These questions may not be answered until other mayors have time to settle into the office. Under the current institutional arrangements however, the city manager's first allegiance almost has to be to the stronger mayor. Mayor Charlie Luken, the city's first stronger mayor, and his successor, Mark Mallory, each offered only one city manager candidate to the council for approval. Although individual members argued that council should be given more candidates to consider, both mayors refused, and both had their choices accepted.

Perceptions are that the city manager lost power to the mayor in this new stronger mayor institutional arrangement. This is as a result of a clearer chain-of-command (the city manager reports to the mayor), an increase in the mayor's formal participation in the budget process, and a lowering of expectations that the city manager will take an active role in developing policy.*

The budget process illustrates how much institutional changes have contributed to the changed relationship between the mayor, city manager, and council. The stronger mayor charter calls for the mayor to present the budget to council, unlike under the previous council–manager form. The budget is perceived to be the mayor's, not the city manager's, and this was Luken's practice. The budget submitted to council by Luken consisted of the consensus arrived at by the mayor and city manager; however this was not the case with the most recent budget (2007). Council received one budget from the city manager and another from Mallory.†

Theoretically, the budget process begins with the city manager and staff developing a budget in response to council's "policy budget." This is submitted to staff at the time that the city's tax revenue is certified, as called for by state legislation. The policy budget provides some broad policy guidelines by which city staff can determine whether department level budgets, which percolate up through the bureaucracy, are in conflict with council priorities. The city manager and a budget committee then develop a draft budget for the mayor's review and comment prior to submission to council.

In reality, Luken and the city manager developed the 2003 budget draft together, and once council received the draft, council's Finance Committee chair was charged with building legislative support. Compromises were made to obtain a unanimous vote on the budget. Unanimity was symbolically important to illustrate the new council's collegial relationship compared to councils in the

---

* One of the primary methods used to determine hierarchical status is the performance evaluation. The city's charter does not state who evaluates the city manager's job performance. It may be that the manager does not receive a formal evaluation. Instead, the mayor (or council) may suggest that the manager receive a salary adjustment. Such an adjustment would, theoretically, require approval by council. If this scenario occurs it may be a symbolic affirmation that the manager has received a positive job performance evaluation.

† According to Gregory Korte of *The Cincinnati Enquirer*, no independent budget from the city manager was published and no records of independent recommendations made by the city manager are available.

1990s, and to demonstrate mayoral leadership and council political support.* Significant budget cuts were made, including the elimination of the city's Planning Department. Along with the city manager's office, the Planning Department was one of the vestiges of the Charter Committee's 1920s contributions to "good government" in Cincinnati. The budget process reveals both the institutional power of the mayor to be involved in administrative matters and his symbiotic relationship with council.

The budget process also illustrates the reality of the mayor and manager's relationship. While it is generally assumed the mayor and manager have a close relationship in the council–manager form (Svara 1986), in Cincinnati, this relationship has taken on a more elevated and formal definition.† Cincinnati's stronger mayor and manager relationship closely resembles those of council–manager cities of comparable size as defined by Morgan and Watson (1992), wherein the mayor and manager form a team with the mayor as the dominant partner. Interestingly, in the budget process of 2006/2007, the new city manager's budget was perceived to be more closely in line with council's agenda than that of Mallory. Yet, the mayor was perceived to have played a significant role in facilitating the compromises that resulted in the adopted budget.

Using his institutional powers, Cincinnati's first stronger mayor named the vice-mayor and council committee chairs, hand-picked the city manager, guided legislation, took leadership on administrative issues and significantly influenced the city's budget. He vetoed two pieces of legislation, threatened veto on other occasions, and became the primary source of formal institutional leadership at city hall. There was little initiative at city hall during this time that was not credited by the press to stronger mayor Luken, who received favorable reviews for getting "a rancorous City Council to behave for the first time in more than a decade" (Korte 2003).

As Cincinnati's second stronger mayor, Mallory has benefited from precedents set by Luken. Like Luken, Mallory too, is perceived as fostering council collegiality. He, too, has threatened vetoes in efforts to enable legislative compromise. Despite his having more conflict with council than Luken did, over both his city manager nominee and the most recent budget process, many continue to see Mallory as the primary leader at city hall. This is a significant departure from the way the weak mayor was perceived in the previous council–manager form.

---

* This process, and analysis, was gleaned from discussions with Gregory Korte of *The Cincinnati Enquirer*, who covered Cincinnati city hall.
† The clearer chain-of-command is also as a result of the adoption of Issue 5 in November, 2001, which gives the city manager the authority to hire and fire future city officials, including the fire and police chiefs, without regard to civil service. This streamlining allows the mayor the potential to determine the future of administrative department heads directly, as a result of exerting control over the city manager.

12.6.2 *Ultimately, the Personality of the Mayor and Council Determine Effectiveness*

Despite the substantial powers that have accrued to the stronger mayor as a result of institutional structural and organizational changes, informed observers indicate that modification to the electoral system was just as important, and arguably more important, in creating change at city hall. The new personalities on council have more to do with "term limits" and electoral modifications than with structural changes. Despite calls for reform, and in spite of the mass media's tirades against status quo government, voters continued to reelect the same council throughout the 1990s. Change did not come about because voters suddenly awakened and wanted a different government, or because of the clarion call of the daily newspapers for more leadership. This is witnessed by the small number of the city's registered voters who bothered casting a ballot on the question of adopting the stronger mayor.

The individual who is elected is a critical element in defining the quality of a governing body. During interviews, comments were often made regarding the weakness of the Cincinnati council in the 1990s. There was a general feeling that the environment had been poisoned, not only by the change to "top vote getter" and the concomitant political conflict it wrought, but also by the arrival of several council members with strong personalities who did not necessarily respect the council–manager form. Whether these two events are coincidental is unknown.* What is known from interviews is that many "informed observers," and much of the mass media, had reached a point of general frustration with the council–manager government as it was. There were a growing number of calls for change. Arguments against the status quo were given further weight by the initially timid political response from the council–manager city hall during a period of racial tensions that erupted into violence in April 2001. An organized political response to the rioting was absent until the fourth day of hostilities when Luken announced that he would fill the political leadership vacuum. Setting in place a dusk-to-dawn curfew, Luken acknowledged the city had serious racial issues and soon began organizing support for a peaceful solution to racial tensions in the community. The following November, despite a second place showing in the September primary to Courtis Fuller, a popular local African-American newscaster, Luken was returned to City Hall as the city's first directly elected mayor in seventy-six years, receiving 55 percent of the vote.

Even with enhanced powers, it is ultimately the individual mayor's personality, political skills, and the context within which they operate that determines

---

* Another institutional change that may have contributed significantly to the way council interacts with the administration was the 1979 adoption of a relatively large council salary for what was considered a "part-time" job. The salary enabled some council members to assume a full-time legislative role. The addition of administrative staff (currently two for each member) further provides council members the opportunity to engage actively in research, policy development, and administrative oversight functions. It enhances their political capacity, including the ability to communicate with, and respond to the concerns of, their constituents.

effectiveness. This is true for mayor–council and council–manager cities alike. Richard Childs states that "outstanding dramatic mayors ... are rare birds in any trade and no system can be concocted as to produce them" (1965). Peter Lupsha's view of leadership suggests that when it does occur it "is more often a product of serendipity" and good fortune "than of any ongoing process or structure of urban leadership or office" (1982). Mayoral case studies often illustrate that successful mayors were able to achieve their successes principally due to their character and personality and, as Ferman (1985) suggests, the political skill to understand what is possible given the political context.

Structure does matter. The stronger mayor structure provides institutional tools to help the mayor push his policy agenda, and it may, perhaps by offering an attractive mixture of power and prestige, attract leaders of strong character. Survey respondents seemed to recognize, as Child's states, that "vigorously assertive personalities seem more to be expected from the direct election model" (1965). Svara found that mayors more often do not offer visionary leadership in council–manager government.* He suggests that additional powers may be necessary to provide the mayor with that capability. "The empowering provisions may enhance leadership first by giving the mayor additional tools to use in assembling a coalition of supporters where it does not naturally emerge and, second, perhaps more important, by attracting more assertive leaders who are put off by the perceived limitations of the mayor's office" (Svara 2001).

While the new stronger mayor provides the office with considerable formal structural powers, how well the mayor performs remains tied to character and personal abilities. The mayor still must build a majority on council to support the mayoral agenda. The mayor must make it difficult for council to override the threat of a veto. The mayor must trust that the chairs of the more critical committees, such as finance, remain allied. This type of political coalition building still demands substantial leadership character traits. The mayor must understand what is possible legislatively and what is not, which issues to leave to council, and how to build coalitions. In this regard, the stronger mayor, in order to be effective, must remain true to Svara's ideal council–manager leader, the facilitative mayor (Svara and Associates 1994).

Luken's extensive legislative experience provided him with the requisite background to build political coalitions.† His history reflected his ability to reach across

---

* Visionary leadership is often lacking in mayor–council cities as well.

† Charlie Luken's political experience is closely tied to his family. His father served on the Cincinnati city council and had seven terms in the U.S. Congress. His uncle was a member of the Ohio legislature, served as a council member in Cincinnati and, in the 1970s, as mayor. Charlie Luken finished tenth, out of nine seats, in his first race for the Cincinnati council in 1979. He was first elected to council in 1981, finishing eighth. Two years later he finished second, and in 1985, 1987, and 1989 finished first. In 1985, Luken was named mayor by council; however, in 1987 and 1989, he won the title via the "Top Vote Getter" system. Luken was the last mayor named by council, the first and last elected by the "Top Vote Getter" system, and the first elected by direct elections (2001) since council–manager government was instituted. In addition to his council experience, Luken was elected for one term to the U.S. Congress in 1990, filling the seat vacated by his father's retirement. Refusing another run, he returned to Cincinnati in 1993.

party affiliations to find common ground. Much of this commonality may be rooted in a shared, conservative, "go slow" approach to change. At the same time, Luken understood from his own legislative experience what political needs council members have; although presiding at most council meetings, he did not comment on every piece of legislation. He appeared to accept council's need to discuss issues, and understood that all elected officials must be able to debate policy publicly. He sparingly used his veto. This suggests that Luken was competently able to build coalitions, and did not feel the need to protect or emphasize his status by participating in all legislative actions.

Though Luken took the lead in hiring the city manager, the removal of certain citizens from mayoral-appointed committees, and in the development of the budget, he appeared comfortable with taking a more hands-off approach publicly to leadership on many other policy issues, preferring to remain in the background. This provided council members the opportunity to take the initiative in several policy areas. It may be that Luken understood that as the first stronger mayor he was setting precedent and purposely did not push the envelope of mayoral power, thereby giving justification to the fears of those who felt that the mayor was given too much power. It may also be that Luken generally preferred a facilitative approach to leadership.

Certainly it was easier for Luken to assume this role given the comparative lack of political experience on the part of council, composed mostly of newcomers who had never held political office. With his broad political history and his many political successes, there was no one on council of the same political stature, no challenger equal to the mayor in the public arena. This situation, combined with the subtlety with which Luken emphasized his stronger mayor powers, provided him with a unique opportunity to define the role of the stronger mayor in Cincinnati. He was able to do so without having to respond to political pressure from other elected officials who had their own idea of how the stronger mayor should act.

Mallory also has an extensive legislative record. Prior to being elected Cincinnati mayor, he served in the Ohio legislature, both as a Democratic representative (1995 to 1998) and as a senator (1999 to 2005). As a member of the minority party, Mallory had to practice the art of compromise and be able to work across party lines to be effective. Like Luken, Mallory's father was also a politician, who served as the Ohio House majority leader while a member of the state legislature. With this history, the perception and expectation of informed observers is that Mallory also should be able to build legislative and political coalitions successfully.

12.6.3 A Note on Council Power and Relationships

Acknowledging that power has shifted from council to the mayor *does not* mean that council has no ability to affect policy. With the mayoralty being separated from council, there may now be a stronger basis for council camaraderie and collegiality in the face of a potential enemy in the form of an aggressive mayor. The overt partisan nature of the mayoral election may also contribute to the development of a "loyal opposition" nurtured by party politics with an eye for future mayoral candidates.

During the summer of 2003 the city of Cincinnati faced an economic development decision that illustrates council's ability to affect mayoral policy. Convergys, a major corporation located in downtown Cincinnati, threatened to leave the city if not given financial inducements to purchase a building for employee consolidation. Luken, stating that Cincinnati could not afford the loss of this employer, took the initiative with "city administrators" crafting a $63.4 million deal (Monk 2003). Sufficient members of council balked, however, that a vote on the mayor's proposal did not occur. Two city council members one, a Democrat, the other a Republican, proposed an alternative deal for $51.8 million.

Although the two proposals appeared to differ greatly in total public dollars, the council proposal allowed Convergys to receive more cash in the earlier years of the deal such that "after adjusting for inflation, both are roughly equal in value" (Monk 2003). The primary difference between the two proposals appeared to be the method used to provide funding, with the mayor's plan dipping deeper into the general fund budget, and council's plan counting more upon property tax payments from downtown to pay off city bonds. The mayor argued that the council plan "would prevent the city from funding other downtown development projects and could ultimately prove more costly than the first Convergys proposal" (Monk 2003). Council members countered that their proposal would put fewer burdens on neighborhoods. Ultimately a compromise was reached and approved (8 to 1) by council, with the mayor's grudging support, for a package that totaled $52.2 million.

While keeping Convergys downtown was a victory for the mayor, council showed its independence, effectively answering the mayor's proposal, crafted by the city's economic development staff, with one of their own, primarily driven by Councilmember David Pepper.* It may be important to note that council argued, just a few months prior to a council election, that their proposal did less harm to neighborhoods. This type of proposal and counter-proposal activity indicates that council has, or at least certain members had, the ability to develop complex alternative proposals to the mayor's, the skill to build consensus, and the willingness to negotiate with the mayor to gain his support.

Relationships among council members have changed significantly from the time of the "top voter getter" mayoral elections to those under the "stronger mayor." Positive perceptions of council relationships found in this study were based on the appearance of a renewed civility that came with council's adoption of a set of general rules to guide conduct between council members. Not only did these rules provide a way for the first stronger mayor council to distance itself from the troubled councils of the 1990s, it also gave the public an alternative picture of council relationships.

Council's institutional powers remain considerable despite the stronger mayor form. Council controls the budget and still plays a major role as an interface

---

* Councilmember Pepper was later elected one of three commissioners for Hamilton County, Ohio. The proposal/counter-proposal was gleaned from an interview with a former staff member of the city's economic development department.

between the public and the city's administrative bureaucracy. Many actions taken by city hall during the Luken administration came as a result of policy leadership on the part of council members.

Council members help to keep the city in touch with the electorate. They serve as a pressure valve that helps to moderate the tension of distraught constituents. They draw attention to specific breakdowns in systems and problems with services. Council members also promote consideration of a wider range of alternatives than professionals might raise; and they deal with the political realities that surround many city government actions (Svara 1999).

Mallory also has been made aware that council retains considerable political muscle in the stronger mayor system and can have a significant impact on legislation. Soon after the last election (2005), five members of council—two Republicans, two Democrats, and a Charterite—formed a majority coalition. They have been active in creating alternatives to legislative proposals put forth by the mayor; a case in point being the city's most recent budget. This "center right coalition of five" is "able to marshal its powers and guard its prerogatives" as a result of a mutual decision that they could have more impact on policy making through a team approach, and Mallory must find a way to work with them (Korte 2007).*

Some informed observers indicate that this council majority's muscle flexing has shifted power at city hall away from the mayor and back toward council. If so, this is a significant change that supports the idea that the character of the individual elected official is more important to understanding the way power is distributed than institutional arrangement. It also means that Mallory may have to generally depend more on his informal powers of persuasion than the enhanced institutional powers that come with being the stronger mayor in order to guide policy making.

12.6.4 Electoral Changes and Term Limits Raise the Level of Expectation

Each of the three methods used to select the mayor in Cincinnati for the last eighty years has influenced the informal powers and expectations of mayoral leadership. Council selection of the mayor provided a natural coalition for the mayor, and a clear understanding of the source of power and status. The mayor was the nominal head of council, meaning that the mayor's ceremonial roles were paramount. The relationship among council members may have been highly collegial because the ability to assume the mayoralty depended on a good working relationship with council, or being a "team player." The mayor's and council's relationship with the city manager was similar to that of a board of directors with a corporate manager, and may have been influenced more by personality (informal power) than formal power.

---

* This coalition of council members is often referred to as "The Fiscal Five" as a result of their work together on the budget.

Expectations of the mayor in this council–manager form were based on the reality of council dominance. As former Cincinnati mayor Eugene Ruehlmann recounted:

> Walton Bachrach was an excellent ceremonial mayor (1963 to 1967). However, when there was a project-based issue raised, like utility rates, business leaders knew that the chairs of the Public Utilities and Finance committees were more important … for downtown growth projects, the chair of the Urban Development Committee.

> *(See also Kotter and Lawrence 1974, 106).*

Expectations of council performance were severely damaged as a result of the conflict generated between members as a consequence of the adoption of the "top vote getter" method for selecting the mayor in 1987. While voters ultimately decided who would be mayor, the process was convoluted, unpredictable, and the council member elected mayor was largely powerless; performance of the mayor was dependent on the collegial support of a majority of council. The "top vote getter" system contributed to a heightened sense of competition among council members, severely straining relationships. Several council members engaged in protracted gambits designed to increase their public exposure for the next council election, all of which was highly publicized, helping to lower public performance expectations and confidence in the council–manager form.

The stronger mayor form has redefined mayoral and council relationships and increased expectation of mayoral performance in particular. Structural modifications have created substantial formal powers that provide the mayor with opportunities to set the agenda, not just play a participatory role. Informed observers understand the significance of the mayor taking a policy leadership role. Expectations are that the mayor will now provide leadership to solve some of the stubborn urban problems that continue to plague Cincinnati. Also, as term limits caused the majority of council to shift from an experienced group of politicians to a less experienced group, there appears to have been a corresponding shift in perceptions away from skepticism and toward a feeling of guarded optimism that council would work together.

Whether these changes, in fact, will improve city hall's response to Cincinnati's problems remains a question, and however important structure may be, the personality and character of Cincinnati's elected officials may well be the key to answering that question.

12.7 Conclusions and Implications

The findings of this study indicate that the change made in Cincinnati's governmental form supports

- The idea that structural problems in municipal government are linked strongly to issues of authority, with accountability and efficiency being a hoped-for by-product of an increase in mayoral power.
- The argument that some large American cities are slowly developing a new form of municipal government, which is a synthesis (or "convergence") of mayor–council and council–manager forms.
- The idea that, in regard to perceptions of mayoral performance, structural change may be secondary to the value of the political leadership skills of the mayor.
- The idea that, rather than there being a preferential model of municipal government that cities will adopt, the form chosen reflects the unique historical political development of a community, and the ability of a proposed form to garner sufficient political support to be implemented.

12.7.1 Accountability and Efficiency

Both prechange and postchange perceptions held by informed observers indicate that the structural changes to Cincinnati's governmental form have not had a significant effect in a number of areas: efficiency, accountability, and the quality of the relationship between city hall and the greater community. After a decade of the "top vote getter" form, and accompanying concerns about Cincinnati's ability to attract private investment and heal conflicted race relations, it should be no surprise that few were ready to say that the stronger mayor form is a cure-all.

However, the compromise between those who wished for an executive mayor and those wanting to preserve the council–manager form has fulfilled, to a great extent, the demand for stronger leadership. The mayor has become, in terms of formal institutional powers, without a doubt, the primary center of power at city hall. Yet those interviewed indicated that the mayor's personality and, thus, his informal power, may be a more significant determinate of leadership, and have a stronger effect on perceptions of power and success than institutional change.

Currently the new stronger mayor, Mallory, is working to consolidate power at city hall. Whether perceptions of accountability (responsiveness to the public) and efficiency (the speed of decision making and the efficacious use of public funds) at city hall have improved may be determined in the future largely by Mallory's personal political skills. Perceptions appear to support the finding that the real argument for changing Cincinnati's governmental form was about enhancing mayoral authority. Increased efficiency and accountability were merely a hoped for by-product of the change.

To gain public support for adoption of the stronger mayor form, it may well have been perceived as necessary to suggest that such a change would enhance values the public already supports: accountability and efficiency. Using such "priming strategies" is not uncommon in attempting to sell potentially controversial solutions to perceived problems.

If it is perceived that the twin concerns of economic development and improved race relations are being addressed in a meaningful way, the new stronger mayor's performance evaluation may well be positive. Correspondingly, the structural changes made to the council–manager system will be considered a successful step forward in the development of a better Cincinnati.

12.7.2 Tradition and Convergence

Structural changes now provide the mayor with increased institutional powers, while protecting council's ability to blunt mayoral prerogatives using their power to override mayoral proposals. Perhaps most important to those supportive of council–manager government, Cincinnati's long-standing commitment to professional administration was preserved by maintaining a city manager. The city's compromise governmental structure represents a "convergence" of elements from the strong mayor and the council–manager forms. In this respect, Cincinnati's new municipal governmental form fits the Type III municipal government discussed by Frederickson, Johnson, and Wood (2004).

In practice, what institutional change a city may adopt could depend more upon which preferences, perspectives, and ideas win the competition for public support, than on an academic analysis of which change best supports the values prioritized by the community at any given time (Frederickson, Johnson, and Wood 2004).

12.7.3 Mayoral Performance and Political Skills

Whether the stronger mayor form was given too much, too little, or just enough power has not yet been determined. An interesting element of this research is that Luken, who was mayor in the former council–manager form, was also the first stronger mayor; he remained a constant. Mallory, then, is the first test case who has served only as a stronger mayor. If, as some suggest, character and political skills are more important than institutional arrangement, judgment as to the success or failure of the stronger mayor form may not be developed until after Mallory has had time to work within the system. This may help explain why the majority of those interviewed were taking a "wait and see" attitude toward evaluating mayoral success. Some complained that Luken had not exercised his new powers enough. They wanted the mayor to be more visionary and set an aggressive agenda for progress. What has been missing at city hall, say some, is a clearly articulated vision for the city's future, and leadership sufficiently strong to develop and implement the policies necessary to make that vision a reality.

Obviously, the transition to stronger mayor is by no means the end of change in Cincinnati, and events may conspire to create additional structural modifications before a deeper analysis of the impact of the most recent changes can occur. In politics, change does not wait for theory. Interest groups, who perceive that they were not well served or could be served better by a different municipal form, will work to "tweak" the system or change it entirely. The way voters respond to additional arguments for change, and the way Cincinnati's political elite perceive the benefits of these arguments, will illuminate further the city's political character.

Ultimately, the informal political skills of the mayor may be most important in determining mayoral performance success. In Cincinnati, Mallory must convince a skeptical public, and the city's elite, that city hall is effectively meeting the challenges of economic development, stemming population loss, and improving race relations. Whether the voters see the need for additional mayoral power and support a call for a strong mayor may be determined in large part by Mallory's ability to create positive perceptions of the city's government. For this he must, to paraphrase Richard Neustadt, depend upon a mayor's single most important political skill, "the power to persuade."

A Note on Methods

Generalized comparison between pre- and post-response sets (pre and post), particularly in terms of direction of change, was made using frequencies. The t-test was selected for measuring statistical significance due to the relatively small sample size. The object of this application was to determine whether or not there was a statistically significant difference in individual respondent perceptions between the two surveys on the same question. Statistical significance was determined at the .05 level.

The difference of means t-test treats ordinal variables as interval. However, the data is "ordered metric" and it is not uncommon to employ this type of analysis using statistical techniques that require interval level data. For the most part, these techniques provide very robust results against modest violations of the assumptions, and still tend to create valid answers even if the assumptions are violated somewhat.

A concern about the measurement level of dependent variables was anticipated. To test this concern, the Wilcoxon signed ranks test was used to verify the analytic findings from the t-test for each and every indicator. This method compares the proportion of individuals with a higher score at the second response to the proportion with a lower score at the second response. Although the t-test is usually robust when the data departs from normality, use of the nonparametric alternative allows verification of the t-test results when the assumptions of normality are violated. The findings indicated that the original t-test results were not distorted by a nonnormal distribution and the direction of relationships was demonstrated.

References

Beaupre, Eugene L. 2000. *The Political and Policy Making Implications of Term Limits: The Case of Cincinnati.* PhD diss., University of Cincinnati.

Blodgett, Terrell. 1998. *City Government That Works: The History of Council–Manager Government in Texas.* Austin: Texas City Management Association.

Childs, Richard S. 1965. *The First 50 Years of the Council–Manager Form.* New York: National Municipal League.

Cincinnati, City of. 1999. Charter: City of Cincinnati, November.

Cincinnati, City of. 2002. Rules and Regulations of the Independent Boards and Commissions, February 4.

Cropf, Robert A. and Todd Swanstrom. 2005. Deja vu all over again: Charter reform fails in St. Louis. *National Civic Review,* (Fall) 24:3, 10–19.

Ehrenhalt, Allan. 2004. The mayor-manager conundrum, *Governing,* October.

Fahy, Colleen. 1998. The choice of local government structure in Massachusetts: A historical public choice perspective. *Social Science Quarterly,* (June) 79:2.

Ferman, Barbara. 1985. *Governing the Ungovernable City: Political Skill, Leadership, and the Modern Mayor.* Philadelphia: Temple University Press.

Fox, John. 1999. The Politics of Politics. City Beat: 15, March 4.

Frederickson, H. George, Gary Alan Johnson, and Curtis Wood. 2004. The changing structure of American cities: A study of the diffusion of innovation. *Public Administration Review* (May/June) 64:3.

Goldberg, Laura. 1996. Shirey shares his concerns with the council. *The Cincinnati Enquirer.* May 22, Metro, C1.

Hansell, Bill. 1999. Revisiting the reform of the reform. *Public Management* 81:7, 27–28.

Korte, Gregory. 2003. Luken still testing his powers. *The Cincinnati Enquirer,* January 30, Metro, C1.

Korte, Gregory. 2007. Personal interview with author, March 22.

Kotter, John P. and Paul R. Lawrence. 1974. *Mayors in Action: Five Approaches to Urban Governance.* New York: John Wiley & Sons.

Lasswell, Harold. 1936. *Politics: Who gets what, when, how.* New York: P. Smyth.

Lupsha, Peter A. 1982. Constraints on urban leadership or why cities cannot be creatively governed. In *Classics of Urban Politics and Administration,* ed. William J. Murin. Oak Park, IL: Moore Publishing Company, Inc.

McGrath, Michael. 2001. An Interview with Terrell Blodgett. *National Civic Review* (Spring) 90:1.

Michaud, Anne.1999. Stronger-mayor here could set standard. *The Cincinnati Enquirer,* April 4, News, A1.

Miller, Zane L. 1968. *Boss Cox's Cincinnati: Urban Politics in the Progressive Era.* New York: Oxford University Press.

Monk, Dan. 2003. Council might look at pair of Convergys proposals. *Cincinnati Business Courier,* July, 22.

Morgan, David R. and Sheilah S. Watson. 1992. Policy leadership in council–manager cities: Comparing mayor and manager. *Public Administration Review,* Sept./Oct.

Morgan, David R. and Sheilah S. Watson. 1996. Mayors of American cities: An analysis of powers and responsibilities. *American Review of Public Administration,* March.

Neustadt, Richard E. 1989. The power to persuade. In *American Politics: Classic and Contemporary Readings,* ed. Allan J. Cigler and Burdett A. Loomis. Boston: Houghton Mifflin Company.

Okubo, Derek. 2005. A time for change: El Paso adopts the council–manager form. *National Civic Review,* Fall.

Radel, Cliff. 1999. Strong-mayor plan is recipe for progress. *The Cincinnati Enquirer,* March 3, Metro, B1.

Schiesl, Martin J. 1977. *The Politics of Efficiency: Municipal Administration and Reform in America, 18001920*. Berkeley: University of California Press.

Sparrow, Glen. 1985. The emerging chief executive: The San Diego experience. *National Civic Review* 74:11, 538–547.

Straayer, John A. 1973. *American State and Local Government*. Columbus, OH: Charles E. Merrill Publishing Co.

Svara, James H.1986. The mayor in council–manager cities: Recognizing leadership potential. *National Civic Review* 75:271–283, 305.

Svara, James H. 1999. The shifting boundary between elected officials and city managers in large council–manager cities. *Public Administration Review* 59: 44–53.

Svara, James H. 2001. Do we still need model charters? The meaning and relevance of reform in the twenty-first century. *National Civic Review* 90:1, 19–33.

Svara, James H. and Associates, 1994. *Facilitative Leadership in Local Government: Lessons from Successful Mayors and Chairpersons*. San Francisco: Jossey-Bass.

Taft, Charles P. 1933. *City Management: The Cincinnati Experiment*. New York: Farrar & Rinehart.

Wheeland, Craig M.1990. The mayor in small council–manager municipalities: Are mayors to be seen and not heard. *National Civic Review,* (July/Aug) 337–349.

Wilkinson, Howard and Robert Anglen. 2001. City embarks on a bold experiment. *The Cincinnati Enquirer,* March 11, Metro, B1.

Wilson, Woodrow. 1912. Issues of reform. In *The Initiative, Referendum, and Recall,* ed. William B. Munro. New York: D. Appleton.

FACILITATION IN THE COUNCIL-MANAGER FORM

C. Very Large City: Where Facilitative Leadership Is Not Expected

Chapter 13

Beating the Odds or Changing the Odds in a Large City: Phoenix, Arizona

Janet Denhardt and Martin Vanacour

Contents

13.1 Introduction

It has long been suggested that large cities with multiple constituencies and complex urban politics are best governed with strong mayors (Banfield and Wilson 1963). That makes the case of Mayor Phil Gordon of Phoenix, Arizona, difficult to explain, however. Although he may be operating in a council-manager system in which mayors do not have the authority of the "strong" mayor–council form, a 2006 *Governing* magazine article declared that Gordon is more than "Strong Enough" to provide leadership to the fifth largest city in the country. The reason? His strength does not come primarily from official grants of power or authority or strong-armed politics. Instead, it is derived from his skillful use of facilitative leadership, supported by a highly effective city management structure and a culture of success.

The city of Phoenix is the hub of a booming metropolitan area that is consistently one of the fastest growing areas of the United States. The current population of 1.4 million represents an almost 48 percent increase since 1990 (http://www.gpec.org/eresponse/phoenix.htm). The city of Phoenix covers over 516 square miles, making it geographically larger than Los Angeles. The surrounding metropolitan area has almost 3.5 million people, and is projected to grow to approximately 4.15 million people by 2010.*

Phoenix has enjoyed remarkable success and recognition as one the best-managed cities in the United States and the world. In 1993, the city was the winner of Germany's Carl Bertelsmann Prize for being one of the two best run city governments in the world along with Christchurch, New Zealand. It is a four-time recipient of the "All-America City" award, and was designated as *Governing* magazine's only "Grade A City" in 2000.

How can a mayor in a council–manager city create such a record of success? Much more than formal grants of authority might suggest. Phil Gordon has played a pivotal and essential role in Phoenix's continued push to meet the challenges of this large and enormously complex metropolitan environment, helping to change the face of Phoenix in ways that will profoundly and positively shape the future of the city and the region.

---

* http://www.ci.phoenix.az.us/ECONDEV/mrktoverpopulation.html

13.2 Background

At present, the city of Phoenix is successful by almost any measure, although, it has an unmistakably checkered past. Phoenix city government was established in 1881, and for the next sixty-seven years the city experimented with mayoral, commission, and manager forms. There were twenty-seven different mayoral administrations between the years 1881 to 1914, a time period characterized by instability, corruption, and poor management. In 1912, Arizona became the last of the 48 contiguous states to join the union. A year later, a new city charter was put into place to establish a commission–manager form of government. Phoenix tried a commission hybrid in which each of four commissioners had certain departments reporting to them while other administrative functions were assigned to the city manager. Unfortunately, the reforms did not work as well as hoped, with a succession of thirty-one city managers over the next thirty-five years (Hall 1982).

By the late 1940s, Phoenix was having serious difficulties. High crime rates and corruption plagued the city. In fact, because of widespread prostitution and venereal disease, Phoenix was declared off-limits to servicemen during World War II (Hall 1982). The instability and short tenure of administrators prevented the city from effectively dealing with financial problems and contributed to crime, corruption, and "reportedly rampant malfeasance, misfeasance, and nonfeasance by public officials" (Altheide and Hall 1983). Under the circumstances, a reform movement launched in the late 1940s had little problem securing support. In 1948, voters approved a modified version of a council–manager form of government that, with some variations, is still the model for Phoenix city government today. The first council under the reformed government continued with business-as-usual, selecting their own manager and retaining administrative authority. In the next election in 1949, however, dissatisfied Phoenix voters elected an entirely new council. This new council selected a city manager that remained in office for eleven years, serving under five mayors and twenty-seven different council members, ushering in a new period of stability and professionalism.*

Over the ensuing two decades, Phoenix began its continuous and meteoric growth. Between 1950 and 1975, the population grew from 107,000 to 669,000, a whopping 525 percent increase. In this same time period, the city grew from 17.1 square miles to 276 square miles. Beginning in the late 1980s and continuing through the 1990s, Phoenix suffered a severe recession, resulting in the collapse of a number of banking institutions, a failing housing market, and an eroding local economy. Nonetheless, between 1990 and 2000, Phoenix' population grew 34 percent, from 983,000 to more than 1.3 million, making it the fastest growing of the ten largest cities in the United States.† Despite the recession, between 1957 and 2005, Phoenix voters approved $3.7 billion in bond issues for construction and improvements to services and facilities, such as the Civic Plaza, Phoenix Sky Harbor International Airport, City Hall, the Phoenix Central Library, the Arizona History Museum, the Arizona Science Center, and the

---

* http://phoenix.gov/CITYGOV/history.html
† http://www.census.gov/prod/2001pubs/c2kbr01-2.pdf

Phoenix Art Museum.* In March 2006, the city passed an $880 million dollar bond issue to fund an array of city improvements including parks and recreation, infrastructure improvements, and perhaps most notably, over $200 million to support the establishment of a downtown Arizona State University (ASU) campus that is expected to ultimately serve 15,000 students.

In addition to the successful passage of major bond issues, the city receives high marks from both its citizens and outside organizations, and economic indicators are positive. Since 1985, the city has regularly commissioned an independent study of citizen attitudes. In 2006, "Nearly nine out of ten Phoenix residents (89 percent) continue to indicate they are either very satisfied (16 percent) or satisfied (73 percent) with the overall performance of the city in providing services" (City of Phoenix 2006, 1). The city's general obligation bonds are rated by Standard & Poor's as AAA+ and by Moody's as Aa1. Phoenix and surrounding cities have experienced positive job growth in fifty of the last fifty-four years, and currently have approximately 1.7 million workers in the labor force, with approximately 680,000 in the city. The median household income is $50, 309. According to 2004 U.S. Census figures, approximately 28 percent of the population is Hispanic and 4 percent black. The economic base is diversified, including major corporate presence in the areas of aerospace, banking, and electronics manufacturing; public sector employment at the city, county and state levels; as well as a strong travel and tourism component. Approximately 77 percent of the workforce is employed in service industries, including business services and tourism.

The Phoenix City Council is made up of a mayor and eight city council members who are elected for staggered four-year terms, with half the council up for election every two years. Elections are nonpartisan, with council members elected by district and the mayor elected at large. At present, the city employs approximately 14,000 employees.

The city has benefited from the long tenure of its recent city managers. The previous city manager, Marvin Andrews, served from 1976 to 1990. Upon his retirement, the council selected a long-time city employee and then assistant city manager, Frank Fairbanks. Fairbanks has served as the city manager since that time.

Although the city of Phoenix is faring very well, it still faces the same problems confronting other large urban areas. Relatively high crime rates, air quality, transportation issues, and poverty have proven to be ongoing challenges to the city and the surrounding areas. In other words, the success of the city of Phoenix cannot be explained by a lack of problems. It is instead a case of the city doing a better job than most in confronting these challenges and gaining the confidence of its citizens.

13.3 Mayor Phil Gordon

Gordon was sworn in as mayor of Phoenix on January 2, 2004. He brought with him a rich background and set of experiences that are clearly important in understanding

---

* http://phoenix.bizjournals.com/phoenix/stories/2006/01/30/editorial2.html (accessed August 2008)

his approach to the office. Gordon was born in Chicago in 1951 and was the oldest of three children. His family moved to Phoenix in the 1960s where he attended local schools and ultimately graduated with a bachelor's degree in education from the University of Arizona and a law degree from Arizona State University. Gordon has long placed a premium on education, a philosophy that he states comes from "a combination of everything I learned from my grandfather and grandmother, who came to this country without speaking English, but who sent all of their children to college." He went on to explain, "My father said 'you have got to go to school—be whatever you want, but go to college.'" This emphasis on education and learning is something that Gordon says guides his actions and informs his vision to this day (Gordon 2006).

Early in his career as an attorney and businessman, Gordon became involved in historic preservation and redevelopment, an experience that he says, "... allowed me to see that city government is there to solve problems. I was drawn to the neighborhood orientation and citizen involvement. I was able to listen and learn how the city, the private sector and neighborhoods can work together—I liked what I saw." In 1996, Gordon took the job of chief of staff for Mayor Skip Rimsza. The experience led him to run for city council in 1997, when he was elected on a platform of fighting crime and protecting neighborhoods. He was reelected in 2001. During his time on the council, Gordon was the driving force behind Shannon's Law, which makes it a felony to discharge a firearm within city limits. He founded the Slumlord Task Force, and spearheaded legislation to help in the fight against neglectful and criminal landlords.

This background, points out City Manager Frank Fairbanks (Fairbanks 2006), gave Gordon the chance to "see both politics and day-to-day operations. As a staff member, he was often involved in explaining administrative matters to council. As a result, he really understands the citizen's view, the staff view, and he has an excellent understanding of council—putting him in a position to work effectively with all of them." Gordon himself observes, "I probably came to this office better prepared than most mayors. I grew up with the elected officials here and I already knew them and the management side personally. I knew how the system worked and didn't work." Besides, he adds with a laugh, "I had a lot of time to lay awake thinking what I would do if given the chance."

Interestingly, he effectively served as the chief of staff for a mayor who had different political views than he did. Fairbanks suggests that doing so helped Gordon understand the role of staff and the idea that "our politics don't matter; it is our job to deliver for the mayor and council. We can make them aware of problems that arise, but it is up to them to create the vision whether it coincides with our personal views or not" (Fairbanks 2006). Because Gordon has experience on both sides of that equation, he has important insights into the relationship between elected officials and staff that help him manage and use that relationship effectively.

13.3.1 Leadership Style

Gordon exemplifies what Svara (1994) describes as the facilitative leadership style: a style that is characterized by consensus building, communication, and shared vision. He may not be in a "strong mayor" system, but he is highly active, visible, and enthusiastic in pursuing this facilitative role. As Assistant City Manager Alton Washington comments, "The mayor is in constant motion. He has shown an energy and passion for the job that is remarkable" (Washington 2007). Fairbanks has a similar assessment: "He is the most energetic and communicative person I've ever met."

13.3.1.1 Building Consensus

While his list of accomplishments is impressive, Gordon is a mayor that is not satisfied with simply "winning." He suggests, "In politics, if you try to show you are right all the time—my way or no way—nothing is going to get done." He reflects, "I don't think there is anything wrong with consensus building. As long as its honest, and you are not sacrificing your core moral beliefs, progress is a benefit. If that means changing direction in the middle of where you are, and at that starts to accomplish what you are trying to do in another manner—then sign on."

So rather than sticking resolutely to a preset plan, Gordon has a broader and more adaptive approach. In other words, he knows where he wants to go, but is flexible and strategic about how he gets there. Gordon has learned, as he puts it, to "anticipate playing chess instead of checkers. Not negatively, not just to win, but in the sense that you can't think one move ahead like in checkers, the end game is more circular. I know where I am going, but the point is to not let the system collapse." As a result, he says, "I assume that what I want is probably not going to happen. You can't draw a line in sand. You keep the parameters, but there has to be fluidity and evaluation."

His commitment to find consensus through this process is strong. In fact, if it is an important issue, Gordon works it until he has a unanimous or near-unanimous vote. He comments that "a one/eight vote is a win, but it means one-eighth of the city is disenfranchised. It's okay to take a no, but if I've got an emotional no, a fight instead of a respectful disagreement—it really starts to affect the management side. If you got two or three 'no' votes, it makes it harder to get things done. That's why the energy to communicate is so important—we have to get people together to talk about it."

Fairbanks echoes Gordon's comments in observing, "It is a challenge, but most of the time, we get 9/0 or 8/1 votes, so there really is a solid consensus." It hasn't always been that way, however. Fairbanks notes that "if you go back to Mayor Goddard, you see that almost everything important that was passed, he did it by 5/4, or 6/3 vote. Phil doesn't like that. He wants to build a team with the council."

The mayor's quest for consensus is not based on control or coercion. Rather, the mayor's style is one of collaboration and cooperation. He says, "You've got to know your partners. You have to know what they want and try to help them without it becoming a "big brother" kind of thing. My philosophy is that everybody is working from good will. There is usually a reason someone is upset, we should have anticipated it, we should have called and communicated more." He also picks his battle carefully, is both persistent and patient, and has a good sense of political timing. As Gordon himself notes, "You have to know when to do battle, and when not to." Co-chief of Staff Ed Zuercher reinforces this point by saying, "If he thinks an issue hasn't 'cooked' enough, he sends it back to get more cooked. So far, he works so hard he usually doesn't let it get to that point. If it's really important, he'll work it, work it, and work it. He'll put it off until its ready. If it is the rare surprise, he assesses how important it is and if it is worth fighting about. If it isn't, he moves on" (Zuercher 2007).

13.3.1.2 Communicating and Sharing the Stage

Communication is clearly the centerpiece of Gordon's leadership style. He talks with members of the council frequently, consulting them about issues and asking for their ideas and opinions. City Manager Frank Fairbanks stresses the mayor's efforts in communicating with others as the basis for his success in collaborating with and empowering others.

> He tries to find ways to support programs that they want. As we try to put together programs and new initiatives, he will talk to every one of them to ask about their concerns and try to find things that appeal to their point of view, priorities, their district, and their particular political views. He communicates extensively with the rest of the council. Talks to every member three to five times a week, sometimes every day. He is touching base with them, asking what is important to them, what they want to accomplish, how he can help them with an issue (Fairbanks 2006).

Council Member Mattox agrees. He says that the mayor "realizes he is a member of the council. He comes over to our side of the building. He stops by my office two or three times a week. He talks to all of us. He is not isolated. He doesn't just expect us to follow his lead because he is mayor; he works with us" (Mattox 2007).

Gordon also places a high premium on empowering and giving credit to others. As City Manager Frank Fairbanks observes, the mayor, "in working with council on major initiatives, will sort of take them in and share public profile with him. He makes sure credit is shared." The city manager emphasized this point as well, saying, "It isn't just the mayor that gets the credit. He shares the stage with the council. It helps avoid the kind of tension you sometimes see between mayors and councils."

Gordon himself explains it this way:

> You have to realize that even if you are solely responsible for something that is very rare, you have to make sure that everyone who deserves

credit, gets credit. I really try to make a point of following through, calling people, thanking people. Particularly those unsung heroes who are sometimes not recognized for their contributions.

Again, his experience is important in this regard. He comments, "I remember how I felt when I was a council member and I'd worked for six months and somebody else took credit for something I did." Clearly this experience shapes his current style as mayor. Council Member Claude Mattox reports that the mayor works hard to see that credit is shared. He says:

> For the most part our votes are unanimous because we all know the direction we want Phoenix to go in. We build on previous decisions and move forward. We understand the value to Phoenix of certain things: light rail, the ASU downtown campus. These accomplishments may be the legacy of the mayor, *but we all share in the success.* He knew he couldn't do it without us.

This quality was amply demonstrated in his September 2006 State of Downtown address. He was clearly center stage, but he talked about the council and showed a video in which each member of the city council was introduced and interviewed. He then proceeded to talk about the role of supporters, such as the then Diamondbacks' baseball player Luis Gonzales, Arizona State University, and the University of Arizona, existing and new downtown businesses by name, city employees, downtown residents, real estate developers, the arts community, and his family.

Those that work with him on the council and in the manager's office report that his interactions with them are characterized by mutual respect and trust. Fairbanks is clear on this point, "He [Gordon] has great respect for the staff in terms of administration and management." This trust has been earned and built, he says, "based on succeeding. Every once in a while, we don't succeed, but to the extent we can deliver on his promises, he is willing to stand behind us and support us. Through this process, we have been able to succeed enough that he trusts us."

Trust is also based on the mayor's inclusive and open communicative style. Council Member Mattox tells us, "When there is a press conference, all of us are invited. In fact, Phil makes his calendar available to us, and if there is something we are interested in, we can attend that meeting. He is clear that the reason he does that is so we can call his office and ask to be included. He has an open door policy, and I have never been refused."

Gordon is also a skilled listener, and he uses that skill with both people he works with in the city and members of the community. Fairbanks explains:

> He will go out and listen to regular citizens, to stakeholders, and once he has heard their concerns, fears, what they hope to achieve, he demonstrates a lot of leadership by putting together solid plans and making the

connections to what's important to them and shows them how this idea doesn't conflict with their goals. So, communication is a really big part of what he does—he starts that communication by being a really good listener.

The mayor admits that sometimes doing so can be difficult. He reflects, "Sometimes it's hard, it's emotional. You go into a crowd and maybe get yelled at. For most people, if they are allowed to vent, and if you are respectful (my grandfather taught me to be respectful), they will come back to the table. I look at it this way: If I'm not in agreement with you today, I will be tomorrow about something else. It is a combination of realizing that, and then believing it. Respect is a big part of my management style."

When there is conflict or disagreement, the mayor works hard to resolve differences and advance mutual interests. He is persistent, open, and always willing to listen. Fairbanks sees it this way: "When the council perceives that when the mayor really wants something, they work and bargain with him to support things they want. He wants to build a team with the council, so he really wants 90 percent agreement on everything." That helps smooth the implementation process, Fairbanks says, "because if everyone is in the tent, then you don't have people publicly dissenting from going in a new direction. His style is to work very, very hard at building this consensus." Co-chief of Staff Ed Zuercher says about the mayor, "He has an intuitive ability to understand what council members are interested in, what is important to them, where they are in their election cycle, where they are in their community, what helps them, what hurts them, what is irrelevant to them. And it's very intuitive—and that's why he's successful."

13.3.1.3 Pursing a Shared Vision and Shared Leadership

Part of the reason this collaborative approach works well in Phoenix is that there is a consistent focus on the big picture and a shared vision for the city of Phoenix. Alton Washington tells us that the mayor "is able to maximize his role through the power of persuasion, a sense of purpose, a sense of direction and reach out to others and convince them of the importance of that direction. Council Member Mattox notes that there are other reasons as well: "Part is Frank (Fairbanks), part is the institution. But a lot is the personality of the mayor; it is really an attitude of openness. Although we agree on many issues, on other issues, we may differ. We don't have 100 percent harmony, but not about things that meaningfully affect the big picture and Phoenix as a whole."

Shared leadership based on a shared vision is the hallmark of Gordon's approach. He is not just participative, he shares leadership with other members of the council, the city manager's office, the citizens of the city of Phoenix, as well neighboring jurisdictions. Co-Chief of Staff Ed Zuercher, in commenting on Gordon's leadership style compared to previous mayors, said, "He is much more collegial with the council. I think that probably translates into more policy initiatives than before because there is not that gulf that you sometimes have between the mayor and council. Now the council can propose and the mayor can propose and they work back and forth." This inclusive and collaborative approach extends to the mayor's relationship with community members as well. Assistant City Manager Alton Washington comments, "He is always inviting people in. For the bond issue, we had over seven hundred citizen volunteers. I was concerned it was too many—it far exceeded anything we had done before. But it worked. People got heard."

Shared leadership is coupled with an understanding on the part of the mayor that there are distinct roles for the mayor and the city manager. Gordon trusts, and is openly and consistently supportive of the city manager and staff. He emphasizes the importance of the city manager's office, stating, "It is important to also have good professional, strong staff. In a manager–council form, professional ongoing management is a huge asset." In fact, the city manager says that the mayor "has almost no interest in day-to-day administration and ongoing management and administrative work of the city." Zuercher agrees: "The mayor is a big picture guy. He is very hands on, but the strength of Frank and the team is that they have the city running so well that the council doesn't even have to worry about or think about it." It works well that way, as Zuercher explains, "Because the mayor understands the role of the city manager and relies on that. And it also works well because the city manager is very smart and very adept at ensuring that he is also in touch with the mayor and members of the council."

The mayor has been openly supportive of the city manager in public, stating, "I want this manager, I like this manager, he's my manager." When we asked Zuercher where this support stems from, he explains, "Frank has been here seventeen years, proving every day to the mayor and council that he is working in the best interest of the city, which ninety-nine out of one hundred times coincides with their best interest. Frank is not dogmatic; he is flexible about finding ways to get things done rather than identifying obstacles or reasons that you can't get things done."

13.3.2 Major Roles

Gordon's leadership style and personality shapes and permeates the various roles he plays as mayor. Of course, Gordon has a number of official roles, such as setting the council agenda and establishing all the committees and subcommittees, selecting the membership on each committee, and choosing who will be the chair. It is the manner in which he carries out these and other roles, however, that is important. The mayor fulfills the traditional roles of performing ceremonial tasks, acting as a spokesperson for the city, presiding over meetings, and acting as the formal liaison with other agencies and jurisdictions.

It is perhaps in his role as representative or promoter of the city where Gordon's style shines through most clearly. Gordon is clearly one of what Wilbur Rich calls "boosters," those with "an ability to sell and promote their cities as exciting and prestigious residential spaces, as business friendly, and as centers of entertainment" (Rich 2000). To be an effective booster, Rich says "gregariousness, humor, and optimism are part of the job description." These are qualities that Gordon possesses in abundance. Alton Washington describes the mayor this way: "He is not ashamed to say this is the city he grew up in and he loves it, and this is the kind of city his children can benefit from as well. He brings it down to the level that the average person can embrace. The mayor has a great style and personality. He operates as the cheerleader for the city."

Traditional roles, such as being spokesperson and promoter of the city, do not fully explain the role that Gordon plays in governing Phoenix. Even in those instances where the mayor has formal authority that would allow him to act unilaterally, he typically does not. Gordon discharges his responsibilities with regard to all his roles with the same attitude of openness and dialogue that he approaches everything else.

13.3.2.1 Policy and Organizing Roles

The subcommittee structure plays a vital role in decision making and consensus building in Phoenix, providing a mechanism and forum to work out many issues and potential problems before they get to the council as a whole. Although he is not required to do so, the mayor makes committee assignments an open and participative process. As Zuercher states, "If people don't feel they are listened to about subcommittee assignments, why would they support him in the future? So, he may formally establish a committee, but first, he informally builds coalitions who agree with that. So, if there is an issue the mayor wants a discussion on, that's fine. But, he needs to go talk to the council members to find out who would like to be on a subcommittee on that topic. Who wants to chair it? Would they trade out other things to do that? What areas would they be interested in?"

Once established, as Washington states, "The mayor sets the charge each year for the committees—sets forth what he would like to see. He doesn't hesitate to talk to members and present his views, and if there is dissent, he looks at ways to work with that." He doesn't try to rigidly control the committees, Mattox says:

> It is communication that is ongoing—constant flow of energy. He doesn't come to us and say this is what we are going to do, he comes in and says this is what I'm thinking about your subcommittee, what do you think? I may say I like it or I don't like it, and make suggestions. He does that with all eight of us, and from that, we come up with the recommendation. Everyone has input.

With this as the backdrop, the subcommittees themselves remain open to participation by other council members. As Mattox explains, "If we're working on an issue in a subcommittee, and another council member had objections, they would come to the subcommittee so we can get a better understanding. Everybody works together to get it accomplished."

While Gordon is open and participative, he also demonstrates leadership in initiating policy and setting goals. His policy priorities are public safety, education, and employment. In setting the charge for each committee, he ensures that key issues get aired and action agendas developed. In doing so, he continues to involve others, but clearly keeps his eyes on the ultimate goal, such as he did with development projects in the downtown Phoenix area.

13.3.2.2 Coordinating and Mobilizing Roles

Gordon fulfills a number of leadership roles with considerable skill, but it is clear that he sees his most important role as that of a communicator and mobilizer. Gordon states, "The key to council–manager government is communicate, communicate, communicate. You cannot overcommunicate. Listening. Listen to the concerns. Go back. Keep all the plates in balance in the air, and keep the philosophy that we can do it!"

As City Manager Fairbanks says, "He works harder at it than most. He is a tremendous communicator. He is calling people in the community, business leaders, union leaders, media leaders, all the time." He talks with "everyone on all sides of the issue and whatever the project, he develops community support first." Through his energy and enthusiasm, he is able to build community support for big, important ideas. As Washington explains, "He reaches out and meets with key players. He likes coffee. He will go to Starbucks and invite people to have coffee. He is not consumed by status, and can humble himself and reach out and go where people are comfortable—it breaks barriers. He brings people into the discussion." As a result, Fairbanks comments, "He is very successful because he wants to be out in the community, developing a good understanding of the tough problems and solving them."

In his role as a communicator and mobilizer, he is very involved in dealing with media, constituencies, and groups, stakeholders to sell ideas and directions, and to listen to them and make sure their concerns are heard. He makes extensive and effective use of the media to get his ideas out to the public. Fairbanks observed, "He is very focused on relationship with the media. It may be his highest priority. He makes sure we are on message and consistent with in what directions the city wants to go."

The mayor also works hard in his role as network builder within the community and with leaders in other jurisdictions and organizations. Washington puts it this way: "The mayor not only facilitates cooperation within the city. In this environment, issues are becoming increasingly regional. He works with other jurisdictions and other mayors to secure agreements to work together on key issues like transportation. He works to find the common interests." In doing so, "he forges partnerships and is able to tap into other organizations and institutions, like ASU. He is able to leverage their talents and resources for our mutual benefit."

The mayor also sees his job as working with the State Legislature to resolve issues of importance to the city. One such issue was a proposed property tax rollback at the state level, which businesses had traditionally wanted, but cities had traditionally opposed because of the resulting loss of revenue. Over time, it had become increasingly clear, however, that the legislature was ready to act. As Zuercher explains, "Mayor Gordon astutely realized what was going on politically and saw earlier than most people that cities could not forever say 'no,' we are not going to allow any tax relief on business property. He recognized that there were a lot of powerful forces who wanted it and that it was going to happen." Under the circumstances then, Zuercher says, "he got himself right in the middle of the discussion and ended up brokering the agreement that was more favorable to cities—it phased in the rollback over time" In Zuercher's view:

> If he had taken a hard line position, he would have lost and he would have made enemies. As it was, he lowered his barriers and tried to seek common ground and through that was able to demonstrate to business and legislative leadership why it was important to mitigate the effects on the city. In the end, the businesses were happy because they got a tax break, the legislature was happy because they were able to deliver on the tax breaks, and he was happy because he had prevented the city from having a catastrophic hit."

In short, the mayor plays a number of key roles, formal and informal in city governance. He develops community support by talking with a broad spectrum of people including business people, neighborhood residents, union representatives, and others to gain an understanding of diverse and varied opinions that may exist with regard to particular issues. He is very focused on working with and using the media in this regard, to both engage the issues and mobilize support for action.

13.3.3 Key Relationships

By all accounts, the mayor's relationship with the city council, city manager, and leaders outside the government, and the community is positive, constructive, and effective. With regard to his interactions with the council, Gordon told us that there are "special ways of working with council, especially when the mayor is a member of council. Even with good-natured people, sometimes it can be difficult. In the weak mayor form, you really have to work to keep it together, sharing ideas." He adds thoughtfully, "It has to come from the heart." Assistant City Manager Washington reports simply, "It's a good relationship" and one that works. "We talk to each other; we agree to disagree about some things. But it isn't personal and we don't circumvent each other. His door is open to any council member. I can walk into his office any time. No invitation necessary."

The mayor's relationship with the city manager seems particularly important in understanding how the city of Phoenix works under Gordon. The success of the relationship between the mayor and the city manager is based in part on tradition, but also is a function of the attitude and approach of both Gordon and Fairbanks. Both try to build on the other's strengths, respect the other's role, and work together to make Phoenix better. In Fairbanks' view, "The key to success is finding a way to effectively work with mayor and council to accomplish their goals and the goals of the community. A lot of what we do is find a way to make those goals a reality. We do that by adapting to the style of the mayor and council."

Fairbanks finds that:

> Gordon is very good to work with. He is committed to supporting the system. He understands that if he were to be pulled into administrative detail, he would have less time and less opportunity to do what he feels is really important, which is communicating and developing future directions ... He has great respect for the staff in terms of administration and management. We use his strengths and work with him to shape goals and dreams for the community that will work.

Strong relationships between the city manager and the mayor's office are aided by structural arrangements as well. Former City Manager Marvin Andrews put a deputy city manager in the mayor's office to act as liaison, and also put a position in the council's office as a council's assistant. These staff play an important role in maintaining open lines of communication and information between the two parts of city government. These "on-loan" staff arrangements have been "very productive," according to Alton Washington, who says, "They can help translate the challenges and priorities, and break down barriers. It sends a signal to the whole organization."

Gordon also has positive relationships with community leaders and the general public. Mattox says about the mayor, "His idea is to bring everyone in, to build consensus. I have found that Phil has success in bringing together people with extremely diverse opinions and groups, and get them to the table to work out their issues. He is really good at bringing together people and getting them to sit down and talk." Zuercher echoes this idea, saying "He is very concerned with understanding people's positions, identifying what's important to them, and then he pushes everyone, especially staff, to find the common ground and work from that."

13.3.4 Positive Impacts and Accomplishments

In his short time in office, Gordon's accomplishments include the start of construction on a light rail system, securing commitments for two new downtown hotels, expanding the Phoenix Convention Center, and the passage of an $878 million bond program. Despite the fact that the University of Arizona (U of A) and Arizona State University (ASU) are traditional rivals, agreement was also reached to locate a U of A Medical School (in cooperation with ASU) in downtown Phoenix. The mayor prides himself on the redevelopment of the downtown Phoenix areas, as well as the revitalization of South Phoenix and West Phoenix. He has also succeeded in increasing the number of police and fire personnel serving the city. Establishing and maintaining a positive and constructive working relationship with the Arizona State Legislature has also been an important accomplishment.

Although all of these accomplishments are important, one of the most visible and in many ways unusual accomplishments has been the development and construction of the ASU campus in downtown Phoenix. Phoenix is the first city in the United States to pass a bond issue specifically to build a major new university campus in the downtown area. Gordon and ASU President Michael Crow came up with the idea through "spontaneous combustion" and worked together to develop a vision, secure the passage of the bond issue, and champion the planning and construction of a new ASU downtown campus (Gullett 2008). Gordon's enthusiasm and keen facilitative skills convinced the Phoenix city council to agree to this project. There was some minor dissent about devoting too much of the bond issue to the university ($223 million, or a little over a quarter of the total $800 million bond issue). In the end, the city council made some small changes and voted to support the construction of a downtown campus.

The mayor was a major force in the passage of the bond issue because of his understanding of every detail of the project, his enthusiasm and salesmanship in acting as "the face" of this project, and his abilities to facilitate cooperation among many constituents and interests. He convinced the city council to select seven hundred-member bond committee, the largest in the history of Phoenix. As soon as the citizen's committee was formed, Gordon spent every day until the election being the chief spokesperson, cheerleader, and fundraiser to publicize the bond issue. The mayor attended almost every public meeting and worked closely with the major newspaper to publicize the importance of this project. Gordon was also the primary facilitator when problems arose between downtown neighborhoods, businesses, and the city. According to Deb Gullett, his chief of staff, the mayor would personally make sure "nothing would blow up." Gordon met with ASU President Crow once every two weeks from the beginning of the program through the construction phase, and continues to meet with him on a regular basis.

13.3.5 Resources and Skills

Gordon draws from many resources in exercising his leadership. Clearly he is a visionary leader, but he is not dogged or inflexible about how that vision will be realized. Further, he pursues a vision that encompasses the variety of concerns, values, and preferences of his fellow council members, community leaders, and the public. He practices, according to Zuercher, "servant leadership in that he doesn't base leadership on enforcing authority through his position. He bases his leadership on the idea that you set aside personal issues and you go and seek the ways that you can help and be a part of things, with the understanding that it pays off in return."

Phoenix does not give the position of mayor much formal power, but Gordon is powerful nonetheless. This power is based on a number of things, but among the most important are (1) his visibility and ability to persuade and mobilize support, (2) keeping people "at the table" to resolve conflict and build consensus, and (3) his seemingly boundless energy.

13.3.5.1 Visibility

Gordon is a highly visible figure in Phoenix. He makes it a point to be present at community events and take advantage of as many opportunities as possible to speak to groups, write columns in neighborhood newspapers, talk with individuals, and serve as the symbol and spokesperson for the community. Although in some ways the mayor is only one vote on a nine-member council, by serving as the primary spokesperson and the most visible symbol for the city among the public, he is able to have much more influence than his formal powers would dictate. It is important to note that the mayor is directly elected in a citywide election, giving him a broad-based "mandate" and strong media awareness. As Zuercher says, "The common person knows the mayor and it is important to them to see him and hear him talk about the issues. The people of Phoenix look to the mayor as the voice of the city."

13.3.5.2 Keeping People at the Table

Gordon handles opposition and controversy with persistence, energy, and an open mind, and by taking on issues one step at a time. He explained to us:

> When you start a hearing, and people say how are you going to do this "impossible" thing? Where are you going to get 200 million to build a university, how are you going to get legislative approval, you've got board of regents, private property—how can you do that? To me, you've got to prioritize. Instead of lining up all those issues up front, my style is to ask, what issue is first, and then solve it. Then the challenge is the next one.

Gordon tries to avoid falling into the trap of treating money as the first and only issue. He says, "Money is always going to be a challenge. But to me it is the least critical challenge. Get everything else right, and we'll find the money. Put the money up front, and you'll never get it through system. So when I am asked who or what are we going to cut, I just say let's just wait, and we'll solve it."

That is not to say that the political waters in Phoenix are always smooth sailing. One of the controversies that Gordon has had to manage involved a proposed condominium development led by the Trump Corporation and others. It was a hotly contested and messy issue, with the developers on one side and the neighbors on the other. Ultimately, the council voted 5 to 4 to approve the development and the neighborhood immediately mobilized in opposition to the vote. The media supported the neighborhood and opposed the development. Citizens were able to get enough signatures to get an initiative on the ballot blocking the project, and it seemed clear that such an initiative would easily pass. If it passed, it would "have been devastating to the city's ability to do zoning on large projects citywide," Zuercher said. The mayor was politically savvy enough to recognize that the issue could create a serious schism in the community. Zuercher stated, "The mayor is really good at evaluating countervailing forces. He assessed that the developers were strong enough that they weren't going to back down, and neither were the neighbors." If a solution were to be found, both sides would have to agree that it was reasonable. So, the mayor went to the council, and asked if they would agree to support an agreement if it could be negotiated between the developers and the neighborhood. They agreed. Zuercher stated:

> Nobody thought you could get those neighbors in a room with those developers and come out with something they would all say was acceptable. But the mayor just said this is too important not to do it, we aren't going to let this blow up, and we are just going to stick it out with each other. And that is what happened. That was a real achievement.

So what resources and skills make Gordon such an effective leader? When Alton Washington was asked that question, he said that the Mayor is "a bridge builder, he has an ability to sit down with people with strong views." That is coupled with the fact, he said, that Gordon "is tireless, he is one of the first people here every morning. His energy is contagious."

13.3.5.3 Personal Characteristics and a Clear Sense of the Job

Gordon has a clear conception of his job and how it works within the larger system of local governance. As Washington explained, "He is able to work within structure. He is policy wonk—he is a person who loves public policy, is not afraid of the complexity and pitfalls of policy. But how you make it work and implement it; he realizes that the management side has expertise to make it work." In fact, the mayor's relationship with the city manager should be emphasized as a critical factor in the mayor's effectiveness. As Council Member Claude Mattox, in commenting on the effectiveness of Gordon's leadership, stated:

> Why does it work? It has to do with Gordon as an individual. But, that being said, part of the good thing about this form is that with a professional city manager, and professional staff, you get quality and consistent management. In some cities, you hear stories about mayors who bring in their friends and supporters from the private sector. But this is a different world. You can't necessarily bring the same skills to the public sector and accomplish it the same way.

With our strong management, we've got people with expertise and training, so they are aware of the requirements of public administration. They come up through the ranks. If I was to throw someone into that mix, they are not going to have the knowledge about how government works and how to make things happen in government. In my opinion, that is one of the downfalls of strong mayor forms.

Of course, Phoenix has a long history of success with the council–manager form, which contributes to the support for this form of government and the apparent ease with which the various players fulfill their respective roles. In no small way, the mayor can concentrate his efforts on mobilizing support and resolving issues because he is free from worrying about administrative matters. As Zuercher puts it, "The strength of Frank and the team he has assembled is that so much of the machine is invisible to the council that they don't even have to worry about or think about it. We know that they are going to be responsive if there are citizen concerns about services; they just have that stuff running so well that the council doesn't even think about it." That sometimes can be a double-edged sword, however. "Because they take it for granted; sometimes they don't appreciate the skill that it takes to make it like that, it seems easy. Kind of the Tiger Woods or Michael Jordon problem—they make it look so easy that you think it is."

Frank Fairbanks warns against becoming "complacent and assuming that it will always work as well as it has. I think the council–manager form is appreciated here, but the second we presume that nothing will happen, then something will happen." He also says, "I think it does work here because we work together as a team, we try to make it possible for the mayor and council to do the work that is truly theirs, which is setting goals, deciding directions, working with [the] community, and reflecting community attitudes in terms of where we go." Once those directions are set, he says:

> We do everything we can to facilitate them and let them be successful. We respect "the line" because it works. If the mayor and council can get program goals achieved and they can get done what they want to do, and we take care of the day-to-day, messy administrative work, then they are going to believe in the system and support it. They set overall direction. We are always pushing them to support things we think will help the community, but whatever they decide, we do our best to make sure it works and help them reach their goals.

13.3.5.4 Mobilizing and Supporting Others

The mayor's ability to gain the confidence and support of the council is obviously also an important resource. True to form, the basis of his support on the council is grounded in his willingness and ability to listen, compromise, and keep after an issue until disagreements can be worked out. All of that is grounded, Zuercher says, "in the fact that he cares." He goes out of his way to keep communication lines open with the council members. Zuercher observes, "He has a small ego in the sense that he doesn't expect that because he's mayor they need to come talk to him. He will go seek out their opinions. He walks around the floor with them, he calls them two or three times a day, he sends his staff to go check with them about things."

So, his support on the council has been carefully cultivated. He expends a lot of energy working with the members to find common ground and ways to work together. Council Member Mattox says that in doing so, Gordon is not heavy-handed:

> If your intent is to shove something down my throat, it is going to be tough; I will fight. The fact that he is the mayor, I respect. He was elected citywide. But he's still only one vote on the council and he is going to need five votes to get something passed. So, to accomplish that, you have to build a team. That means sharing my interests. He and I work together so there is a balance.

For example, Mattox said, "I want development in West Phoenix. But investment downtown also helps because it builds the tax base for police and fire that benefits the area I represent. He understands the problems in my area." It is not a quid pro quo arrangement, Mattox said, "but it is working together for both of us to attain each others goals and make both of us successful. He is very good at that."

In his work with the council, the manager's office, and the community, in some ways, Gordon can be seen as navigating the waters of the perfect storm. He has worked tirelessly to build community support and awareness of issues, he has cultivated the trust and cooperation of the council, and he can count on a professionally managed city run by a highly accomplished, professional and politically savvy city manager. By openly respecting the important role of the city manager, Gordon enables that office to do its job effectively. Zuercher summarizes it as follows: "The mayor and council in Phoenix might not all be formal students of council–manager form, they might not cite the literature, but they get it. That's just the DNA of Phoenix government—that the mayor and council do get the big picture, and the staff execute it."

13.4 Conclusion

Mayor Phil Gordon of Phoenix presides over the fifth largest city in the United States. As he gears up his campaign for reelection, he continues to be a highly popular, visible, and enthusiastic figure in Phoenix politics. His success as mayor demonstrates the power of the facilitative leadership model (Svara 1994) in explaining the roles and style of effective mayors in council–manager cities, even if those cities are as large and complex as Phoenix. In the 1994 edition of his book, Svara stated:

"The emergence of mayors who use a collaborative style to overcome dissension and drift ... suggests that the facilitative model may be effective in very large cities if the right kind of leader appears." That seems to be exactly the case in looking at the city of Phoenix and the experience of Gordon. Through his use of collaboration, communication, and facilitation, coupled with his boundless energy, Gordon serves as a focal point and catalyst for what is arguably one of the best-run cities in the United States. Importantly, his influence has not led to the diminishment of the role of the city manager or council. In fact, his facilitative style of leadership supports and builds a similar collaborative and facilitative style demonstrated by the city manager and the council, all of which works to the great benefit of the city and the citizens it serves.

References

Altheide, David and John Hall. 1983. Phoenix: Crime and politics in a new federal city. In *Crime in City Politics*, ed. Anne Heinz, Herbert Jacob, and Robert Lineberry. New York: Longman, 193–238.

Banfield, Edward and James Wilson. 1963. *City Politics*. Cambridge, MA: Harvard University Press.

City of Phoenix. 2006. Community Attitude Survey. ftp://phoenix.gov/pub/payf/attsurvey.pdf (accessed June 2006).

Fairbanks, Frank. 2006. Personal interview by the author. September.

Gordon, Phil. 2006. Personal interview by the author. September.

Gullet, Deb. 2008. Personal interview by the author. March.

Hall, John Stuart. 1982. Phoenix, Arizona. In *Decentralizing urban policy: Case studies in community development*, ed. Dommel and Associates, 47-83. Washington DC: Brookings Institution.

Mattox, Claude. 2007. Personal interview by the author. February.

Rich, Wilbur. 2000. Vincent Cianci and Boosterism in Providence. In *Governing Middle-Sized Cities: Studies in Mayoral Leadership*, eds. James Bowers and Wilbur Rich. Boulder, CO: Lynne Rienner Publishers, 197–214.

Svara, James H. and Associates. 1994. *Facilitative Leadership in Local Government: Lessons from Successful Mayors and Chairs*. San Francisco: Jossey-Bass.

Washington, Alton. 2007. Personal interview by the author. February.

Zuercher, Ed. 2007. Personal interview by the author. March.

FACILITATION IN THE MAYOR–COUNCIL FORM

Chapter 14

Building Trust and Developing a Vision: Akron, Ohio

Raymond W. Cox III

Contents

14.1 Introduction

In January 1987, in the middle of his term as mayor, Tom Sawyer was sworn in as a member of Congress. Don Plusquellic, the chair of the city council, was elected by the council to serve the remainder of Sawyer's term. In November 2005, Plusquellic was reelected for the fourth time, thus extending the longest service as mayor in the history of Akron, Ohio. Few would have expected that anyone would survive for more than a term or two in the office.

14.2 Governmental and Community Context

When Plusquellic was initially selected as mayor, the city of Akron was changing—mostly for the worse. The mid-1980s saw one of the longest strikes by rubber workers in the city's history. Corporate decisions were already in place that would transform the erstwhile rubber capital from a manufacturing city to a near ghost town. Tens of thousands of jobs would disappear during the 1980s. The population, which peaked at some 290,000 in the late 1960s, was already falling and would settle at just above 210,000 at the start of the twenty-first century. That Akron would survive and to some extent even thrive was in sharp contrast to the experience of countless "Rust Belt" cities in New York, Pennsylvania, Ohio, and Michigan.

Akron seemingly was an unlikely place to launch a political career. Nothing about government in Akron in the past two decades would prove to be easy. In a very real sense, the city had to be *re*created. The economic and social pillars that dominated political life in Akron would be swept away in a wave of layoffs, corporate takeovers, and social distress. While such problems faced a myriad of midwestern industrial cities, Akron seemingly was one of the most disadvantaged. It was smaller than the great steel cities, such as Pittsburgh and Cleveland, or manufacturing cities, such as Rochester and Buffalo in New York, or Gary, Indiana, or Cincinnati and Toledo in Ohio. Ultimately, it was more dependent on a handful of companies and a single-industry, tire manufacturing, than its neighbors.

Reshaping the city of Akron was not the result of the work of a single individual. Nor for that matter has the shape and direction of the change been the result of consistent and broad agreement about that change. This has been a change that has been bruising and contentious. The single constant in the transformation has been the presence of Mayor Plusquellic. It would be his vision of a renewed Akron that would prevail. His success stems in part from outliving his opponents, but voters in five elections reaffirmed his approach. The consistency of his message has played a key role in the recovery of the city. It is the quality of persistence more than the correctness of individual decisions that has won the day. While the interplay of ideas and practices that are the realm of policy making are critical in reshaping the city of Akron, *persistence* and *consistency of vision* are the key attributes of the mayor and, therefore, essential to policy implementation. No economic recovery plan (no plan in general) unfolds as one expects; that is the dilemma and fascination of policy implementation. We know what we want to happen, we even have an inkling of what will happen, but events surprise us. It is the capacity to persist, to see projects through (maybe not in the same form), and to judge outcomes by consistency with a long-term vision, not by specific outcomes and meeting target dates that is for this mayor the definition of leadership.

14.2.1 Political Profile of Akron

The government of the city of Akron is a product of the late Progressive Era. Shortly after the end of World War I, the city revised its Charter to create a commission form of government, but this form was only short-lived being replaced by the mayor–council form in 1924 (a return to the form that existed before 1920). The state of Ohio represents an interesting dichotomy in the forms of local government that operate within its boundaries. Local government political reform that was the hallmark of the Progressive Era seemingly halted with the emergence of charter cities in the first quarter of the twentieth century. Only one of eighty-eight counties is a "charter county" and that status was not approved until 1979. The state also is different, in that politically and governmentally it is two states with strong-mayor–council governments operating in the northern and northeastern regions of the state, and council–manager governments dominating the central and southwestern areas. In effect, geography is a key determinant in understanding the role of the municipal chief executive officer (CEO). The scope of executive authority is the same, but in the northern part of the state, the selection of the CEO is the result of election by the citizenry, while in the southern part of the state, selection of the CEO is the result of the appointment by the council of a professional manager.

Seemingly, the only consensus on government organization in Ohio has been in the creation of strong civil service systems. Thus, Akron, despite shifting back to the strong-mayor form in its Charter of 1924, nevertheless continued the civil service commission system, which was created as part of the Charter of 1920. The Civil Service Commission controls the hiring and promotion of all but a handful of employees in the government. The mayor controls the appointments of "cabinet" officers and their deputies, who head the operational departments of the city (e.g., Finance, Planning and Urban Development, Public Service, Law, and Public Safety), and a few "deputy mayors." Otherwise, the control of recruitment, appointment, and promotion rest with a three-member Civil Service Commission and a director appointed by the commission. Effectively the mayor, as envisioned by the Charter, was no more influential than the city managers being appointed at the other end of the state, who often have authority to appoint a wider range of department heads than granted through the Akron Charter.

The mayor's influence would not be over the "bureaucracy," but rather through the budget. By 1924, common political wisdom was that the budget should be an executive-developed document. The mayor presented the budget to council and could veto portions of the document after it was enacted. While public policy was *set* by council, the scope and direction of policy implementation was based on the budget. In this, the mayor had control.

As with many other Rust Belt communities, the politics of the city has been a study in contrasts. The early decades under the 1924 Charter were to be dominated by the emerging economic problems brought on by the Depression and the growth of unionization in the later part of the 1930s. In a city dominated by a single industry (though there were nearly a dozen tire manufacturers in the 1920s and 1930s), labor–management disputes could be both contentious and complicated. A mayor was inevitably caught between the "rock" of corporate influence, and the "hard place" of union demands. On the other hand, at least in theory anyway, city politics would be a "nonpartisan" affair until the 1960s when party designations were added to the ballot in mayor and council elections. The first two "partisan" mayors of the city were Republicans, reflecting the dominance of the party in Ohio and in the boardrooms of the city. The city council, in contrast, was controlled by the Democratic Party. In 1983, Sawyer, until then a member of the city council, won an upset victory over the incumbent and the mayor's office (and council majority) has been in the hands of the Democratic Party ever since.

The Charter of 1924 has been changed a number of times, but only three changes have had direct impact on the office of the mayor. The first, as mentioned above, was the shift to partisan elections. It is also the only change introduced before Plusquellic assumed office. The second was an initiative-driven change (later partially overturned as unconstitutional) that placed severe limits on campaign contributions to candidates for either mayor or council. The third change gave authority for the selection of the police and fire chiefs to the mayor. Until the year 2000, those positions were filled through the Civil Service Commission.

14.2.2 Economic Profile of Akron

To understand Akron it is necessary to understand the economic and social diversity that has shaped this region. Akron exists because it is the terminus of two canal systems that were the economic engine of the lower Midwest until the Civil War. The capacity to move goods, both agricultural and manufactured, east from Akron was critical to its growth. Yet, from its beginning, Akron was never merely a transportation node. New ideas and new products seemed to emerge, establish themselves,

and then move west to flourish. Industries as varied as processed grains (the predecessor of Quaker Oats) and harvesting machines (the predecessor of International
Harvester) would start in Akron in the early and mid-nineteenth century.* The city
was often a place where ideas (and products) were given birth, even if that early history would be forgotten. Everything from the first American toy company (a manufacturer of marbles) to the first professional American football championship team,
to the first electric railway and the first automobile used as a police wagon, to the
first public school system to differentiate students into "grades," came into existence
first in Akron. As each new idea, invention, or product would emerge, Akron would
reassert itself upon the American consciousness as a place of creativity.

The emergence of Akron as a major manufacturing center came at a price. The
canal that was once Main Street was filled in and paved over. The factories were
built close to the canal terminus and, thus, were virtually downtown. Between three
shifts of workers, a city-funded university on the hill across the railroad tracks, and
a downtown that had once been a significant regional retail and commercial center,
the city was a vibrant, busy place as the automobile industry expanded nationally.
The city boomed. The population jumped from less than 70,000 to over 200,000
in the decade from 1910 to 1920. Importantly for the future of the city, the various
tire companies that dominated the social, political, and cultural landscape did not
operate in the monopolistic and aggressive style that typified the company towns
of Appalachia or the western United States. The tire companies found themselves
competing for workers. Each sought to encourage workers with recreational amenities.† Tracks of land were sold to employees, not leased. Parts of the city, while
dominated by one tire manufacturer or another, were also economically relatively
"blended" communities in which, on one street, small homes would be adjacent
to larger homes and then still larger homes to reflect the salaries and status of the
homeowners. The result was that Akron was a city of homeowners. The city in the
late 1950s was the prototype of the burly, middle-class, blue-collar city that was
common in the Midwest.

Yet that same story has a negative side. Each new idea that produced a new
invention or product came of the necessity of an old idea passing into history
or simply moving on. By the 1980s, it was no longer clear whether or not a new
idea or new product would emerge to resurrect the Akron economy. Certainly the
"numbers" did not look good. The population peaked in the 1960s when rapid
suburbanization and some "white flight" caused a decline of more than 18 percent
between 1965 and 1980. Between 1970 and 1980, some 35,000 tire manufacturing jobs would also disappear. The often sooty and smoggy air of Akron was
being cleansed, but for the wrong reasons. Simultaneously, the tire factories that

---

* In a sense, the *devolution* of tire manufacturing in Akron in the 1970s and 1980s was simply a
  repeat of history.
† The world famous Firestone Country Club began as a facility accessible to any and *all* Firestone
  employees.

operated close to downtown began to empty. The retail stores had followed the wealthier residents into the suburbs, and the commercial operations simply found fewer customers to serve. By the time that Plusquellic became mayor in January 1987, the south end of downtown looked more like London or Berlin after a World War II air raid.

The demographic description of Akron today reflects both the positive and negative elements. Having lost its connection to the blue-collar middle class, the city is neither as vibrant nor as economically secure as it was immediately after World War II. According to the 2000 U.S. Census

- Per capita income is about 55 percent of national average.
- Cost-of-living at national average.
- Sixty-two percent homeownership in city.
- September 2006 unemployment rate of 4.7 percent.
- Thirty-four percent "minority" (primarily African American) population, but with a suburban ring that is 90 to 99 percent white.
- Immigrant population speaks some 90 languages.
- Percentage of population with a bachelor's degree or higher is only 75 percent of the state level and 86 percent of the national level.
- Economic and employment growth index for 2006 is the highest among the large cities of Ohio.
- Population is relatively stagnant, having declined by about 2 percent since 2000, in contrast to declines of 20 percent between 1965 and 1985, and another 9 percent between 1986 and 2000.
- In 1960, Akron represented 70 percent of the county population; in 2005 it represented slightly less than 40 percent of the county population.

As suggested above, the numbers are not always positive, but the high homeownership rate, a relatively low unemployment rate, and high employment opportunity projections are strong foundations from which to build a new economic base for the city and the region.

Two aspects of the Ohio tax code have played a critical role in the redevelopment of the city of Akron. The first is that cities in Ohio are permitted to level a gross income tax on those who work in the city. This income tax, which is fairly elastic and, therefore, sensitive to economic change has been relatively stable and even growing over most of the past decade, suggesting that Akron remains a strong economic center, even though the manufacturing jobs are gone. The second is that various economic development tools, such as Tax Increment Financing (TIF) and Joint Economic Development Districts (JEDD) have been used successfully to create new jobs within the city and the surrounding area. Both the income tax and the economic development tools will be discussed in detail later because they have played an important role in the rebuilding and reshaping of the city.

14.3 Mayor Donald Plusquellic

Plusquellic is a native of Akron, having grown up in the working class Kenmore area of the city. He attended the University of Pittsburgh School of Engineering, and graduated from Bowling Green State University School of Business. He earned his JD from The University of Akron School of Law. His foray into politics began even before he completed law school, when in 1973 he was elected to the city council. He would be reelected to that seat (Ward 9) at each biennial election, and then to an at-large seat until he was appointed mayor in January 1987. He held the post of council president for the three years prior to his appointment as mayor.

Not unlike a number of young politicians who grew up in the 1960s, Plusquellic holds out the memory and image of President John Kennedy as the inspiration for seeking public office. The generation that was to heed Kennedy's words was also a group that felt connected to the political figures of the past. He felt the call to help solve the problems of society through the collective response of government. Working together to define and resolve problems was not merely a slogan, but an expectation of behavior (Plusquellic 2006–2007).

Upon entering government, the advice of veteran members of the city council resonated with Plusquellic. "Getting along" by going along and learning from seasoned veterans was still the expectation in the 1970s. The lessons of trust and mutual support that are embedded in the legislative process had to be learned and practiced. To this day, when the mayor discusses politics in Akron, the images that are invoked are of a generation of city councilmen who applied a traditional legislative approach to the overwhelming problem of holding the city together through the economic trauma of the 1970s and 1980s. It is that style of consensus-based decision making founded on experience and *trust* that continues to shape his style today.

Becoming a "big city" mayor in the 1980s was not necessarily a prize. The economic downturn of the late 1980s would hinder redevelopment and wither state and federal aid for even thriving communities. In 1987, Akron was just coming off the longest and most destructive strike by rubber workers in the city's history. Retail and commercial buildings in downtown were being abandoned, lending to the air of being a ghost town. Recreating the downtown was not going to be easy. The new mayor understood that economic redevelopment is an agonizingly slow process. Projects may be in the planning stage for years and may take still longer to implement. A time horizon of decades, not years was needed. Picking up from the projects begun by his predecessor, Sawyer, and looking to promote more projects, Plusquellic began the long process of rebuilding. In this endeavor, he needed not only the support and cooperation of former colleagues on the city council, but also of the business community.

His views were apparent from the beginning of his tenure as mayor. In a newspaper story about the party primary in his first mayoral campaign, Plusquellic is quoted as saying:

The city of Akron is truly at a crossroads ... the challenges and opportunities are great. Fresh ideas and innovative plans are fine when the ideas are presented and the plans are formulated with experienced leadership behind them. I have that experience. I have exhibited that leadership. I am able to face those challenges and grasp the opportunities that will, ultimately, bring Akron safely and successfully through the crossroads (*Akron Beacon Journal*, February 6, 1987, A1).

The years would suggest that Plusquellic met his own challenge. In an article written at the time of his inauguration as the 62nd president of the United States Conference of Mayors, it was noted that:

Most visibly, Mayor Plusquellic has transformed downtown Akron. From luring the National Inventors Hall of Fame to its new child-friendly headquarters in Akron to the construction of a new minor league baseball stadium and a new convention center, downtown Akron has experienced somewhat of a renaissance in the years of Plusquellic's leadership. As a result, more than a dozen new restaurants and clubs with an eclectic blend of music and nightlife have invigorated downtown. As the principal employment center of the county with some 30,000 workers, Downtown Akron has produced significant increases in revenue generated from downtown businesses, which in turn have helped Akron to continue investing in neighborhoods to make them even stronger (*Akron Beacon Journal*, June 29, 2004).

In a line that is typical of his leadership style, the mayor pledged during that inauguration speech to the conference to work in a "collaborative," bipartisan manner to do "America's business" for the people of Akron and the nation (*Akron Beacon Journal*, June 29, 2004).

Mayors in Akron are elected on an odd-year cycle for a four-year term. The ten members of the council who represent the wards of the city are elected on a two-year cycle, so every other election they run at the same time as the mayor. On the other hand, the three at-large council members serve four-year terms that are held in the opposite cycle from the mayor. Thus, the race for mayor is the "highlight" of the campaign in the years when the office is being filled. Relatively little attention is paid to the ward council races. With more than thirty years in public office, one might expect that Plusquellic has had his share of campaign battles. Yet the reverse is true. His campaigns for mayor have rarely been true contests. As the *Akron Beacon Journal* noted after his reelection in 2003 to affirm his place as the longest sitting mayor in the history of the city, he inevitably seems to garner nearly three-quarters of the votes in each election (*Akron Beacon Journal*, November 6, 2003). It is more accurate to say that after twenty years as mayor no one is *undecided* about the mayor.

In the words of an editorial after the November 2003 election:

All those years and still Plusquellic has seen little erosion of support. That says much about the way he has guided the city. The mayor often notes the futility of waiting for the perfect plan, say, for downtown development. His style has been to plunge into a problem, accepting the challenge and the risk. That can be messy. It also has yielded positive results.

At the core of the approach has been an invaluable ability to articulate what is best for the city as a whole. Call it vision, or whatever. Plusquellic has a passion for the city and a firm sense of where it should be headed. That drive has been present in his work downtown, of course, but also in his interest in the schools, neighborhoods and regionalism (*Akron Beacon Journal.* November 6, 2003, B2).

This driven man has been able to take a city that was almost moribund and reshaped it into a successful, if not yet thriving, mid-size city with a solid reputation for the quality of life. In 1999, Plusquellic received the highest honor bestowed on city leaders by the U.S. Conference of Mayors, the City Livability Award, for the mayor's leadership in creating and developing Joint Economic Development Districts (JEDD) for Ohio (U.S. Conference on Mayors, 2004).

14.4 Leadership Style, Roles, and Relationships

14.4.1 Defining Leadership

As public sector management texts have come to define leadership, a great deal of emphasis is placed on two attributes: concern for others and concern for the future (see, for example, Burns, 1978). This is especially true when we connect leadership to position. The attributes of a good leader, who is also a "boss," are different from the specific characteristics and behaviors of the *exercise of leadership at a moment in time.*

14.4.2 New Leadership Styles

The literature on management and leadership, even if one were to filter out those examinations directed to the private sector, is quite extensive. Even a cursory look at that body of work would consume far more space than is appropriate here. In keeping with the general theme of two decades of change, the review of leadership that follows will look at perspectives that have emerged roughly in that period.

Robert Behn (1991; 2001) has written extensively on the topic of leadership in the pubic sector. He offers us two important perspectives. First, he clearly articulates the *necessity* of leadership. He argues that organizations fail, not because of the lack of technical competence of employees or managerial acumen of senior administrators, but due to a lack of leadership. Second, is the importance of *luck.*

There is an old saying, "I would rather be lucky than good." Behn (1991) turns this notion around by suggesting that those who are lucky are also those who are good. We can never control everything that happens now or in the future. Decisions need to be made, even though we have little sense of the implications of the future on those decisions. Luck is in how things play out over time. The successful manager is the one who knows what to do when confronted by the unexpected.

Kiel (1994) takes the notion of the unexpected a step further. By borrowing from the literature on what is popularly referred to as "chaos theory" in physics, Kiel develops a management perspective that is designed to help managers successfully navigate in a chaotic world. The point is to discover the underlying order within the seeming chaos of the organization. Once we identify the underlying order, we can see that seemingly divergent behavior may still fall within the boundaries of acceptable behavior. Variability of performance is the norm. Trying to make things fit into narrow confines of behavior (the one-best-way of scientific management) cannot succeed. In fact, trying to straightjacket the range of acceptable performance may only create problems. Furthermore, things are most chaotic at the point when change is happening. The goal is not to control change or to control the future. Those are impossible tasks. The goal is to take advantage of the chaos (Kiel prefers instability) to impel change.

Two keys to successful application of chaos theory to management are to encourage participation and to create a diverse workforce. Participation becomes a way of stirring the pot, and the conflict of ideas and cultures gained through diversity is necessary to "achieve" instability. The nonstable organization is a creative organization. These are not easy notions for managers who have been taught that control is key. Yet, intuitively we see the connection between instability and change, even as we resist or fear to try it as practice. Furthermore, notions such as strategic management apply some of the same principles about the uncertainty and allusiveness of the future. Strategic management emphasizes guiding toward a broadly defined future, not a narrow path to a single point. There is another old saying, "only time will tell." Kiel uses this saying to illustrate the central point of chaos theory. We cannot know ahead of time the path we will take or the final destination. We may plan to go to a destination, but only when we "arrive" can we look back to see how we got there, or even where "there" is.

Helping an organization follow an unknown path of change and innovation is not an easy task. It takes a manager of insight and courage. The attractiveness and resulting persistence of old notions of control and direction as key attributes of management practice are because this is a safer course. Especially if the final goals are so far into the future that those who set the goals will not be around to be judged by the outcome, a more controlling style seems a wise course. That may be the path of the manager, but beginning with the seminal work of James MacGregor Burns (1978) in a book simply titled, *Leadership*, an alternative approach was clearly articulated. Burns introduced the idea of "transformational leadership." The key tenets of transformational leadership are

- Importance of active leadership
- Change organizational performance by changing its culture
- Future orientation

Burns (1978) emphasizes that a leader accomplishes this through

- The articulation of a vision that defines the direction, values and outlook for the organization
- The joint development of a mission that defines the outcomes to be achieved
- Empowerment of employees by granting authority to decide and act at the lowest level possible
- Broad participation in the above activities and all decision making

The keys to success are in creating an ethic of accomplishment and mutual support that is founded on trust.

Drawing on these varied ideas, it can be said that the successful leader

- Possesses determination
- Is future-oriented
- Seeks partners, but recognizes nothing lasts forever
- Works from strength
- Ignores the naysayers (Cox, 2004)

14.5 Plusquellic on Leadership

In conducting interviews with Plusquellic, it is quickly apparent that he is the prototype of the successful leader as described above. His political career reflects the five attributes of successful leadership. His views on leadership, as they emerged from the interviews, emphasize the attitude of trust and respect and the culture of visioning that are central to Burns' (1978) definition of transformational leadership. It is clear that he has sought to transform, economically, politically, and socially, the city of Akron because that is what he believes that politicians should do.

While it is not surprising that a politician might see leadership from the perspective of chaos theory, Plusquellic's style is subtler than implied by that orientation. Yes, he is determined and quite willing to ignore naysayers. He would aggressively assert that he does not suffer "fools" well. Yet, he is also quick to recognize that he does not always have the answers. He embodies Behn's notion of luck (luck is in how things play out over time). As will be discussed in more detail below, his relationship with the city council is a critical component of his leadership. Furthermore, the fact that some of his most senior people have served with him for nearly all of his twenty years in office is a testament to his behavior as a "boss." No one would mistake him for being "easy." Yet, as demanding as he is, with as high expectations as he has, there remains a core of senior managers (and a large segment of the citizenry) who place their faith in his judgment. When he plunges "into a problem, accepting the challenge and the risk" (*Akron Beacon Journal,* November 6, 2003), he is also taking those deputy mayors and many others along.

The report on his speech at his swearing-in ceremony on December 31, 2003, noted that:

> … the awards he's received personally and those that have been bestowed on the city and its various organizations are because of people pulling together for the betterment of the city.
>
> He praised the level of cooperation he has in working with the all-Democratic City Council—something he said puts him in a rare position compared with other cities.
>
> He also hearkened back to that speech he made at that very first swearing-in—a speech in which he pledged to build bridges and bring people together. In that address, he promised to become the "best damn mayor Akron's ever had," a remark that got him into trouble with his grandmother for his language.
>
> "So tonight, I want to say that I want to be an even better darn mayor than I have been in the past," Plusquellic said. "And together, working with you, I know we can accomplish even greater things for the city" (*Akron Beacon Journal,* December 31, 2003, B1).

Aided by his own experience as a member of council for thirteen years, including three as council president, Plusquellic sought out the council on a number of ideas as they unfolded. While the extra-majority of Democrats on the council (and, for that matter, a Democratic majority in the state legislature in the mid and late-1980s) helped to encourage cooperation, Plusquellic sought allies on council to help promote his agenda of development. Where conflict existed it was more likely to be with the business community and/or political opponents.

14.5.1 City Council Relations and Council Performance

Possibly the most telling comment about Plusquellic's relationship with the city council is that, when I asked both the mayor and the council president to tell a story that illustrated his relationship to the council, both men independently of each other told the same story (Plusquellic 2006; Sommerville 2006). In a sense, the particulars of the story are not relevant. It was a story of the close working relationship between two long-time political figures from quite different backgrounds. The point both men sought to convey was that the mayor's first instinct is to include the council, not exclude it.

The relationship between any mayor and any city council will be tense. The charter-defined roles require that the mayor and council share authority. This is no different than the inevitable conflict between governor and state legislature or president and Congress that is so much a part of the American political landscape. Despite the limited control over the civil service system mandated by the Akron Charter, the conflict between mayor and council is tilted heavily in favor of the mayor. As noted earlier, the staggered election cycle serves only to highlight the office of mayor and downplay the council elections. And, after fully twenty years in office, the mayor can get everyone's attention simply by calling a press conference. In a political tug-of-war with the council, the mayor will win. As such, the tactics for political success are often public confrontation rather than old-fashioned arm-twisting and political horse-trading. The roughshod practices of budget manipulation or service delivery changes are not part of his repertoire, not because he would not hesitate to apply such pressure if he thought it would help, but because he does not need to use such tactics. That being said, such tactics would be used only in the *extremis,* because the mayor would see the need for such behavior as a sign of weakness in his position. He is not going to put himself through the exhausting effort to achieve change if he is in serious jeopardy of losing.

The decision to consult with the city council before major policy decisions is at the option of the mayor. This does not mean that he does not consult, but it does mean that it is an informal process with selected individuals on council, not the full body. In February 2007 (*Akron Beacon Journal,* February 21, 2007), the mayor presented to council a proposal to increase the city sales tax. Members of council knew this was coming because of both private consultations and because the proposal was first released to the press the week before. The more pertinent question would be whether the proposal would have gone forward if the recommendation of members of the city council had been overwhelmingly negative. The simple answer is "yes," the proposal would have gone forward. It is not that he would not accept the advice of the council, but that on an issue as politically charged and controversial as a tax increase, the mayor can only go forward, he cannot back down from the controversy.

When the shoe is on the other foot, i.e., when a member of council is developing a major initiative, it is expected that the mayor will be involved. Even this categorization is not completely accurate. When the council president began looking at the issue of a police advisory board, the mayor supported the effort by agreeing to have members of council travel to other cities to study how those programs were working in those locales. The mayor was less than enthusiastic about this issue, and if asked directly would say so, but he did not try to interfere in the development of the legislation to authorize such a program (*Akron Beacon Journal,* January 5, 2004).

The point of these two events—the tax increase proposal and the police advisory board proposal—is that the behavior of the mayor reflects respect for the separate and distinct role of city council vis-à-vis the office of mayor. Each has the responsibility to act, but neither is fully independent of the other. Cooperation is borne of respect for the institutions. Nevertheless, neither the council nor the mayor must sacrifice their independence in the name of cooperation. And, in this environment, the mayor would simply assume the mantle of leadership.

14.6 Positive Impact

To understand Plusquellic's leadership style, it is necessary to trace some of his most important decisions of the past twenty years. The economic turnaround that resulted in Plusquellic accepting the Livable City award from the U.S. Conference of Mayors can be traced to three distinct development projects, all of which have their origins in his first term as mayor, but each of which took nearly a decade to come to fruition. It is his ability to focus on the long term, what the newspaper calls "vision," but which are probably more accurately the traits of determination and a strategic, future orientation. The mayor knew these were projects that would take years to unfold. While conventional wisdom suggests that politicians can never see past the next election, this was clearly an example of a politician who knew that if he was to have an impact on the community, then he had to think about the community one and two decades into the future not four years out.

Early in this chapter the economic conditions in Akron in the mid-1980s were described. The city faced innumerable obstacles. Housing had been torn down near the center of the city to accommodate roads and businesses, but the businesses were gone and the roads underutilized. Yet for all of the decline in the center city, the reality was that Akron was then, and even more so today, "land poor." The available land for either housing or business development was virtually nonexistent. Parcels larger than a small residential lot did not exist. Downtown had to be transformed, but new job opportunities would not come merely from downtown. While two major downtown initiatives to address both housing and downtown revitalization were begun during his first years in office, the signature program for the mayor was to be the establishment of the first-in-the-state Joint Economic Development District (JEDD). According to the city, a JEDD is "an economic development alternative to annexation and provides municipalities and townships with an opportunity to work together to mutually benefit their communities." The rationale and method for this tax sharing arrangement is

- Township provides developable land and existing commercial and industrial businesses in need of services.
- Township retains their property taxes (does not affect political or school boundaries).
- City provides access to central water and sewer services.
- City receives new JEDD income taxes from businesses and persons employed in the District.*

---

* http://www.ci.akron.oh.us/News_Releases/2004/0721.html

The first two JEDDs took some six years to negotiate, but then three more were announced in November, 1994. The districts represent a unique method of promoting regional cooperation between the city and its neighboring townships. By giving the communities a reason to cooperate rather than fight about annexation and development issues, it meant that all could prosper. Currently, the city has four such districts covering some 3,000 acres in which some 20,000 people are employed. The JEDD contracts negotiated by Plusquellic with the townships served as the model for a state law, which authorizes the creation of such districts across the state.*

Two additional development projects have been underway for some two decades with varied success. The revitalization of downtown has been driven by multiple efforts to build new public and private facilities in the downtown area. These efforts have neither been easy, nor without controversy. In a manner that has proven typical of Plusquellic, some of these efforts have been tried and failed, but often come back in a slightly different guise or form.

The strategic outlook of revitalization (and in-fill housing) remains a constant, but the location, scope, and form of the initiatives under the strategy have varied. Three downtown projects, all supported by public funds, illustrate the strategic approach of the mayor. When Plusquellic became mayor, plans were already underway to create a downtown convention center. As a member of the city council, Plusquellic supported this effort. On becoming mayor, he vigorously sought state aid in the construction of the center. But, shortly after that Plusquellic decided that the convention center, as designed, would be too small (it was being designed to fit available dollars, not to reflect actual use). He immediately began pushing for a convention center/arena that could serve the city and the university. The new, larger facility would require changing the location of the center. By eliciting the support of the president of the University of Akron, he was able to get the university what it wanted—the acquisition of an old department store to serve as the downtown anchor of the campus. This, in turn, gave him the "excuse" to abandon the original convention center site (the parking garage that would have served the building the university wished to acquire). He got his convention center, though not quite in the configuration he envisioned (it was not large enough to serve as a sports venue, though this idea would emerge later at another site).

At virtually the same point in time, a proposal surfaced that permitted the city of Akron to bid to be the site of a proposed "Inventors' Hall of Fame." Seizing upon this issue, Plusquellic quickly added this facility to his wish list. Akron's successful bid as the new home for the facility was greatly aided by Plusquellic's ability to garner both local support and the promise of funds from the state.

The third facility proved more controversial. In the mid-1980s Akron was in competition with Canton and Youngstown to be the site of a new minor league baseball park. The original idea was quite modest—a $1 million facility for about 5,000 fans. Canton was the odds on favorite, but no one planned for the mayor.

---

* http://www.ci.akron.oh.us/News_Releases/2004/0721.html

Rather than a relatively small facility on the fringe of Akron, or in Canton, the mayor saw a major facility that would be an anchor for a downtown entertainment district. This was not to be a small, low-priced park. This was going to be a large (over 8,500 seats that could be expanded to 12,000) facility built to very exacting specifications and, most importantly, it would quite literally be on Main Street. By the time of its completion, it would be a $30 million plus, publicly funded facility (*Akron Beacon Journal,* December 8, 1995). Many thought it was a waste of money. They did not see what Plusquellic saw. They saw an expensive "white elephant" that would simply make a bad situation downtown worse. He saw the anchor for a revival of downtown with restaurants and other establishments. His simple logic was that the ballpark gave people a reason to be downtown. He lobbied both the state (from which he got $5.8 million) and the local business community to back the proposal. They set a goal of 5,000 season tickets for five years as assurance that the team and the stadium would be a success. The ballpark opened to a sell-out crowd in April 1997, yet many were convinced that a majority of the original season ticket holders would withdraw support in 2002. Despite a weak economy, a relatively small number dropped their season ticket-holder status, and the team continued to maintain high attendance that year and into the next few years. The team is one of the most successful in all of minor league baseball with total attendance consistently over 400,000 each year. Restaurants that would be only marginally successful if they depended on the Monday to Friday lunch crowd, thrived as people who came down for a ball game came back for dinner. An aborted attempt to create a hockey/basketball arena in the same area (harkening back to his original vision for the enlarged convention center) made sense as the logical extension to the success of the ballpark (now people would be coming down year-round rather than just during baseball season).

14.6.1 In-Fill Housing

The economic picture of Akron in the 1980s was glum. As the city would prove over the next two decades, its transformation would be the result of innovative and bold thinking. These new and innovative ideas were not always successful. Experimentation has been a basic strategy. As described earlier, Akron is a city that seemingly has had to reinvent itself every forty years or so. The influence of tire manufacturing had a long run—seven decades. But, as the tire industry declined, it was not merely the employment base that was threatened, it was also the basic housing stock. The population boom in Akron was from 1910 to 1925. During that period the population nearly tripled. As old homes were razed to make room for more factory space, new housing had to be built along the fringes of the city to keep up. The core of the housing for the city was built in response to the housing demand of the first decades of the twentieth century. A second post-World War II boom pushed the boundaries of the city still farther. But, by the 1960s, new housing was being built nearly exclusively in the suburban ring.

The core of the current housing stock in the city is sixty to nearly one hundred years old. Furthermore, because of first the canals and then the cereal companies, and finally the tire companies, housing in downtown Akron was comparatively sparse. As the tire industry faded, it left both a business and a residential hole in the center of the city. If Akron was to respond to its decline, it would have to reverse what was already two decades of population loss. The city needed to renew interest in both working and living downtown. Some of the earliest speeches by the mayor (*Akron Beacon Journal,* February 6, 1987) discussed the need for housing in the inner city. As would be typical of his style over the next two decades, Plusquellic did not permit "old" methods and "old" ways to limit his thinking about how to encourage new housing and new homeownership in the city. He found willing a partner in the Alpha Pi Alpha fraternity to build moderate-income housing near South Main Street. He worked with Children's Hospital to build new townhouses near the hospital with low interest loans to encourage hospital staff to move there. Later, he would support the Akron Metropolitan Housing Authority in its HOPE VI projects to replace public housing with mixed priced housing with special arrangements to facilitate homeownership by the former residents and others. Recently, in cooperation with the University of Akron, another new housing development targeted to faculty and staff is being developed with the active support of the city. Not all of these efforts have succeeded; the hospital decided it needed more parking and quickly moved to buy the new townhomes so they could be bulldozed for a new parking garage. On the other hand, two new private developments, one of which is pricing condominiums at up to $1 million are now being built near downtown (*Akron Beacon Journal,* January 12, 2007). It has been a slow and often frustrating process, yet the city (because of the mayor) has never lost sight of the goal, even as some projects have been less successful than others.

14.6.2 Public Schools—City Cooperation

The State of Ohio has one of the most fragmented public school systems in the United States. Summit County, of which Akron is the county seat, has seventeen school districts for less than 550,000 residents. The state law that controls school district operations encourages such fragmentation and separate administration. When school districts coincide with city boundaries, the temptation is for the city to take control. That is what happened in Cleveland in the mid-1990s. When the state changed the formula for funding school construction, the financial underpinning of the Akron School District meant that the district might not be able to participate in the state program. Rather than follow the Cleveland model (some had speculated that he would follow that path), the mayor chose a quite different direction. He announced, in cooperation with the county executive, that he would back an unprecedented ballot initiative to increase the county sales tax to fund construction and remodeling in all eighteen school districts in the county. He campaigned for the proposal, but in November 2002, it lost in virtually every suburb (*Akron Beacon Journal*, January 10, 2003). The proposal was dead, but the need for funding remained. The mayor shifted gears and now sought an Akron-only solution (*Akron Beacon Journal*, January 10, 2003). This time he proposed an increase in the city income tax, with the additional funds being transferred to the school district for the construction of new schools that would simultaneously serve as community centers. In May 2003, this proposal passed, permitting the school district to undertake the largest school construction and remodeling effort in its history (*Akron Beacon Journal*, May 8, 2003).

Rather than push a solution that would increase his authority, the mayor opted to experiment with unique funding arrangements. Rather than assume control himself, he supported efforts that kept the school district administration in the hands of the Akron School Superintendent. As with many other problems he has faced over the past twenty years, the school-funding issue represented an opportunity to think creatively. The mayor stayed focused on the problem as narrowly defined: funding. In doing so, he *twice* developed unique arrangements that delivered exactly what the schools needed. His willingness to experiment ands his persistence paid off for the public schools.

14.7 The Nature and Sources of Leadership

14.7.1 Future Vision

From the very outset of his political career, Plusquellic has been noted for his willingness to look at the long-term implications of programs and policies. His capacity to envision a new way of doing things, as well as to envision new economic, political, and social arrangements is key to understanding Plusquellic's leadership style. He is always much more interested in tomorrow than he is in today; and he quickly forgets yesterday. The past influences the present and even the future, but it is *past*. The needs and desires of the public are the *future*. He is neither reluctant nor timid in his depiction of the future. It is something to strive toward. Those who are too deeply rooted in the past ways of seeing and thinking and, therefore, reluctant to seek change find the mayor combative and even startling in his expectations. It is not *trying* that is the greatest sin. On the other hand, it would be a mistake to see the mayor as reveling in change for the sake of change. His decisions may imply change, but they are well thought out. There is a clear theme of economic and social renewal to his efforts. Whether the issue is supporting the Akron Public Schools, affordable housing, or Canal Park baseball stadium, each effort had the potential to yield significant economic and social benefit to the city. It is as though he prefaces each decision by asking the question: "Will this make the City better in the long run"?

14.7.2 Securing Support for His Vision

While his relationship has been spotty with regard to the business community, his relations with the city council, the county government, and the school district have demonstrated a considerable talent for bringing disparate groups together to reach a common goal. The two initiatives in support of the Akron Public Schools proved to be Plusquellic at his best. Not unlike other public school systems, the Akron schools were viewed as in disarray and failing. He could have chosen the path of taking over the public school system as was done in Cleveland in the late 1990s. Plusquellic chose instead to create a partnership, which included two innovative revenue sharing proposals.

The mayor enjoys exceptional relations with the council. After twenty years, it would be expected that more than a few council members would have felt stifled in trying to advance their political careers. Certainly those strains were apparent in 2004 and 2005 when speculation that Plusquellic would run for governor was strongest, but on the whole he has continued to receive strong support on policy initiatives from the council.

The perception among the council is that his efforts to include them are genuine. But also, as an old political hand with long experience with the dance of legislation and the policy process, he does not take policy disputes personally. He understands that your ally today may be your opponent tomorrow. In this sense, there are two Don Plusquellics: the aggressive, even pugnacious, visionary who puts his heart and soul into the City, and the Don Plusquellic who well understands that compromise is part of making a policy. The first Don Plusquellic will battle those who do not share his vision. This is the Plusquellic portrayed in the press (he is good press). He can be acerbic and even critical of opponents. But the second Don Plusquellic is one who prizes action over debate. Once the debate is over and it is time to shape the "deal," he will readily engage even those he has vilified to get the project going; and, then, forget the battle the next day as he begins shaping the coalition that will promote the next policy. For those on council who are similarly program- and policy-oriented, this duality makes the mayor a valued ally and advocate for the city. While he never said it in so many words during the interviews, it is clear that Plusquellic makes a clear distinction between the behavior during the discussion about the policy to follow, and the discussion about how to design an implementation plan for that policy. His forte is in the former. Getting to the decision of *what* needs to be done dominates his thinking. The discussion about *how* to get it done is of less interest. Once the policy is set, he is likely to be able to envision several paths of implementation. He will be quite open to taking any of those paths.

The mayor rarely has had to resort to the kind of arm twisting and political maneuvering that is the stereotype of all political decision making. On the other hand, he has on at least two occasions interjected himself (behind the scenes) into the issue of city council leadership, guiding council toward officers who were supporters of his programs and policies (*Akron Beacon Journal* December 17, 1995, and February 21, 2007)

14.7.3 Sources of Leadership

The position of mayor in Akron will never be the same. As the CEO of the city for fully twenty years, Plusquellic has come to embody in the minds of many in Akron what a mayor should be. His influence extends well beyond the formal authority of office. His support is critical to the success of policy initiatives in the city and in the public schools. Having twice been recognized for his leadership by the U.S. Conference of Mayors, Plusquellic has gained stature as a major policy figure on urban issues in the United States. Others across the country look to him. Also, because, in a very real sense Akron is a very large *small* town, the simple fact that he was born in Akron and has remained in Akron lends credence to his vision of what can be achieved in the city—politically, socially, and economically.

14.7.4 Key Support

The base of the mayor's political support is in the middle-class sections of the community, but the true source of his capacity to secure change is in his relationship to the business community. Especially in his early years as mayor, his proposals for change and revitalization met with considerable skepticism and even outright opposition from the business community. As a Democratic mayor in a city that had experienced considerable labor–management upheaval in the years before his selection as mayor, this distrust should be expected. While they are often reluctant to say so, the business community recognizes that Plusquellic's mayoral leadership has been the driving force behind the renewal of the city. There is considerably more individual and collective support for the mayor in the business community than might be expected in a city with partisan elections. Therefore, it has been his ability to win over much of the business community to his vision of a better city that is the key to his success.

14.7.5 Communicating with Citizens

The mayor uses all the tools available to reach citizens. He has not sought out new ways to reach citizens, though departments within the city have used citizen surveys and other methods to get citizen input. Akron is the second largest city (behind Newark, New Jersey) to not have a television station based in the city. Therefore, Akron remains a newspaper town (also fitting in that the recently defunct Knight–Ridder chain began in Akron in 1839). While Plusquellic has the appearance and presence to do well on the television, the opportunity to discuss positions at length makes him more appropriate for the radio and television. While he is quite capable of speaking in "sound bites," he is especially effective at discussion and debate. He has the politician's frustration with the filtering of his message that is the inevitable result of communicating through the newspaper, or any other media. He inevitably invites the dialog that can emerge as the newspaper reports and critiques policy proposals. The forcefulness and passion of his arguments come through even in the newspaper.

14.7.6 Opposition and Adversity

Plusquellic represents an interesting dichotomy when we examine the notion of facilitation. As noted earlier, his initial reaction to the word is to reject it. To him, facilitation is simply a way of making sure that implementation goes smoothly. It is not a key behavior. On the other hand, he will cooperate with any who share his concern to set the policy.

By temperament and experience, Plusquellic was born to be a mayor. He would be less effective as a city manager, not for lack of capacity and capability, but for the simple reason that managing and administration are not paramount concerns. He places considerable trust in his deputy mayors,* and even his department heads (those still appointed by the Civil Service Commission). He is appreciative of their skill in managing and implementing programs. He relies on them to be competent and professional. As noted earlier, the five department directors and deputy mayors (plus, since 2002, the police and fire chiefs) are his only appointees. As would be expected in a group that is by their nature "political," the deputy mayors share a common bond of elected political experience. For example, the current and most previous directors for Public Service (utilities, sanitation, public works, etc.) had served on the city council. It should also be noted that several recent deputy mayors dealing with economic development came through the ranks and served as department heads. Depending on the position and needs, the mayor is as likely to select the "senior" department civil servant as he is to select an outsider to be a department director. The skills and knowledge gained in the policy area as a civil servant are appreciated and recognized. Because these individuals have policy roles and are not necessarily involved in the direct operations of city departments (again, most department heads are selected through the Civil Service Commission), they are valued for the advice they can offer the mayor and the broad management control they offer. While it certainly would be a stretch to suggest that professional management skills are not needed, these are first policy coordination positions and only secondarily management positions. The parallel is to the U.S. president's cabinet, not a city manager's management team.

The more critical question then is the relationship between the deputy mayors and the department heads. To the extent that political necessity and administrative professionalism clash, it would most likely be seen in those relationships. The "hands-off" stance of the mayor with regard to program implementation is replicated in the relationship between the deputy mayors and the department heads that report to them. It should also be remembered that, after twenty years as mayor and a dozen years on city council, the mayor has as much experience with and in city government as any senior civil servant. His views, his expectations, and his priorities are well known by all—especially senior public servants, many of whom never worked in city government at a time when Plusquellic was not a driving force.

The kind of political pressure and the manipulation of the administrative system that is the stereotype of the clash between the values and attitudes of administrative

---

* There are currently five deputy mayors, including the deputy mayor of administration and chief of staff to the mayor, and deputy mayors for economic development, intergovernmental relations, labor relations, and public safety.

professionals and the political ambitions and goals of elected officials is abated in an environment in which the assumption of "experience in government" is the reverse of the norm. This mayor has greater knowledge of how the city works than many administrative professionals. It is by dint of experience of how things work, not the exercise of political power, that Plusquellic dominates government. Although by personality he is not deeply interested in administration and management, it would be a mistake to think that he does not understand those processes. His standards of performance are not based on political prejudices, but rather on long experience of the operations of city government. Controlling the appointments of department heads and other senior officials is not realistic, nor necessary. He doesn't need to be manipulative. The better question will be the relationship between administrators and the next mayor. At that time, knowledge of "administrative feasibility," which many (from Long to Waldo) have identified as a key source of administrative influence, will rest again in the hands of the senior civil servants. That is when the clash of politics and administration will emerge.

14.8 Conclusions

Plusquellic's leadership still involves inclusion and considerable dialog in the shaping of public policy. Despite his unease with the term, he is a facilitative leader. On the other hand, he is also an "executive." He makes decisions and then expects that his staff and department heads have the know-how and capacity to implement the policy. He is not blind to the financial constraints faced by his community, but he does have considerable trust in his staff. He would expect them to tell him that it won't work the way he expects (this would not be a comfortable conversation for the staff person). If they say they can do it, he moves on. He cannot be easy to work for, yet people are very loyal precisely because they know he trusts them.

References

Behn, Robert. 1991. *Leadership Counts.* Cambridge, MA: Harvard University Press.

Behn, Robert. 2001. *Rethinking Democratic Accountability.* Washington, DC: Brookings Institution Press.

Burns, James McGregor. 1978. *Leadership.* New York: HarperCollins.

Cox, Raymond W. III. 2004. On being an effective local government manager, in *The Effective Local Government Manager, 3rd ed.*, Charldean Newell, ed., Washington, DC: ICMA, 1–19.

Kiel, Douglas. 1994. *Managing Chaos in Government.* San Francisco: Jossey-Bass.

Plusquellic, Donald. 2006, 2007. Personal interview by the author, June 20, July 25, August 31 (2006), and June 13 (2007).

Sommerville, Marco 2006. Personal interview by the author. May 12.

Chapter 15

The Power To Persuade: Philadelphia, Pennsylvania

Craig M. Wheeland

Contents

Two point nine, four, and thirty-one. Nine, twenty-five, and seventy-four. The numbers seemed cryptic … . The first set, Rendell explained, was for Cumberland County, Pennsylvania, where the jobs [from defense support facilities] would go under the proposed relocation and consolidation plan: 2.9 percent was the unemployment rate, 4 percent was the poverty rate, and 31 percent was Clinton's share of the votes in the presidential election. The second set was for Philadelphia: 9 percent was the unemployment rate, 25 percent was the poverty rate, and 74 percent was Clinton's share of the votes in the presidential election. Clinton laughed. If there is another politician in the country who would make an appeal to the president this way, it was hard to know who it was.

Buzz Bissinger
Prayer for the City

15.1 Introduction

Mayors serving in traditional strong mayor cities have a portfolio of formal powers giving them a privileged position in bargaining among officials to shape the policy of the jurisdiction. A simplistic understanding of leadership posits that strong mayors can govern by reliance on the exercise of formal powers. Careful consideration of Richard Neustadt's analysis of presidential power offers lessons apropos to mayoral leadership (Neustadt 1980). Neustadt explains that the president's formal powers are advantages (1980), "checked by the advantages of others. Continuing relationships will pull in both directions. These are relationships of mutual dependence." A strong mayor's power correctly understood through the lenses Neustadt provides is not the power to command, but rather the power to persuade. For mayors as much as for presidents, formal powers are advantages in bargaining relationships, but do not obviate the need to tap other sources to be persuasive. Over his two terms, Edward Rendell demonstrated adroit abilities to build relationships among officials, use pragmatic appeals to interests to reach agreements, and search for compromise and conciliation to be persuasive. He understood the exercise of power as persuasion. The attributes of facilitative leadership appropriate for mayoral leadership in council–manager government provide an important complement of power resources to the formal powers available to mayors in strong mayor cities to bargain with other officials. Rendell's performance is one case demonstrating the value of wedding some of the attributes of facilitative leadership to strong mayor systems.

15.2 Community Context

Since the Colonial era, Philadelphia has been a city at the center of the economic, social, and political development of the United States (Warner 1987; Weigley 1982). By a state law, Philadelphia consolidated with Philadelphia County and the other municipalities within the county in 1854 to form a city of about one hundred thirty-five square miles (Geffen 1982). The city now sits at the heart of a nine-county metropolitan area (four counties are in New Jersey). After World War II,

Philadelphia experienced the major trends transforming many Frostbelt cities in the United States:

- Deindustrialization and disinvestment
- Out-migration of affluent white residents to the growing suburbs
- Increasing African American in-migration to the city
- Declining neighborhoods and a declining downtown
- Becoming home to the metropolitan region's poor
- High rates of violent crime
- Declining tax base
- Increasing demand for services

These eight trends contributed to Philadelphia's population decline from 2,071,605 in the 1950 census to 1,586,000 in the 1990 census. The city's current population is 1,517,550 (U.S. Census Bureau 2000). The in-migration of African Americans since 1950 combined with the loss of white residents changed the percentage of the African American population to 40 percent in 1990. By 2000, Philadelphia's white, non-Hispanic share of the population fell to just under 50 percent (U.S. Census Bureau 2000). This demographic change combined with a racially influenced settlement pattern turned Philadelphia into the third most racially segregated central city in the United States (Kasarda 1993). In addition, in the early 1990s, Philadelphia ranked seventh out of one hundred central cities for having the most neighborhoods with high rates of poverty, and fifth for the number of neighborhoods experiencing distress (Kasarda 1993). David Rusk (1995) labeled Philadelphia a "zero-elasticity" city because of its inability to expand its boundaries via annexation and because of the high-density settlement pattern, and is as such a city drastically limited in how it can address social and economic problems. Indeed, Rusk (1995) suggested cities like Philadelphia will need "life support" and ultimately the intervention of national and state governments to help manage their problems.

15.3 Political and Governmental Context Before 1947

The practice of politics in Philadelphia in the 1990s reflected the lingering effects of more than a century-old tradition characterized as partisan and pragmatic at its best, and as unethical and criminal at its worst. The Republican Party dominated city politics from the Civil War era through World War II. During this era, Lincoln Steffens (1904) labeled the city "corrupt and contented" even after having thrown out the notorious "Gas Ring" in the 1880s. Steffens lamented the fact that the machine retained power after having the state impose a strong mayor charter in 1887 to enable the election to the office of mayor a "good business man, who with his probity and common sense, would give them that good business administration which is the ideal of many reformers" (1904). Republican boss Matthew Quay had supported the charter's passage in the state legislature in order to use the new charter as a means to take over control of the city's government from a rival faction in the Republican Party (Burt and Davies 1982). Although two businessmen were elected mayor under the new charter, by 1893 Quay and the Republican machine were firmly in control. Not until after World War II would Democrats take power in the city under the leadership of reformers Joseph Clark, who was elected controller in 1949 and mayor in 1951, and Richardson Dilworth, who was elected city treasurer in 1949 and district attorney in 1951 (Clark and Clark 1982). Clark and Dilworth led the effort to adopt a new home rule charter in 1951, which remains the basis of Philadelphia government today.

15.4 Political and Governmental Context After 1947

The 1951 Home Rule Charter (City of Philadelphia 1951) established a strong mayor form of government with a civil service system covering most jobs, an elected treasurer, an elected controller, an elected district attorney, and a position for professional executive management called the managing director. An organization chart is provided in Figure 15.1. The mayor is directly elected by voters in partisan elections to a four-year term and is limited to two terms. The mayor's formal powers include the following: calling special meetings for the council to consider legislation; promoting the city; proposing legislation; preparing and submitting the budget; using the veto power; submitting reports on the city's performance; appearing before council or council committees any time to express views on issues being considered; executing the law; appointing citizens to boards and commissions usually without council approval; and appointing/removing assistants (e.g., chief of staff and deputy mayors), the finance director, the city representative (who performs ceremonial activities on behalf of the mayor), and the managing director, all without council approval.

The charter specifies the managing director to have "had such experience for at least five years as an executive either in public service or private industry as shall qualify him for the duties of his office" (City of Philadelphia 1951), but otherwise leaves qualifications to the mayor's discretion. The managing director has the formal authority to appoint, supervise, and remove, with the approval of the mayor, department heads, such as the police commissioner, health commissioner, streets commissioner, the fire commissioner, and recreation commissioner. Because the managing director works at the pleasure of the mayor and appointments/removals must be approved by the mayor, mayors have routinely exerted control over these administrative positions.

The Home Rule Charter created a seventeen-member city council with ten members elected by ward and seven members elected at-large. The city council members are elected in partisan elections, serve four-year terms and are not limited in the number of terms they may serve. Two of the at-large seats are reserved for the minority party to guarantee representation and possible oversight of the majority

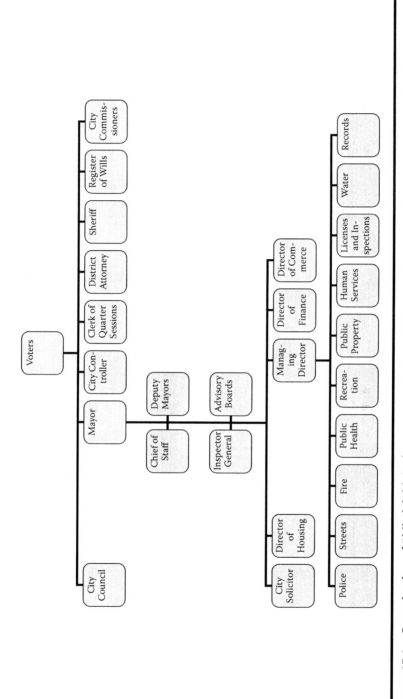

Figure 15.1 Organization of Philadelphia's city government May 1992. (From Department of Records, July 27, 2007.)

party. Since 1951, the Republican Party has held the two at-large minority seats and usually has held at least one ward seat on council. Council members elect a council president to preside at meetings and to represent them in discussions with the mayor. Council also adopts rules as to how the work of the council will be organized. The factions within the Democratic Party often are represented among the council members, and occasionally council members will struggle over committee assignments, resources, and who will be council president. Often the Republican members are swing votes.

After the 1951 charter change, the partisan and pragmatic character of city government remained, and to some extent the unethical and criminal character as well, only now the Democratic Party dominated with about a three-to-one registration advantage among voters. Factions formed within the Democratic Party based primarily on race and the support or opposition to machine-style politics (Keiser 2003). Reformers wanted to eliminate the practices supporting job and contract patronage, otherwise known in Philadelphia parlance as pay-to-play, and to bring about social and economic reform as well. They competed with leaders loyal to the Democratic organization interested mainly in jobs and contracts. The reform and organization factions competed for African American votes.

In the 1963 and 1967 elections, Mayor James Tate, an organization loyalist, won two terms with the support of African American voters by delivering jobs and other particularistic-type rewards, but he did not share leadership positions with African Americans (Keiser 2003). In 1971, Tate's police commissioner, Frank Rizzo, appealed to organization loyalists and white, blue collar voters using highly charged racial statements driving African Americans and reformers to support the candidacy of Republican Thacher Longstreth. Rizzo won the election by a mere 50,000 votes and won reelection in 1975, but the racially divisive character of his campaigns, mayoral rhetoric, and policies moved the majority of African American voters and leaders to the reformers' camp (Keiser 2003). The election of Bill Green in 1979 brought a reform, biracial coalition to power. Green named Wilson Goode as managing director, the first African American to hold this position. Goode emerged as a popular, visible, and effective managing director and a perfect candidate to run for mayor with the support of the newly formed white liberal reformer/African American biracial coalition.

In 1983, Goode narrowly defeated Rizzo in the Democratic primary and narrowly defeated Republican John Egan in the general election to become the first African American elected Philadelphia's mayor. Philadelphia's African American population had achieved full political incorporation defined as having "an equal or leading role in a dominant coalition that is strongly committed to minority interests" (Browning, Marshall, and Tabb 2003). In 1985, Goode and his administration mismanaged an effort to arrest members of a radical group named MOVE in a densely settled neighborhood of row homes. Goode approved dropping a bomb on the house and the resulting fire destroyed homes and killed members of MOVE still in the home. The MOVE disaster tarnished an otherwise effective first term for Goode. In the aftermath of the MOVE disaster, Goode ran for reelection and won a narrow primary victory over Ed Rendell, who had finished two terms as district attorney, and a narrow general election victory over Rizzo who ran as a Republican.

Keiser (2003) suggests that the organization loyalists generated enough white votes in the 1987 general election for Goode to prevent Republicans from winning the mayoral election, even if it meant that their old champion, Rizzo, would lose. The possible loss of jobs and contracts motivated enough organization loyalists to join white liberal reformers and African Americans to elect Goode twice. Keiser (2003) argues that entering the 1991 election period, Philadelphia's faction-based politics within the Democratic Party had evolved into two biracial coalitions: African American voters and leaders were split between the reformers/good government faction and the organization/jobs/contracts faction of the party. Coalition politics shaped Ed Rendell's second run for mayor in 1991 and his effort to govern once elected.

15.5 Profile of Edward Rendell

Rendell grew up in New York City and came to Philadelphia to attend the University of Pennsylvania. He graduated from Penn as a political science major in 1965 and earned his JD from Villanova University in 1968. Philadelphia District Attorney (DA) Arlen Specter hired Rendell out of law school to be chief of homicide (Duvoisin *Philadelphia Inquirer*, November 6, 1991). When Specter lost reelection in 1973, Rendell left the DA's office to enter private practice. He did legal work for the Democratic Party until 1977. Rendell decided to challenge incumbent Emmet Fitzpatrick in the Democratic primary for DA in 1977. Rendell ran as a reformer and revealed the high energy, gregarious, buoyant campaign style that would eventually help in his bid for mayor. Rendell won the primary and general election in 1977 and voters reelected him in 1981. Rendell ran unsuccessfully for the Democratic nomination for governor in 1986 and lost in the 1987 Democratic primary for mayor of Philadelphia. Rendell's challenge to Goode in the primary hurt his reputation with African-American leaders, especially the African-American clergy of Philadelphia.

Seemingly at a crossroads in his political and professional life, Rendell entered the crowded Democratic primary for mayor in 1991 as the front runner, but he had to compete with four candidates: Peter Hearn and three African Americans—Lucien Blackwell, George Burrell, and James White (eventually White dropped out). Rendell won the primary with 49 percent of the vote, but he only attracted about 15 percent of the African-American vote. The Republican Party again nominated Frank Rizzo after a tough three-way primary with Ron Castille and Sam Katz. As the general election campaign began, Rizzo featured the crime issue and began to attract "organization" Democrats who were his strongest supporters in the 1970s, and African-American voters who remained unhappy with Rendell for challenging Goode in the 1987 primary. But Rizzo died on July 16 and Republican

Party Chairman, William Meehan, chose relatively unknown Joseph Egan to replace Rizzo, rather than one of the two losing candidates from the primary (Paolantonio, *Philadelphia Inquirer*, November 3, 1991). Not choosing Katz is considered a strategic error driven by Meehan's anger at Katz for not dropping out of the primary once Meehan endorsed Castille. While Republicans were in disarray, Rendell focused on his policy proposals and his performance as district attorney fighting crime; appealed to voters across racial lines; received the endorsement of prominent African-American clergy; and easily defeated Egan in the general election with 66 percent of the vote, the largest margin of victory since Richardson Dilworth's reelection in 1959.

During the 1991 primary and general election campaigns, Rendell used a campaign strategy that provided a foundation for governance once elected. He focused on his proposals to address the main issues: the city's budget crisis, high taxes, the declining economy, and high crime rates (Saving Philadelphia: A Special Report, *Philadelphia Inquirer*, May 5, 1991). He avoided personal criticism of his opponents stating: "I'm not going to talk about my opponents. I'm going to talk about my plan for digging us out. This is not a trivial time for the city of Philadelphia where we can worry about rhetoric or personal kinds of mudslinging" (Carvajal and Dubin, *Philadelphia Inquirer*, May 23, 1991). He raised more money for the primary and general elections than his rivals so he had the resources to deliver his message (Paolantonio, Holman and Samuel, *Philadelphia Inquirer*, May 11, 1991; Paolantonio, Carvajal, and Duvoisin, *Philadelphia Inquirer*, November 6, 1991). And he was gracious after each victory, calling all of the other candidates and reaching out to leaders of the various factions in the city, especially African Americans. For example, Rendell's twenty-eight-member transition team included representatives from a wide array of the city's factions, with the exception of representatives from council member John Street's faction (Paolantonio, *Philadelphia Inquirer*, November 10, 1991). Once in office, Rendell would adeptly adjust this "oversight" on his part to reach out to Street.

Rendell's reelection in 1995 was practically a foregone conclusion. He did not face a serious challenge in the Democratic primary and the African-American clergy again endorsed him. Rendell was so popular by the fourth year of his term that some Republican leaders considered endorsing Rendell for reelection rather than running a candidate (Kaufman and Rubin, *Philadelphia Inquirer*, November 8, 1995). Eventually Republicans nominated Joseph Rocks, a former state senator who tried to reach out to disgruntled city employees upset at the union contracts Rendell negotiated, and who promised to cut the wage tax dramatically, to "get tough on crime" rather than continue Rendell's community policing, and to shift resources to neighborhoods away from Center City, which was an area Rocks claimed Rendell favored to the detriment of neighborhoods (Williams, *Philadelphia Inquirer*, February 17, 1995). Rock's campaign lacked money and his proposals could not counter Rendell's record as mayor, Rendell's promise for more of the same, or the overwhelming amount of money Rendell had at his disposal to spend on his campaign as well to use to support the election of other officials. Two weeks before the general election Rendell still had $2.3 million to spend which was forty-two times the amount Rocks had left to use (McCoy and Marder, *Philadelphia Inquirer*, October 28, 1995). Rendell won reelection with 77 percent of the vote, the largest margin of victory since 1932, and he won all sixty-six of the city's wards, also a first since 1932 (McCoy, Nicholas, Kaufman, Williams, and Jones, *Philadelphia Inquirer*, November 12, 1995).

15.6 Leadership Style, Roles, and Relationships

The mayor's formal powers defined in Philadelphia's Home Rule Charter set expectations for executive-style leadership (Wheeland 2002). Svara (1990) suggests "by establishing direction, forging coalitions, galvanizing the bureaucracy— in general, by managing and resolving conflict in all dimensions of the governmental process—the executive mayor becomes the driving force in this form of government." The charter gave Rendell all the formal features needed to be a successful executive-style leader, yet achieving success depended on the influence of contextual variables, such as the city's political culture, fiscal resources, interest group activity—and of proximate variables, such as Rendell's skills, personality, vision of the job, and legislative program (Wheeland 2002). As Megan Mullin, Gillian Peele, and Bruce Cain (2004) argue:

> … the structure in which a mayor operates helps to determine the odds of success for a given set of political strategies. The formal rules setting the balance of power among city officials create a set of opportunities and constraints for mayors not just by defining their authority and jurisdiction but also by influencing how other city officials and the public respond to mayoral activities.

Although formal powers gave him an advantage in the bargaining among officials, Rendell needed to tap informal sources of power in order to be a successful executive-style mayor and the dominant actor in city government.

Over his two terms, Rendell combined executive and facilitative styles of leadership, effectively tapping both formal and informal sources of power. He excelled at the traditional roles filled by mayors in both the strong mayor–council and the council–manager forms of government, such as ceremonial activities, public relations, and promoting the city. His willingness to work for the city included symbolic actions like having photos taken of him literally cleaning bathrooms in City Hall to demonstrate his commitment to improve city government; traveling to the home of donors to ask for money to help fund the transformation of South Broad Street in Center City into the Avenue of the Arts; meeting with business leaders planning to invest or disinvest in the city; and lobbying the national government for an Empowerment Zone and the retention of defense facilities in the city. As an executive style leader, he clearly presented himself to the public and media as a "driving force" in city politics. He used the formal powers of his office to control the staffing of the leadership positions in his administration, prepare city budgets, develop policy initiatives, set goals and objectives, and perform as the city's main crisis manager.

During Rendell's two terms, he relied extensively on the talent of his chief of staff rather than on the managing director. David L. Cohen served as Rendell's chief of staff until April 1997, when Greg Rost succeeded him. Cohen was part of every major decision and negotiation while he served as chief of staff. Even after he resigned in April 1997 to pursue his legal career, Cohen continued to advise Rendell, to resolve public conflicts using his mediation and negotiation skills, and to attend Tuesday morning meetings Rendell had with council President Street (Nicholas, *Inquirer Magazine*, October 18, 1998). Cohen's influence was so pronounced that he earned recognition among the city's leadership and the media as the city's "co-mayor." Rendell commented that: "As long as I'm mayor, David will always be part of the decision-making process" (Goodman, *Philadelphia Inquirer*, May 27, 1997). When Rost replaced Cohen, he welcomed Cohen's ongoing involvement. Rost continued to perform the main responsibilities Rendell expected of his chief of staff. In contrast to Cohen's legal background, Rost had pursued a PhD in government, joined Rendell's 1991 campaign as a policy advisor, and then worked in Rendell's administration as a policy advisor who authored many key reports and proposals (Goodman, *Philadelphia Inquirer*, March 30, 1997).

The expansive role Rendell gave to his chief of staff, as well as his deputy mayors, to develop and implement his initiatives limited the managing director's responsibilities to coordinating day-to-day operations.* Rendell appointed R. Gene Shipman, who had served as city manager in Hartford, Connecticut, as his first managing director, but Shipman resigned after two years allegedly because of the role of the chief of staff and deputy mayors (Williams, *Philadelphia Inquirer*, December 13, 1992). Rendell subsequently appointed Joseph Certaine to the position. Certaine had worked for the city for more than fifteen years in various management positions and came to the city with a background in Democratic Party politics and community activism (Loeb, *Philadelphia Inquirer*, May 26, 1994). Some critics questioned his appointment because he did not have a college degree or extensive professional experience, but others saw Certaine as providing an appropriate focus

---

* Rendell began with eight deputy mayors, but the total number varied throughout his two terms (Meyers, Philadelphia Inquirer, January 12, 1992). Rendell relied on deputy mayors more so than did his predecessor, Mayor Goode, who had only a couple (Editorial, Philadelphia Inquirer, January 13, 1992). Rendell appointed deputy mayors to focus on his reform agenda as well as liaison with important constituencies. For example, in 1992 he appointed deputy mayors for Housing, Management, and Productivity; Labor Relations; Community Development; Economic Development; Criminal Justice; and Operations. His appointees came from business, government, and labor and were demographically diverse. Policy coordination across the disparate areas was provided primarily by Rendell's chief of staff, David Cohen.

on day-to-day service delivery. Certaine served through Rendell's second term without controversy. Although Rendell's managing directors did not have the scope of work previous mayors had given their managing directors, his approach did not undermine the competence of the city's leadership.

Rendell used the veto power on a few occasions. He vetoed a bill to create an independent civilian review board to investigate police misconduct in 1993; a bill to shorten the time permitted to rehabilitate a city-owned house in 1995; a bill to require banks who do business with the city to stop charging ATM fees in 1998; and a bill to raise pension benefits for retired city employees in 1999 (Loeb and Gammage, *Philadelphia Inquirer*, June 4, 1993; Marder, *Philadelphia Inquirer*, May 19, 1995; Burton, *Philadelphia Inquirer*, September 24, 1998; Yant, *Philadelphia Inquirer*, January 15, 1999).

Rendell also threatened vetoes; for example, a proposal to repeal the 10 percent liquor-by-the-drink tax used to fund public schools in 1996 (Marder, *Philadelphia Inquirer*, April 30, 1996). Council sometimes won these battles, such as overriding the police review board veto, but most of the time Rendell prevailed (Carvajal, *Philadelphia Inquirer*, June 11, 1993).

Rendell also used his influence over mayoral appointees to the governing boards of various authorities to influence or block actions he deemed detrimental to the city. For example, in 1997 he did not want the Southeastern Pennsylvania Transportation Authority (SEPTA) to allocate funds in mass transit services toward the suburbs and neglect city needs, so he ordered the two city appointees on the SEPTA board to veto SEPTA's capital budget if adjustments were not made. The threat worked (Sipress, *Philadelphia Inquirer*, June 18, 1997).

Rendell's selective use of the veto power helped him to maintain good working relationships with council members and governing boards. He rarely had to resort to this confrontational tool to influence action, preferring instead to compromise, logroll, persuade, or cooperate with city council and boards on most matters facing the city.

Rendell skillfully adapted his leadership style to include roles and practices traditionally associated with facilitative-style leadership, especially as an articulator and mobilizer, as well as a team relations and network builder among the city's elected officials (see Svara 1994 for a discussion of these roles). Journalists affirm Rendell's skill using facilitative roles and practices. After reviewing Rendell's first year in office, Charles Mahtesian (1993) described Rendell as "a man who decides which politicians he must have on his side, and then does what it takes to get them." Mahtesian (1993) concludes, "In an era of technocratic mayors, [Rendell] adheres to the notion that political power is the basis for governmental action. This idea lies behind all the stunts and promotion; all the stroking of egos and twisting of arms; all the consolidation of control." Rob Gurwitt (1993) called Rendell an "adept facilitator." He was able to overcome a long period of dissension "by carefully sharing both the spotlight and his thinking" with other elected officials and sharing his power to achieve a consensus. At the beginning of his second term, Howard Goodman (*Inquirer Magazine*, April 20, 1997) suggested Rendell "has enlarged the role of the mayor to include political godfather, municipal Mr. Fix-It, festival impresario, fundraiser, cheerleader, spokesman for urban causes."

15.7 The Sources of Leadership

In addition to his detailed knowledge of city policy and the formal powers available to him, the keys to understanding Rendell's approach include: (1) his commitment to respect and consult with other elected officials, especially council members; (2) his commitment to share credit for successes with other officials; (3) his use of financial contributions to other officials in order to build relationships; (4) his commitment to forge a biracial administration and to promote good race relations citywide; and (5) his personality.

Rendell's partnership with Council President John Street epitomizes his willingness to respect, consult, and share power with other officials. After winning in 1991, Rendell supported Street's rival for council president, but after Street won, Rendell immediately reached out to form a partnership. The two met regularly during Rendell's two terms, often in Street's office, to discuss initiatives and develop strategies (Mahtesian 1993; Bissinger 1997). In 1992, Street helped Rendell reach an agreement with the city's four labor unions (Bissinger 1997). Street secured passage of the operating budget well ahead of statutory deadlines and helped get seven of Rendell's eight budgets approved unanimously. The only exception was when two council members, Cohen and Blackwell, voted against the fiscal 1995 budget over spending priorities (Motley, *Philadelphia Inquirer*, March 25, 1994). Street traveled with Rendell to New York to meet representatives of bond rating firms to assure them that the city's budget success and pattern of council–mayor cooperation would continue into Rendell's second term and to ask to have the city's bond rating improved from junk bond status to investment grade (Rosenberg, *Philadelphia Inquirer*, March 13, 1995). After five years with junk bond status, Moody Investor's Service approved Rendell and Street's request for an investment grade rating on March 15, 1995. Rendell could not have been successful carrying out many initiatives without the help of John Street.

Rendell's willingness to share power with the council president, as well as to share credit, stands in contrast to the strained, often combative relations other mayors in Philadelphia's recent past had with city council and with other city officials, such as the district attorney. For example, Goode's relationship with the city council deteriorated during his second term. Goode allowed the fiscal year 1991 budget to become law without his signature (Diaz and Meyers, *Philadelphia Inquirer*, June 1, 1990). In addition, city council passed nonbinding resolutions asking the mayor to submit monthly reports explaining how his administration spent money and also asking the mayor to submit plans on how he would address the city's anticipated budget deficit in fiscal year 1991 (Diaz and Meyers, *Philadelphia Inquirer*, June 1, 1990). During negotiations over the fiscal year 1992 budget, Goode threatened to veto the council's budget, only to decide two weeks past the statutory deadline to sign it (Turcol and Meyers, *Philadelphia Inquirer*, June 14, 1991). Rendell knew he had to avoid the acrimony surrounding Goode's budget travails. He did so by reaching out to Council President Street and other council members within the first month of his first term.

Rendell's approach to cultivating relationships with Street compare favorably to Giuliani's working relationship with Council Speaker Peter Vallone during Giuliani's first term as mayor of New York (Kirtzman 2000). Giuliani needed Vallone's help to secure passage of his proposals. Like Rendell and Street, Giuliani and Vallone met regularly to discuss strategy and proposals. And Vallone successfully secured council support for Giuliani's proposals. However, other than an effective relationship with Vallone, Giuliani's leadership style was nearly the opposite of Rendell's. Giuliani was confrontational, credit-claiming, and often blunt to the point of being abrasive when commenting on the proposals offered by other city leaders. Giuliani showed little interest in personally developing relationships with other council members, while Rendell worked to bring council members and other city leaders into his coalition.

In addition to sharing credit, consulting officials, and sharing power, Rendell also relied on his fundraising prowess to cultivate relations with city, state, and national elected officials. Rendell once commented, "I raise money all the time," and so he did, amassing more than $16 million during the decade of the 1990s, which is more than any Democrat running for any office in Pennsylvania during that time period (Zausner, *Philadelphia Inquirer*, December 12, 1999). Rendell used these resources to support officials seeking election, and nearly always supported incumbents who had supported his initiatives. For example, Rendell raised nearly $4 million for his reelection campaign prior to the 1995 primary, while his Republican opponent raised $45,000 (McCoy, Marder and Roche, *Philadelphia Inquirer*, May 6, 1995). Rendell shared his campaign funds with city council members and other officials. Before the 1995 primary, he gave about $170,000 to council members seeking reelection, $101,000 to the Pennsylvania Democratic Committee, and $55,000 to the Philadelphia Democratic Committee (McCoy, Marder and Roche, *Philadelphia Inquirer*, May 6, 1995). Not surprisingly, once in office, these officials who received Rendell's support were at least respectful toward the mayor if not loyal.

Rendell won in 1991 with a biracial coalition. In order to sustain the coalition, Rendell used his appointment powers to create an administration that reflected the diversity of the city. During his two terms he appointed African Americans to key leadership positions, including the managing director, city solicitor, police commissioner, public health commissioner, and fire commissioner. Rendell also took political risks to promote better race relations, such as helping to resolve a highly charged racial dispute in the Gray's Ferry neighborhood of South Philadelphia. Rendell mediated the Gray's Ferry conflict by appearing at an event to promote racial harmony with The Nation of Islam's controversial leader, Louis Farrakhan, in exchange for Farrakhan calling off a march through the neighborhood (McCoy and Goodman, *Philadelphia Inquirer*, April 9, 1997). Finally, Rendell's partnership with Council President Street not only unified the Democratic Party and the leg-islative and executive branches of the city's strong mayor form of government, it created an effective biracial partnership between the city's two most visible leaders. During Rendell's two terms, African Americans continued to be incorporated into the governing of the city.

Finally, Rendell used his charisma and sometimes volcanic personality to praise or confront officials, journalists, and employees, and to promote the city. Rendell's passion for politics, his exuberance for the city's sports teams, and his streetwise banter generally created an image appropriate to the city he governed. However, Rendell readily admitted to being prone to angry outbursts, although rarely in public, and occasionally his banter would have sexual and often pro-fane content that seemed to even stretch beyond the wide latitude the tolerant culture of Philadelphia allowed (Bissinger 1997; Goodman, *Inquirer Magazine*, April 20, 1997). When challenged for having crossed-the-line in a conversation or action, Rendell would apologize, readily admit to his imperfections, and try to move on. For example, after newspapers reported Rendell's sexual banter with a female reporter, Rendell responded at a press conference: "I am what I am. Again, I'm not perfect. I do like to joke around and kid around. This job is a crusher. It's a high-pressure job. I do certain things to have fun and release tension. If I felt this would have been offensive to the reporter, I never would have done it … . Let me repeat, I've never intentionally, or with great negligence, done something to offend someone" (Bissinger 1997). Rendell's *mea culpa* was accepted and such incidents were forgiven, especially in light of the positive effects his personality had on his performance as mayor.

15.8 Rendell's Accomplishments

Svara (1990) posits that executive-style mayors should excel in policy initiation and implementation if they are to have fully and adeptly used the powers of the office. Svara (1990) suggests policy initiation "includes the formulation of policy and the generation of sufficient agreement and support to secure its approval. Initiation presumes that the mayors have imaginative ideas (or supporters who will gener-ate them) and the desire to undertake change." And Svara (1990) defines policy implementation as "getting things done and making government work, that is, the manipulation of administrative staff, organization, and resources to execute policies and direct programs to accomplish policy objectives." Judged according to Svara's criteria, Rendell used the powers of his office fully to initiate and implement numerous policy objectives.

Rendell was successful in part because he understood the need to articulate a vision and set priorities. He believed "running the city, you have got to have priori-ties, you have to set goals, you have to communicate well with your constituency what your goals are and why they are important, and you have to have the political courage to stay the course to achieve those goals" (West 1999). Rendell's vision for the city included:

- Restoring fiscal stability
- Lowering taxes to attract and retain businesses and the middle class
- Offering a full range of city services
- Reducing the cost of managing the city
- Investing in Center City in order to make Philadelphia a destination for tourism and conventions
- Securing state and national resources to address poverty and neighborhood revitalization
- Promoting good race relations

A review of three prominent accomplishments will document Rendell's effectiveness as mayor.

15.8.1 Fiscal Stability

The budget battles during Goode's second term left the city on the brink of financial collapse. The city experienced five straight years of deficits from 1988 to 1992 (Loeb, *Philadelphia Inquirer*, October 24, 1994). Although at first opposed, Goode eventually welcomed state intervention in part because of his inability to find a resolution with council (Meyers, *Philadelphia Inquirer*, June 2, 1991; Zausner and Meyers, *Philadelphia Inquirer*, June 6, 1991). On June 5, 1991, Governor Robert Casey signed legislation to create the Pennsylvania Intergovernmental Cooperation Authority (PICA). PICA's purpose was to oversee Philadelphia's finances and to raise a one percent sales tax in the city in order to pay for $350 million or more in bonds to be issued by PICA to pay off the city's obligations (Meyers, *Philadelphia Inquirer*, June 9, 1991). In order for the city to have access to the money, and as long as PICA had bonds outstanding, PICA had to approve the city's five-year financial plan. PICA did not have the power to tell the city how to spend money or raise revenue; rather if the five-member PICA board did not approve the plan, or the city did not adhere to the plan, then PICA could have withheld funds from the sale of bonds. Rendell had to submit the first annual update of the city's financial plan within three months of taking office (the due date was March 22, 1992).

Rendell addressed the city's long-term financial challenges primarily through spending restraint, reducing the cost of administering the city, and by reducing the costs of labor contracts. From fiscal year 1993 to Rendell's final budget, fiscal year 2000, spending increased incrementally from $2.3 billion to $2.7 billion—only a 17 percent increase over eight years (Meyers, *Philadelphia Inquirer*, April 23, 1992; Benson, *Philadelphia Inquirer*, March 19, 1999). In addition to restraining spending, Rendell cut the cost of administration. For example, in his first two years in office, he contracted out about 26 different services including sludge hauling, grass cutting, custodial services, and food services. By doing so, he eliminated more than 1,200 city jobs and generated about $25 million in annual savings (Loeb, *Philadelphia Inquirer*, October 6, 1994). Rendell also modernized technology available to employees with the help of John Carrow, the mayor's appointee to be the city's first-ever chief information officer. Carrow brought his private sector experience from General Electric Corporation to overhaul the city's computer systems, bringing efficiencies to the management of various departments, and earning *Governing* magazine's honor as the 1996 Public Official of the Year (Cohodas 1996).

Finally, Rendell negotiated tough four-year agreements with the District 33 union (blue collar) and the District 47 union (white collar). Rendell saved the city $374 million by cutting holidays from fourteen to ten; cutting sick days from twenty to fifteen for new hires; reducing the city's contribution to the union managed health care plans; providing no raise in the first two years of the contract, a 2 percent raise in the third year, and 3 percent in the fourth year of the contract; and securing greater flexibility in work rules to allow the city to contract out and introduce productivity-enhancing technology and practices (Duvosin, *Philadelphia Inquirer*, October 7, 1992). The four-year contracts awarded via arbitration to the police and firefighters in 1993 followed the structure of the contracts with Districts 33 and 47, producing savings of about $22 million annually from the police contract, and about $30 million total from the firefighters contract (Purdy and Gammage, *Philadelphia Inquirer*, March 31, 1993; Goldman, *Philadelphia Inquirer*, November 24, 1993). All four unions did better in the next set of four-year contracts negotiated during Rendell's second term. For example, the contracts in 1996 with District 33 and District 47 raised costs by $128 million over four years, but these costs along with the increased costs of the police and firefighter contracts were an affordable way for Rendell to reward labor for having helped the city achieve fiscal stability (Nicholas, Sataline, and Jones, *Philadelphia Inquirer*, July 1, 1996).

As a result of cost cutting and spending restraint, Rendell achieved surpluses in the budget the final three years of his first term, an accomplishment that stands in dramatic contrast to the deficits of Goode's second term (Loeb, *Philadelphia Inquirer*, October 24, 1994). Beginning in fiscal year 1996, Rendell became the first mayor in fifty years to get council to approve cuts in the wage tax: .10 percent cut for city residents and .08 percent cut for residents of suburbs (Marder, *Philadelphia Inquirer*, March 24, 1995; Williams, *Philadelphia Inquirer*, January 29, 1995). He also secured an 8 percent cut in the business privilege tax in the fiscal year 1996 budget (Marder, *Philadelphia Inquirer*, March 24, 1995). The tax cuts continued the rest of Rendell's second term. Although taxpayers received small amounts of money, the tax cuts became important symbols of the city's effort to become more competitive with suburban locations as a place to live and do business.

15.8.2 Economic Development

Rendell's tenure featured initiatives to develop Center City, the Navy Yard, and some of the economically distressed neighborhoods. Rendell saw the need to pursue all these projects, saying in May 1994 that "when you look at how to develop a city … you have to have a diverse plan. Certainly, I think almost immediate payoff can be in tourism, hospitality, conventions—becoming a great destination city. And a lot of our efforts are designed for that. But on the other hand, you can't go on that track without thinking about the Navy Yard, thinking about the neighborhoods, the need to rebuild our infrastructure, the need to keep economic vitality in our neighborhoods …" (Noyes, *The Philadelphia Daily News*, May 2, 1994).

Rendell's approach to the development of Center City featured promoting the use of the new Convention Center, the building of the National Constitution Center, and developing the Avenue of the Arts. The grand opening of the state- and city-financed Pennsylvania Convention Center occurred late June 1993 and was part of the first Welcome America celebration that lasted through the Fourth of July (Fish, *Philadelphia Inquirer*, March 31, 1993). Rendell supported projects related to the use of the Center, such as hotel construction, and persuaded the Republican Party to hold their quadrennial convention in Philadelphia in 2000. During his two terms, Rendell also supported and promoted the building of the National Constitution Center (NCC) on Independence Mall. The NCC opened on July 4, 2003, after three years of construction (National Constitution Center 2007). Although the Avenue of the Arts was an idea dating back to the 1970s, Rendell gave new life to the proposal to change South Broad Street into the Avenue of the Arts (Hine, *Philadelphia Inquirer*, September 13, 1992). Rendell created the Avenue of the Arts Inc. in November 1992 to be the nonprofit organization to mobilize support for a dozen related projects (*Philadelphia Inquirer*, Editorial, November 23, 1992). Since Rendell's launching of the initiative, the Avenue of the Arts effort has generated nearly $650 million from national government, state, city, and private sector donors in order to build The Kimmel Center, home to the Philadelphia Orchestra; to refurbish the Academy of Music, home to the Opera Company of Philadelphia; to build new theaters; and to install a new streetscape for the area (Downtown Visions for the Arts 2007).

With the closing of the Navy Yard in 1995, the city had the opportunity to develop this large parcel. Although initial efforts to recruit the German-based Meyer Werft to continue building ships in a portion of the Navy Yard failed, in part due to Governor Tom Ridge's opposition, eventually the state and city reached agreement with a private company, Kvaerner ASA, in 1997 to continue shipbuild-ing at the site (Gorenstein, *Philadelphia Inquirer*, December 17, 1997). In 2001, Aker, a Norwegian shipbuilding firm, purchased Kvaerner ASA and continues to build ships at the site (Holcomb, *Philadelphia Inquirer*, July 13, 2006).

Rendell addressed neighborhood concerns by offering his Philadelphia Plan in 1994. The Philadelphia Plan created partnerships with nine corporations and community development nonprofits to fund the rehabilitation of existing housing and the building of new housing in low-income neighborhoods (Bissinger 1997, 313). Rendell also aggressively pursued one of the national government's nine Empowerment Zones in partnership with Camden, New Jersey, and the effort suc-ceeded (McCoy, Ott and Goldstein, *Philadelphia Inquirer*, December 21, 1995).

Rendell not only sought new investment, he also met with business and national government leaders planning to close facilities to try to persuade them to stay. In 1993, Rendell created a unit in the Commerce Department to proactively identify businesses who might be planning to disinvest in the city (Nicholas and Rozansky, *Philadelphia Inquirer*, August 19, 1995). His efforts met with mixed results. For example, he tried to convince Unilever's executives to reverse their decision to close the Breyer's ice cream plant and save the 240 jobs the city would lose (Nicholas, *Philadelphia Inquirer*, August 24, 1995). But the plant closed, as did many other Philadelphia landmark businesses, such as After Six Formal Wear, Whitman's Chocolates, and Mrs. Paul's Kitchens (Bissinger 1997). Rendell did have some successes keeping private sector investment, such as preventing PNC Bank from moving nearly twelve hundred jobs to Camden, New Jersey (Bissinger 1997). Rendell also effectively lobbied national government officials to keep administrative operations in the city. For example, Rendell's personal appeal to President Clinton in a car ride from Philadelphia Airport to the city helped keep the Naval Aviation Supply Office, the Defense Industrial Supply Center, Naval Air Technical Services Facility, and the Defense Personnel Support Center in Philadelphia, saving a total of 8,444 jobs (Bissinger 1997).

15.8.3 City Services

As with economic development, Rendell met some successes and some disappointments in the delivery of city services. Rendell was able to

- Restore funding to libraries so they could expand hours of operation to weekends and evenings
- Provide full custodial staffing for the city's recreation centers and funds to build several new facilities
- Open city pools in the summers
- Expand lawn care in the city's parks
- Hire more police officers along with increasing funding to Town Watch and other neighborhood-based public safety organizations (Cipriano, Marder, Rubin and Sitton, *Philadelphia Inquirer*, January 27, 1995)

These quality of life services provided direct evidence to the city's residents that the city was headed in the right direction. However, the public schools were a greater challenge for Rendell.

Although he was not directly responsible for the operation of the public schools, Rendell persuaded city council to adopt a liquor-by-drink tax to generate more money for the schools in 1994. And even though he had appointed only three of the nine members of the school board, in May 1994, Rendell endorsed the appointment of David Hornbeck as superintendent over the other remaining candidates. This move generated controversy because some members of the school board thought Rendell was meddling improperly in what they believe to have been a process driven by merit rather than politics, and also because the other leading candidate was African American and Hornbeck was white (Mezzacappa and Rosenberg, *Philadelphia Inquirer*, May 25, 1994). The school board was evenly split racially, and under the leadership of Board President Rotan Lee, had tried to avoid race as a factor in appointing a superintendent ((Mezzacappa and Rosenberg, *Philadelphia Inquirer*, May 25, 1994). Rendell believed Hornbeck would be the kind of leader to reform the school system and bring about significant improvement in school performance, and so he joined with some of the business and child-advocacy leaders to lobby the school board. Eventually Hornbeck's rival withdrew so the school board chose Hornbeck (Mezzacappa, *Philadelphia Inquirer*, June 14, 1994). Even with the new revenue and with Hornbeck's leadership, the Philadelphia public school system remained a problem throughout Rendell's two terms and eventually the state intervened to take over the school system in 2001, two years after Rendell left office.

15.9 Conclusion

Throughout his adult life Rendell has exhibited a passion for public service via elected office. Rendell served two terms as Philadelphia's district attorney, and ran losing campaigns in Democratic primaries for governor and for mayor, before finally winning the mayoral election in 1991. He served as mayor in a city with long-term economic and social problems and on the brink of fiscal collapse. In eight years, he achieved fiscal stability, cut taxes, expanded city services, addressed neighborhood revitalization, maintained a biracial coalition, and transformed Center City into a place to do business as well as a place to visit for entertainment. Rendell's success rests on his adapting an executive-style leadership appropriate for a strong mayor form of government to include roles and practices featured in a facilitative style of leadership appropriate for the council–manager form of government. Rendell understood that power derives from formal and informal sources. Although he used these sources of power to become the "driving force" in city politics, he did so paradoxically by consulting, sharing success, and often being supportive of other city officials. Rendell's case illustrates how advantages accrue to the elected executive when he or she understands the skillful exercise of power to be a matter of persuasion more so than of command.*

---

* Ed Rendell ran successfully for governor of Pennsylvania in 2002 and won an easy reelection in 2006. Rendell's easy success running for reelection for district attorney, mayor, and governor after having to win competitive elections to a first term to each office is evidence of his political and managerial competence and his ability to disarm if not always win over his opponents.

References

Benson, Clea. 1999. City council gives unanimous nod to $2.7 billion budget mayor Rendell's final spending plan includes small cuts in some taxes. *Philadelphia Inquirer*, March 19, B2.

Bissinger, Buzz. 1997. *A Prayer for the City, New York*. New York: Random House.

Browning, Rufus P., Dale R. Marshall, and David H. Tabb, eds. 2003. *Racial Politics in American Cities*. 3rd ed. New York: Addison Wesley Educational Publishers.

Burt, Nathaniel and Wallace E. Davies. 1982. The Iron Age: 1876–1905. In *Philadelphia: A 300-Year History*, ed. Russell F. Weigley. New York: W.W. Norton, 471–523.

Burton, Cynthia. 1998. Council ends its effort to counter ATM fees, mayor Rendell had vetoed legislation, saying the city needed the targeted banks' business. *Philadelphia Inquirer*, September 24, C1.

Carvajal, Doreen and Murray Dubin. 1991. Rendell and Rizzo praise each other, prepare for battle. *Philadelphia Inquirer*, May 23, A24.

Carvajal, Doreen. 1993. City council voids veto police panel councilmen W. Thacher Longstreth was the pivotal vote. *Philadelphia Inquirer*, June 11, A1.

Cipriano, Ralph, Diana Marder, Daniel Rubin and Lea Sitton, 1995. Neighborhoods welcome the news, but are wary too. *Philadelphia Inquirer*, January 27, A16.

City of Philadelphia. 1951. *Home Rule Charter*. www.phila.gov/personnel/homerule (accessed November 15, 2006).

Clark, Joseph S., Jr. and Dennis J. Clark. 1982. Rally and relapse, 1946–1968, in *Philadelphia: A 300-Year History*, ed. Russell F. Weigley. New York: W.W. Norton, 649–703.

Cohodas, Marilyn. 1996. *Reengineering the City*. http://www.governing.com/poy/1996/ptcarrow.htm (accessed November 15, 2006).

Diaz, Idris M. and Dan Meyers, 1990. Schools get their tax hikes council passes '91 budget. *Philadelphia Inquirer*, June 1, A1.

Downtown Visions for the Arts. 2007. *Cities: Executive Summary for Philadelphia, PA*. http://downtownvisions.com (accessed November 15, 2006).

Duvoisin, Marc. 1991. The high point in a career full of ups and downs. *Philadelphia Inquirer*, November 6, A9.

Duvosin, Marc. 1992. City pact is a gamble on economy, state aid and the other unions. *Philadelphia Inquirer*, October 7, A1.

Fish, Larry. 1993. Convention center will open with a gala festival vice president Gore will open the hall. *Philadelphia Inquirer*, March 31, B3.

Geffen, Elizabeth M. 1982. Industrial development and social crisis 1841–1854. In *Philadelphia: A 300-Year History*, ed. Russell F. Weigley. New York: W.W. Norton, 307–362.

Goldman, Henry. 1993. Pact sets engine staffing levels the firefighters' contract contains a wage freeze and reduces starting pay. *Philadelphia Inquirer*, November 24, B1.

Goodman, Howard. 1997. City Hall understudy sets stage to take over the starring role. *Philadelphia Inquirer*, March 30, B1.

Goodman, Howard. 1997. He is not forgotten, and he's not gone, either. *Philadelphia Inquirer*, May 27, R1.

Goodman, Howard. 1997. Rendell's gamble, can he make Philadelphia fun?. *Inquirer Magazine*, April 20, p. 18.

Gorenstein, Nathan. 1997. Deal to revive shipyard officially signed, Kaverner ASA will get almost $400 million aid. *Philadelphia Inquirer*, December 17, D1.

Gurwitt, Rob. 1993. The lure of the strong mayor. *Governing,* 6:10 (July), 36–41.

Hine, Thomas. 1992. The arts as an avenue restore south broad street's leading role. *Philadelphia Inquirer,* September 13, N1.

Holcomb, Henry. 2006. Aker delivers 4th Phila. Ship – full speed ahead with more underway at shipyard. *Philadelphia Inquirer,* July 13, C3.

Kasarda, John D. 1993. Cities as places where people live and work: Urban change and neighborhood distress. In *Interwoven Destinies: Cities and the Nation,* ed. Henry Cisneros. New York: W.W. Norton, 81–124.

Kaufman, Marc and Daniel Rubin. 1995. It was an all-Rendell affair in the mayor's race, *Philadelphia Inquirer,* November 8, A14.

Keiser, Richard A. 2003. Philadelphia's evolving biracial coalition. In *Racial Politics in American Cities,* ed. Rufus P. Browning, et al. New York: Longman, 77–112.

Kirtzman, Andrew. 2000. *Rudy Giuliani: Emperor of New York.* New York: William Morrow.

Loeb, Vernon and Jeff Gammage. 1993. Mayor vetoes police review panel sets up weaker board by executive order. *Philadelphia Inquirer,* June 4, A1.

Loeb, Vernon. 1994. A managing director who's out and about. *Philadelphia Inquirer,* May 26, B1.

Loeb, Vernon. 1994. City privatization lowers costs while raising eyebrows. *Philadelphia Inquirer,* October 6, A1.

Loeb, Vernon. 1994. City turns in a 2nd surplus, sees another. *Philadelphia Inquirer,* October 24, A1.

Mahtesian, Charles.1993. Rendell-mania. *Governing,* 6:7 (April), 34–38.

Marder, Dianna.1995. Council passes wage tax cut and Rendell budgets the new tax rate takes effect Jan.1. *Philadelphia Inquirer,* March 24, B2.

Marder, Dianna. 1995. Housing proposal is vetoed by Rendell the mayor felt the bills were flawed. *Philadelphia Inquirer,* May 19, B2.

Marder, Dianna. 1996. 3 councilmen seek to end city drink tax, it brings in 19 millon a year for city schools. *Philadelphia Inquirer,* April 30, B3.

McCoy, Craig R., Peter Nicholas, Marc Kaufman, Vanessa Williams, and Richard Jones, 1995. Rendell's victory: just how overwhelming was it?. *Philadelphia Inquirer,* November 12, B2.

McCoy, Craig R., Dianna Marder, and Walter F. Roche, 1995. Rendell ahead in fundraising – by nearly $4 million. *Philadelphia Inquirer,* May 6, A1.

McCoy, Craig R. and Dianna Marder, 1995. Mayor's fund lead immense. *Philadelphia Inquirer,* October 28, A1.

McCoy, Craig R., Dwight Ott, and Steve Goldstein, 1995. Chosen for new poverty aid plan. *Philadelphia Inquirer,* December 21, A1.

McCoy, Craig R. and Howard Goodman, 1997. Tenacity, charm: how deal was made. *Philadelphia Inquirer,* April 9. A1.

Meyers, Dan. 1991. How the city bristled at, then embraced authority, sinking day by day, the city grasped for a control board. *Philadelphia Inquirer,* June 2, C8.

Meyers, Dan. 1991. Putting city back on its feet, new oversight board is the key for Phila. to recover fiscal health. *Philadelphia Inquirer,* June 9, E1.

Meyers, Dan. 1992. Getting down to work, the mayor enjoyed an upbeat week. *Philadelphia Inquirer,* January 12, C1.

Meyers, Dan. 1992. Budget sails through council, Rendell's plan set for final approval. *Philadelphia Inquirer,* April 23, A1.

Mezzacappa, Dale and Amy Rosenberg. 1994. Rendell's letter tiles school board. *Philadelphia Inquirer*, May 25, B1.

Mezzacappa, Dale. 1994. Unity urged on new chief of schools in the 10-month selection process, sides had made endorsements. *Philadelphia Inquirer*, June 14, B1.

Motley, Wanda. 1994. Mayor promotes Certaine to city's managing director. *Philadelphia Inquirer*, March 25, B3.

Mullin, Megan, Gillian Peele, and Bruce E. Cain. 2004. City Caesars? Institutional structure and mayoral success in three California cities. *Urban Affairs Review*, 40:1, 19–43.

National Constitution Center. 2007. *About Us*. http://www.constitutioncenter.org (accessed January 30, 2007).

Neustadt, Richard E. 1980. *Presidential Power: The Politics of Leadership from FDR to Carter*. New York: John Wiley & Sons.

Nicholas, Peter and Michael Rozansky.1995. Mayor hustles to save Breyers plant. *Philadelphia Inquirer*, August 19, A1.

Nicholas, Peter. 1995. Rendell can't stop Breyers closing. *Philadelphia Inquirer*, August 24, B1.

Nicholas, Peter, Suzanne Sataline, and Richard Jones, 1996. City, unions reach accord on contract. *Philadelphia Inquirer*, July 1, A1.

Nicholas, Peter. 1998. An indispensable man. *Inquirer Magazine*, October 18, p. 9.

Noyes, David. 1994. Rendell on economic development we have to do everything. *The Philadelphia Daily News*, May 2, p. 28.

Paolantonio, S.A., Laurie Hollman, and Terence Samuel. 1991. Mayoral campaign contributions biggest ever. *Philadelphia Inquirer*, May 11, B3.

Paolantonio, S.A. 1991. The climax of a campaign full of surprises a political season that seemed to go Rendell's way. *Philadelphia Inquirer*, November 3, A1.

Paolantonio, S.A. 1991. Rendell aims to solidify his political foundation. *Philadelphia Inquirer*, November 10, E2.

Paolantonio, S.A., Doreen Carvajal, and March Duvoisin. 1991. Rendell wins in a landslide. *Philadelphia Inquirer*, November 6, A1.

Philadelphia Inquirer. 1991. Saving Philadelphia: A special report, May 5, F1.

Philadelphia Inquirer. 1992. The Rendell team has enough deputy mayors to field a softball squad, but can they play ball?. Editorial, January 13, A6.

Philadelphia Inquirer, 1992. The culture biz. Editorial, November 23, A12.

Purdy, Matthew and Jeff Gammage, 1993. Police given contract. *Philadelphia Inquirer*, March 31, A1.

Rosenberg, Amy. 1995. The city's bond rating gets a boost. *Philadelphia Inquirer*, March 13, A1.

Rusk, David. 1995. *Cities without Suburbs*. 2nd ed. Washington, DC: The Woodrow Wilson Center.

Sipress, Alan. 1997. Rendell gets action on SEPTA budget, he had threatened rejection of the capital spending plan. *Philadelphia Inquirer*, June 18, B7.

Steffens, Lincoln. 1904. *The Shame of the Cities*. New York: Hill and Wang, Inc.

Svara, James H. 1990. *Official Leadership in the City: Patterns of Conflict and Cooperation*. New York: Oxford University Press.

Svara, James H., and Associates. 1994. *Facilitative Leadership in Local Government: Lessons from Successful Mayors and Chairpersons*. San Francisco: Jossey-Bass.

Turcol, Thomas and Dan Meyers, 1991. Goode signs budget. *Philadelphia Inquirer*, June 14, A1.

U.S. Census Bureau. 2000. *Demographic Prof le Highlights.* http://factfinder.census.gov (accessed August 23, 2004).

Warner, Sam Bass. 1987. *The Private City: Philadelphia in Three Periods of Its Growth.* Philadelphia: University of Pennsylvania Press.

Weigley, Russell F., ed. 1982. *Philadelphia: A 300-Year History.* New York: W.W. Norton.

West, Darrell. 1999. *An Interview with Philadelphia Mayor Edward Rendell.* http://inside politics. org/intrendell.html (accessed November 15, 2006).

Wheeland, Craig M. 2002. An institutionalist perspective on mayoral leadership: Linking leadership style to formal structure. *National Civic Review,* 91:1 (Spring), 25–39.

Williams, Vanessa. 1992. Managing director has been a quiet mystery at city hall. *Philadelphia Inquirer,* December 13, B1.

Williams, Vanessa. 1995. Rendell launches bid for 2d term. *Philadelphia Inquirer,* January 29, A1.

Williams, Vanessa. 1995. Rocks starts uphill drive to be mayor. *Philadelphia Inquirer,* February 17, A1.

Yant, Monica. 1999. Rendell vetoes pension increase, council failed to override. *Philadelphia Inquirer,* January 15, A1.

Zausner, Robert and Dan Meyers, 1991. Casey signs Phila. rescue bill new board, city sales tax established. *Philadelphia Inquirer,* June 6, B1.

Zausner, Robert. 1999. Mayor keeps cash machine in high gear. *Philadelphia Inquirer,* December 12, A1.

CONCLUSION

Chapter 16

Advancing Facilitative Leadership in Practice

James H. Svara

Contents

16.1 Introduction

The concluding chapter in *Facilitative Leadership in Local Government* (Svara 1994) stressed the importance of facilitative leadership in council–manager cities and suggested that it is potentially useful in elected executive forms as well. The case studies and new survey research presented here support a revised summary. Many cities, regardless of form, have effective leadership to which the mayor is a central contributor. In all cities, it is important for the mayor to help shape a shared vision for the city and draw together the support inside and outside government to advance it using a facilitative approach. Mayors who do not promote vision or use facilitative leadership are likely to be less effective than those who do. Thus, rather than seeing facilitative leadership as a specialized style appropriate to a particular governmental setting, the "visionary facilitator" is the preferred type of mayor in all cities.

Facilitative leadership rests on and promotes cooperative relationships. It is "natural," i.e., induced by structural characteristics, to find cooperation in council–manager cities. Several case studies demonstrate, however, that cooperation can be lost and that capable leadership is needed to restore it. This pattern seems to be present in Midway, Auburn, Stockton, Winston-Salem, and Cincinnati during the time periods covered by the case studies. Cooperation among officials is typically found in the other case study cities, even one as large and complex as Phoenix, but constructive working relationships are not automatic. Sustaining cooperation requires active leadership, monitoring, and corrective adjustments by the mayor, council, manager, and staff to take advantage of the structural features in a form with unified powers. In mayor–council cities, mayors usually determine whether a cooperative relationship is present. Separation of powers in the city charter and American cultural values tend to stimulate conflict as mayors seek to drive city government, and councils seek to protect their position and prerogatives. Mayors can choose, however, to use a facilitative approach that recognizes council goals, and share information with the council along with the restrained use of their formal authority. Mayors, despite their powers, can be more effective by building bridges with the council and making full use of the contributions of administrative staff.

The impact of leadership on restoring or finding the basis for a positive working relationship seems to resolve the chicken–egg quandary regarding facilitation and cooperation in local government. Although facilitation promotes cooperation, it is not always true that cooperation is necessary to permit facilitation. The mayors who successfully restored cooperation and the appropriate functioning of the council–manager form used facilitation in the face of conflict, dysfunctional disagreement, and disjuncture between the council and manager. The positive conditions they created are likely to be stable assuming that leaders continue to monitor and adjust relationships. In mayor–council cities, a facilitative leadership style is even more important in eliciting constructive working relationships because the "default" position is conflict over the interests of office induced by separation-of-powers provisions. As Wheeland observed about Rendell (Chapter 15), he overcame a long period of conflictual interactions by sharing the spotlight and seeking to persuade.

It is important to recognize that disagreement and conflict are not bad. There are fundamental differences among the actors and interests in local government, and substantial imbalances in resources. These factors will be expressed in differing values, preferences, and priorities. Disagreement is a cuing mechanism that alerts participants and the public that important issues are being considered. The public should pay attention at least, and possibly join the fight on one side or the other.

These various forms of disagreement and difference in perspectives, however, do not necessarily produce serious conflict unless two others characteristics are present: the participants "perceive that their goals are incompatible," and they take active measures to "achieve their own goals (at least in part) by blocking the goals of others" (Zeigler, Kehoe, and Reisman 1985). Disagreement becomes conflict (or minor conflict becomes major conflict or conflict escalates depending on your choice of terminology) when incompatible goals cause some participants to seek to impose their preferences on others and block opponents from achieving their own goals (Svara 1990). It is not in their interests to do otherwise because they cannot trust the choices that a competitor with incompatible goals will make. The situation is seen as zero-sum, either there is only one winner or the gains of one participant represent losses for the others. When the governmental process is highly conflictual, differences are resolved by imposed solutions or by compromises that reflect the relative strength of the opposing parties. Alternatively, there may be impasse in finding any solution, or stalemate when an action by one participant can be blocked by another. Dysfunctional conflict magnifies the level and scope of conflict and increases the incompatibility of the participants. Leadership is required to resolve conflict, especially by changing the way that the parties to disputes define their opposing goals or finding new goals that arch over the differing views.

In many mayor–council cities, the basis for serious and recurring conflict is the difference in the interests and official prerogatives of the mayor and council because powers are separated between them. In council–manager cities, serious conflict is uncommon because of unified authority, but there is not necessarily a high level of cooperation. In other words, the working relationship, level of communication, coordination of functions, and ability to govern effectively may be low. Just as mayoral leadership can be important to relieving conflict, it can also be important to increasing cooperation (Svara 1990).

Rather than focusing on the accomplishments of the mayor alone, the approach we are taking is to assess the combined leadership of all officials, i.e., the capacity of the governmental "system" in a city to identify needs and meet goals. Following a distinction made by Stone (1989), the focus is on the "power to" rather than the "power over." It is possible that we should reverse the standard way of differentiating forms of government by restating the "despite" clause. For example, Klase observes that Mayor Joines in Winston-Salem exercises leadership despite possessing the limited authority of a mayor in a council–manager city. Greenblatt (2006), commenting on Mayor Gordon in Phoenix, expressed the same sentiment this way: "Some mayors have it easy. They can write their own budgets and dismiss department heads who don't want to follow orders. The mayor of Phoenix can't do that." Rather than assuming that mayoral powers are always an advantage, the potential for the mayor to provide leadership should be assessed in terms of the overall capacity of the governmental system to address problems and deliver solutions on a sustained basis. It may be just as appropriate to explain the effectiveness of certain mayors in a mayor–council city by arguing that *despite* having formal powers, the mayor is able to develop effective partnerships with the council, administrative staff, and other leaders outside city government to get things done. The council–manager mayor starts with the likelihood that the internal partnerships are strong and can be used to achieve positive results. In this view, the potential for leadership by all officials in a council–manager government—with effective guidance by the mayor—matches or even exceeds that of mayor–council cities.

Mayoral leadership can have shortcomings in each major form of government. Some mayors in mayor–council cities get caught in the trap of power or are disabled by endemic conflict with the council that is induced by separation of powers. When faced with conflict, it is easy to look for power resources to use against opponents or to expand ones support base. The more one uses a power-over approach, the more power is needed to overcome resulting resistance. This is the power trap. It is not the lack of powers per se that limits these mayors, but not having enough power to be able to rely completely on rewards and sanctions to get things done. Put differently, so-called "strong" mayors may need to seek more partnerships and be more inclusive rather than seeking to be more powerful.

In council–manager cities with a predisposition to a power-with approach, some mayors are unable to develop partnerships with the council and manager, or they drive away potential partners by attempting to control them. In either case, it is usually not the lack of power that leads to ineffective mayoral leadership in council–manager cities, but rather a lack of vision or the inability to guide others to set goals and act on them. Americans have a cultural preference for strong leaders—a topic to be explored later in this chapter—and by extension for the structural arrangements that promote autonomous executive action. The conclusion that emerges from leadership research, however, is that a facilitative style along with a clear sense of purpose is more likely to lead to success in public and private organizations than is a top-down, authoritarian style of leadership.

Forms of local government vary in the extent to which they support collaboration among officials. The council–manager form may be viewed as providing a positive climate for individual and collective leadership rather than being viewed as a drag on leadership (Pressman 1972). In cities that use the mayor–council form, the mayor has to make a greater effort to offset the structural features that can induce conflict and pursue facilitative leadership. The separate powers and independence of the executive and legislature are not abandoned, as Cox observes in Akron, but the mayor and council have found ways to cooperate.

Knowledge and insights from the case studies suggest some revisions in the way we think about the mayor's office and support refinements of the facilitative leadership model. In the following section, there is a review of leadership roles and types and the resources that support leadership. In the remainder of the chapter, we consider some important issues in mayoral leadership and form of government.

16.2 Summary of Key Points in the Case Studies

The case studies add to our description and understanding of the roles filled by mayors.

16.2.1 Mayoral Roles

As noted in Chapter 1, there are three sets of roles: traditional/automatic, coordinative, and policy and organizing. The case studies also clarify broad types of facilitative leadership. In the review of roles and types of leadership that follows, the examples that are offered from the case studies are illustrative, but not exhaustive.

16.2.1.1 Roles: Traditional/Automatic

These roles are built into the office and all mayors will fill them. There is variation, however, in how well they are filled. Mayors spend a lot of time performing *ceremonial* tasks. John Nalbandian of Lawrence noted in his log, "I have been mayor now for over a month, and I cannot believe how time consuming it is. The ceremonial duties alone take up a lot of time." New mayors commonly make the same remark. The ceremonial activities can be a curse, if accepted without any constraints, and they can consume a lot of time with little return if the mayor does not put the appearances to good use. These ceremonial occasions, however, can also be an asset in generating a wide range of audiences for the mayor and a chance to provide a service that is appreciated by constituents. They provide the opportunity for developing personal support and sharing information about what city government is doing.

These activities blend with the mayor's role as *link to the public*. Mayors stand out as the spokesperson for city government. They have the opportunity to announce and explain positions taken by the council and to put these decisions in the context of ongoing goals and commitments. In filling this role, it is important that mayors be able to separate their own preferred positions from the decisions made by the council, as Kevin Foy did in Chapel Hill. Once a policy decision is made, this is the position presented by the mayor. In addition, the mayor by virtue of the nature of the office receives a large volume of comments and complaints from citizens and has extensive dealings with the media. These activities taken together make government more accessible and visible to citizens. Pat Evans of Plano capitalized on her frequent audiences with constituents to maintain active communication with them. Phil Gordon of Phoenix emphasizes public appearances and media events of all kinds as a way of generating support for city initiatives as well as creating a personal bond between citizens and city government. A means of formalizing the linkage role (and an opportunity for educating the public and goal setting as we shall see) is the mayor's state of the city address—or the state of the downtown or whatever the mayor wishes to focus attention on.

As *presiding officer*, the mayor obviously fosters discussion and resolution of business in council meetings. In this role, the mayor also sets the tone for how city government conducts itself. Delores Madison of Midway took on a dysfunctional council in a small town facing bankruptcy and dissolution and fostered a constructive and civil attitude in the way meetings were run. Not all mayors will prepare a letter with "directions and instructions" for the council (although they might want to), but those who fill the presiding officer role well help the council to develop a style that promotes a high level of performance. Jan Dempsey of Auburn came onto a city council that was embroiled in conflict in most matters that came before it, and she gradually changed the tone of public discourse. Allan Joines of Winston-Salem changed the "circus" atmosphere in city council meetings by working with council members to establish procedural rules for how council meetings should be run. In the way council members conduct themselves in meetings, the council members send important messages about how seriously they take their work, their attitude toward citizens and what kind of citizen participation is expected, and the level of respect and standards of performance for staff members. Based on extensive observation of city council meetings and comparison to other indicators of performance, Halter (2002) concluded that well-run meetings are linked to better functioning of city government overall.

Finally, the mayor plays a critical role in external relations as *representative/promoter*. This role builds on the other traditional ones, as well as including the contacts the mayor as titular head has with other local governments and with state and federal government agencies. The general task of promoting the jurisdiction includes official contacts with civic and nonprofit organizations, meetings with prospective investors and developers, and various activities to create a positive image for the city. All mayors fill this role, and some give it great prominence, attracting attention to themselves and their cities. The effectiveness of Gordon and Ed Rendell of Philadelphia is based in part on their success as unabashed promoters of their cities.

16.2.1.2 Roles: Coordination and Communication

The second set of roles involves active coordination and communication—active in the sense that the mayor must recognize these roles and choose to fill them. Furthermore, filling them well requires a higher level of creativity and strategic thinking than that found in the basic roles. Some of the roles can blend together seamlessly, such as promotional activities and network building, but the higher-level role is not necessarily pursued by all mayors. In the coordination and communication roles, the qualities emerge that differentiate the active and effective mayor from the passive and ineffective mayor. Filling the coordinative roles well does, however, build on the foundation provided by a high level of performance in filling the basic roles.

The first is the *articulator/mobilizer*. It blends efforts to educate with efforts to convince or win support. A key aspect of this role is raising awareness by articulating issues and promoting understanding of problems. These activities are often undertaken with the intent of prompting action. A dramatic example of filling this role is provided by Mayor George Heartwell of Grand Rapids. He transformed the State of the City Address in Grand Rapids into a day-long conference at which members of the community participate in workshops and policy discussion groups as well as hearing the mayor's address. Heartwell has used these sessions to emphasize education and environmental, economic, and social sustainability. Evans (Plano) sought to increase awareness of the needs of growing ethnic and racial minority groups in the city and to promote support for diversity by creating the Multicultural Outreach Roundtable (MCOR). The mayors who are effective at goal setting, discussed below, have usually started by identifying issues and raising awareness of the need to act.

The role of *liaison with the manager* reflects the way that the mayor shapes the interaction between the council and the city manager, as well as the partnership that may be present between the mayor and the manager as individuals. Delores Madison provided a shield to help the new town manager establish sound operations and protect him from criticism when he was doing what the council had instructed him to do. She was available to talk to citizens when they came to city hall to complain. She told the city manager, "let them call me" if they have questions. Jan Dempsey understood and appreciated the "professionalism, wisdom, and knowledge that the city manager brought to the organization." She and city manager Douglas Watson developed a strong and trusting working relationship, and she valued his involvement in all aspects of the policy process. At the same time, she invested time in developing relationships with key staff members in order to foster a team approach to generating ideas and planning city projects. As a former career city administrator, Allan Joines understands that the city manager provides advice about policy, but does not determine policy. Furthermore, he sees the need for elected officials to provide oversight of administration while staying out of the details of management. The close relationship and the clarity of the city's vision achieved through the strategic plan helped the mayor focus the efforts of the manager and staff on high priority areas. In Phoenix, the interaction between the mayor and the city manager is both personal and institutionalized, with a city staff member assigned to work in the mayor's office. In these interactions between the mayor and manager, the objective is to strengthen the support of the manager for the council as a whole and to achieve a high level of communication between the council and the manager.

In two cities, it was possible to observe the role of the mayor in handling a transition in the city manager's office when a successful and respected long-term manager retired. In contrast to the many instances when a mayor receives guidance from a city manager about how to handle a challenge, with the selection of a new city manager, elected officials must set the parameters and determine the process for the search. Although organizing the search for a new manager clearly overlaps the organizing/delegating role to be considered later, it also sets the tone for future mayor–council–manager relations. Joines in Winston-Salem presided over the process by suggesting the use of a search firm and assisting in the negotiation and approval of a contract. The council as a whole developed selection criteria and participated in initial screening and final interviews. Although the city manager who was retiring in Chapel Hill continued to handle his administrative responsibilities during the search for his replacement, Foy had to "step forward, be the leader and take the reins" to handle the search and the transition in a way that would create the foundation for the future working relationship between the council and the new city manager. The mayor oversaw a process that was inclusive of a wide range of internal and external stakeholders.

The *team relations and network builder* role covers interactions including those with the city council and various forms of external networking. Effective mayors coalesce the council and establish a positive tone.* A central activity of mayors in council–manager cities is helping others accomplish their goals. John Nalbandian observes that one of his responsibilities was helping others get things they wanted to initiate—and which he favored—on the political agenda. Gordon places a premium on achieving consensus even when he has a majority. In his view, getting the broadest possible support is worth the extra time it takes to make a decision. Many mayors use retreats to strengthen understanding of council roles and working relationships as well as to develop goals.

Even when mayors have powers they could use to line up support by offering inducements or threatening sanctions, they may choose the facilitative approach of including council members in determining policy goals and seeking to persuade rather than overpower them. Rendell used this approach in forging coalitions in stages with the city council. After initially backing another candidate for council president, he developed a strong partnership with the winner, John Street, as well. Don Plusquellic of Akron chooses to "consult" informally with selected members of the city council before developing major policy proposals. If lines are drawn, he is aggressive in advancing his position and attacking those who oppose him. Once a decision has been made, however, and it is time to convert an idea into action, he will readily engage those he attacked to get the project going. Although Steen Dahlstrøm of Middlefart could control the vote and fill all cabinet positions

---

* In the case of Midway, Florida, the mayor's informal communication with other council members is considerably constrained by the Sunshine Law. This has the practical effect of rendering coalition building a strategy that the mayor cannot explicitly pursue.

with members of his party majority, he puts a strong emphasis on consensus. The exchange and mutual adjustment that leads to a shared agreement is valued as well as getting acceptance for his policy ideas. Art Prochaska of Yorkville, on the other hand, appeared willing to rely on his majority in the council and was viewed with suspicion by the minority.

A key part of the mayor's leadership, regardless of form, is developing communication and support networks that extend outside government, and actively involving the community and neighboring governments. Gordon expanded citizen involvement in planning and campaigning for a large bond issue in 2005. Having over seven hundred participants broadened the scope of the bond issue and helped build support for its passage. Joines has been effective in creating groups to work on problems and support initiatives in Winston-Salem. He has made community unity and racial healing one of his highest priorities. Foy contributed to the creation of a new downtown partnership with the business community, the university, and city hall. Joan Darrah of Stockton was effective at getting people to work together to resolve crime, to improve ethnic relations, and to accept or reject plans for future development. Evans in Plano and Heartwell in Grand Rapids were active and generally successful at regional networking. Plusquellic negotiated Joint Economic Development Districts with neighboring townships. There are other examples of networking in support of policy initiative mentioned in the next section. Mayors not only establish linkages, they help shape and guide the interaction, as Foy demonstrated in being a moderator of complex processes of involving the community in rewriting the land use ordinance and working through a decision that generated substantial racial tension.

16.2.1.3 Policy and Organizing Roles

The three policy and organizing roles reflect the distinction between making the process of governance run smoothly in the coordinative roles, and altering or adjusting the process and shaping the ends of governance in the policy and organizing roles.

Filling these roles well creates the highest level of activism by a facilitative mayor and produces the greatest impact. The *delegator/organizer* assigns tasks and adjusts relationships as needed to strengthen performance. In the *goal setter* role, the emphasis is on ensuring that goals are established and the city has a sense of direction and shared mission regardless of whose goals are chosen. In the *policy initiator* role, the mayor advances and advocates policy solutions and offers a vision for the city. The mayor offers and promotes his or her own goals, although a facilitator is open to the goals advanced by others as well.

Delegating and organizing involves the general tasks of orchestrating, aligning the contributions of various actors, and assigning tasks to ensure that coordination is maintained. The mayor monitors the governmental process and makes adjustments as needed. The actions can include assigning council members to committees deciding whether to create a citizen task force, or looking to staff for a recommendation. It involves getting council members "on board" in order to move forward to a decision by the council as a whole. The mayor can also take steps to reinforce the values and division of functions in council–manager government or spanning the separation of powers in mayor–council cities. The mayor can seek to improve the amount or kind of information provided to the council by the city manager regarding proposals or performance. For example, Joines has emphasized monitoring staff progress in achieving goals. The council is regularly updated by the mayor on the overall status of all the action items, and the city manager and staff regularly communicate the status of all action items. In a broader sense of organizing, the mayor can provide a bridge (or occasionally a buffer) between governmental officials and the public and help to orient staff in a more positive way to citizens. Prochaska expanded interaction with citizens by holding "Coffee with the Mayor" meetings every other Saturday at different locations throughout the community. In many cities, the mayor, a council member, and staff have meetings with citizens around the city as part of an effort to increase the accessibility of city government, e.g., Winston-Salem's "Talk of the Town" meetings.

Two mayors offer examples of using the organizing role to change the tone and operation of city government. Madison found governmental systems that were not functioning appropriately. The council was not making coherent decisions, and the staff was not handling administrative responsibilities or providing services. She set about restoring order first in the council and then in the administrative sphere by hiring a city manager who provided leadership, competence, and commitment to professional standards. She worked with citizens to make them understand how the reconstruction process would work and who was responsible for what. Finally, she monitored the process and sought to ensure that the council–manager–citizen exchanges were functioning properly, intervening as necessary to deal with pressure points. For example, as noted earlier, she took on an expanded role in communicating with citizens who might have overwhelmed the administrative staff with complaints. Similarly, Dempsey inherited a city council torn by controversy that gave poor direction and oversight to the city manager. Despite operating from the weak position on the periphery of the city council at the beginning, she first instilled a new sense of values about how the council would conduct itself and then guided the council to the selection of a new city manager who would provide more support and responsiveness to the council. She promoted a charter change that made the mayor presiding officer on the city council and strengthened the potential of the office to provide facilitative leadership. Through change in process and structure, she contributed to institutionalizing the effective functioning of council–manager government in Auburn, a dramatic expression of the organizing/delegating role. In addition to these cases, mayors in Stockton (twice) have altered internal working relationships by influencing the hiring of a new city manager and establishing a working relationship with the new person.

Yorkville and Cincinnati offer examples of how mayors have used a change in structure to reorient working relationships. Although the Yorkville mayor has considerable authority and influence as the only at-large elected official and the chief executive officer in the mayor–council city government, Prochaska and the council experimented with giving more responsibility to a professional city administrator. In 2006, the city administrator position was codified by ordinance to be a position hired by the mayor with the advice and consent of the city council and accountable to both the mayor and the city council. The city administrator, acting on behalf of the mayor, can assume substantial executive authority and also has the responsibility to advise and inform all elected officials on any and all policy issues. Still, there are incentives for the mayor to act as an executive leader who treats the city administrator as an assistant responsible to him or her. Valerie Burd, elected in 2007 in Yorkville, will have the potential to shape the city administrator office and its relationship to the mayor and council as part of the way she fills the organizing/delegating role.

In Cincinnati, charter changes that strengthened the mayor and made the city manager's position more dependent on the mayor's support have provided the framework within which two different mayors have operated. The first was criticized for not exercising his new powers enough. The second has encountered a city council that has altered its practices in part as a reaction to the changes in structure. A working majority has emerged that is able to offer alternatives to the mayor's proposals. Many continue to see Mark Mallory as the primary leader at city hall, but he is having difficulty organizing the process to coordinate the contributions of the mayor, council, and city manager as mayors in other cities with less formal power have been able to do.

In the *goal setter* role, the mayor ensures that the city has goals, but the ideas can come from any source. Goal setting is accomplished by some leaders through drawing out and melding the goals of the council and the staff, through retreats for the council, and through fostering community strategic planning efforts. For example, Dempsey appointed committees and organized two strategic planning efforts that looked forward to the years 2000 and 2020. For the facilitative mayor, goal setting is a collaborative process in which all share. Still, the mayor may have a catalytic effect, enabling coalitions to emerge that would not have been possible through efforts of the council members alone. Council members commonly defer to the mayor for strategic leadership, and they are more likely to come together in a goal-setting process if the mayor is supporting it. They will not necessarily follow all the mayor's ideas, but they are likely to accept a goal-setting process organized by the mayor.

In the *policy initiator* role, the mayor advances and advocates policy solutions and offers a vision for the city. There are numerous examples in the case studies of both specific new projects and changes that improved the climate and reputation of the city. Evans promoted the tri-city Performing Arts Center with neighboring jurisdictions. Foy advanced the idea of sustainable downtown development and changing the plans for a major thoroughfare to make it more pedestrian friendly as part of a vision for Chapel Hill that encompasses environmental protection, affordability, and sustainability. Joines pushed the creation of a baseball stadium in a mixed-use project downtown as part of promoting a positive economic environment in the city. Prochaska promoted the commercial growth of the city, particularly a new shopping center. Gordon built on the decisions made under previous mayors to construct downtown sports and entertainment venues and a light rail system linking downtown Phoenix to its suburban neighbors. Gordon promoted a vision of a revitalized downtown with educational institutions, research, and residences alongside its office buildings. Podesto built on the groundwork laid by Darrah to achieve the redevelopment of the waterfront. As well, Dahlstrøm pushed the creation of the "Culture Island," a community center on the waterfront with a public library, tourist office, restaurant, and cinema. Rendell pushed the development of Center City as a place for tourism and conventions with a new Convention Center, National Constitution Center, and Avenue of the Arts.

Not all initiatives are successful, especially when they move beyond existing institutional boundaries. In Akron, Plusquellic was not successful in a referendum to approve a county sales tax to fund construction and remodeling in all eighteen school districts in the county, but later was successful in getting increased funding for schools in Akron. In Grand Rapids, Heartwell elevated the importance of sustainability on the community agenda and expanded the network of participants in a sustainability network. He has also increased public support for the independent school district and has gotten many city employees to volunteer in tutoring programs. He has not, however, succeeded in persuading the city council to support seeking legislative approval for the creation of an Education Renewal Zone, a tax increment authority to divert an increment of local property tax increases to the public schools. Heartwell demonstrates that visionaries need to be patient and take the long-term view: "It's a good piece of work," he argues, "whose time has not quite yet come."

Focusing on specific initiatives and emphasizing the contribution of the mayor alone is misleading. Nalbandian promoted a creative approach to financing local government needs with a countywide sales tax that funded the city and county's projects and permitted reduction in the property tax equivalent to the school district property tax increase to build a second high school. He was essential to the development and success of the initiative; however, it was not his idea alone. He convened interested parties who came up with the idea, and he helped assure success by lending his status to the persons whose projects would be funded by the new tax. Furthermore, a specific project may be part of a combination of activities produced by the actions of many people inside and outside of government. Policy breakthroughs can be based on community building, and success at policy initiation often depends on effectively filling all the other roles. As supported by the data in Chapter 1, visionaries can have a positive impact based simply on the quality of their ideas and their determination, but the visionary who draws on the other facilitative roles can achieve greater success. A policy initiative by the mayor that is accepted by the council and community is often the proverbial tip of the iceberg sitting on the submerged mundane ceremonial tasks, attention to the quality of council meetings, promoting the image of the city, contacts with developers and meetings with leaders in other cities, identifying issues and raising public awareness, making the most of the relationship with city administrators, expanding teamwork on the council, establishing networks in and beyond the community, making certain that the parts of the governmental system work together, and fostering a goal-setting process that encourages sharing of goals. The roles are mutually reinforcing and success in one enhances success in others. Furthermore, they go on concurrently.

The roles may impact different spheres in the mayor's relationships—council, staff, and community—and different aspects of role performance can affect more than one sphere. These points are illustrated in Table 16.1. The activities carried out to fill most roles have impacts in more than one sphere and affect "higher" ranking roles as well.

In sum, the case studies clarify the roles and offer a wide range of activities to illustrate them. The specific content and activities selected to fill roles will vary with the individual mayor, the community setting, and the circumstances. It makes a difference how many roles are filled and how well they are filled. Another way to appreciate the importance of the roles is to consider what is missing if a role is not filled well or does not target certain spheres. For example, what is lost when the mayor helps to raise the awareness of other council members about the importance of an issue, but does not have the same effect on the staff or the public? Roles are the palette mayors use to paint the portrait of their leadership.

16.2.2 Types of Leadership

Each mayor fills the roles and combines them in different ways, but there are several distinct clusters of attributes that differentiate general types of mayors. As noted in Chapter 1, a classification of leadership types in council–manager cities divides mayors into the categories of caretaker, coordinator, and director. The caretaker mayors do not move beyond the automatic roles and often fill even these roles in a minimal way. There are no examples of the caretaker mayor in the case studies in this book.

Some mayors stand out for their leadership. As Loomis, quoted by Nalbandian, says, "On occasion ... a city commissioner becomes mayor and actually functions as more than a ribbon cutter, presiding officer, and symbolic head." The general perception of mayors in council–manager cities among the public and most academic researchers is that this kind of effective leadership is a rare occurrence. Evidence presented in Chapter 1 indicates, however, that effective leaders—those who make an important positive contribution to the performance of the city council—are the norm rather than the exception, although there is variation in the extent and nature of this contribution.

Table 16.1 Examples of Mayoral Role Activities and Impacts

Role Dimensions	Spheres		
	Council	*Staff*	*Community*
Traditional/Automatic			
■ Presiding officer	Leading meetings and setting tone for the council	Shaping the agenda and setting tone for relationships with staff	Setting the tone for involving public
■ Ceremonial	Celebrating accomplish-ments	Spotlighting staff contributions	Expanding citizen familiarity with city projects and develop support for the city
■ Link to public	Spokesperson for the council who unifies the city	Informing staff of citizens, interests and needs	Providing channel for proposals and complaints and providing information about programs and policies
■ Promoting/representing	Making the city visible and conveying council views to outside parties.	Communicating positions/concerns of staff to outside audiences; providing information to staff	Generating support for city projects and creating interest in the city
Coordinative			
■ Team relations/network building	Promoting cohesion and effective teamwork	Promoting partnership with council	Developing networks inside and outside community
■ Articulator/mobilizer	Raising council awareness about community problems	Raising staff awareness about community problems	Raising citizen awareness about community problems and mobilizing support

(Continued)

Table 16.1 (Continued)

Role Dimensions	Spheres		
	Council	Staff	Community
■ Liaison with manager	Informing council members of developments within the administration and informing manager of council member interests/ concerns	Improving communica- tion between the council and the manager	Promoting public understanding of city manager's role and contribution
Organizing and Policy Making			
■ Monitoring/ adjusting	Delegating tasks to council	Improving staff-council interaction	Ensuring that citizens are involved in developing, implementing, and assessing programs and services
■ Goal setting	Helping the council share goals and carry out goal setting process	Ensuring that staff knowledge about community conditions, needs, and trends is conveyed to council	Ensuring that citizen goals are identified and incorporated into council and staff goal setting activities.
■ Policy initiation	Articulating vision, proposing specific projects, and winning support	Signaling to manager priority areas for research and policy development	Articulating vision, proposing specific projects, mobilizing support, and building coalitions

The distinction between the "coordinator" and "director" based on previous research is further clarified in the case study cities. Both types create an atmosphere that promotes cohesion and improves communication among officials and strengthens the capacity of the council to identify problems and make decisions.

The coordinators (Darrah and Madison are examples) are not strongly associated with a policy agenda of their own, even though they contribute to fashioning and acting on an agenda. The directors have their "own" policy agenda, although it reflects to a greater or lesser extent the views of other officials. This is a subtle distinction in the sense that neither type is a solitary leader and both have broad goals for their cities. The distinction is captured, however, by Winner's (1994) observation that former Mayor Noel C. Taylor of Roanoke, Virginia, "believed he knew what was best for Roanoke, wanted to be progressive, but did not have a specific agenda." Also, Wheeland (1994) made this observation about former Mayor Betty Jo Rhea of Rock Hill, South Carolina: Although she "cares about policies, she does not try to develop them and then seek other public officials and community leaders to adopt them." Thus, coordinator-type mayors ensure that goals are set, but are not the source of the goals. Facilitative mayors may shift between types of leadership. For example, Foy clearly took the lead in some areas, but approached other issues without promoting any particular ends, focusing instead on engaging others and gaining input across the community.

The study of Stockton provides a careful analysis of the distinction between the types of leadership in a single city. When comparing Darrah and Podesto, Podesto had greater strength in articulating issues and mobilizing support and in policy initiation. Darrah was stronger at team relations and network building, as well as delegating and organizing. Darrah described her contributions as strengthening interpersonal relationships and building support for action on the city's problems. Podesto described his accomplishments in terms of specific, concrete changes that advanced economic development and heightened recognition of the city, although his accomplishments were often accompanied by conflicts with the council and he turned the city manager into a hard-charging implementer of the mayor's initiatives. Benedetti and Lambuth conclude that coordinators and advocates alternate as mayor, each responding to the particular challenges they encounter and perhaps to the elements missing in the previous mayor. Darrah fostered a process from which a vision shaped by engaged citizens emerged, and Podesto focused on accomplishing specific projects in that vision. It could be argued that Podesto illustrates an intermediate type that can be labeled the "policy advocate." Whereas the coordinator focuses primarily on process and is weak at policy initiation, the policy advocate concentrates primarily on policy initiation and gives less attention to process. In contrast, a director combines coordination *and* policy direction.* Based on Stockton's experience, Benedetti and Lambuth view the director as an ideal type, not attainable by "mere mortals" and not observed in Stockton.

---

* For a typology of mayoral leadership based on the interaction of policy guidance and process coordination, see Svara (1990). I contrasted the activist/reformer, who is strong on policy but weak on coordination, with the coordinator who has the opposite characteristics. As in the current classification, the "director" type is effective in both areas.

It is certainly difficult to effectively handle both active dimensions of leadership. The coordinator may strain positive relationships by being an advocate for policy initiatives, and the policy advocate may be disinclined to broaden his vision or incorporate the preferences of others in goal setting. In this sense, the two types are potentially in conflict with each other. Podesto may have been fortunate to achieve the success he did without alienating support on the council. Despite the difficulty, however, the director type is attainable when the skillful leader uses all the facilitative roles to foster a cohesive process and fashion a shared vision that incorporates the mayor's own goals and those of other key actors. Both coordination and policy direction are or were provided by Dahlstrøm, Dempsey, Evans, Joines, Heartwell, Gordon, and Nalbandian. Their experience indicates that mayors can integrate the coordinative dimension with effective organizing and policy role performance to achieve the director type of leadership. They are all remarkable leaders, but they are still mortals.

In Cincinnati, there has been a struggle to achieve a viable, constructive version of mayoral leadership that offers a variation on the coordinator versus director dilemma. The city had failed to take the step that most larger council–manager cities had taken long ago in moving to direct election of the mayor. The city continued the traditional practice of selecting the mayor from within the council, a practice that makes visionary leadership less likely. Starting in 1987, the council designated the top vote getter in the at-large city council election as mayor. Thus, in effect all candidates were competing for the mayor's position in the campaign, and their next attempt to become mayor could begin as soon as the election was over. The Cincinnati city council demonstrated an extreme form of fragmentation, and critics claimed that the council was dysfunctional. By changing the charter to give the mayor additional powers as well as being directly elected, the assumption seemed to be that an effective leader would emerge. In a sense, leadership would be anointed by the charter. Summarizing the perceptions in the city after the charter change, Spence observes that the mayor became the "unquestioned leader" who would be evaluated by his or her effectiveness at developing policy, setting goals, delegating, and organizing. It could be argued that all mayors should be evaluated by these criteria, not just those few that have enhanced powers. Furthermore, having more powers does not automatically achieve the result of creating a director-type mayor. It appears that Luken put continued emphasis on coordinative leadership, and Mallory finds that he does not have enough power to control a majority on the council that has preferences different from his own. Empowering the mayor does not eliminate the need for mayors to work with the council. According to the typology developed here, Luken could not be a director without having a vision, and Mallory cannot be a director without incorporating the council in setting goals. Neither of these qualities is likely to be produced by the city charter, but rather depend on the leadership qualities of the individual who holds the office.

The mayor–council mayors require different classification than that developed for council–manager cities. As executive mayors, they may either choose to pursue strong mayor types of leadership (Svara 1990) or those that draw extensively on the facilitative style. Mayors can use their powers to be brokers—determining who will win policy contests without being the initiator of policy proposals—or they can be innovators who use their power to secure approval and implementation of their own policy agenda. Prochaska and especially Plusquellic and Rendell appear to be facilitative innovators who made extensive use of inclusionary methods in shaping their programs and securing support for them. They are policy initiators and, rather than being constrained by conflict with the council, they attempt to build trust and work with council leaders and members.

The discussion of types of leadership in cities with different forms of government raises some puzzling questions. How can a mayor be a director if he/she is not in charge? If a mayor is in charge, why would he/she choose to be a facilitator and share power with others? These combinations of characteristics seem anomalous because they run counter to certain shared cultural values regarding leadership and power within the United States. In order to better understand the leadership differences related to this form of government, it is useful to examine these values and how they differ in the United States and other countries. This exploration is inspired by the case study from Denmark and introduces some new concepts before returning to examination of key points from the other case studies.

16.2.3 *Cultural Values and Expectations of Leadership*

Cultural values that shape how people think about relationships and social control have a powerful influence in defining leadership, but the variation of these values across countries has not been widely recognized. The case study from Denmark illustrates the importance of operating within a cultural context that differs significantly from prevailing norms in the United States. A facilitative leader fits in the structural and cultural context of Danish local government. Structural factors (i.e., the quasi-parliamentary form of government with unified authority rather than separation of powers) and cultural factors are aligned in support of a facilitative style, as we observed in the case study of Dahlstrøm. He was not just demonstrating his individual preferences when he chose not to use his majority power to the fullest extent; he was also reflecting the cultural values that prevail in Denmark. In contrast, the collaborative leader runs against (or perhaps across) the currents of cultural values in the United States. Even though facilitative mayors match the *structural* characteristics of council–manager government, they are at odds with underlying cultural values.

Research by the Dutch psychologist, Geert Hofstede, has identified key characteristics that can affect the way people relate to each other in organizations and in the political process. These values can differ greatly across countries. Of particular relevance is the degree of emphasis that a society puts on "power distance" and the extent to which there is a "tolerance for ambiguity" within a society. Hofstede defines *power distance* as "the extent to which the less powerful members of institutions and organizations within a country expect and accept that power is distributed unequally" (Hofstede 1997). A large power distance in a country indicates that subordinates are dependent on their superiors and accept and expect the upper echelons of the hierarchy to give them direction and control them. Centralization is common and people generally accept hierarchy, and the powerful are expected to have privileges and to look as impressive and powerful as possible. In countries with small power distance, subordinates expect and receive consultation with their superiors, hierarchies are looked upon as inequalities established for the convenience of those on top, the ideal boss is a democrat, decentralization is popular, and the powerful try to look less powerful than they are (Hofstede 1997).

Uncertainty avoidance is defined as "the extent to which the members of a culture feel threatened by uncertain, unknown, ambiguous, and unstructured situations" (Hofstede 1997). In societies marked by high uncertainty avoidance, individuals generally feel uncomfortable in ambiguous situations and have an emotional need for rules. Society is characterized by many precise laws and rules, administrators are negative toward the political process, and citizens have a low trust in institutions. Individuals from low uncertainty avoidance countries generally have a high tolerance for ambiguity, do not like rules, and are not afraid of breaking them if it is considered to be necessary. They are positive toward politics and political institutions and exhibit a subjective feeling of well being (Hofstede 1997).

Among the countries studied by Hofstede, who examined staff members in business organizations, Danes have very low scores for power distance and also low scores for uncertainty avoidance, i.e., a very high tolerance for ambiguity. These results are also confirmed in surveys of local government top administrators (Mouritzen and Svara 2002). In this kind of setting, a political leader is less likely to be ill at ease when his or her exact powers and responsibilities are not clearly superior to followers or subordinates. According to cultural norms, leaders are expected to share power and be inclusionary. They are likely to be egalitarian and flexible. Thus, the "ideal" leader in Denmark approximates the characteristics of the facilitative leader.

In comparison, the United States has intermediate level scores on both of these cultural values. With intermediate power distance scores, leaders want and are expected to be in charge although they cannot be autocratic and must be sensitive to democratic conditions. Struggles over power (as opposed to power sharing) are common. With a tendency to avoid uncertainty, there is discomfort when authority relationships are ambiguous. Leaders are likely to push for clarification of status and test the limits of power in order to determine how far they extend. The tendency to spell out authority in constitutions and charters helps to clarify the powers each actor has and also the limits on their powers. Moderately high power distance and uncertainty avoidance scores contribute to distrust of leaders. Thus, the "ideal" leader is likely to be (or appears to be) the out-front, solitary leader, the

Lone Ranger, who steps in to solve problems that others cannot, but there is always scepticism about whether we trust the leader who has this power. In Parks' view, "the heroic image of leadership that prevails in the conventional mind" has the power of a "myth" (2005). Like Hofstede, Parks sees myths as "powerful stories that arise from, pervade, and shape the cultures we breathe" (202).

In keeping with these cultural values, there is a slogan often heard in support of strong executive forms of government that captures this sentiment: "We need to have one person who can be held accountable." This statement implies that ultimately one person has control over others and that the person can be held to account by followers or the public who at once depend on but don't fully trust the leader. It is consistent with a moderately strong inclination to accept power, and it eliminates ambiguity about who is in charge. In comparison, the facilitative approach presumes that the leader has the responsibility to ensure that all can contribute and that decisions reflect shared goals. Although this appears to be the appropriate leadership style in a country with the cultural values of Denmark, it does not square well with the American context. Despite the widespread use of unified authority and shared power forms in school systems, other special districts, nonprofits, and voluntary organizations (as well as a majority of governments in cities over 5,000 in population), in the political process, there is a tendency to expect separation of powers and to prefer a leader who is in charge. From this perspective, the facilitator may not appear to be a real leader.

Not surprisingly, in view of American cultural values, the popularly perceived "ideal" leader is still close to the image of the "strong" executive at the national, state, and urban levels of government. Officials who share power and operate in ambiguous relationships, e.g., having influence but not being in control or being the first among equals, may not be recognized as complete leaders or perhaps leaders at all. They are widely perceived to be saddled with liabilities. The activities they engage in and the governing arrangements they foster may be missed when identifying leaders. The resources they use may not appear to be the stuff from which leadership can be fashioned. For the same reason, there may be a tendency to overlook or undervalue the facilitative aspects of leadership used by leaders who have formal powers. In contrast to these views, the case studies indicate that these visionary facilitators are "real" leaders and that the mayors supported by powers can usefully employ facilitative methods to strengthen their leadership rather than relying entirely on their powers alone.

Recent scholarship advances a model of leadership drawn from the arts that is based on collaborative values rather than control, and creativity rather than power. The facilitative director type of mayor is similar to the orchestra conductor, the choreographer of a dance troupe, or the director of a play or movie. These persons are typically in charge and they do represent the one person who can be held accountable, but these are not the characteristics we focus on when we view them as leaders. They lead by creating a vision of what is to be accomplished and by aligning, coordinating, and melding the contributions of the participants in the process. Drawing particularly on dance, Denhardt and Denhardt (2006) conclude that leaders connect with followers, create an emotional bond, and energize the group. "The act of leading," they observe, "results in a flow of human energy in a particular direction and at a particular speed and tempo." Leadership is necessarily collaborative. Drawing on theatre, Parks (2005) observes that the director uses authority to maintain "equilibrium in a social system" and uses leadership to mobilize the "social system to create a new reality."* The other participants are essential to success because they must make their own creative contribution and devote their energies to achieving the desired result. Parks (2005) concludes that "theater, leadership, and teaching are all communication arts requiring constructive feedback in a demanding, consultative mode." The director type of mayor is a leader in this sense. Like conductors, they use batons to guide, blend, and direct rather than using the proverbial big stick. Handy (1996) conveys a similar view about the business sector when he observes that "the softer words of leadership and vision and common purpose will replace the tougher words of control and authority because the tougher words don't bite anymore."

The facilitative approach is also associated with a feminine style of leadership. The qualities associated with facilitative leadership are more commonly manifested by women than men. According to Fisher (2005, 138), these include:

> web thinking, mental flexibility, the ability to embrace ambiguity, intuition, imagination, a penchant for long-term planning, verbal acuity, executive social skills, the capacity to collaborate, and empathy.

Although these traits, which are essential in a new global economy or, we might add, in an era of new governance, are not associated exclusively with women, they are more likely to possess them. Men, just as they may have more difficulty setting aside a power-over approach to leadership, may also have more difficulty developing these skills.

An approach to leadership that stresses collaboration and shared vision will probably always be outside the conventional views of what leadership means in the United States. Obviously, it is possible for American mayors to manifest this kind of leadership, but they should be sensitive to the possibility of perceived discrepancies between their approach and the expectations of the media and the public.

16.2.4 Resources and Mayoral Attributes

The discussion of resources for leadership is shaped by the cultural context and the leadership style that is being enhanced. In an influential article on the "preconditions" of mayoral leadership, Pressman (1972) concluded: "Without governmental

---

* One could argue that the formal features of the council–manager form of government contribute to maintaining equilibrium in the governmental process.

jurisdiction, staff, and financial resources, it is hard for any mayor to direct, or even influence, the actions of others." If one accepts "direct" to mean give orders, the first half of the statement is a truism, but the second half overlooks the potential of shared leadership to influence how others behave. To repeat the distinction made earlier, there is a tendency to think of the leader's "power over" other actors rather than thinking of the shared "power to" address problems and implement solutions. The resources needed for each approach to leadership will be different, and our focus will be on power-to leadership. In this section, a complete inventory of resources will be identified and then special attention will be given to the importance of vision and dealing with conflict.

16.2.4.1 An Inventory of Resources

In contrast to Pressman, who identifies the preconditions of enhancing the influence of the mayor *compared to other actors*, we seek to identify the preconditions for enhancing the *capacity of all actors* through facilitative leadership, i.e., bringing officials, citizens, and leaders in the community and other governments together to establish and carry out policies that address the aspirations and needs of the city. The case studies indicate that this kind of facilitative leadership does not depend on a superior power position. There are resources available in the mayor's position, in the form of government, and within the personal qualities of the incumbent to develop leadership in the areas of coordination and policy guidance. Below is a summary of the factors that contribute to effective performance of mayors who expand the power of city government to meet the aspirations and needs of its citizens (expanded version of Svara 1994, Figure 11.2).

- **Resources derived from position**
  - Public roles: presiding officer, ceremonial leader, spokesperson, official representative
  - Strategic location to secure and channel information and to build relationships
  - Access to information
  - Support of and interaction with city manager
  - Staff support necessary to fill demands of office
  - Powers/duties that enhance visibility and support director style of mayor/chairperson (e.g., direct election, state of city/county address, appointment to boards and commissions, voting), but do not isolate him/her from other members of the governing board as powers, such as veto and staff appointment authority, would do

- **Informal resources**
  - Support of key groups in community
  - Contacts and connections; desire to expand network
  - Media attention and support

■ **Personal resources, attributes, and characteristics**
  – Clear conception of the office
  – Understanding of how to fill roles appropriately and how to use automatic and coordination/communication roles as the foundation for organizing, goal setting, and policy initiation
  – Clear sense of purpose
  – Vision of the future
  – Time to devote to office
  – Energy
  – Positive attitude
  – Resourcefulness
  – Integrity and fairness
  – Commitment to full involvement of members of governing board through inclusiveness, sharing of information, supporting expression of divergent views, and accepting the initiative of others members
  – Respect for authority and prerogatives of city/county manager

■ **Skills**
  – Ability to communicate, particularly active listening and effective speaking
  – Ability to set goals and priorities, and keep sight of broad goals while making specific choices
  – Ability to develop strategies to achieve goals
  – Ability to enlist and motivate others
  – Ability to resolve conflicts and differences
  – Flexibility—ability to shift the emphasis placed on different roles

The initial resource is the mayor's position itself. John Nalbandian noticed that the same problem-solving skills he had employed as a council member could be used to greater effect as mayor. The explanation is simple but essential to understanding the potential of the office: "… people listen to you—they think you have more power than you actually have." Mayors often remark that people think that they can do things over which they have no direct authority, and that perception is a powerful resource. Other actors expect the mayor to be a leader and accept leadership from them. Nalbandian notes that his predecessor dismissed his position by reminding people that he had just one of five votes. In effect, he was dispelling the ambiguity of his position by asserting that he has no potential for leadership. In contrast, Nalbandian promoted the ambiguity: "I don't remind anyone of that fact. I just try to move things along, focusing especially on inclusive projects."

The mayor's presiding officer and other public roles give the incumbent voice and visibility, and the mayor's strategic location provides the opportunity to shape the content and direction of discourse. The public and the media expect the mayor to be the person who speaks for the city, not simply the equivalent of a press secretary or media relations officer. The mayor sits at the middle of four key inter-action channels with the (1) other members of the council; (2) the city manager or administrator; (3) citizens, community leaders, and the media in the city; and (4) leaders in other local governments and at other levels of government. In this strategic location, mayors have a high level of information and can help inform and guide these diverse actors. The mayor is in a position to lend support to others and generate support from the person whose proposal is supported, as Nalbandian observes. Similarly, the mayor can share an idea with others and let them get credit for proposing it. Mayor Keno Hawker of Mesa, Arizona, advises mayors to get someone else to propose a policy or program the mayor is strongly interested in. It spreads the credit and secures another supporter from the beginning.*

Support of and interaction with the city manager is a great asset. Mayors and city managers have a wide-ranging exchange of information and views on all aspects of city government affairs. In Denmark, this aspect of the relationship is captured by referring to the top administrator as the "sparring partner" of the mayor. City managers are expected to display professional independence and integrity in their one-on-one interaction with the mayor. In the council–manager form, the mayor has a special relationship with the city manager, but not an exclusive relationship, as noted previously in discussion of the liaison role of the mayor. The relationship with the manager requires the mayor have tact, respect, ability to share authority, and trust in the manager's commitment to advance the goals of the city and to achieve the highest performance from government as a whole.

For executive mayors, having a professional chief administrative officer (CAO) expands the resources and perspectives of the mayor. Executive mayors are not well served by CAOs who simply tell them what they want to hear (Chase and Reveal 1983). Furthermore, the mayor builds support on the council by allowing the CAO to keep the council fully informed. In addition to the high-level advice and assis-tance provided by the city manager or CAO, mayors need to have personal profes-sional staff support necessary to fill the demands of office for public appearances and preparing policy ideas.

Mayors may have other formal powers and resources as well. Despite the instances of empowering the mayor in council–manager cities, a distinction should be made among kinds of enhancements to the position. Powers/duties that enhance visibility and support the director style of mayoral leadership are valuable, e.g., direct election, delivering state of city/county address, making appointments to boards and commissions, voting. However, powers that isolate the mayor from other members of the governing board may undercut the mayor's ability to be a facilitator, e.g., veto and staff appointment authority and voting only to break ties (Wheeland 2002). When one considers the extraordinary accomplishments of some mayors with no additional powers (or even less than normal as in the cases

---

* Presentation by Keno Hawker at the Workshop on Mayoral Leadership and the Future of Council–Manager Government, Arizona State University, April 18, 2007.

of Dempsey and Nalbandian), and the limited results from some mayors who have more powers, proponents of empowerment should be cautious in their claims about what will be accomplished by assigning more powers to the mayor; and they should recognize that having certain powers may be counter-productive. Probably all mayors wish at times that they had more power over others, but as Joines observes, "You have to cooperate with everyone, and you have to keep that in mind … . People appreciate the fact that you have included them in what is going on, and in the long run, it will be easier to get a resolution to a problem."

Council–manager mayors who have extraordinary powers, such as nominating the city manager to the council or initiating the removal of the city manager, may have a harder time securing cooperation from the council. The formal connection to the mayor could jeopardize the perceived objectivity of the manager's recommendations to the mayor and council and the manager's commitment to serve the entire council. Expanding the mayor's power over the city manager can reduce the shared power to solve the city's problems. In mayor–council cities, executive mayors need to explore how to keep from becoming dependent on their powers and engendering increased conflict with the council. In many cities, the drag of mayor–council conflict offsets the mayor's resource advantage (Svara 2006).

Mayors with a clear conception of the job—its possibilities, interdependencies, and limitations—are more likely to be able to take advantage of the inherent opportunities of the mayor's office. The mayor must be willing (and have the ability) to use the "power of persuasion" in dealings with other actors, as Rendell did, and "moral suasion," as Nalbandian recommends and Madison practices, to remind council members of their obligation to do what is right for the future of the city.

Willingness and ability to commit time can give the mayor a relative advantage over other officials, but this does not mean that the amount of time per se determines effectiveness. Mayors must use their time strategically. Jonathan Howes, former mayor of Chapel Hill, observed that over his years in office, a number of council members began spending more time in their position than he did as mayor.* Mayors cannot become leaders simply by spending a lot of time on the job, but a substantial commitment of effort is a precondition for success. The time must be used well and converted to other resources like knowledge or networks.

The importance of personal qualities in determining the inclination of individuals to seek leadership and their ability to exercise it was confirmed by the cases. Energy, resourcefulness, contacts and connections, ability to communicate, a clear sense of purpose, and the ability to keep sight of broad goals while making specific choices are important for leadership in any setting. Effective leaders have a positive attitude and are able to convey that orientation to others (Goleman, Boyatzis, and McKee 2001). These qualities must be channeled, however, into appropriate role behavior. In council–manager governments, the automatic and coordinative

---

* Jonathan Howes, former mayor and special assistant to the chancellor at UNC-Chapel Hill, made these comments at a symposium in 1991.

roles support goal setting, organizing, and policy initiation. The highly committed, assertive, and impatient mayor may jump into the higher level roles without developing the others, but runs the risk of having only short-term success or being isolated from the council although, as we have seen, Podesto was effective as a policy advocate. Elected executive mayors may conclude that they can rely on their formal powers and do not have to build relationships and trust with members of the council.

Information is a key resource. By self-education, staff support, and briefings by the top administrator, the mayor stays on top of issues. A high level of knowledge strengthens the mayor in interactions with the rest of the council, staff, and citizens, and is a source of influence in working with others. For example, Dempsey held herself to the standard of always being well prepared, and Evans studies issues before deciding what she thinks are the best answers for Plano.

Another resource is integrity. It undergirds the trust other officials and citizens have for the mayor. Nalbandian observes that "respect and loyalty leading to trust count above all other elements for a facilitative mayor." Joines built up trust in the black community that gave him credibility when pledging support for persons dislocated in the stadium project. Danish mayors can earn credits by building good will that they can use to move the council forward and in the direction of the mayor's preference.

To be effective as a coordinator or director, certain interpersonal skills are needed for leadership. The mayor must be effective at working with others and accept certain responsibilities to them. Inclusiveness, sharing of information, listening, encouragement of the expression of divergent views, and ability to resolve differences are important traits for mayors to have in their dealings with the council.

The mayor must also bring the force of personality and a commitment to persist in the face of opposition or reluctance. Mayors can be more effective if they are not shrinking violets. As an observer in Auburn commented, Dempsey was determined not to simply be in the parade, she wanted to lead the parade. She also was credited with being able to be forceful in enlisting support. She used a direct approach that and could be "intimidating, but engaging." Other personality styles can be effective as well. It appears that Evans' "gentle style of persuasion" was just as effective in securing acceptance of a number of projects, although she is also described as being "tough as nails" in pursuing a goal once she concludes that a course of action is the right one. As an effective facilitative mayor, she is proactive in seeking out people who might oppose her position and making efforts to co-opt them. Gordon is effective at keeping people at the table despite their differences. Many of the mayors in the case studies work hard to develop consensus on key issues before a decision has been made, even when they have majority support. Effective mayors need to be willing to share credit, as Gordon is adept at doing.

Finally, mayors need to be flexible and capable of shifting how they fill roles and the relative emphasis they place on different resources depending on the needs and opportunities in the city, the strengths and weaknesses of the council members, the characteristics of the city manager or city administrator, and myriad other factors. A mayor acts as a stabilizer who attends to those areas where contributions are needed at a given time. As a consequence, mayors need to be able to shift the extent to which they are central to decisions, visible to the public, and assertive of their own point of view depending on conditions. For example, mayors can remain in the background when there is extensive support for a shared goal, but must be able to move forward and build the support if it is lacking. Despite the flexibility, however, one constant should be a clear sense of purpose, which is conveyed by the mayor to all participants in the governmental process.

The list of resources is a long one. Not all mayors will possess or display all the resources at any given time. The list is intended to suggest to mayors the wide variety of resources they can draw upon to shape their own leadership activities, i.e., their efforts to guide and work with others. As just noted, they need to be able to draw on the resources flexibly and strategically, keeping in mind their goal of making the governing process purposeful, participative, inclusive, and efficient. There is considerable interaction among the factors, and the personal attributes and skills are more numerous and important than formal or informal resources. There is one resource that deserves additional discussion.

16.2.4.2 Importance of Vision

Mayors who have a vision for the future of the city can blend their goals with those of others and ensure that elected officials have a strong impact on the civic agenda. In *The Facilitative Leader*, the mayor's vision was incorporated in the discussion of the policy advocate role and was assumed to be part of the director type of mayoral leadership. It is important to give separate attention to vision for three reasons. First, vision is not necessarily the same thing as advocacy. A mayor could stress the importance of adopting certain programs or approaches without having a general orientation that connects the proposals for new policies or programs. Being a visionary implies that one is able to connect specific ideas with a broad view of what a desired future would be. Advocacy often divides and engenders countering proposals. Vision can provide the basis for agreement. Second, empirical evidence presented in Chapter 1 supports the recognition that the approach mayors take to interacting with others is different from their ability and inclination to be visionary. Vision and facilitation are two distinct qualities that can be combined in various ways. Third, acquiring the ability to be visionary and the ability to be facilitative require two different kinds of training and personal development.

It makes a difference for mayors to have a vision of the future. A vision guides their efforts and creates a framework for members of the city council. Council members may not agree with all elements of the mayor's vision, but it gives them a frame of reference into which they can place their own goals. Without the mayor's vision, each member of the council could have his/her own separate view of where the city should go, or they might focus entirely on dealing with present concerns and reacting to immediate problems. The requirements of facilitation remind the mayor that his or her vision should incorporate the goals of others. If the mayor lacks vision, however, the facilitative mayor may try to secure commitment from council members to engage in a process that will generate a shared set of goals.

16.2.4.3 Resources for Dealing with Conflict

An important change in the past decade is the increased independence of council members, their expanded activism, and their increased attention to constituent concerns (Svara 2002). The increased use of district elections contributes to these conditions. Whereas council members in council–manager cities once had a strong commitment to the governance function and less interest in the representational function, they now are just as interested in the representational function as their counterparts in mayor–council cities. In some cities, councils with no official who has power over them can be severely divided and incapable of exercising their governance function (Gurwitt 2003). The Cincinnati council probably fit this description before changes in the charter, and perennially fragmented councils in Hartford and Richmond were a major contributing factor to change of form of government in these cities. This is not, however, a widespread condition. Overall, council members in council–manager cities rate themselves as more effective in governance activities than their mayor–council counterparts (Svara 2002).

Still, due to the changes in the orientation of council members, it is important for mayors to be capable of displaying what might be called "facilitation with an attitude." They need to be strong, assertive, persistent, and capable of mobilizing outside groups to influence the behavior of members of the council. Even facilitative leaders must be able to use "forceful interventions" when the group is floundering (Cufaude 2004). Podesto, who took an independent course vis-à-vis the council, used these methods, and Dempsey was "in the face" of persons on and off the council, who did not work together. With softer insistence, Evans, Heartwell, Joines, Madison, and Gordon exerted pressure on their colleagues to work together to achieve overriding goals. Mayors should not assume that these behaviors will be necessary, but they should be capable of pursuing them if the members of the council insist on going their separate ways. The ultimate but high risk method of acquiring influence is to endorse candidates, share campaign resources with supporters, and even to work against the reelection of incumbents who oppose the mayor.

If the mayor wants to maintain facilitative leadership, he or she should avoid being forceful to the point of driving away potential supporters or disempowering other actors, for example, by browbeating members of the council. The mayor who tries to isolate or freeze out an independent council member by turning other members against him or her is also using power-over methods. There may be instances when a council member is obstructing initiatives supported by the mayor, and the mayor is able to use the committee appointment power to keep the opponent off a key committee. Mayors, however, should examine their attitudes toward an

independent council member and consider whether working with rather than trying to isolate or denigrate this person will be more effective. Furthermore, mayors
need to be aware of the risk of isolation if they antagonize a majority of the city
council. The point is not to be nice for its own sake, but to practice leadership in
ways consistent with the context and the facilitative style. It appears that successful
mayors seek supporters and are willing to work with everyone who is willing to help
meet shared goals. They recognize the power of invitation and the creative energy
that can be created by collaboration and inclusion.

The case studies provide evidence of mayors turning around conflictual situations by patiently, persistently, and assertively promoting communication and clear
division of roles, drawing out shared goals, and promoting the accomplishment of
goals. Facilitative leaders are less likely to view differences as zero-sum and appear
to be capable of drawing together persons with differing views.

16.3 Issues In Mayoral Leadership

In the discussion of roles, types of leadership, and resources, some general issues arise.
Here we consider the arguments concerning the use of collaborative leadership techniques, the nature of the mayor's contributions in different structural settings, and
the distinctive challenges to mayoral leadership in each major form of government.

16.3.1 Recognizing Leadership by Council–Manager Mayors

The contribution of mayors in council–manager cities is often ignored because it is
collaborative and also because it is subtler and less visible than the kind of leadership
displayed in mayor–council cities. It is important to examine these factors in order
to address the presumed political leadership deficit in council–manager cities.

As discussed in Chapter 1, collaborative leadership is widely recognized in the
literature as more effective than an authoritarian or power-over style (Denhardt and
Denhardt 2006). "It has become almost a cliché among leadership theorists," Parks
(2005) observes, "to disavow a heroic command-and-control model of leadership."
Despite the record of accomplishment demonstrated in these case studies, popular perceptions support the view that controlling leaders are most effective. The
evidence for this conclusion is the popularity of charismatic turn-around CEOs
in companies, and take-charge leaders in the governmental arena (Collins 2001).
This notion is often translated into the claim that cities, particularly large ones,
should have "strong" mayors. The discrepancy between research results and popular
perceptions is produced in part by cultural norms that lead city residents to expect
certain kinds of behavior from the mayor and incumbents to offer behaviors that
meet these expectations.

It is common in general descriptions of council–manager cities to denigrate
the contribution of the mayor and council and exaggerate the impact of the city

manager. The manager, Pressman suggests, will bypass the mayor and relate directly to the council, pursue a personal/professional agenda, and take cues from outside influentials, but not provide leadership responsive to elected officials nor supportive of their exercise of democratic control. From this perspective, city managers placate council, and only the mayor is capable of curtailing the manager by limiting his or her scope of responsibilities and expanding the mayor's activities. Some argue that there is inherent conflict between mayors and managers (Kammerer 1964), and some observers may perceive power as a hydraulic system "whereby decrease in the manager's power would result in increased mayoral power" (Sparrow 1984). From this zero-sum view of power, mayoral leadership is essential to securing political control and curtailing the power of administrative staff. What is missing in this perspective is the possibility that mayors can make constructive contributions to leadership in cooperation with the city manager.

Survey data and the case studies presented here offer a different view. Top administrators who were surveyed in Europe, Australia, and the United States report that their influence is positively related to the influence of the mayor. City administrators who work for mayors with little influence may have a greater relative influence, but it is a bigger piece of a smaller influence pie. Their influence ratings are lower than those who work with high influence mayors (Mouritzen and Svara 2002). More often than not, mayors enhance the position of the manager rather than supplanting them. The mayor is essential to providing a sense of direction, maintaining alignment and coordinating the parts of council–manager form, and restoring working relationships when they are out of balance.

When effective working relationships are in place, the conditions seem natural and the contribution of mayoral leadership to preserving the smoothly working "system" may not be apparent. There are no obvious breakthrough accomplishments for which the mayor might claim credit when things work well. There are no dramatic victories over opponents and, thus, the mayor's image is not elevated. The contribution of the mayor to forging agreement within the council is easy to ignore. Unlike the situation in mayor–council cities where it is commonly perceived that new mayors battle the bureaucracy (Flanagan 2004) and get credit when they shift priorities (Siegel 2005), the mayor in a council–manager city expects to have a cooperative city manager who is responsive to the policy directives of a new mayor and council. Unlike mayors who get attention from the battle with bureaucrats, there is not a dramatic boost in reputation for a mayor who works with a city manager to shape goals and accomplish them. Indeed, the mayor and council may be dismissed as "rubber stamping" the city manager's recommendations. Thus, the political leadership that is integral, along with professional leadership, to a smoothly functioning council–manager city can be easily overlooked.

It is a mistake to assume, however, that other leadership contributions cannot be identified. In the case study cities, there are four kinds of situations regarding the ongoing relationship between the mayor and city manager. First, the city manager has served for an extended period and works effectively with the current (and previous) mayor (Grand Rapids, Lawrence, Phoenix, and Plano). Second, the city manager retires after extended service and a strong working relationship with the mayor, and the mayor oversees the selection of a new city manager (Chapel Hill and Winston-Salem). The mayor preserves a strong working relationship by guiding the transition to a new city manager. In both of these situations, the mayor profiled in the case study is a catalyst who provides the critical new element that helps a city council undertake policy initiatives that had not been possible before. Despite continuity in the city manager's position, elected officials were capable of new accomplishments because of the presence of an effective mayor.

In the third kind of situation, the mayor takes advantage of a resignation by the city manager (Dempsey in Auburn, and Darrah and Podesto in Stockton) to find a person who relates differently to the mayor and/or the council than the departing manager. Similarly, in Cincinnati, the current mayor had a vacancy to fill when he began his term, as did his predecessor at the point that he assumed new charter powers. Finally, in the fourth situation, the mayor enters office with a vacancy and a leadership void and guides the process of selection and the restoration of working relationships (Madison in Midway). In these cases, the mayor makes a substantial contribution. The mayor helps to preserve a relationship or contributes to reorienting the relationship between the city manager or administrator and the city council, as well as enhancing the performance of the city manager. It is not necessary for the mayor to change city managers to have an impact as the continuity situations illustrate. The possibility, however, of changing the city manager at any time is an essential tool for achieving accountability.

The Midway case illustrates that the mayor and city manager can develop a synergistic relationship that enhances the effectiveness of both, but the leadership team may be unstable. If a substantial number of council members are opposed to the mayor and consider the manager to be the mayor's agent, then the mayor–manager relationship may be a cause of resentment among members of the "out" group. The effectiveness of the mayor–manager leadership team may be temporary unless the mayor can win over opponents on and off the council.

Mayors are part of the overall representative democratic leadership that is combined with professional leadership in the council–manager form of government. Elected officials introduce some new policies, review and approve the policy recommendations of city managers, bring current problems to the governmental agenda, oversee administrative performance, link citizens to government and investigate their complaints, and hire and appraise the city manager. Mayors along with other council members propose new policy initiatives and help to refine and, on occasion, redefine the vision of their city. Typically, mayors and city managers work through policy proposals together, but at times it may be necessary for the mayor to make adjustments to offset resistance to new ideas. On occasion, Nalbandian perceived the need to generate support for new ideas before talking about them with the manager who had the reputation of being politically cautious. The form is certainly not the "city manager" form of government, as it is sometimes inappropriately called. The council–manager form combines political and professional.

The mayor can be helpful in goal setting and determining direction, policy initiatives, and priorities. As we observed in Chapter 1, less than half of councils perform well at goal setting when the mayor is neither a visionary nor effective at helping the council set goals. Most of the councils have a high level of performance—good or excellent—when the mayor has one of these qualities, and almost half of the councils achieve excellent performance when the mayor is both a visionary and goal setter. Thus, mayors can make a direct contribution to determining the direction of government, and an indirect contribution through enhancing council performance.

There is no controversy about the argument that mayors in mayor–council cities make a contribution. Indeed, the form depends on their doing so.

16.3.2 Distinctive Challenges to Mayoral Leadership by Form of Government

In this analysis, I do not mean to be advocating one form of government over the other. Rather I am arguing that mayors must adopt a leadership style that is consistent with and appropriate to the form in which they operate, while at the same time consistent with the universal practices that contribute to effectiveness. Both kinds of mayors must operate "against type" in some respects and maintain a delicate balance between potentially contradictory forces. Following the example of Dahlstrøm in Denmark, mayor–council mayors can choose not to use all their powers or rely only on their powers. This mayor must avoid the tendency to take charge in a preemptory way. The logic and structure of the form require that mayors use their powers, and they are likely to have to deal with conflict that will require them on occasion to use resources to reward supporters or sanction opponents. Still, if they rely on power and only try to build partnerships after first asserting control, they may find that few want to join the partnership, that powers are insufficient to win many contests, and that they are locked in a stalemate.

Examples of an excessive reliance on power would include attempting to promote their agenda unilaterally, lining up rather than enlisting the council, and seeking to secure unquestioning compliance from administrators. In response to these tactics, the other actors are often inclined to resist. Without allies, the prospects of success are reduced both in the acceptance of the mayor's initiatives and in the effectiveness of their implementation. On the other hand, mayors who seek to incorporate the goals of council members as well as their own, and who tap into the experience, accumulated knowledge, and public service commitment of administrators, have greater prospects for success. Most mayors in mayor–council cities will find that they must choose whether or not to utilize a dual mode of leadership styles—both power-based and facilitative. Given their context, using either mode alone is likely to cause problems. They must seek to establish trust, to treat all fairly, cultivate relationships, as Rendell did, and to be open to alliances with each new policy issue, as Plusquellic is. If the mayor only treats his friends well and is viewed with distrust by opponents, the opponents will always look for ways to defeat the mayor. Circumstances can arise that permit them to do so, as the Yorkville experience shows. Thus, mayors in mayor–council cities face a power paradox: The mayor's power over others is inversely related to their "power to," i.e., the systemic capacity to get things done.

This dilemma is also present in the mayor's relationship to the CAO or other top administrators. In only half of the mayor–council cities is there formal provision for an official who provides comprehensive policy advice to the mayor and central supervision and coordination of all departments in city government. When the CAO position is present, mayors must choose what kind of person to appoint or nominate for the office.* The mayor who emphasizes a power-based approach may choose to appoint a person who extends the mayor's control throughout the organization and focuses exclusively on accomplishing the mayor's agenda. Alternatively, to increase governmental capacity, the mayor would broaden the purpose of the position and the criteria for appointment. A key issue is whether the person chosen to be CAO expands the mayor's knowledge and is willing and able to be honest in communications with the mayor. The mayor should expect loyalty from the CAO, but also accept shared responsibility to the council and a professional relationship and two-way communication with department heads. These choices will determine whether the mayor can establish and maintain effective working relationships with the staff and the council.

The council–manager mayor can take advantage of the partnerships that are readily available in the form, but they must perform a balancing act as well in two areas. First, these mayors must be able to balance the individualistic features of leadership with the collective. It is just as important that they have a personal vision as it is that they incorporate the goals of others into it. Second, mayors are typically highly visible which means that they will get more attention from the public and in the media than the other members of the council. Council members may be envious, but mayors have implicit prominence and authority, and council members usually expect leadership from the mayor. As long as the mayor is sensitive to the need to spread credit and share the spotlight, it is likely that council members will accept the mayor's more prominent public position.

In the relationship with the city manager, the mayor should expect support but not personal loyalty. The broader the support for the mayor's policy goals on the council, the more the city manager can help to advance them. The mayor must accept the manager's responsibility to the entire council and recognize that this shared communication helps rather than hurts the mayor. The manager's

---

* Based on a survey in 1997, in council–manager cities over 5,000 population with a CAO, 12 percent are appointed by the mayor alone, 35 percent are appointed by the council, and 53 percent are appointed by the mayor with the approval of the council (Svara 2001).

communication with council members contributes to social capital—the social connections that tie the council and mayor together—and reinforces the linkage of council members to each other and the city. It is not the mayor alone who has to generate partnerships. New mayors should give an incumbent manager a chance to be responsive; they should not assume that the manager supports the previous mayor's goals or is only interested in promoting a "bureaucratic agenda." Mayors should ensure that a constructive assessment process for the manager is in place and used seriously. Through periodic formal review and ongoing interaction, mayors can make certain that the council is utilizing its formal power to make managers continuously accountable and to change the city manager when performance consistently falls short of the standards that the council has established. An essential feature of the council–manager form is that change in performance of the executive and change in the occupant of the executive's office can occur at any time. The council can act on its own to get answers from the manager, but the mayor is ultimately responsible for ensuring a high level of administrative accountability.

16.4 Conclusion: Expanding Mayoral Leadership and the Implications for the Public Sector

Most cities need more leadership and better leadership to improve performance in serving their citizens. The same can be said for government generally. After examining what has been learned about improving the contributions of mayors in both forms of government, we will examine the implications of the evidence for public sector leaders generally.

The world is increasingly complex, and cities increasingly require a wide range of contributors inside and outside government and across jurisdictions to ameliorate or solve their problems. In addition, people are less connected to their communities and less involved in public affairs. In view of these challenges, the mayor can make a special contribution by being the embodiment of the community, engaging citizens in public affairs, and conveying a sense of purpose, direction, and shared commitment. The same characteristics that create this need for increased leadership also shape the kind of leadership that will be effective. The times call for leaders who have vision and facilitate collaboration. Americans accept this kind of leadership in some settings and they can appreciate it when it is effectively practiced in public office as observed in the case study cities. Still our cultural values incline us to expect governmental leaders to be out front even if they are not in charge. Selfless and low profile leaders can leave citizens feeling adrift. Effective political leaders find a way to blend these tendencies. Through their words or actions, they convey the "mixed" message that "*I* will take the lead in developing a *shared* vision, and *I* will make sure that *we* work together cooperatively to achieve it." We want mayors to convey a sense of power, but we should recognize that it is the combined power to address the problems of the city that offers the greatest prospects of successful action rather than the power of the mayor over other actors.

In the past decade, there has been increased attention given to whether the mayor in council–manager cities should have more formal powers. The evidence presented here indicates that elevating and emboldening the leadership of the mayor is more important than empowering the mayor. Officials, citizens, reporters, and scholars should recognize that in a fundamental sense mayors already "run" their cities. They do not control their cities, i.e., they do not solely or unilaterally determine the agenda, and they do not have direct control over city staff and operations. They do, however, have the ultimate responsibility to ensure that their cities have a clear purpose and that the laws are properly executed, i.e., they ensure that there is proper oversight by the mayor and council of the performance of administrative staff. Furthermore, they take whatever actions are necessary to make sure that all the conditions that contribute to effective execution are in place and properly functioning, and they take responsibility for identifying and seeking to remove any factors that impede proper performance. They are free from the distraction of administrative detail and operate above the limited perspective of day-to-day decision making to focus on the big elements of leadership.

Overall, mayors are responsible for promoting the council as an effective governing body. They interface with the city manager who is charged with linking strategic and operational management. They inspire, organize, and intervene as necessary to ensure that the city has direction, that the city can deal with problems and make clear decisions, that policies are effectively carried out, and that the organization is well run. At the same time, they also have broad linkage responsibilities. They speak for and to citizens and seek to engage them in city government. They form networks with leaders in the immediate and broader community and those who might join the community. They relate to governmental leaders in other jurisdictions in their regions and at other levels of government. The mayor's domain is as broad as they make it. In carrying out these responsibilities, the mayor must pay attention to maintaining the delicate balance between self and collective. Mayors should not abuse their elevated status by taking an "I'm-in-charge" attitude. This advice is not meant to remind mayors that they are constrained and must guard against exceeding the bounds of their leadership. Rather the advice recognizes that American cultural values about leadership are ambiguous. When displaying intense, visible, visionary leadership, it is easy to get pulled back into a leader-centered mode and it is common for actions to be misinterpreted by other actors. Because collaboration is essential to effective leadership, it is appropriate to behave in ways that make it apparent that the mayor is really collaborating. As a general approach, it is useful for mayors to establish a foundation for relationships by facilitating first and then providing vision.

The council–manager mayor can exercise a modest dual mode of leadership styles. The mayor does not need power to subdue bureaucracy or beat the council into submission (and, as we've seen, mayors with powers who take this approach are not likely to be successful). Still, the mayor has ways to assert, win over, and compel. They can apply pressure directly—"I want you to do this"—and indirectly through others who can influence the actor to be persuaded—"I need your help in persuading your council member to support this proposal." The stronger the popular understanding and support for the mayor's initiatives, the greater the mayor's political weight in the council. Mayors can work to get agreements in principle regarding goals and operating procedures on the council and use them to get agreement on specifics. Mayors can provide positive strokes when support is present and express disappointment or anger when it is absent. They can win support by promoting the ideas of others. Mayors use their enhanced access to the media to engender support or apply pressure. They can also win allies among council members by including them in favorable public relations activities. None of these methods of asserting personal leadership depends on formal empowerment, and all must be carried out in a way that is consistent with the underlying facilitative approach. Mayors increase the likelihood of acceptance of their initiatives when they inspire and enlist, when they spread credit, and when they stress what is shared in the ideas they are promoting rather than simply advocating their own preferred outcomes.

There are some aspects of formal empowerment that can be advantageous to the mayor, but it is important to remember the power paradox. Current day mayors, to an even greater extent than in the past, personify their cities whether or not they are unilaterally in charge of their cities. They should formally report to citizens on the state of the city and its future. It is clear that mayors in moderately large and large cities are full-time officials, although the Grand Rapids case shows that defining the position in this way can still engender sufficient opposition to block formal recognition of the time commitment required to fill the position. Mayors should be directly elected, have an adequate salary, and have staff support. The manager and staff should contribute to publicizing the mayor, recognizing that in the process they are promoting the city as well. The mayor and city manager must be able to make deals for the city with appropriate review and approval by council. There are some powers that give the mayor leverage and enable them to bestow benefits while guiding the deliberative process. These include giving the mayor authority to appoint members of council committees and to appoint citizens to serve on boards and commissions without council concurrence. These may be useful and enhance the mayor's position without negative consequences. In contrast, powers that strengthen mayors by distinguishing and separating them from the council may be counterproductive. These include exercising the veto and receiving the annual budget prepared by the city manager, and subsequently presenting it with comments and suggestions to the council (or preparing a mayoral budget in addition to the manager's.) Powers that may be perceived to weaken the responsibility of the city manager to the council as a whole, such as giving the mayor authority to nominate the city manager to the council for approval or permit only the mayor to initiate the dismissal of the manager, are highly questionable. They enhance the mayor's power to control the manager, but they potentially weaken the manager's responsibility to serve the entire council. The special formal ties to the mayor could call into question the manager's commitment to professional standards and the long-term interests of the community as a whole, and weaken the capacity of city government to identify and address its problems and operate at the highest level of accountability and competence.

An alternative to empowering the mayor in council–manager cities is for mayors to commit themselves to achieving effective leadership, i.e., offering ideas and adopting behaviors that will contribute to the highest possible level of performance by city government. As the case studies make clear, effective mayors have a vision for the future and they facilitate the contributions of the council, manager and staff, and citizens. Facilitation entails empowering and enlisting, coordinating and enhancing communication among the actors in city government, and ensuring that there is a process for setting goals and implementing them. The mayor leads actively and collaboratively. These characteristics are not inconsistent with being visionary, but the lower proportion of visionary mayors in council–manager compared to mayor–council cities suggests that many incumbents and potential and actual candidates for the office perceive a contradiction between the two dimensions of leadership. Those who recognize the facilitative nature of the position may feel that it is better not to have strong views about the future of the city, or that they must give up their personal agenda to be mayor. Among potential candidates, those with strong views may feel that they don't belong in the mayor's office in a council–manager city or that they will experience too much frustration (or tension) trying to push their own agenda in this setting.* The city is not best served by either those who are totally selfless or completely self-centered. Balancing the tension between serving self and others generates energy. The literature on leadership provides a clear picture of the ideal leader, and the case studies provide examples in city hall. The best leaders blend their own aspirations with the preferences of others; they augment their own drive to succeed by enlisting the contributions and energies of others, and they expand the organization's power to meet its goals.

Council–manager cities have many mayors who meet these ideal standards, but they need many more. Thus, this message should go out: "Wanted—the best leaders in the city to be candidates for mayor." Due to our incomplete understanding of the mayor's office (even, I concede, too much emphasis on facilitation without sufficient attention to vision), this message has not been clearly enunciated or fully understood. More candidates who are visionaries as well as facilitators should step forth to run for the mayor's office. In most council–manager cities, the victorious candidates will have the assurance of knowing that they will move into a city

---

* On occasion, the person with a strong commitment to a personal agenda decides to run, is elected, and then tries to change the form of government rather than channeling his or her leadership through the form.

government that is well run, and have a management team already in place that is capable of translating the goals of new elected officials into reality.*

In mayor–council cities, the ideal leader is the same, and mayors improve their prospects for success by combining vision and facilitation with modifications and additions appropriate to the form of government. A commitment to effective leadership means building partnerships, expanding capacity, and using the powers of the office in ways that are consistent with the facilitative approach. Naturally, mayors should be visionaries (a characteristic that is already found more often in the mayor–council form, but still in only three of five cities), but they must recognize the potential for expanding their impact by not relying on their powers alone or assembling a team of loyalists to be advisers and top administrators. They should not limit themselves to the backing of supporters on the city council for an agenda they have devised on their own. They have more tools, but also more burdens and liabilities than their counterparts in council–manager cities. Often, new mayors inherit problems from their predecessors. They must assemble their management team and face a greater transition challenge than mayors in council–manager cities. Finally, they must resist the temptation reinforced by the media and popular expectations to go it alone. Mayor–council cities have many mayors who meet these ideal standards, but they need many more, and the effectiveness of city governments that use this form is much more dependent on the quality of the mayor. Thus, the message should go out in mayor–council cities that the best leaders are needed—not just the most assertive or forceful. Due to our one-sided understanding of the mayor's office (even, I concede, an exaggerated emphasis on the mayor as a "driving force"[†]), this message has rarely been enunciated, although mayors like Rendell and Plusquellic have realized the possibilities of a different leadership style. Better understanding of facilitative leadership may expand the range of candidates for the mayor's office and broaden the scope of leadership styles.

The argument that the same dimensions and style of leadership are preferred in both major forms of government does not imply that the forms are converging. Mayors in each form operate within a different context and, as noted, have different options, opportunities, and constraints. It will be harder for mayor–council mayors to display and maintain facilitative leadership. It may be harder for council–manager

---

* In the 2001 survey of council members, the performance of mayors and city managers was compared in three areas: providing the council with sufficient policy alternatives, accomplishing the goals of the council, and providing sufficient information for assessment of performance. In council–manager cities, 71 to 81 percent of the council respondents in three city size categories gave the city manager an excellent or good rating depending on the specific measure and the size of the city. In mayor–council cities, the range of good to excellent ratings for the mayor on these measures was 35 to 47 percent (Svara 2002).

† In *Official Leadership in the City* (Svara, 1990), I characterized the mayor–council mayor as the "driving force" in city government in contrast to the mayor as "guiding force" in council–manager cities.

mayors to emerge as visionary leaders. The message of this study, however, is that both are possible.

The case studies and survey data from council members taken together provide a transforming view of the mayor's office and suggest a reinterpretation of leadership issues in the form of government debate in American cities. Two important themes emerge that run counter to standard assumptions about mayoral leadership. First, mayors in council–manager cities are at least as well and may be better positioned to develop positive and effective leadership than the power-oriented "strong" mayor in mayor–council cities. Second, mayors in mayor–council cities can enhance their effectiveness and long-term impact by incorporating facilitative approaches in their leadership behavior. These themes are not exactly the equivalent of "man-bites-dog" stories, but they run counter to popular perceptions and the bulk of the academic literature. It is well established in the general literature on leadership in all kinds of organizations that collaborative approaches to leadership are preferred to authoritarian and power-based approaches. The facilitative approach and visionary leadership are the preferred characteristics in studies of businesses, nonprofits, and public organizations. The major exception has been studies of elected political leaders. This book does not turn the mayoral leadership literature on its head, but it turns it on its side and demonstrates the need for more attention to the horizontal dimensions of leadership—vision, empowerment, collaboration, engagement, and coordination—rather than the vertical dimensions of hierarchy, power, and control.

These observations have important implications for leadership in government generally, and there may be increased receptiveness to the message. The Democratic Party nomination contest in 2008 between Hillary Clinton and Barack Obama focused widespread attention on differing approaches to leadership. As noted earlier, there is increasing recognition in business and public administration that leadership styles associated with women can be more effective than assertive masculine styles of leadership, and this view was mentioned in the media. As Ellen Goodman (2008) observes, "The transformative inspirational, collaborative, 'female' style has become more attractive. Especially to a younger generation." Ironically, that style was modeled more clearly by Obama than Clinton,* but the point remains that an approach to leadership that stressed the characteristics associated with facilitation emerged for the first time in the national political arena.

The lessons of successful mayors reinforces this alternate rhetoric and avoids the confusion of style and gender. Men and women effectively used the facilitative style in varied settings: harmonious, contentious, or highly complex. Leaders in the public sector can share responsibility and empower others rather than trying to overpower them. They can inspire and at the same time incorporate the goals of others in their vision. They can emphasize making systems work rather than feeling

---

* Goodman (2008) observes that the collaborative style can be more effective "when it is modeled by a man" because women still encounter the double bind in politics or corporate leadership of appearing to be soft and not strong enough when manifesting a style that may come naturally to them.

compelled to replace them. Finally, political leaders can collaborate with public administrators rather than trying to control, distance, or marginalize them. The last point is consistent with studies of political appointees in the federal government who over time come to respect—sometimes grudgingly—the staff with whom they work as "civil servants" (Aberbach and Rockman 2000; Ferrara and Ross 2005). The experience of local leaders who pursue the facilitative approach is that the effective working relationship can be expected and pursued from the beginning, rather than emerging slowly in a cautious process of give and take.

We all need to be more sophisticated and less cynical observers of leaders whether we are members of the public, reporters, teachers, or administrators at high, middle, or low levels in public organizations. We should allow candidates and incumbents to be less heroic, less certain of the rightness of their proposals, more open to accepting the ideas of others, and more willing to work with others. We should encourage them to be bold and visionary without having to claim that their ideas alone must be accepted. To the cynics who say that this will never happen and that this approach to leadership will never work, we have the large number of facilitative mayors to offer as evidence that it can work. Visionary facilitation is not the only approach to effective leadership, but we have come a long way from the time that it was not even widely recognized as a possible approach to leadership.

References

Aberbach, Joel D. and Bert A. Rockman. 2000. *In the Web of Politics: Three Decades of the U.S. Federal Executive*. Washington, DC : Brookings Institution Press.

Chase, Gordon and Elizabeth C. Reveal. 1983. *How to Manage in the Public Sector*. Reading, MA: Addison-Wesley.

Collins, Jim. 2001. The Misguided Mix-up between Celebrity and Leadership, http://www.jimcollins.com/lib/articles/10_01_a.html (accessed October 2007).

Cufaude, Jeffrey. 2004. The art of facilitative leadership: Maximizing others' contributions. *The Systems Thinker Newsletter,* 15:10. http:/www.pegasuscom.com/levpoints/facilitativeleader.html (accessed October 2007).

Denhardt, Robert B. and Janet Vinzant Denhardt. 2006. *The Dance of Leadership: The Art of Leading in Business, Government, and Society*. Armonk, NY: M.E. Sharpe.

Ehrenhalt, Allan. 2004. The mayor–manager conundrum. *Governing,* October.

Ferrara, Joseph A. and Lynn C. Ross. 2005. *Getting to Know You: Rules of Engagement for Political Appointees and Career Executives*. Washington, DC: IBM Center for The Business of Government.

Fisher, Helen E. 2005. The natural leadership talents of women. In *Enlightened Power*, eds. Linda Coughlin, Ellen Wingard, and Keith Hollihan. New York: Jossey-Bass, 133–140.

Flanagan, Richard M. 2004. *Mayors and the Challenge of Urban Leadership*. Lanham, MD: University Press of America.

Goleman, Daniel, Richard Boyatzis, and Annie McKee. 2001. Primal leadership: The hidden driver of great performance. *Harvard Business Review*, Reprint (December): 43–51.

Goodman, Ellen. 2008. "Obama Uses 'Female' Style to Win," *Boston Globe* (February 21). http://www.Boston.com/Bostonglobe/Editorial_Opinion/Oped/Articles/2008/02/21/Obama_Uses_Female_Style_To_Win?Mode=Pf (accessed February 26, 2008).

Gurwitt, Rob. 2003. Are City Councils a Relic of the Past? *Governing*, April, 20–24.

Halter, Gary. 2002. The mayor in council–manager government: Leadership potential as presiding officer. Paper delivered at the Southwest Political Science Association annual meeting, New Orleans, LA.

Handy, Charles. 1996. *Beyond Certainty: The Changing Worlds of Organizations.* Boston: Harvard Business School Press.

Hofstede, Geert, 1997. *Cultures and Organizations. Software of the Mind.* New York: McGraw-Hill.

Kammerer, Gladys M. 1964. Role Diversity of city managers. *Administrative Science Quarterly*, 8: 421–442.

Mouritzen, Poul Erik and James H. Svara. 2002. *Leadership at the Apex: Politicians and Administrators in Western Local Governments.* Pittsburgh: University of Pittsburgh Press.

Parks, Sharon D. 2005. *Leadership Can Be Taught: A Bold Approach for a Complex World.* Cambridge, MA: Harvard Business School Press.

Pressman, Jeffrey L. 1972. Preconditions of mayoral leadership. *American Political Science Review*. 66: 511–524.

Siegel, Fred. 2005. *The Prince of the City: Giuliani, New York and the Genius of American Life.* San Francisco: Encounter Books.

Sparrow, Glen. 1984. The emerging chief executive: The San Diego experience. *Urban Resources*, 1984, 2 (Fall): 3–8.

Stone, Clarence. 1989. *Regime Politics: Governing Atlanta.* Lawrence, KS: University of Kansas Press.

Svara, James H., 1990. *Official Leadership in the City: Patterns of Conflict and Cooperation.* New York: Oxford University Press.

Svara, James H. 1994. Leadership issues and the future of council–manager government. In Facilitative Leadership in Local Government: Lessons from Successful Mayors and Chairpersons in the Council–Manager Form, James H. Svara and Associates. San Francisco: Jossey-Bass, chap. 11.

Svara, James H. 2001. Do we still need model charters? The meaning and relevance of reform in the twenty-first century. *National Civic Review*, 90: 19–34.

Svara, James H. 2002. Council roles, performance, and form of government. In *The Future of Local Government Administration: The Hansell Symposium,* eds. George Frederickson and John Nalbandian, Washington: International City and County Management Association.

Svara, James H., 2006. Mayoral leadership in one universe of American urban politics: Are there lessons for (and from) the other? *Public Administration Review* 66: 767–774.

Wheeland, Craig M. 1994. A profile of a facilitative mayor: Mayor Betty Jo Rhea of Rock Hill, South Carolina. In *Facilitative Leadership in Local Government: Lessons from Successful Mayors and Chairpersons in the Council–Manager Form*, James H. Svara et al., San Francisco: Jossey-Bass, chap. 7.

Wheeland, Craig M. 2002. An institutionalist perspective on mayoral leadership: Linking leadership style to formal structure. *National Civic Review*, 91:1, 25–39.

Winner, Linda C. 1994. Leadership making a difference: The Honorable Noel C. Taylor Mayor of Roanoke, Virginia. In *Facilitative Leadership in Local Government: Lessons from Successful Mayors and Chairpersons in the Council–Manager Form*, James H. Svara et al., San Francisco: Jossey-Bass, chap. 6.

Zeigler, Harmon, Ellen Kehoe, and Jane Reisman. 1985. *City Managers and School Superintendents.* New York: Praeger.

Index

A

Accountability issues, 275, 372
    expectations *vs.* reality in Cincinnati, 263–264
    and mayoral empowerment in Cincinnati, 24, 275–276
Adapted mayor-council form, 96
    in Yorkville, Illinois case study, 75
Administrative modernization, 44, 45
    gap between civic engagement and, 45
    in Midway, Florida case study, 179–180
    by Rendell in Philadelphia, 342
    in Yorkville, Illinois case study, 76, 78
Administrative partnerships, in Danish case study, 68–69, 69
Administrative staff
    open communications in Chapel Hill, North Carolina, 160–161
    relationships in Chapel Hill, North Carolina case study, 159–162
Administrator role, switching to mayor from, 109–110
Adversity
    in communities with council-manager form, 167
    Plusquellic's handling of, 324–326
Advocate role, in Stockton, California case study, 234, 250–251
African Americans
    and Chapel Hill mayoral elections, 161
    endorsement of Ed Rendell, 334
    in-migration to Philadelphia inner city, 329
    in Midway, Florida case study, 170
    Rendell's appointment of, 339, 340
Akron, Ohio case study, 305–306, 364
    annexation and development issues, 319
    Charter of 1924, 307, 308

city context, 306–310
city political profile, 307–308
cooperation in, 317
dependence on tire industry, 306
deputy mayors and city admininstration relationships, 325
economic downturns in, 306
economic profile, 308–310
handling of opposition and adversity, 324–326
high home ownership rate, 310
historical creativity of Akron, 309
in-fill housing issues, 320–321
Joint Economic Development District (JEDD), 318–319
key support for Plusquellic, 324
land-poor issues, 318
leadership styles in, 313–315
long-term visioning in, 307
Mayor Donald Plusquellic, 311–313
mayoral influence on budget, 308
minor league baseball park development, 319
nature and sources of leadership, 322–326
Plusquellic on leadership, 315–318
Plusquellic's impact, 318–322
police advisory board proposal, 317
public schools-city cooperation issues, 321–322
roles and relationships in, 313–315
rubber workers' strike, 313
shift to partisan elections, 308
support for mayoral vision, 322–323
tax increase proposal, 317, 321–322
U.S. census data, 310
Altamont Commuter Express, 235
Ambiguity, cultural comfort with, 371, 372
Andrews, Marvin, 286

395

G